Never Mind the Bollards
Max Wooldridge

Introduction

The idea for a book about England's rock and pop music landmarks, the places that have inspired lyrics and where album sleeves were shot, came to me on a drunken evening a few years ago. Or maybe even further back, in the early 1990s, when I worked on a staff newspaper for a major high-street retailer. Most weeks we had to spin bad news stories such as '100 staff about to lose their jobs' under devious headlines like 'Meeting the Challenges Ahead'.

But there was a bright side to the job – the diary column. Staff would sometimes ring in with details of famous customers they had served. One morning an assistant manager of a central London branch telephoned to say a colleague had sold a rhyming dictionary to the Aussie pop princess Kylie Minogue. It made me giggle, but as a musical landmark it hardly competed with Abbey Road, The 100 Club or Bristol's Colston Hall. The initial concept was probably planted in my mind that day. A more recent equivalent of the Kylie snippet might be the location of the woods where Amy Winehouse buried her pet canary. There are, however, far more important musical landmarks in England and that's where this book comes in.

Then there was the aforementioned drunken Friday night in a pub in Kentish Town, when some friends and I had the sozzled idea of a book that recreates some of the best album covers of the last four decades: *Ziggy Stardust*, *The Clash*, maybe even that Kevin Rowland one where he is decked out in lingerie? The working title was *Cover the Cover*, or *Cover Me*, or something like that. Still half-drunk we managed to tick off the easiest and most obvious one – *Abbey Road* – the next morning before hitting the nearest pub to the relief of St John's Wood motorists.

The idea faded but in true male anorak style, one half of my brain now seemed reserved for amassing rock and pop landmarks and trivia. What finally convinced me to pitch the book was a trip I made to Lithuania. In the capital, Vilnius, I asked a local man for directions to the Frank Zappa statue. When I told him I was from London he said to forget about

Zappa and told me in broken English how the music of Ray Davies and The Kinks had changed his life. He wanted to know all about Muswell Hill and Waterloo Bridge – and he couldn't wait to visit London to embark on his own Kinks pilgrimage.

I've always been fascinated – and hope you have too – by songs that marvel in the magic of the everyday, attempt to tap into the English soul, or lyrics that evoke a sense of place or time – or just tell a darn good story, be it "a bustle in your hedgerow", *My Pink Half of the Drainpipe*, *Town Called Malice*, *Teddy Picker*, *Penny Lane* or *Itchycoo Park*. And the work of natural heirs to music hall heroes and our modern-day Noël Cowards and Lionel Barts, songwriters who rhymed "noblesse" with "Shoeburyness" (Ian Dury), "Balzac" with "Prozac" (Damon Albarn) and "ghastly" with "Rick Astley" (Nick Lowe). Some of the best English songs conjure up images of a long-vanished England, chronicle ASBO Britain, or recall a spot of argy-bargy in the taxi queue.

I once took a girlfriend on a surprise country drive into deepest Hampshire. She was excited because I'd promised her a visit to a spa hotel and hadn't told her where we were going. When the car stopped, her face dropped. Imagine her horror when she discovered we were outside Headley Grange, where Led Zeppelin 'IV' was recorded. "But I thought you'd be pleased," I protested. She soon decided she wanted to be a former girlfriend and shacked up with her yoga teacher. She would probably hate this book, but if you can identify with my actions that day, or have done anything similar yourself, then this book is for you.

The eagle-eyed amongst you will spot the book's one deliberate mistake (for others it's in chapter 4: The South.) Despite my best efforts it has been impossible to include every single English act or band ever, or landmark, so my apologies if you're a big Modern Romance fan, or actually do want to know where Ms Winehouse's pet is buried. There just wasn't room to squeeze it in.

MW, September 2010

Contents

LONDON

London, the big shopfront, where everything happens. You can press your nose against the window, or just march straight on in. England's capital promises the chance to be part of the latest scene, or better still, at the forefront of the next one. There's always the promise of a good evening, or something legendary happening. A late night of wild abandon, unthinkable in the suburbs where we live.

But you're a long way from net curtain twitchers, Neighbourhood Watch schemes and suburban banality here. Outside central London cafés, young hipsters thumb the pages of glossy magazines telling them what's in, what's not; others sell celebrity lifestyles now supposedly accessible to everyone. On weekdays in the big smoke nearly every doorway is occupied by office workers dragging on cigarettes, savouring a precious few moments away from their bosses. Then there's the London look, where eye contact can be rare. Watch two Londoners talk and one's attention will often shift over the other's shoulders on the look-out for a new style, the next best thing, or just someone more interesting to talk to. When you are staring in the film of your life there's no time for extras. And underneath those grey clouds, amid the sometimes maddening hustle and bustle, there's a vibrancy here that makes most other capital cities seem like provincial backwaters.

London's diverse musical energy means you don't need to stare over London's shoulder; you can look it right in the eye. Mods, Glam Rock, Punk, Britpop; whatever the scene may be, you can be sure London will be at the heart of it.

West End

OXFORD STREET
LONDON W1

Overloaded with chain stores, booby-trapped with charity muggers and heaving with human cattle, Oxford Street is for most Londoners, hell on earth, but it does hold some musical interest.

At 150 Oxford Street is HMV's very first store, officially opened in July 1921 by the celebrated British composer, Sir Edward Elgar, and now the company's flagship.

At 214 Oxford Street are the former Air Studios of legendary Beatles producer, Sir George Martin (they have since moved to Hampstead). The Pretenders recorded their 1984 *Learning to Crawl* album here, in 1984. Taking a leaf out of The Beatles' book, the Pretenders didn't travel far for the cover; they simply took to the roof of the building.

The 100 Club, a boiling hot stuffy cellar at 100 Oxford Street, is one of London's most important venues and is still thriving today. Launched as a jazz club in 1942, it saw visits from Glenn Miller and Louis Armstrong. Over the years, it became a trad pad, then a blues venue frequented by such greats as Bo Diddley, Muddy Waters and Freddie king, before, in the '60s, transforming itself into a a Brit-Beat hotbed boasting gigs by The Who, Animals and Kinks. The following decade it achieved infamy as the site of the two-day Punk Festival on 20-21 September 1976, with acts like The Clash, Sex Pistols and The Buzzcocks. Siouxsie and the Banshees formed especially for the gig and played just one song – a 20-minute recital of the Lord's Prayer. During the festival, Sid Vicious lashed a bike chain at Nick Kent after Kent asked him to "move aside" because he was blocking his way; he also smashed a glass that blinded a member of the audience, and was then arrested for carrying a knife. At the end of May 1982, The Rolling Stones played an unannounced gig at the 100 Club as a warm-up for their European tour and, in 1986, Metallica played a secret gig here to "break in" Jason Newsted when he joined the band as bass player after the tragic death of Cliff Burton.

In Argyll Street, off Oxford Street, is the London Palladium, once famous as the setting for 'Sunday Night at the London Palladium' and now better known as home to big West End musicals such as Andrew Lloyd Webber's *The Sound of Music*. The Palladium was a fitting last venue for Ian Dury, given his love of music hall. Ian's old painting teacher, Sir Peter Blake, was in the audience that night. Journalist Nik Cohn's famous observation: "Elvis became God…Tommy Steele made it to the London Palladium", still resonates.

Steele returned to the Palladium to star in *Scrooge – the Musical* in 2005/6. In May 2007, Marty Wilde celebrated 50 years in music with a concert at the Palladium.

SOHO SQUARE
LONDON W1

Leading off Oxford street, Frith Street leads into Soho Square, where a bench is dedicated to the singer/songwriter, Kirsty MacColl, killed by a power boat whilst scuba diving with her children at Cozumel in Mexico in December 2000, aged just 41. Her mother Jean (Newlove) campaigned for justice for Kirsty but ceased the campaign nine years after her daughter's death when their legal options ran out. Kirsty's

father was the famous folk singer, Ewan MacColl. Despite a string of hits (including *Soho Square*) she is perhaps most famous for her duet with Shane MacGowan on *Fairytale of New York*, which has become a perennial Christmas favourite. The bench aptly features lines from her song, *Soho Square*.

A magnificent evocation of Soho's seedy romance is The Pogues *A Rainy Night in Soho* (1985), recalling the first stirrings of a love affair as the wind whistles through the late-night streets. Written for Shane MacGowan's on-off girlfriend (and eventual wife) Victoria Clarke and produced by Elvis Costello, with its sweeping strings and lonesome trumpet it's often viewed as a prototype for *Fairytale of New York*.

At 1 Soho Square, Sir Paul McCartney's music publishing business occupies three stories in an elegant eighteenth-century building. He owns rights to more than three thousand songs and Broadway shows, including Buddy Holly's catalogue and the musicals *Annie*, *Guys and Dolls* and *Grease* – all part of a show-business empire that, along with the royalty he earns on every Beatles record sold, has made him one of the richest men in England.

At the height of Beatlemania, when his band mates were buying large country mansions to escape the glare of publicity, Paul McCartney lived in an attic room at 57 Wimpole Street in the house owned by his girlfriend Jane Asher's parents. He didn't waste his time inside though: during his stay in the house, he wrote *Yesterday*.

Above: Kirsty MacColl was tragically killed in Mexico in December 2000.
Opposite page: The 100 Club, Oxford Street.

Sex and clubs and rock 'n' roll

BOHEMIAN Soho has always attracted writers and artists. William Blake was born on Marshall Street and returned to the area later in life; Shelley was sent down from Oxford and came to Poland Street; William Hazlitt's house (now a cosy and exclusive hotel) remains on Frith Street; and a seven year-old Mozart touted his talents on Dean Street, while Verlaine and Rimbaud lodged briefly on Old Compton Street. In the Sixties, Soho was where the great and the good of London's music scene came to party.

Bag O' Nails This was *the* musicians' after-hours hang-out, just off Regent Street. Punters sat next to the likes of The Beatles, Rolling Stones and Hollies. A favourite club of Paul McCartney's, he met his future wife Linda Eastman here. Soul star Geno Washington met his wife here and it's where her sister met Peter Noone of Herman's Hermits.

The Scene Club This basement club with padded walls in Soho's Ham Yard, Great Windmill Street, was a hang-out for the pilled-up finely-dressed mod elite in the early 1960s.

The Flamingo Located in a basement in Wardour Street, off Shaftesbury Avenue, Rik Gunnell's Flamingo club was famous for its all-nighters fuelled by alcohol (and sold without a licence). Mods popped pills here but the club had a multi-cultural fan base who grooved to modern jazz, R&B, soul and ska.

Ad Lib This was the the in club of the mid-1960s. Situated at the top of 7 Leicester Place (the building also housed the offices of the council refuse collectors). A regular haunt with the pop glitterati of the day as well as fashion designers like Mary Quant and Jean Muir and actresses like Hayley Mills and Julie Christie. John Lennon and George Harrison turned up here after having their drinks spiked with LSD while having dinner with their dentist.

The Speakeasy Famous musician's haunt in Margaret Street, where bands like the Jimi Hendrix Experience, Deep Purple and Thin Lizzy jammed regularly. Cream drummer Ginger Baker once beat another musician in a bet to bed the entire waitressing staff. The club lasted well into the 1970s and it was where, in 1977, The Who's Pete Townshend famously told Sex Pistols Steve Jones and Paul Cook they were the only hope for rock.

The Scotch of St James Pop aristocracy held court at the Scotch of St James in Masons Yard in Westminster, so named because the decor was decked out in tartan. In September 1966, Jimi Hendrix played his first English gig here, jamming with the house band.

FRITH STREET
LONDON W1

On Frith Street is the Bohemian nirvana that is Bar Italia, a little bit of Naples in the heart of Soho. Like most things that Londoners really enjoy, it reminds us of being abroad, as eloquently lamented by Pulp on their *Bar Italia* track on the album *Different Class*:

> 'There's only one place we can go/
> It's around the corner in Soho/
> where other broken people go.'

Above the door a blue plaque reminds customers that in this very building, on 26 January 1926, John Logie Baird gave the first public demonstration of television. (Would he have continued if he'd know that people would be watching the likes of X Factor 80-odd years later? You be the judge.)

At 47 Frith Street is the 'new' Ronnie Scott's jazz club (the original was at 39 Gerrard Street until 1965). For decades, Ronnie Scott's has been the home of British jazz. It has hosted British and US legends through the years, including Georgie Fame and Stone's drummer Charlie Watts and Jimi Hendrix made an appearance on the eve of his death to jam with War on the songs *Mother Earth* and *Tobacco Road*.

WARDOUR STREET
LONDON W1

The legendary Marquee Club, where the Stones first made an impression 40 years ago, no longer exists in any form. Between 1964 and 1988, 90 Wardour Street was one of the world's greatest music venues and at the forefront of every scene; R&B, psychedelia, mod and punk. The Marquee was sweaty but atmospheric with its floors sticky from beer and various bodily fluids. The late Malcolm McLaren said in 2002: "The Marquee was home to so many outlaws and heroes of another era and plenty of rock 'n' roll ghosts inhabit its basement […] Back in the 1970s The Marquee opened its doors to the Sex Pistols for one chaotic night: Johnny Rotten was thrown off the stage, and the Pistols were subsequently banned from ever playing at the Marquee again."

Above the door at number 90 Wardour Street is a blue plaque dedicated to Keith Moon. The Ship pub, at 116 Wardour Street was where The Clash manager, Bernie Rhodes, famously screamed "I want complete control!" at The Clash and Mick Jones went home and wrote the song.

Tucked away down a backstreet, at St Annes Court, off Wardour Street, are the legendary Trident Studios, where The Beatles recorded *Dear Prudence* and where David Bowie recorded *The Rise And Fall of Ziggy Stardust And The Spiders From Mars*. It was also used by Elton John, Marc Bolan, Queen, Lou Reed, Genesis, Supertramp, and many more. The Beatles used this studio because it had an eight track: Abbey Road at the time was only a four-track.

In the early Seventies Marianne Faithfull, by now a heroin addict, was living homeless on a wall in St Anne's Court (for two years).

De Lane Lea Studios, now at 75 Dean Street, was where Jimi Hendrix recorded *Hey Joe*. Originally at 129 Kingsway, other bands that recorded there include The Beatles, The Stones and Deep Purple.

At 49 Greek Street was Les Cousins, an acoustic mecca, opened by Andy Matteou in the basement of his parent's Greek restaurant in the spring of 1965. The Soho folk club launched the likes of John Martyn, Ralph McTell, Bert Jansch and Al Stewart. Bert Jansch went to form Pentangle with John Renbourn.

BERWICK STREET
LONDON W1

In between clouting photographers and brotherly shoves, Liam Gallagher and brother Noel found time to record some fine music and their 1995 album *(What's The Story) Morning Glory?* was arguably Britpop's highpoint. The road featured on the album's cover is Berwick Street in Soho, best-known for its fruit and vegetable market and specialist record shops. Marc Bolan's mother, Phyllis Feld, once manned a fruit and veg stall on the market and Elton John worked weekends, at number 44, in a Musicland record shop. Noel Gallagher wanted the album cover to be less light-hearted than usual and to have an 'urban' feel. The idea was to have a street scene with two men passing each other, one glancing at the other. Oasis sleeve designer Brian Cannon stood in for Noel who wasn't well at the time. "He reckoned the backs of our heads were pretty similar," Cannon says. A friend of the band, Sean Rowley, is the figure walking towards the camera. The shoot started at four-thirty in the morning and used around 300 frames. "We ended up using the very first one taken," says Cannon. "If I'd known, I would have sacked the shoot after five minutes."

If Walker's Court at the south end of Berwick Street epitomises the sleazy face of red-light Soho, then Soft Cell's debut album *Non-Stop Erotic Cabaret* must be its musical soundtrack. Released to great success in 1982, its trash-life tracks include *Seedy Films*, *Sex Dwarf*, *Bedsitter* and, photographed on the album's back cover, *Walker's Court*.

OLD COMPTON STREET
LONDON W1

At 59 Old Compton Street is a blue plaque marking this as the original site of the legendary 2i's Coffee Bar, which opened its doors on 22 April, 1956. Founded by Australian wrestlers Ray Hunter and Paul Lincoln and christened by their landlords,

two Irani brothers (it was originally the 3i's but the third sibling got cold feet), the dark basement cafe would soon become a focal point for British skiffle and the emerging rock 'n' roll scene. On its tiny stage many legendary musicians began their careers: The Vipers, Toomy Steele, Cliff Richard and The Drifters, Adam Faith, Marty Wilde, Vince Taylor and Terry Dene all performed here early on in their careers. Wee Willie Harris, who waited orange juice and coffee, paid tribute to the place with his 1957 single, *Rockin' At The 2i's*. The bar appeared in 1959 film *Expresso Bongo*, starring Cliff Richard and Laurence Harvey. Marc Bolan, then Feld, served coffee there in '63. With the advent of The Beatles the music scene moved on and the 2i's finally closed in 1970.

CITY OF WESTMINSTER

SITE OF THE
2i's COFFEE BAR
(1956-1970)

BIRTHPLACE OF
BRITISH ROCK 'N ROLL
AND THE POPULAR
MUSIC INDUSTRY

ROBERT MANDRY

CHINATOWN
LONDON W1

The late American singer-songwriter Warren Zevon name-checked an actual Chinese restaurant in Soho – Lee Ho Fook, formerly at 15-16 Gerrard Street in the heart of London's Chinatown – in his classic 1978 track, *Werewolves of London*. Long-suffering staff were used to diners' "ah-woo" werewolf impressions in between mouthfuls of beef chow mein, the dish mentioned in the song. The song also features the lines:

> 'He's the hairy-handed gent who ran amuck in Kent/ Lately he's been overheard in Mayfair.'

At the end of Gerrard Street, at number 48, was a basement bar that closed in 2004 but not before inspiring one of the Pet Shop Boys' biggest hits. In the early 1980s, Neil Tennant and Chris Lowe used to drink in the downstairs dive bar of the King's Head pub, later immortalising it in *West End Girls* as "a dive bar in a West End town".

In a studio in Lisle Street, in August 1968, The New Yardbirds rehearsed together for the first time. Within a few months they would change their name to Led Zeppelin. Jimmy Page came up with their name, based on a Keith Moon crack that "they'd go down like a lead zeppelin".

Opposite page top: Ronnie Scott's jazz club.
Opposite page bottom: Dr Feelgood at The Marquee Club.

Left: Modern day Carnaby Street
Below: The Pet Shop Boys.

CITY OF WESTMINSTER
IMPRESARIO
DON ARDEN
AND MOD BAND
"SMALL FACES"
(STEVE MARRIOTT, RONNIE
LANE, KENNEY JONES,
IAN MCLAGAN AND
JIMMY WINSTON)
WORKED HERE
1965-1967

CARNABY STREET
LONDON W1

HEDDON STREET
LONDON W1

Much beloved of Japanese camera-toting tourists, Carnaby Street was the epicentre of 1960s fashion, where the rock elite bought their clothes, and centre of Swinging London. The street famously inspired The Kinks' *Dedicated Follower of Fashion*, and later The Jam song *Carnaby Street*. It was also where U2 shot the video for *Even Better Than The Real Thing*.

On 8 September 2007 a commemorative plaque dedicated to Don Arden and The Small Faces was unveiled at 52-55 Carnaby Street, Arden's former offices. Kenney Jones, ex-drummer of Small Faces, said: "To honour the Small Faces after all these years is a terrific achievement. I only wish that Steve Marriott, Ronnie Lane and the late Don Arden were here to enjoy this moment with me."

In the early 80s this was the offices of *Smash Hits* magazine, where Neil Tennant was working when he launched the Pet Shop Boys.

The nearby Courthouse Hotel, at 19-21 Great Marlborough Street, virtually opposite Liberty's, is now a Hilton-run hotel (Courthouse Doubletree by Hilton), on the premises of the former Marlborough Street Magistrates Court (site of many a rock star appearance, including Brian Jones in May '68.). The former courtroom is now an aptly-named restaurant Silk.

Glam rock's first concept album made an unlikely rock landmark out of Heddon Street, a quiet blink-and-you'll-miss-it side-street off Regent Street. The doorway of number 23 was the precise location for the cover of the *The Rise And Fall of Ziggy Stardust And the Spiders From Mars* (1972), the record that broke David Bowie worldwide.

On a miserable February evening photographer Brian Ward helped to conceptualise David Bowie's notion of an alien visitor seduced by the trappings of excess, fame and flamboyant ambiguity. Designed by Bowie's ex-King Bee bandmate and friend George Underwood, with artwork by Terry Pastor, the sleeve juxtaposes glam hedonism with backstreet grime.

There's no rubbish or boxes outside nowadays as the ground floor is a Moroccan tea room (with solicitors and architects offices occupying upper floors). Ward shot the original photographs in black and white but later tinted them to achieve the desired effect. When Bowie revisited Heddon Street in 1993 a woman stopped him in the street: "They took your phone box away. Isn't it terrible?" The old red telephone box in question – featured on shots on the album's back cover – was sold to an American fan in the late 1970s. As for the famous K West sign, under which Bowie's alter ego stands with his foot up on rubbish, this was auctioned off as a part of a sale of rock 'n' roll memorabilia. Bowie commented later that it was a shame the sign went. "People read so much into it. They thought K West must be some sort some sort of code for 'quest.'" Not for first time album covers were imbued with all manner of hidden mystical meanings.

DENMARK STREET
LONDON W1

From its origins as a sheet music supplier in Victorian times to recording studio heaven in the 1960s, Denmark Street is London's Tin Pan Alley, famous for its music shops and studios where The Beatles, The Rolling Stones, The Kinks and Jimi Hendrix recorded in basements in the 1960s, where Elton John (then Reg Dwight) worked as an office boy at Mills Music, and where Bob Marley bought his very first guitar.

1970s soft-rock band, Sad Café, were photographed here, at number 6, for the cover of their 1979 album, *Facades*, which gave them their one-and-only hit, *Every Day Hurts*. Number 6 Denmark Street, for years a Greek Booksellers, is now aptly a guitar shop in a street that still specialises in musical instruments and printed music. During punk, the Sex Pistols used a rehearsal room behind the shop and small studio flat above was home to Steve Jones and Paul Cook. Living upstairs in the early 1980s were Bananarama. Cook helped the new wave girl-group record their debut single, *Aie a Mwana*, as well as acting as producer on their 1982 debut album *Deep Sea Skiving*.

At number 9 is a gastropub, which used to be the famous Giaconda Café, haunt of many '60s bands and, later, The Clash and The Slits. And at number 29 is the famously 'intimate' 12 Bar Club, still going strong.

Nearby, at 15 St Giles High Street, is the new Intrepid Fox. When the original Goth HQ on Wardour Street closed in 2006 many thought that it was last orders for one of London's longest-running rock bars, but it just shows you can't keep a good Goth down.

CHARING CROSS ROAD
LONDON W1

Until it closed in January 2009 to make way for a Crossrail station at Tottenham Court Road, The Astoria was one of the true great London venues. Many bands made their debut here, most recently Arctic Monkeys. Not bad for a building that started life as a pickle factory.

Below: Jarvis Cocker (top left) and Glenn Matlock (bottom) both went to CSM while the 12 Bar Club (top right) is a famous venue on Denmark Street.

St Martin's College of Art (CSM), on Charing Cross Road, was immortalised in Pulp's *Common People*. Jarvis Cocker dated a sculpture student who revealed to him she'd always wanted to "sleep with common people like you". This was the inspiration for the band's 1995 hit *Common People*:

"She came from Greece she had a thirst for knowledge, she studied sculpture at Saint Martins College, that's where I caught her eye."

Jarvis Cocker really was too smart for Britpop. While the press made out that the bickering and competition between Oasis and Blur was symbolic of the class divide in Britain, Cocker summed it up in three minutes of pure pop, layered upon a simple keyboard riff. "You will never understand, how it feels to live your life, with no meaning or control" spat Cocker, with the conviction of one who knows. Words that took on an extra signficance two years later when, after years of struggling in pop wastelands, Pulp headlined Glastonbury. The ultimate vindication for the people's champions.

Apart from Jarvis Cocker, other famous musicians who have studied here include the original Sex Pistols' bass player Glen Matlock. The college played host to the Pistols' debut gig on November 6, 1975. On the night the college's horrified social secretary pulled the plug after only five numbers. Pistols manager, Malcolm McLaren also studied here, as did Sade and PJ Harvey, Faris Badwan (the Horrors), MIA, Billy Childish, Joe Strummer and Vivian Stanshall.

Off Charing Cross Road, on Manette Street, is the Borderline, a great place to catch bands on the up before they get screwed by their record company. The late American lost country hero, Townes van Zandt, played his last ever show here. Spinal Tap auditioned for a new drummer here (true) after the old one spontaneously combusted (might not be true), and Oasis shot the *Cigarettes and Alcohol* video here.

TOTTENHAM COURT ROAD
LONDON W1

Pink Floyd played many early concerts at the UFO Club at 31 Tottenham Court Road where they were the house band (see opposite).

The street is namechecked by The Pogues in their 1984 song *Transmetropolitan*, written by Shane MacGowan:

> 'From a 5 pound bet in William Hills/
> To a Soho sex-shop dream/
> From a fried egg in Valtaro's/
> To a Tottenham Court Road ice cream.'

The Centre Point building is visible in the beginning of the music video for *Check the Meaning* by Richard Ashcroft.

It also appears in the background of the music video for *Midnight Madness* by The Chemical Brothers, and during the video of *Bang* by Blur.

Just off Tottenham Court Road is the site of the former Whitfield Street Studios, where The Clash recorded their first album in 12 days in 1977. The studio, once owned by CBS, opened in 1972, with the Byrds, Iggy Pop and Mott the Hopple among the first artists to use it. Iggy Pop recorded *Raw Power* there.

At the top of Tottenham Court Road is Warren Street, site of The Prince of Wales Feathers pub. It was here, in December 1976, that TV presenter Bill Grundy retired to after the infamous interview with the Sex Pistols (see also page 23). "I have just been f***ed. I need a drink!" regulars heard Grundy say. "He did not say anything about his career, he did not have to," said one regular. The disastrous broadcast wrecked Grundy's television career.

TRAFALGAR SQUARE
LONDON W1

The Dire Straits song, *Lions*, was inspired by songwriter/guitarist Mark Knopfler's nocturnal wanderings about the "Wild West End." Knopfler moved to the capital after completing an English degree at Leeds University.

Aural Sculpture, The Stranglers' eighth studio album from 1984, features the southern (Mall) side of the square at the feet of Nelson's column.

PICCADILLY CIRCUS
LONDON W1

Northern Irish punk band Stiff Little Fingers had a different song of the same name from their 1981 album *Go for It*, a true story about a friend of theirs migrating to London to escape the Troubles in Belfast only to be stabbed by strangers in Piccadilly Circus. A compilation album from the British pop/rock band Squeeze released in 1996 was titled *Piccadilly Collection* and showed a picture of Piccadilly Circus on its cover.

The Morrissey song *Piccadilly Palare* from the album *Bona Drag* recounts the life of male prostitutes by employing the use of "palare" (alternatively spelled 'polari'), argot used by this subculture and by gay men generally. Jethro Tull

night trippin': the UFO club

EVERY musical genre needs its HQ. For R&B it was the Crawdaddy, for punk it was The Roxy, for New Romantics it was Blitz. The psychedelic scene was no different and, in the 1960s, Hippy Central was the incense- and hash-infused interior of the UFO Club in the basement of 31 Tottenham Court Road, opposite the Dominion Theatre. This hugely influential club lasted less than a year but during that time became the nocturnal haunt of the '60s counter-culture and spawning ground of Pink Floyd and Soft Machine.

London's UFO club (pronounced 'You-Fo', not You-Eff-Oh, which marked you out as hopelessly unhip) was founded by John Hopkins (usually known as "Hoppy") and Joe Boyd in an Irish dancehall called The Blarney Club. Pink Floyd performed on the opening night, on 23 December, 1966, billed as UFO 'Presents Night Tripper', and would go on to feature as the club's 'house band'. Floyd would soon become the toast of London's underground music scene but their tenure at UFO was short lived. As their fame grew they were able to play bigger venues for higher fees. The new house band were Soft Machine but other acts who were attracted by the club's reputation included The Incredible String Band, Arthur Brown, Tomorrow, and Procol Harum, who played there when *A Whiter Shade of Pale* was No 1 in the charts.

The club was popular with rock luminaries of the day. Pete Townshend used to hang out at the side of the stage when the Floyd played, no doubt also entertained by erotic dancer Suzy Creamcheese, who was immortalised in a Zappa song.

In his book, *White Bicycles*, Joe Boyd, says "unlike conventional gigs at the time it had more going on than just music – there was body painting, a light show, motorbikes." There was rather too much going on for some tastes, though, and, in June 1967, Hopkins was imprisoned for drug offences. Police pressure on the club increased in the following weeks, and the landlords revoked the lease. The club moved into The Roundhouse for a few months but, despite the building being almost derelict, the rent was exorbitant. In October 1967 the UFO Club at the Roundhouse folded.

Left: Pink Floyd at the psychedelic UFO club in 1966.

mention Piccadilly Circus in *Mother Goose* on the album *Aqualung*: "And a foreign student said to me/was it really true there are elephants and lions too/in Piccadilly Circus?"

Bob Marley makes mention of Piccadilly Circus in his song *Kinky Reggae* on the album *Catch A Fire*. The Sundays mention Piccadilly Circus in their song *Hideous Towns* on their 1990 album *Reading, Writing, and Arithmetic*.

A terrific illustration of Piccadilly Circus adorns the cover of the 1971 *Howlin' Wolf Sessions* by blues legend Howlin' Wolf, who influenced the likes of Led Zeppelin, The Rolling Stones and Cream. Eric Clapton himself was invited to play on the album while bassist Bill Wyman and drummer Charlie Watts from The Rolling Stones made up the rhythm section.

Steven Georgiou (formerly Cat Stevens) was the third child of a Greek-Cypriot father, Stavros Georgiou and a Swedish mother, Ingrid Wickman. The family lived above Moulin Rouge, the restaurant that his parents operated on Shaftesbury Avenue, a few steps from Piccadilly Circus. Shaftesbury Avenue also features on the cover of *From The Heart Of Town* by early '90s band, Gallon Drunk.

MAYFAIR & PICCADILLY
LONDON W1

At 23/25 Brook Street in Mayfair is the Handel House Museum. Ok, so why should Handel's London home be important for a Rock Pilgrimage? Simply, because as well as belonging to an important classical composer, this house was occupied by the legendary Jimi Hendrix. Hendrix reported seeing Handel's ghost, and stories set in the house are the stuff of rock legend. This was Hendrix's first London residence, which he got through Chas Chandler (half of his management team and ex-Animals bassist) and the apartment originally belonged to Ringo Starr. Keith Richards notoriously fell down a flight of stairs here, and broke a leg. Hendrix spent most of his time with the curtains drawn, which accounted for his nickname 'The Bat'. This is also the flat where Hendrix first performed to a tiny but elite group of 1960's British Rock Royalty, and where he penned many of his earliest hits from *Are You Experienced*. An English Heritage blue plaque marks the former residence of the guitar legend, as well the other bloke.

ENGLISH HERITAGE
JIMI HENDRIX
1942~1970
Guitarist and Songwriter
lived here
1968~1969

The unluckiest address in England?

KEITH Moon and Mama Cass died in the same London flat. The flat, which belonged to (American singer-songwriter) Harry Nilsson, was at 12 Curzon Street, in Mayfair. When he was away Nilsson would often loan out the place to friends. Cass Elliot used it when she headed the bill at the London Palladium in 1974. On 29 July that year she went back to the flat after a Palladium performance and died from heart failure in a bedroom. Keith Moon died in the same room on 7 September 1978 returning with a girlfriend after attending a party hosted by Paul McCartney for the film premiere of *The Buddy Holly Story*. He watched a video and took Heminevrin, a drug prescribed to combat alcoholism, then died in his sleep. An autopsy revealed that the number of pills in Moon's stomach added up to 14 times the recommended dosage. In the wake of these tragedies, Nilsson sold the flat to Pete Townshend.

In the 1960s Indica Gallery was a counterculture art gallery in Mason's Yard (off Duke Street), in St. James's. It was in the basement of the Indica Bookshop, co-owned by John Dunbar (husband of Marianne Faithfull), Peter Asher and Barry Miles (who helped set up the UFO Club, see page 13). It hosted poetry readings and experimental art exhibitions, and John Lennon met Yoko Ono at her Unfinished Paintings And Objects show there in 1966 (a meeting hilariously recreated in The Rutles' film *All You Need Is Cash*).

The Pigalle Club, in Piccadilly is one of London's most famous live music venues where The Beatles played in the 1960s. With green and black diamond-shaped wallpaper and crisscrossed mirrors it has the extra glamour and glitz of a nightclub. It alternates between jazz, soul and swing, with seven live acts a week including performances by a house band. There are occasional showcase acts from major stars like Van Morrison, Shirley Bassey and Ruby Turner.

At 3 Savile Row is the site of The Beatles' last live appearance – on top of the building, which was then Apple Records, on 30 January 1969. These days, by the way, it's the Council of Mortgage Lenders. The Fab Four played for only 40 minutes before the Royal Bank of Scotland, opposite, complained to the police (the last track played was *Get Back*). This was the most famous residence of The Beatles' company Apple Corps, used as their HQ from 1968 to 1972. When the band sold the building in 1976, John and Yoko had the front door shipped to New York where it was housed in their Dakota apartment. The same door was also photographed and appeared on the back cover of Ringo's *Rotogravure* album. John Lennon married Yoko Ono in March 1969 and a month later held a brief ceremony on the roof of the Apple offices to legally change his name to John Ono Lennon.

A Nightingale Sang in Berkeley Square is one of the most famous songs of the Second World War. It was written by Eric Maschwitz for singer and stage actress, Judy Campbell (mother of Jane Birkin) in 1940; it has also been covered by Vera Lynn (in the same year), Frank Sinatra, Nat King Cole and Rod Stewart.

Hard Rock Café, at 150 Old Park Lane, boasts some excellent rock memorabilia – including Mötley Crüe's original drum kit and guitars; Janis Joplin's black knit shawl she wore in concert and on the back cover of the 1967 LP *Cheap Thrills*; and Eric Clapton's Fender Lead II guitar. It also serves a decent burger.

HYDE PARK
LONDON W1

A wave of emotion rolled over Hyde Park in May 1969 when The Rolling Stones took over the park for a massive free concert. It may have been a bit of a dodgy performance but Mick and the boys (featuring new guitarist Mick Taylor) lived up to the hype surrounding what turned into a memorial concert in Brian Jones' name after his shock death. Hells Angel's provided the security, thousands of butterflies were released… a truly fitting hippie memorial in the last summer of love.

Hyde Park was also the major venue for the Live 8 string of benefit concerts. The Red Hot Chili Peppers played in Hyde Park and made a multi-million selling live album from the concert. Queen played here in one of their most popular shows, in 1976. It is estimated that between 150- and 200,000 people turned up for the event, which is still a record for Hyde Park to this day.

The lyrics of Dire Straits' song *Industrial Disease* (from the *Love Over Gold* album) refer to Speakers' Corner: "I go down to Speakers' Corner, I'm thunderstruck; they got free speech, tourists, police in trucks. Two men say they're Jesus; one of them must be wrong. There's a protest singer, he's singing a protest song…"

Top right: The Rolling Stones' memorial in Hyde Park to the death of Brian Jones.
Bottom right: The legend of Jimi Hendrix lives on in Mayfair.

...plosion of punk
...y, but not all. What
...t to stick a safety pin
...eave gigs covered
...had enjoyed the Sex
...all over and as the
...he Eighties, there was
...rs' strike, riots and

...ople looked for
...ulture movement
...lash against both its
...music that had gone
...ung from a small club in

...o, where DJ Rusty Egan
...ided the setting for
...signers and neglected
...sic featured Roxy Music,
...wie, whose song

Heroes would become the club anthem
and people here dressed very strangely.

"High street fashion was rubbish," said
Egan. "You went to charity shops and thrift
stalls, made your own outfits. It was a week's
achievement to look the way you looked. You
could live out your fantasies, become a film
star… You had to glamorise your glum, horrible,
boring existence with no future on the dole in
Thatcher's Britain." Strange would turn people
away from the door if they weren't looking
flamboyant enough (including Mick Jagger).

Popularity meant the club needed bigger
premises and they relocated to 4 Great Queen
Street, in the heart of Covent Garden. They
named it the Blitz Club and the whole scene
took off. Strange and Egan joined Midge Ure
(of Ultravox) to form Visage, future members
of Spandau Ballet were regulars and the club's
cloakroom attendant, Boy George, would go

on to sire Culture C...
stealing money fro...

The Blitz Kids w...
Romantics and bef...
full of pop stars wit...
men wearing make...
highwaymen. While...
other than its glam...
was pioneering, fav...
drum machines ove...
Duran Duran becam...
give birth to dance...
adding disco beats...

It was fun and v...
lasted, but electrop...
pop and the hedor...
of some.

If punk meant r...
dressing down the...
were working clas...

COVENT GARDEN
LONDON WC2

THE STRAND
LONDON WC2

Neal Street in Covent Garden today could be any pedestrian-friendly drag in an affluent 21st century European metropolis. Chain fashion outlets predominate, while café and sandwich bars vie to peddle the most authentically Italian cup of coffee in London. In 1977 things were different. Covent Garden was shabby and neglected, the local economy still reeling from the relocation two years previous of the wholesale fruit and vegetable market to Nine Elms, just south of the Thames.

At 41-43 Neal Street in a tiny erstwhile gay club, was The Roxy, which would become the crucible of the UK punk scene, until it was forced to close its doors in 1978. The Clash – with Strummer sporting bleached blonde hair and '1977' hand written across his shirt – officially opened London's first punk rock venue on 1 January, 1977. With punk banned from most London venues like the 100 Club, the Marquee and various pub gigs in the wake of the furore that followed the Pistols' TV appearance on the Bill Grundy Show on December 1, 1976, the burgeoning scene had found itself with few live outlets. Enter accountant Andrew Czezowski (he handled the books for King's Road boutiques Sex and Acme Attractions plus a stint as The Damned manager) and make-up consultant Susan Carrington. Don Letts was the resident DJ.

Rock dinosaurs Robert Plant and Jimmy Page once paid a visit to Roxy to check out The Damned. When The Damned left the stage after a 20-minute set a drunk John Bonham ordered The Damned back on stage. A vodka-sizzled Bonzo had to be carried out. Today 41-43 houses the flagship London store of Speedo swimwear.

Ever wondered why Mancunians like The Smiths ended up signing to Rough Trade, a London-based record company, rather than Factory Records? The answer lies here, at the former Rock Garden (6/7 The Piazza, Covent Garden, London, WC2E), their debut London gig, which directly led to their signing.

The Middle Earth Club, at 43 King Street, was where Marc Bolan held a gig after leaving John's Children. Re-named as the Middle Earth, however, it became the resident venue for Tyrannosaurus Rex. 16 Bruton Place, was the office of Lupus Publishing Company, Marc's publishers. The Tyrannosaurus Rex Fan Club formed in February 1969, was also run from those premises.

The Lyceum Ballroom, on the Strand, is the legendary London music venue and pop shrine, where Bob Marley and the Wailers recorded their landmark live album which spawned his breakthrough hit *No Woman No Cry*. By the late '70s it was doing discos on Saturdays and weird new wave hootenanny's on Sundays. Bauhaus, the Birthday Party and their like took the 2,000-plus crowd to new musical tangents and German industrial noiseniks Einsturzende Neubauten accompanied their cacophony by making huge holes in the stage with a road drill. Soon after, sadly it closed its doors to live gigs. The Lyceum inspired The Kinks' song *Come Dancing*: Ray Davies's oldest sister, Rene, died of a heart attack whilst dancing on the Lyceum dancefloor the day before his 13th birthday.

The famous video for Bob Dylan's *Subterranean Homesick Blues* (1965) was filmed in the street at the back of the Savoy Hotel on the Strand after he and Donovan had sat up all night writing the caption boards! The care-in the community looking geezer in background was poet Allen Ginsberg.

Gary Numan's first post-Tubeway Army single *Cars* (1979) was inspired by a road rage incident, when he was attacked by a group of men and locked himself in his car to escape. A synth-driven exercise in urban dystopia with an irresistible dance-rock rhythm, Cars sees the robot-cockney feeling safe in his car, yet, still, "nothing feels right". Timeless enough in both sound and alienated mood to have hit the UK charts in the 70s, 80s and 90s.

A disused tube station, Aldwych is regularly used for filming – and, in particular, has been used in two pop videos – The Prodigy's *Firestarter*, and Everlast's *Black Jesus*. The Prodigy threw lots of bits of shiny foil about in the tunnel (which are still there), while Everlast threw lots of feathers around (which aren't). If you're looking for it now, the canopy has gone, and it says "Strand Station", which was the original name.

Proud Galleries, in Buckingham Street, just off the Strand (also Chalk Farm Road in Camden) frequently puts on photographic shows featuring stunning images of top rock 'n' pop icons, from Jimi Hendrix to Keith Richards to Freddie Mercury, from the Beatles to the Libertines. They are also popular hang-outs for up and coming bands.

Central London

BUCKINGHAM PALACE
LONDON SW1

The Sex Pistols crashed Her Majesty The Queen's Silver Jubilee party big-time in 1977. In March, the band's very public signing to A&M Records occurred outside the front of the gates of Buckingham Palace. Not long after the ink had dried on the contract, A&M walked away from the partnership. At just six days, the record company's dealings with the punk band lasted even less time than a royal marriage. A year earlier, Jamaican reggae star Dillinger (aka Lester Bullock), mentioned by Joe Strummer in The Clash's *White Man in Hammersmith Palais*, wrote a song called *Buckingham Palace* in which he imagines blazing up his chalice (smoking pipe) in the palace.

WESMINSTER & DOWNING STREET
LONDON SW1

The Who were pictured underneath one of London's best-known landmarks, The Palace of Westminster and its famous clock Big Ben, on the sleeve of *The Who Sings My Generation*, their 1965 debut album. Twelve years later in 1977, The Jam copied their exact pose wearing Union Jack jackets. If you want to recreate it with some mates the photograph was taken from Bridge Street with Big Ben in the background. That was the sleeve for The Who's US album release anyway; the cover for the UK album – called just *My Generation* – was shot amongst some oil drums further south at Surrey Docks.

No punk squat this: number 10 Downing Street is the former residence of failed musician and Labour Prime Minster, Tony Blair. Whilst studying law at Oxford University in the early 1970s, budding guitarist Blair, complete with long hair and an early Slash-style top hat look, formed a student band playing Bad Company numbers. The band names The Quango Chiefs and War Mongerers were already taken so they called

themselves Ugly Rumours. A grinning Blair invited a handful of English pop stars to an official reception at Number 10, in July 1997, soon after Labour's landslide victory in 1997. Guests included Creation Records boss Alan McGee and Oasis songwriter Noel Gallagher, then at their Britpop peak.

That same year, usually reticent Geri Halliwell, the artist usually known as Ginger Spice, described former Conservative prime minister Baroness Thatcher as the original girl power icon. The statement didn't go down well and a few years later she had switched to New Labour. Big Audio Dynamite punned on the Prime Minister's official residence on their second album, *10 Upping Street*, released in 1986, while *Mr Prime Minister*, a track on North London hip-hop star Ms Dynamite's 2005 album *Judgement Days*, was a critique of Blair's government. Number 10's current lodger – former Eton pupil David Cameron – was attacked by Paul Weller in The Jam's *Eton Rifles* (see Berkshire, page 152):

> 'Thought you were clever when you lit the fuse /
> Tore down the House of Commons in your brand
>   new shoes.'

VICTORIA
LONDON SW1

The Jam can be seen at the entrance to Victoria underground station at the start of the video for their 1979 single, *Strange Town*. It's worth a look on YouTube just to clock bassist Bruce Foxton's shocking near-Teutonic mullet.

> 'Found myself in a strange town /
> Though I've only been here for three weeks now /
> I've got blisters on my feet /
> Trying find a friend in Oxford Street.'

David Bowie did some strange things in the 1970s, not least commenting that Hitler was "one of the first rock stars".

When arriving at Victoria Station in early May 1976 he gave a Nazi salute to a crowd of gathered fans (see Rock Against Racism, page 39)

Near Victoria station, but round the corner in Vauxhall Bridge Road, was where the cover of Ian Dury's breakthrough 1977 album, *New Boots and Panties!!* was shot. A long since been demolished clothing shop, Axfords, at number 306, was the store Ian Dury posed outside with his young son Baxter, nowadays a songwriter in his own right. Dury's son wasn't even supposed to be in the cover photo and wandered into shot.

PIMLICO
LONDON SW1

The Small Faces' communal Pimlico home in the mid-1960s was located at 22 Westmoreland Terrace, a four-storey Georgian bachelor pad. With no shortage of house guests and non-stop partying until the early hours, only drummer Kenney Jones elected to live elsewhere else. Meanwhile Steve Marriott, Ronnie Lane and Ian McLagan lived the mod dream: they listened to sounds, paraded around in newly-bought clothes and got high. Their chatty cleaner Marge provide the inspiration for the 'How's Your Bert's Lumbago?' line in the band's song *Lazy Sunday Afternoon*.

EMBANKMENT
LONDON SW1

In 1971 Jethro Tull frontman Ian Anderson posed for some photos along the Embankment by the Thames. With a battered old overcoat and long, messy hair, he was made up to look like a tramp.

Above: The Sex Pistols signing to A&M Records in March 1977.

The photographs formed the basis for the sleeve of Jethro Tull's *Aqualung* album – a painting of a scrawny down-and-out. The album takes its name from the tramp's nickname of Aqualung after the heavy breathing and gurgling sound of phlegm in his lungs.

SOUTH KENSINGTON
LONDON SW7

First opened in 1871 as a memorial to Queen Victoria's husband, the glass-domed oval of the Royal Albert Hall on Kensington Gore is one of the capital's instantly recognisable landmarks. Each year it hosts the summer proms but for over four decades it's also been a top rock venue. Supergroup Cream bid farewell from here in 1968 but guitarist Eric Clapton didn't say goodbye for good. The Hall has latterly been home to a series of annual gigs by Slowhand: "After Midnight, we're gonna let it all hang down", though with his audience getting older by the year, they're more likely to be tucked up with their cocoa after midnight.

BELGRAVIA
LONDON SW1

The Beatles manager Brian Epstein lived at 24 Chapel Street, off Belgrave Square, his main London home that he bought in December 1964. He also died here in late August 1967 after an overdose of pills. Aged just 32, his death was a bitter shock to many. The Pretty Things' London abode was located at 13 Chester Street from the summer of 1964. The address was also the name of a track on the band's eponymous debut album. The house briefly became the epicentre of Swinging London with Christine Keeler, the Kray Twins, Diana Dors and an increasingly unpredictable Brian Jones as regular visitors.

CHELSEA
LONDON SW3

The Who posed for their *The Who Sell Out* sleeve at David Montgomery's Chelsea studio in Edith Grove in October 1967.

The sleeve includes a shot of Roger Daltrey submerged in a bath of Heinz Baked Beans: the beans were so cold the singer almost caught pneumonia. Three of The Rolling Stones – Brian Jones, Keith Richards and Mick Jagger – lived at 102 Edith Grove in Chelsea in 1962 and 1963 before they hit the big time. Brian Jones had lived in the middle floor flat when the Stones had first formed but Jagger and Richards soon moved in. The Beatles visited the flat for a party in April 1963 after seeing the Stones play at Richmond's famous Crawdaddy Club. Later, in the late '60s, the songwriting duo both moved to Cheyne Walk; Keith lived at number 3 and Mick resided at number 48 (by this stage in their career they could afford separate houses). Home to Jagger between 1968 and 1975, his Cheyne Walk residence was busted by the Chelsea Drugs Squad in an infamous raid in 1969.

Sir Peter Blake designed The Beatles' famous *Sgt Pepper* cover at his studio at Chelsea Manor Studios, 1-11 Flood Street, off the Kings Road. In late March 1967, photographer Michael Cooper lined up the Fabs in Studio Four in front of a remarkable collage designed by Blake and posed for other shots that appeared on the inner sleeves.

Chelsea was the name of a punk band led by singer Gene October (not his real name) that included the Bromley Contingent's Billy Idol on guitar and Mick Jones' former London SS comrade, Tony James on bass.

The American actress and singer Judy Garland's final residence, and the place she died following an accidental overdose of barbiturates, was at 4 Cadogan Lane in Chelsea. She passed away in late June 1969, just three months after she had married her fifth husband, nightclub manager Mickey Deans.

Opposite page: Cream at the Royal Albert Hall in 1967, and Eric Clapton there in 2009.

Street life

STARTING at Sloane Square and running for nearly two miles southwest through the borough of Chelsea, to Waterford Road in Fulham, is the King's Road, so named for its use as Charles II's private road from Westminster to Kew. Though you'd never guess it today from the preponderance of high street chains, the King's Road was at the core of virtually every London happening. In the 1960s it spawned the mini skirt at Mary Quant's Bazaar, and dandy decadence at Nigel Waymouth's Granny Takes A Trip, and from 1971 onwards it housed Westwood/McLaren's flamboyant experiments with safety pins and bondage.

'I went down to the Chelsea Drug Store/
To get your prescription filled.'

The Rolling Stones' *You Can't always Get What You Want* (1969) is probably the most famous song to be associated with the King's Road. The Chelsea Drug Store was situated on the corner of Royal Avenue and the King's Road, over three floors of bars, record stores, newsstands and, yes, a chemist. The store offered a 'flying squad' service with young ladies in purple catsuits delivering punters orders by motorbike. You can still visit the site today, order a Big Mac from a terminally bored teenager, and weep.

There are other songs to name this most famous of streets: *Walking Down The Kings Road* by Squire is the ultimate mod London song, while *King's Road* is the title of a song by Tom Petty and the Heartbreakers from the 1981 album *Hard Promises*.

At the west end of the King's Road is a district known as The World's End, based around the pub of the same name. This was an unfashionable and relatively poor part of SW3 but the Fashionistas who had made their home at the other end of the King's Road found it was the perfect place to open the legendary 1960s boutique, Granny Takes a Trip. The World's End then became the centre of the counter-culture world of the 1960s, and this continued in the late '70s and '80s with the opening of the Let it Rock (see also next page) boutique started by Vivienne Westwood in the 1970s at number 430 (it is now known as Worlds End).

FOUR LADS WHO SHOOK THE WORLD

THE BIRTH OF BRITISH PUNK

IT'S 1976. You've just heard the opening chords of *Anarchy in the UK* and life will never be the same. Ditch the flares. Cut the hair. Stop listening to your older brother's Yes and Genesis albums. This is Year Zero.

Like all great movements, punk rock was a reaction: against the austerity measures introduced by Callaghan's Labour government in the wake of the oil crisis; and against the bloated, overblown, self-indulgent noodlings of prog rock superstars such as Rick Wakeman (who wore a cape) and Pink Floyd. "Never trust a hippy", said John Lydon, and he meant it, man.

The seeds of punk in the UK were sown in London's King's Road when two teenagers, Steve Jones and Paul Cook started hanging out in Too Fast To Live, Too Young To Die, a retro clothes shop run by Malcolm McLaren and Vivienne Westwood. Jones and Cook asked McLaren to manage their band, The Strand, and then recruited Glen Matlock, who sometimes worked in the shop, as bassist. Before departing for New York – where he would briefly manage The New York Dolls – McLaren and Westwood renamed their shop SEX (later Seditionaries), and renamed The Strand as the Sex Pistols.

On his return to the UK in May 1975, McLaren began the search for a singer, after being turned down by Dolls' vocalist Sylvain Sylvain. A series of auditions followed (including Midge Ure and Kevin Rowlands), before McLaren's friend, Bernie Rhodes (who would go on to manage The Clash) saw John Lydon on the Kings Road wearing a Pink Floyd T-shirt with the words 'I hate' scrawled above the lettering, and holes poked through the eyes. Lydon was introduced to the band and the rest, as they say, is history.

It was at an epoch-making Pistols gig supporting Eddie and Hot Rods at the Marquee on 12 February 1976, that punk began to spread from the capital to the rest of the country. In the audience were Howard Devoto and Pete Shelley, who were inspired to form their own punk group, Buzzcocks, and take the message to the northwest (see page 252). Also in the audience was Mick Jones, who would go on to form The Clash with Joe Strummer (in April the Sex Pistols supported Joe Strummer's 101'ers at the Nashville), Paul Simenon and drummer Terry Chimes (later replaced by 'Topper' Headon). Around this time The Ramones, leading lights in the New York punk scene, released their debut album, though Lydon claimed they had no bearing on the Sex Pistols direction, declaring: "I didn't like their image, what they stood for, or anything about them."

Lydon, who would become Johnny Rotten (due to his poor dental hygiene), would define the Sex Pistols with his singular stage persona, described by Jon Savage as " a cross between Uriah Heep and Richard Hell." On 26 November, 1976, the Pistols released their first single, *Anarchy in the UK*, a powerful piece of punk politics that defined an era and would change the face of popular music for ever (it wasn't the first punk single; that honour went to The Damned's *New Rose*, which was released a month earlier).

A week later punk had already grabbed the headlines for different reasons, during a live interview on Thames Television's Today programme when Steve Jones swore on air. The tabloid press were apoplectic with rage, with the *Daily Mirror*'s front page screaming 'The Filth and the Fury'. This led to national uproar as punks were labelled as 'inhuman' and 'nauseating', and council officials up and down the country banned them from playing in their towns. Such publicity only succeeded in hastening punk's arrival and, as the nation drowned in a sea of uncollected rubbish, Johnny Rotten's sneering two fingers to the establishment resonated with a generation growing increasingly disillusioned as the dole queues lengthened.

BAKER STREET & MARYLEBONE
LONDON W1

Best known for Gerry Rafferty's eponymous 1978 number three hit, Baker Street has its own rock credentials. At 94 was the building bought by The Beatles in 1967 to sell psychedelic clothes. It was called the Apple Boutique and when it first opened, it had a huge psychedelic mural painted on the side wall, but the council ordered it to be painted over so it was then painted white with 'apple' printed simply in black paint. Once, Paul McCartney wrote 'Hey Jude' with white paint on the window to promote The Beatles' new single. It failed to be successful and eventually all the clothes were given away in 1968 to anyone who queued up outside. The building is now a branch of Reed Employment.

Number 34 Montagu Square, in Marylebone, was a true rock 'n' roll shrine. This was the home of Ringo Starr and the place where John Lennon first lived with Yoko Ono. Their nude *Two Virgins* cover was shot here in the basement and Paul recorded a demo version of *Eleanor Rigby* in a temporary studio. But it wasn't all good. They also got busted. John was charged with possession of cannabis. Ringo later rented the house to Jimi Hendrix but then had to throw him out for trashing the place.

The Beatles rarely travelled far for their album covers. The cover shot for their first album was taken at 20 Manchester Square, in the stairwell of the old headquarters of EMI Records. EMI have long since moved to Hammersmith and the original building and stairwell has been demolished and completely rebuilt. A later photograph, featuring a remarkably more hirsute Fab Four, was taken in exactly the same spot at the end of their career and these two contrasting images shots are used on their two Greatest Hits compilations. The new Manchester Square complex houses ICI's head office.

Left: The Apple Boutique opened for business in 1967, complete with psychedelic mural.

EUSTON & ST PANCRAS
LONDON NW1

Hold Still, on Jarvis Cocker's 2009 album *Further Complications*, conjures up every parent's nightmare – the horror of losing a young child in a public place. The song is based on a traumatic few moments at St Pancras International station when Cocker thought he'd lost his son – and worst-case scenarios flooded his imagination. The British Library's Sound Archive, now housed at 96 Euston Road, next to London's St Pancras station, is the UK's greatest reference point for things musical, with over three and half million recordings.

Roy Harper was once arrested for climbing the clock tower of St Pancras station in 1960. "I ended up being fished off the roof because I was trying to change the time", he said.

When Damon Albarn first moved to London he worked at Le Croissant shop at Euston station.

HOLBORN
LONDON WC2

In Studio 9 in Television House on Kingsway, the '60s TV music show *Ready, Steady, Go!* was first broadcast, in August 1963. The first song performed was *Twist And Shout* covered by Essex's Brian Poole and the Tremeloes.

The members of Coldplay met at the University College London (UCL) in September 1996. Chris Martin and Jonny Buckland were the first members of the band, having met one another during their orientation week. They spent the rest of the college year planning a band, with their efforts culminating in a group called Pectoralz. Later, Guy Berryman, a classmate of the two, joined. By 1997, the group, who had renamed themselves Starfish, performed gigs for local Camden promoters at small clubs. Martin also had recruited his longtime school friend Phil Harvey, who was studying classics at Oxford, to be the band's manager. (To this day, Coldplay consider Harvey to be the fifth member of the group.)

Suede's Brett Anderson and Justine Frischmann of Elastica also met while studying at University College London and became a couple soon afterwards.

NEXT time you slag off an Underground busker for murdering *Stairway to Heaven* or *Streets of London* bear in mind that they are transport troubadours, carrying on a musical tradition that dates back to Roman times.

For years, the only sound you'd hear at Tube stations was an Orwellian two-tone signal followed by a muffled mumbled announcement about delays. Busking on the Underground was illegal and it wasn't until 2003 that London Underground granted permits through their busking scheme. Now nearly 400 buskers entertain the travelling public throughout the week, with up to 3,000 weekly time slots.

So flash them a smile and flip them a couple a coins if it's a song you like. And if it's *Lady In Red* they're playing, try to refrain from attacking them.

Down in the Tube Station at Midnight, The Jam (1978)

A tale of violence on the Underground as a commuter makes his way home with a "takeaway curry" and is attacked by neo-Nazi thugs: "They smelt of pubs and Wormwood Scrubs, and too many right wing meetings." The Jam used Baker Street Underground Station for the cover and the intro and outro train sounds were taped by producer Vic Coppersmith-Heaven at St John's Wood underground station.

Smithers-Jones, The Jam (1979)

Another Tube reference by The Jam, this time penned by bassist Bruce Foxton: "Here we go again. It's Monday at last. He's heading for the Waterloo line. To catch the 8 am fast, It's usually dead on time…"

Fugazi, Marillion (1984)

This title track off their second studio album, is full of London locations: "Drowning in the liquid seize of the Piccadilly Line, rat race scuttling through the damp electric labyrinth."

Twelve Stops and Home, The Feeling, (2006)

The album's title refers to the 12 stops on the Piccadilly Line of the London Underground from Leicester Square to Bounds Green. Lead singer Dan Gillespie Sells grew up in Bounds Green and lived a short walk from the tube station.

GOING UNDERGROUND

North London

ISLINGTON
LONDON N1

The 18-storey Kestrel House on Islington's City Road estate is the tower block that graces the artwork of The Streets' widely-acclaimed debut album, *Original Pirate Material*, released in 2002. The album introduced The Streets – aka producer and MC Mike Skinner – as a chronicler of mundane modern Britain with a hybrid accent; a mix of his hometown Birmingham and adopted London. His wryly-observational songs about urban England tell of KFC and McDonald's, PlayStations and pills and he blazed a trail for the likes of Arctic Monkeys, Jamie T, Lily Allen and Dizzee Rascal.

Inspired by David Bowie and Marc Bolan, Gary Kemp wrote all of Spandau Ballet's 23 hit singles. Before that the Islington boy attended Rotherfield Junior School, in Rotherfield Street, and the Anna Scher Children's Theatre drama club. Kemp saw the Sex Pistols at Islington's Screen on the Green (where The Clash played their first gig, on 29 August, 1976) and immediately quit his jazz-funk band. "In 1979, this little club called Billy's appeared in (Meard Street, Soho)," he recalled, "run by Steve Strange (later of Visage) and Rusty Egan (later of The Rich Kids). I went to a Bowie night where Egan played this extraordinary mix of music. It was Bowie and Iggy Pop, but mixed with Kraftwerk and Gina X and Telex from Belgium – all these pulsing electronic rhythms. I bought a synthesizer." See also page 312.

Pink Floyd built the original Britannia Row Studios, Britannia Row, Islington (since relocated to Fulham), after their 1975 album *Wish You Were Here* was released. They recorded their next album *Animals* and parts of 1979's *The Wall* here. The children singing the famous, anarchic chorus line, "We don't need no education" on *Another Brick In The Wall*, were from nearby Islington Green school. The school's new head teacher was the progressive-minded Margaret Maden who'd employed the unconventional Alun Renshaw

as music teacher. Renshaw smoked in class and swore at students and he jumped at the chance to help out when Roger Waters called into the school for help. Waters said he still has "hairs standing up on my arms and everywhere just remembering the sound… hearing those kids sing." But kids joyfully singing about rejecting education didn't go down so well. "When I saw what the lyrics were, of course I went: 'Oops,'" says Mr Renshaw. "I had to go and talk to Margaret about it. By that time of course it was a bit too late to back down." It kicked up a bit of a stink. The pupils were more upset that, without Equity cards, they weren't allowed to be in the video and stage-school students mimed the words in their place. In a 2007 BBC documentary, Ms Maden says she regrets letting the children get involved now and, in 2004, some of them launched a bid for thousands of pounds in unpaid royalties. The case is still pending.

Tales From Turnpike House is a 2005 concept album by pop group Saint Etienne, about life in a block of flats (including guest vocals from David Essex). Turnpike House is a high-rise

Below: Spandau Ballet's Gary Kemp.
Opposite page: The Clash.

block of flats in Goswell Road, an area of (ex)-council blocks between fashionable Clerkenwell and Upper Street.

Islington's Hope & Anchor pub, 207 Upper Street, is a seminal pub-rock venue that hosted the likes of Dr Feelgood and Kilburn and The High Roads, The Clash, The Damned and The Stranglers. London debuts were made here by Joy Division and U2 – with only nine people in the audience. Local boys Madness played their first proper gig here, for an agreed fee of £40, but as Suggs put his foot through a monitor and was charged £45 for the privilege they ended up £5 down. The Union Chapel, Compton Avenue, is also one of the capital's top smaller venues.

Mott The Hoople's *The Journey* is about nearby Archway. Written by Ian Hunter, the song about the suburb's 'suicide bridge', started life as a poem and ended up an eight-minute epic.

CAMDEN
LONDON NW1

"Four skinny indie kids," sang Half Man Half Biscuit on the track of the same name, "drinking weak lager in a Camden boozer." Welcome, indeed, to Camden: indie kid heaven. The north London suburb became the centre of the music universe for a year or two during Britpop (see page 30) but some of its claims to rock fame go back a little further.

The Clash used an alleyway near Camden Lock for the now-iconic cover of their eponymous 1977 debut album. Photographer Kate Simon snapped Paul Simonon, Joe Strummer and Mick Jones posing like ne'er-do-wells on a stairwell opposite their oddly-named Rehearsal Rehearsals studios. The back cover shot comes from west London and a news photo of rioters clashing with police under the Westway during the 1976 Notting Hill Riots. (Ironically, the cover of a Clash album with London in its title, 1979's *London Calling*, was shot in New York – the black-and-white

here, while The Doors performed their only UK gig here, in 1976 (released as bootleg album *5 Go Mad At The Roundhouse*).

Taking full advantage of the early-1980s ska revival Camden Town seven-piece Madness dominated the singles charts in the early '80s with their 'nutty' sound and image. Blending influences like music hall, fairground, Prince Buster, The Kinks and Ian Dury, Suggs (aka Graham McPherson) and boys had six top 10 albums and spent more weeks in the singles chart (214) than anyone else (except UB40, who racked up the same number). They loved to showcase their neighbourhood in their songs and videos. Their *Liberty of Norton Folgate* album for example refers to a short length of street connecting Bishopsgate with Shoreditch High Street. The album's second track *We Are London* reads like an A to Z of the capital; mentioning Regent's Park, Baker Street, Camden Lock, Compton and Carnaby Streets, even Camden's Marathon Bar kebab house, latterly Amy Winehouse's pit stop for aggro 'n' chips.

They were pioneers of the still-new pop video medium, especially when it came to making funny footage. Their first video, *Baggy Trousers*, was shot in Kentish Town and showed Lee Thompson playing his sax while 'flying' (well, suspended from a crane) and the group playing at Islip Street school. In *House of Fun* a shamefaced adolescent, played by Suggs, attempts to buy his first packet of condoms. *Our House* was filmed at 47 Stephenson Street, Harlesden, in a terraced house with a purposefully ghastly décor. The building was often used to hire out to film crews and the owner, who lived there, kept it looking that way because of this, so it remained the same until it was sold in 1999. As a solo artist Suggs paid tribute to his neighbourhood in 1995's number 14 hit, *Camden Town*.

Elsewhere in Camden, Carl Barât, who went to Brunel University with Pete Doherty's sister, set up flat in Camden Road with Pete Doherty after the terrible twosome were introduced and fell in musical love. They formed the Libertines and began playing gigs in their living room. Another post-Britpop Camden-phile is Editors' frontman Tom Smith. He wrote *Walk The Fleet Road* about becoming a father, as well as the Camden street near the home he shares with his partner, Radio 1 DJ Edith Bowman.

When it comes to venues Camden is king, with the legendary Good Mixer, in Inverness Street, where members of Blur (who decamped here after signing their first contract with

---

Top: The cheeky chappies of Madness.
Bottom: The Libertines met in a Camden flat.

live image with retro pink and green typography a clear tribute to Elvis Presley's 1956 debut album sleeve).

The first major rock 'n' roll event in Camden took place close by, on 15 October, 1966, at the Roundhouse, a converted former railway engine shed at the top of Chalk Farm Road. Pink Floyd and the Soft Machine performed in front of a star-studded audience of 2,000. The gig set the pattern for events at the Roundhouse and artists such as Jimi Hendrix, Marc Bolan, Cream, Hawkwind and The Clash all started playing

Food Records), Oasis (though not at the same time as Blur) and, er, Menswear used to drink at the height of Britpop. Other patrons include Neneh Cherry, Finley Quaye, The Libertines, The Darkness and Travis. The venue is still going strong today. The Dublin Castle, 94 Parkway, was an early venue for Blur, as it was for local nutty boys Madness who also shot the video for *My Girl* here. Now part of the Camden Crawl festival, Amy Winehouse played a chaotic set here in 2007.

An early venue of The Police and Siouxsie and the Banshees gigs, Koko, in Camden High Street, was formerly the Camden Palace. It still hosts big-name acts like Coldplay, Madonna and Babyshambles. Hawley Arms, 2 Castlehaven Road, gained notoriety in 2007 as Amy Winehouse's favoured local, though Razorlight like to drink here too. The pub suffered from a disastrous fire in 2008, but it produced great headlines such as: 'Amy's Winehouse Burns Down'. She chanted 'Camden Town ain't burning down!' when she heard the news, which probably made very little sense to her Los Angeles audience. Formerly known as the Monarch, Barfly, in Chalk Farm Road, is where some of the biggest UK rock and indie stars started out and still a great place to catch up-and-coming bands. Right next to the tube, the Electric Ballroom is often missed by the tourists who flock up and down Camden High Street. Even on the sunniest of days, when you walk through the rabbit warren of corridors into the half-light of the ballroom, it's easy to imagine the likes of Sid Vicious and The Pogues jamming on the stage.

Each May the Camden Crawl sets up camp along Camden Town's two-mile stretch of high street with a programme of up-and-coming artists, contemporary bands and after-show parties across more than 40 venues, including the Jazz Café.

KENTISH TOWN
LONDON NW5

Kentish Town's Bull & Gate pub, 389 Kentish Town Road, featured early performances by Blur, The Housemartins, Suede, PJ Harvey, The Pogues, The Libertines, Muse, Manic Street Preachers and Coldplay. Kentish Town is also home to The Forum, for many years one of the area's most popular and comfortable cinemas, and now a popular live music venue.

As Madness grew up and went to school nearby it was natural that the cover of their second album *Absolutely* be shot at Chalk Farm Tube Station, Haverstock Hill. They wanted to use Camden station but were unable to, due to crowds.

A rock critic recommends

TAKE it from a man who knows. Guest contributor David Smyth, the chief rock and pop critic for the *London Evening Standard*, chooses his top five venues in the capital – and the one he misses the most:

1 O2 Shepherd's Bush Empire
It has been a nicely scuffed rock venue since the Nineties. It's small enough to feel intimate but admired enough to attract A-list stars on a weekly basis.

2 Royal Festival Hall
The South Bank Centre's main venue is the place to go for a sit-down chin-stroking session, especially during the annual Meltdown festival. Space-age boxes along the sides make it look spectacular too.

3 Koko
After a thorough polishing, the former Camden Palace is also now a wonderfully ornate, deep red, thoroughly modern venue with balconies that go up to the moon.

4 Bush Hall
A world away from the traditional toilet venue, the Bush Hall in Shepherd's Bush is small but as plush as they come. Gazing at its intricate white ceiling feels like being inside a wedding cake.

5 The Roundhouse
Another refurb gone right, this train shed from 1846 hosted psychedelic spectaculars in the Sixties and reopened in 2006 as a smart but characterful space for gigs, including the BBC Electric Proms."

6 (and one that's no longer with us…) The Astoria
A classic rock venue, from its black walls to its sticky floors. It didn't need to look classy to host historic gigs from the likes of U2, The Rolling Stones, Nirvana and Oasis. It finally closed to make way for the Crossrail development in 2009.

Looking back in anger:
BRITPOP

IN the early Nineties Madchester had fizzled out, Nirvana were everywhere and US rock and grunge bands filled the UK charts. British pop was at an all-time low. America ruled the (air) waves.

Debts had forced Blur on a reluctant two-month tour of the US in 1992, which they loathed and their homesickness had them longing for all things Britain. Their next three albums would be about their country, its curiosities and caricatures. Like The Beatles, Blur would sing about Britain's everyday life; Bank Holidays, 18-30 holidays, Sunday dinners, suburban sex-swaps and feeding pigeons. "If punk was getting rid of hippies," said ever-modest frontman Damon Albarn, "then I'm getting rid of grunge."

Britpop – a term that makes most people cringe now – started in the spring of 1992 when Blur and Suede released *Popscene* and *The Drowners* respectively. (The bands' frontmen hated each other after Elastica's Justine Frischmann left Brett Anderson, and Suede, for Albarn.) Suede's eponymous

debut album would shoot to number one the following year, but the mainstream wasn't paying attention quite yet. It took vocal protests from the music press to convince Brit award organisers to make Suede a last-minute addition, joining the likes of Enya, Genesis and Stigers. But a mood was growing.

If one album defined Britpop it was Blur's *Parklife*, propelled upward in 1994 by the success of their benchmark single, *Girls and Boys*. "When it happened, it wasn't a shock," guitarist Graham Coxon told Britpop chronicler John Harris. "It was something that we'd all been half-expecting. It was, 'When is the world going to realise that we're making excellent pop music?' And they'd finally twigged."

Soon, Pulp, who'd been at it for over a decade already, Elastica, Sleeper, Suede, Supergrass, Dodgy, The Bluetones, Shed Seven, Oasis, Gene, Echobelly, Cast, even Menswear, were all making impressions on the charts and at Brit award ceremonies.

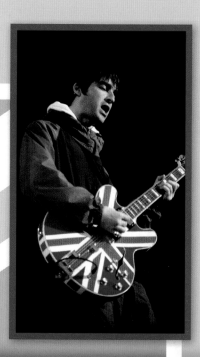

Oasis' *Definitely Maybe* went straight to number one as the UK's fastest-selling debut album in 1994. With the help of John Peel's patronage, Elastica would break that record the following year.

Britpop was openly retro, a nostalgic call to bygone eras of great pop music. The influence of David Bowie, The Jam, The Smiths, The Kinks, Small Faces and The Beatles was unmistakable. And, Oasis notwithstanding, it was mostly a London thing: Pulp, Blur, Suede and Elastica were all based in the capital and Camden became Britpop Central. *Melody Maker* declared: "Camden is to 1995 what Manchester was to 1989." The Good Mixer pub, 30 Inverness Street, in particular soon had Britpop groupies turning up, hoping to catch regulars like Coxon and members of Menswear.

There was a real sense of optimism afoot in the country in the mid-'90s; football's European Championships were held here in '96, Chris Evans was doing his best to emulate

The Tube on his *TFI Friday* TV show and everyone could sense the imminent end of the long, long Tory regime.

However, many of the bands genuinely despised each other. "The whole thing was so bitchy," remembers Frischmann. "I always feel kind of dirty after I've talked about Britpop". Then along came 'the Battle of Britpop'. Albarn decided to release Blur's single *Country House* on the same day as Oasis's *Roll With It*, in the summer of 1995, a deliberate confrontation, which made the ITN news. Blur 'won', but it was all getting a bit silly.

Oasis's mega-successful *(What's The Story) Morning Glory?*, and hit singles like *Wonderwall*, appealed directly to the lad mag crowd and Britpop felt like it had been hijacked. The *Country House* video, featuring Matt Lucas, Keith Allen, *Loaded* pin-ups and a Benny Hill homage, seemed to be a metaphor for what Britpop had become: over-indulgent, self-parodying and in love with itself.

When New Labour came to power in 1997 the good music had pretty much dried up and slow-off-the-mark, air-kissing luvvies were using phrases like 'Cool Britannia'. When arch rock 'n' roller Noel Gallagher went to Number 10 for drinks with Tony Blair it signalled the end of a musical era. Indie had sold its soul.

Almost all the Britpop bands have since split up. But the movement's influence can be clearly seen today in the likes of Kaiser Chiefs, The Libertines and Coldplay. Britpop wasn't built to last, but it sure was good fun while it did.

Top left: Justine Frischmann and Elastica play live.
Above right: The rivalry between Oasis and Blur found its way onto the pitch.
Opposite page: Noel Gallagher's trip to 10 Downing Street and the 'Cool Britannia' culture signalled the end of Britpop.

The futuristic-looking estate that adorns Richard and Linda Thompson's 1979 album *Sunnyvista* is Rowley Way, near Swiss Cottage, not far from the far more famous Abbey Road. On the album the king and queen of folk-rock are joined by Gerry Rafferty and Squeeze's Glen Tilbrook.

Sinead O'Connor's 1997 *Gospel Oak* was her first recording since her acclaimed 1994 album, *Universal Mother* and the cover features the bridge at Gospel Oak station looking up Mansfield Road close to Hampstead Heath. The world seems to have since given up on Sinead O'Connor after the infamous incident when she tore up a photograph of the Pope on television.

No shrine marks the spot, but Morgan Studios once stood at 169-171 Willesden High Road, Brent, and it's where Rod Stewart cut his first album, *An Old Raincoat Will Never Let You Down*. Lou Reed, Paul McCartney, Eric Clapton and The Kinks also recorded here.

Below: Ralph McTell.
Opposite page: Abbey Road is synonomous with The Beatles.

Streets of London: songs about the capital

Baker Street, Gerry Rafferty (1978)
Scottish troubadour Rafferty pays tribute to a largely unremarkable road. It seems a mate of his had lived here: "this dream about buyin' some land / He's gonna give up the booze and the one-night stands." A number three hit in the UK and number two in the US.

For Tomorrow, Blur (1993)
"It's about being lost on the Westway," explained Damon Albarn, "It's a romantic thing, it's hopeful." The song mentions driving to Primrose Hill – "It's windy here and the view's so nice" – and having a cup of tea in Emperor's Gate. He used to visit his parents in their Emperor's Gate flat.

LDN, Lily Allen (2006)
A nod to Lord Kitchener's *London Is The Place For Me*, Allen's gathering of crack dealers and ASBOs is a dystopian alternative to Kitchener's optimistic Windrush anthem.

London's Burning, The Clash (1977)
Written by Joe Strummer as he paced the city at night, he's said: "There was nothing to do in those days. Television stopped at 11pm, all bars stopped at 11pm, and that was it… I was walking around a lot in West London, and 'London's Burning' came to me all at once."

London Song, Ray Davies (1998)
"If you're ever up on Highgate Hill on a clear day," sang north the Londoner and ex-Kinks frontman, "You can see right down to Leicester Square."

Play With Fire, The Rolling Stones, (1965)
"Now she gets her kicks in Stepney, not in Knightsbridge anymore". The song is credited to Nanker Phelge, a pseudonym used when the entire band composed a track, even though Mick Jagger and Keith Richards are the only Stones to appear on the track.

Sheila, Jamie T (2006)
Sheila samples John Betjeman's poem *The Cockney Amorist*, about how he used to walk the streets of London with a girlfriend. "It sounds fragile and romantic," said Wimbledon's Mr T. "I like the way he's an old man talking about it and he's almost pining for olde England… he thinks about churches and old buildings and the beauty of the place."

Strange Town, The Jam (1979)
Part of the video was shot at Victoria Station's underground section. Lonely Surrey boy Paul Weller sings:

'Found myself in a strange town/
Though I've only been here for three
  weeks now/
I've got blisters on my feet/
Trying find a friend in Oxford Street'

Streets Of London, Ralph McTell (1969)
The most recorded London song of all time possibly isn't what you think it is. "I grew up in post-war Croydon," explained McTell. "I used to go to Saturday morning pictures at the end of Surrey Street, which was a busy bustling market, and collect boxes for firewood while they were clearing away the stalls. But late at night there was this old chap who used to wander up, kicking up the papers and picking up the rubbish from the market, just the odd bit of stuff that had been dumped, and it was an image that I always remembered.

You're the One for Me, Fatty, Morrissey (1992)
"All over Battersea / Some hope and some despair," sings Mancunian Moz in a song about Chas Smash from Madness. Morrissey once asked Smash to be his manager but the Madness man wasn't that mad, saying: "I don't fancy having to iron his socks."

Hear also:
Waterloo Sunset, The Kinks (1967); *London*, The Smiths (1987); *Hold Tight London*, Chemical Brothers (2005); *Leave the Capitol*, The Fall (2004); *Hometown Glory*, Adele (2007); *Come Back To Camden*, Morrissey (2004); *London Loves*, Blur (1994); *Has It Come To This?*, The Streets (2001); *Upon Westminster Bridge*, Half Man Half Biscuit (2005); *London Lady*, The Stranglers (1977).

PRIMROSE HILL
LONDON NW1

John Lennon had a PA system of sorts fitted to his white Rolls-Royce so he could shout at passers-by. Once, while driving through London's Regent's Park, he startled Rolling Stone Brian Jones by yelling, 'You are under arrest!'

Few places in England, let alone London, can claim as much rock heritage as Primrose Hill. If The Rolling Stones look a bit worse for wear on the cover of 1967's *Between the Buttons* it isn't surprising. Photographer Gered Mankowitz shot them early one cold November morning in 1966 after the band had been recording all night at Olympic Studios in Barnes and the photo is deliberately fuzzy around the edges. The album spawned two hits, *Ruby Tuesday* and *Let's Spend The Night Together*, but headline-grabbing drug busts that year largely overshadowed the band's musical output.

Madness made it further up Primrose Hill for the cover of 1982's *The Rise And Fall*, which featured the hit single *Our House* (also the name of West End musical featuring the band's music). The Camden Town band included a song on the album named after the hill, which starts with the line "A man opened his window and stared up Primrose Hill." On the cover each band member is pictured with a prop depicting a different song title. The nutty boys name-check the Hill again on 1982 single *Driving In My Car*.

The video for Blur's 1993 single *For Tomorrow* – which includes the lyric "Let's take a drive to Primrose Hill it's windy there and the view is so nice" – shows the band at Trafalgar Square and on a red London bus before flying kites on Primrose Hill. The black and white footage, the image of World War II fighter planes on the single's sleeve and the band's mod garb, shows Blur turning demonstrably pro-British, sewing one of the first seeds of Britpop (see page 30).

In a show of harmony deemed ironic given what was to come, the cover for Oasis single *Wonderwall* was also shot on Primrose Hill. The artwork was inspired by Belgian surrealist René Magritte and the sleeve's art director Brian Cannon's hand holding the picture frame. The original idea was to have Liam in the frame but Noel vetoed the idea at the last minute and Anita Heryet, a Creation Records employee, stood in as cover star.

Billy Bragg says he felt inspired to write *Upfield*, which includes the line "I dreamed I saw a tree full of angels, up on Primrose Hill", by William Blake. The Emilíana Torrini song *Unemployed In Summertime* begins with the lyrics "Let's get drunk on Saturday / Walk on Primrose Hill until we lose our way." It's also thought Sir Paul McCartney penned *Fool On The Hill* after a fleeting encounter with a mysterious man up here who suddenly disappeared.

St Augustine's Church hides the former Victorian church hall, Wessex Sound Studios, at 106A Highbury New Park, from the street yet it was the venue for two of punk's greatest albums. In the summer of 1977 the Sex Pistols laid down *Never Mind the Bollocks, Here's The Sex Pistols*, while two years later, The Clash recorded *London Calling* at the same studios. Queen, The Rolling Stones and XTC have also used the recording facilities.

ST JOHN'S WOOD
LONDON NW8

The Beatles' *Abbey Road* album cover has produced the Fab Four's most enduring image – and London's most famous rock 'n' roll landmark. The Beatles were barely on speaking terms when they stepped on to the zebra crossing outside the Abbey Road studios in St John's Wood, northwest London, for the 10-minute photoshoot in August 1969. The cover fuelled bizarre rumours that Paul McCartney had actually died three years earlier and the cover portrayed a funeral procession: John Lennon, dressed in white was a priest; Ringo Starr, all in black, represented an undertaker while McCartney, barefoot and out-of-step, was the deceased. Meanwhile George, in denims, was the gravedigger. Originally Abbey Road was going to be called Everest, after the brand of cigarettes smoked by the engineer Geoff Emerick. Many have paid homage to Abbey Road's zebra crossing, including the Red Hot Chili Peppers cavorting around with socks strategically positioned over their manhoods.

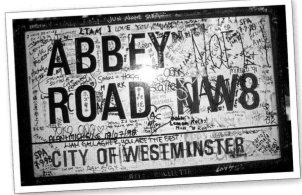

HAMPSTEAD
LONDON NW3

Hampstead may have been the place for music millionaires like Boy George and George Michael in more recent times, but it used to house rock stars of a very different calibre. Johnny Rotten shared a squat with fellow Sex Pistol member Sid Vicious, at 42A Hampstead High Street, in 1975 and reported that, despite the lack of running water, it was better than home. Elsewhere, Mick Jagger and Keith Richards shared 10A Holly Hill in the Sixties. On the back of the cover of 1994 compilation *Way To Blue* Nick Drake can be seen walking down to the pond at Hampstead Heath, near where he lived during his time in London.

HIGHGATE
LONDON N6

Whilst still attending William Ellis School in Highgate, guitar legend Richard Thompson formed his first band, Emil and the Detectives (named after a book and a movie by the same name), with classmate Hugh Cornwell, later lead singer and guitarist of The Stranglers, on electric guitar. Highgate Cemetery is also where punk svengali Malcolm McLaren was laid to rest after a day-long series of events which brought north London to a standstill in 2010.

It was in The Archway Tavern, 1 Archway Close, Highgate, that The Kinks signed their first recording contract and later immortalised the inside on the sleeve of their 1971 album *The Muswell Hillbillies*, a homage to the *Beverly Hillbillies* TV show and the nearby area of north London where Dave and Ray Davies grew up.

FINSBURY PARK
LONDON NW4

When Frank Zappa did a cover of The Beatles' *I Want To Hold Your Hand* as an encore at Finsbury Park's The Rainbow in 1971, Trevor Howell, the jealous boyfriend of a female fan, leapt on stage and pushed Zappa into the orchestra pit. Zappa took a 10-foot fall, followed by a monitor which fell on top of him breaking his leg in several places and causing other injuries including a fractured skull and damage to his larynx and. It was said to change his singing voice forever.

Formerly the Finsbury Park Astoria, the Rainbow Theatre was a major venue in London during the Sixties and Seventies. The building (now the UCKG UK headquarters) still stands out from its surroundings near Finsbury Park tube station. The venue played host to the first Beatles Christmas Show in 1963. Fans saw Jimi Hendrix set fire to his guitar on stage for the first time here in 1967. In 1973 The Rainbow was the venue chosen by The Who's Pete Townshend for Eric Clapton's comeback concert. Queen, Bowie, Floyd and the Grateful Dead have all played here too.

Born in 1956, John Lydon spent his early years in a two-room Victorian flat with an outdoor toilet in Benwell Road, Finsbury Park. The eldest of four boys, he often looked after them as his mother was frequently unwell. He wasn't very healthy himself and has a bent spine as the result of childhood meningitis, which kept him in hospital (St Anne's Hospital, Highgate) for a whole year, also giving him his fearful 'Lydon stare'. The Sex Pistol has since described his young self as a "very shy" kid who was "nervous as hell" and hated going to Sir William of York Catholic School, where he had several embarrassing incidents. "I would shit my pants and be too scared to ask the teacher to leave the class. I'd sit there in a pants' load of poo all day long."

Finsbury Park has become an established music venue and notable events have included the Sex Pistols comeback gig in 1996 and 1992's Madstock concert. There Morrissey was heckled off stage when fans took exception him coming on stage draped in a Union jack, which was often used by far-right groups at the time.

Above: John Lydon aka Johnny Rotten grew up in Finsbury Park.
Opposite page top: Amy Winehouse: a modern-day rock 'n' roll lifestyle.
Opposite page bottom: Ray Davies and The Kinks in their local area of north London.

CROUCH END
LONDON NW8

Bob Dylan once called in for a drink at Banners, 21 Park Road, Crouch End, but was told he would have to eat if he wanted to drink as they only had a restaurant licence. They wouldn't bend the rules for him and he left, though a little plaque saying 'Bob Dylan sat here' marks the spot where he briefly sat down. Both Ray Davies, of The Kinks, and Adam Ant went to Hornsey College of Art, in Crouch End. *Konk*, the second album by indie rockers The Kooks, is named after the studio where it was recorded (at 84-86 Tottenham Lane, Crouch End), owned by the same Ray Davies.

MUSWELL HILL
LONDON N10

Ray Davies, mastermind of The Kinks and writer of *Waterloo Sunset,* is London's unofficial poet laureate, chronicling the city's glitz and gloom and its homely suburbs. *Muswell Hillbillies* is about his home turf up on the hill. It's here that Ray was born in 1944 and grew up at 6 Denmark Terrace, a Victorian semi-detached which was cramped for a large family. It was a musical home, with a piano that his parents would gather round with friends for a hearty singsong after coming back from the Clissold Arms. Here, in 1964, Ray and brother Dave worked out the chords to *You Really Got Me*, the song that first put them at the top of the charts.

"Mum would shout and scream when dad would come home drunk," sang Dave Davies on *Fortis Green*. "When she'd ask him where he'd been, he said 'Up the Clissold Arms', chattin' up some hussy, but he didn't mean no harm.' The Clissold Arms, 105 Fortis Green, has a display of Kinks memorabilia, including a signed copy of the band's first single, a cover of Little Richard's *Long Tall Sally*, a guitar, a wall of photographs and a small brass plaque which reads: 'Site of 1957 performing debut of Ray and Dave Davies. Founding members of The Kinks.'

Number 87 Fortis Green Road was the home Ray bought when he married Rasa, whom he'd met when she was still a Bradford schoolgirl and a Kinks fan. It's Rasa's falsetto on the backing vocals of *Sunny Afternoon*. Ray and Dave used to go rock and rolling at the local hop, The Athenaeum, where Sainsbury's now stands.

Vivian Stanshall, of The Bonzo Dog Doo-Dah Band fame, was found dead in his Muswell Hill flat in March 1995 (one hundred years to the day after the death of the original Sir Henry Rawlinson). Though Stanshall often smoked in bed and once set fire to his ginger beard, the coroner found this fire was caused by faulty wiring.

Amy Winehouse grew up in Southgate, a quiet suburb, before going to theatre school. She moved on to another, Sylvia Young Theatre School, but was allegedly expelled at 14 for "not applying herself" and for piercing her nose, but not before she'd appeared in *The Fast Show* in 1997, with other members of the school.

BACK TO BASICS
THE PUB ROCK SCENE

SOMEWHERE between 1970s prog rock's self-indulgence, glam rock's androgyny and the filth and fury of the punk rebellion thrived a beer-swilled, anti-showbiz musical genre known as pub rock.

Instead of stadiums or large venues, pub rock bands played in the sweat-soaked back rooms of old Victorian boozers reeking of best bitter.

They played different musical styles – R&B, soul and country-rock – but their ethos was the same. They wanted to return to playing real songs in small venues using just basic equipment. They set out to breathe life into a music scene that had become far too pompous for its own good.

The pub rock scene was the 1970s first musical backlash, a resistance to rock becoming a spectator sport. It was a rallying cry against the bombastic lyrics and fancy theatrics of progressive rock. You'd never see a pub rock guitarist sitting on a stool whilst he played on stage.

Pub rock was a reaction to prog's silly capes, pointed wizard hats and dry ice in favour of a more vibrant, stripped-down sound. For musicians and fans alike it was a welcome return to roots rock 'n' roll. They replaced meandering solos that seemed to go on for hours with three-minute, rapid-fire, back-to-basics rhythm and blues.

The scene also removed the barriers between bands and audiences. Artists performed only inches away from their fans.

These were bands you could watch with a pint in your hand and stand next to at the bar afterwards. If you were lucky, they might even have bought you a drink.

Bands even functioned as live jukeboxes. Fans would call out the names of songs they wished to hear and the bands would play them – an interaction unthinkable at large venue prog gigs, where requests failed to make it over the wall of Korg synthesizers.

THE roots of the English pub rock scene were in early 1970s north London, and, ironically, its trailblazers were an American country rock band called Eggs Over Easy. In 1971, they got the ball rolling when their manager put them up in an empty house in Kentish Town.

Until then London's pubs had hosted jazz, folk and country and western gigs, but Eggs Over Easy changed all that. Originally they travelled over from Greenwich Village to record with Jimi Hendrix's ex-manager and Animals bassist, Chas Chandler. Tired of studio work, one night they walked into their nearest local that put on live music and secured a regular gig.

Unwittingly the Tally Ho in Fortess Road became the home of pub rock. It stood opposite what is now the Forum but was demolished in 2006, replaced by, yes, you've guessed it, a housing and retail development.

A Monday night residency for Eggs Over Easy followed and soon grew to four gigs a week. The Tally Ho soon ditched its jazz-only policy in favour of pub rock, inspiring other bands to follow them.

The country rock outfits Bees Make Honey and Ducks Deluxe, a band made up almost entirely of former roadies, joined the scene. There was also Brinsley Schwarz, featuring musician and producer Nick Lowe. The group were named after the group's guitarist and swapped their instruments like the Canadian rock group, The Band.

By early 1973, they were joined by Chilli Willi & The Red Hot Peppers, managed by Jake Riviera, later the co-founder of Stiff Records along with pub rock's prime mover Dave Robinson. Their growing ranks would include Ace and Ian Dury's Kilburn & the High Roads, spotted by Robinson at London's Speakeasy club.

Also, by Essex's Dr Feelgood who made their London debut at the Tally Ho later that summer. With Dr Feelgood, a new generation of rock fans found icons in raspy-voiced singer Lee Brilleaux and former Essex schoolteacher turned guitarist John Wilkinson, better known as Wilko Johnson.

It wasn't long before the Tally Ho was packed to the rafters. The pub rock scene soon became based around a small circuit of large Victorian pubs in London and its beer-swilling fans saw gigs almost every night of the week. Back then, most pubs were run as tenancies, allowing landlords more freedom. Many jumped at Dave Robinson's 1960s-style gig packages, with several bands on the same bill.

DR FEELGOOD, 1975

DIRE STRAITS LIVE, 1970

While pub rock was largely a London scene, some of its leading lights hailed from – and sung about – Essex: Dr Feelgood was from Canvey Island and the Kursaal Flyers and Eddie & the Hot Rods were both from Southend-on-Sea. The Kursaal Flyers were typical of pub rock bands, starting out as a country rock group, with a pedal steel guitar and banjo, before adding original material to their shows. And, even before his Blockheads days, Ian Dury sang about Essex. There were also some provincial venues, like JBs in Dudley and Sheffield's Black Swan.

Pub rock culminated in the mid-1970s with the *Naughty Rhythms* Tour, organized by Jake Riviera, with Dr Feelgood, Chilli Willi and the nine-piece soul band, Kokomo.

THE majority of venues were in north London: the Lord Nelson in Holloway Road, the Cock Tavern in Kilburn High Road (a suitably apt venue for Ian Dury's Kilburns), Camden's Dublin Castle and Islington's Hope & Anchor. This was a folk venue until Hope manager Fred Grainger met Dave Robinson, who built an eight-track upstairs studio above the venue. All of these except the Lord Nelson still exist today. Although Kentish Town's Tally Ho was the first pub to put on a pub rock band, Islington's Hope & Anchor became the venue most associated with the scene, when the Tally Ho changed la—rds and ditched rock for Irish bands.

Way out west, there was the Kensington, the Windsor Castle and the Nashville, originally a large country and western venue (hence the name) that later became an important punk venue, with early appearances by the Sex Pistols, the Stranglers and The Clash.

Peckham's Newlands Tavern was the solitary pub rock venue south of the river, where former mod Graham Parker and his band The Rumour rehearsed and made their debut.

NICK Lowe has amusingly summed up the whole pub rock scene: it was "the regrouping of a bunch of middle-class old mods who had been seduced by the hippie scene and then realized they'd made a terrible mistake." It wasn't until pub rock that these musicians were able to reconnect with an audience.

ROBINSON and Riviera aside, another key player was the late broadcaster, Charlie Gillett, who died in March 2010. Starting in 1972, his influential Honky Tonk radio show on BBC Radio London was required listening for music fans and musicians. The programme's gig guide became an invaluable bulletin board for bands looking for new members. And, when he wasn't managing Kilburn & the High Roads, he played demo tapes by new bands, including, in 1977, one by Dire Straits. Two months later they were signed to Phonogram Records and would become the only pub rock, style group to achieve world domination.

Apart from Ace's transatlantic chart-topper *How Long*, none of the original pub rock groups achieved any real chart success. Bands found it difficult to recreate a sweaty pub night in the studio. The exception was Canvey Island's Dr Feelgood. Pub rock reached its commercial highpoint in October 1976, when their live album *Stupidity*, stormed into the UK album chart at number one.

But by this time pub rock was on the wane and a new and snarly revolutionary music was ready to take on the rock establishment.

Bees Make Honey had already thrown in the bar towel, as had Ducks Deluxe and Brinsley Schwarz. These pub rock pioneers were replaced by younger new bands like the 101'ers, the Count Bishops and four teenagers from Southend-on-Sea called Eddie and The Hot Rods. They worked the same R&B as their contemporaries like Dr Feelgood but their energy, super-fast rhythms and songs about adolescent depression attracted a younger crowd. They were a hit on the pub circuit and were soon described in the music press as 'punk rock'.

The transition from pub rock to punk had begun. The 101'ers started to play in pubs alongside the emerging Sex Pistols, inspiring singer Joe Strummer to quit and join The Clash, and this more or less sounded the death knell for pub rock.

Many pub rock musicians went on to greater success elsewhere. Ducks Deluxe's Nick Garvey and Andy McMaster formed The Motors; ex-Kilburn & the High Roads Ian Dury became hugely successful with the Blockheads; Nick Lowe of Brinsley Schwarz became a Stiff Records' house producer and had a successful solo career that included an inspired lyric that rhymed 'Rick Astley' with 'ghastly'. And, what of Flip City, whose singer was a young man called DP Costello? Well, he later took the first name Elvis.

PUB ROCK'S legacy was to lay the foundations for punks to take rock 'n' roll to the next level with three chords and lots more attitude. Fresh, harder-edged bands were poised to declare a musical Year Zero and overthrow all that had gone before. And they would mean it, Ma'am.

CHARLIE GILLETT, 1973

East London

MILE END & AROUND
LONDON E1/E3

The cover of Morrissey's 2003 compilation *Under The Influence* sees the Mancunian miserablist standing outside the Grave Maurice pub at 269 Whitechapel Road, E1, once popular with the infamous Kray Twins and Diana Dors.

Why the Dickens are they smiling? The cover of The Jam's 1983 singles collection *Snap!* saw the trio strolling through the courtyard of The Dickens Inn public house in St Katherine's Docks, a popular tourist attraction near Tower Bridge. The docks were built by Thomas Telford in the early nineteenth century and because of their proximity to the City were one of the most important docks in London. First opened in 1858, Wilton's Music Hall, in Graces Alley, is the world's oldest surviving music hall, and is still a venue today.

Sheffield son, Jarvis Cocker wrote a 1995 Pulp song about squatters, called *Mile End*:

'We didn't have nowhere to live/
We didn't have nowhere to go/
Till someone said 'I know this place off Burditt Road'/
It was on the fifteenth floor/
It had a board across the door.'

SHOREDITCH & AROUND
LONDON E2

One sure way to fast-track yourself to the nearest Accident and Emergency ward in London's fashionable East End is to recreate The Verve's 1997 video for *Bitter Sweet Symphony*. The busy street Richard Ashcroft marches down, barging into passers-by and narrowly avoiding being hit by a car, is Hoxton Street in trendy Shoreditch. Ashcroft begins his walk outside the Golden Fried Chicken takeaway at the junction of Falkirk Street and Hoxton Street, before continuing north along the east side of Hoxton Street. Extras were brought in after Ashcroft was attacked by one man he bumped into who didn't realise a music video was being made. The idea was inspired by Massive Attack's *Unfinished Sympathy* video, where a more considerate Shara Nelson walks down West Pico Boulevard in downtown Los Angeles.

The Macbeth pub in Hoxton Street is where Amy Winehouse's ex-husband Blake Fielder-Civil and his friend Michael Brown were accused of assaulting barman James King in June 2007. Girls Aloud recorded a 2008 song called *Hoxton Heroes*, on the B-side of their single *Can't Speak French*.

Shoreditch's Old Blue Last pub, in Great Eastern Street, is a good venue. There are bands and DJs every night and it has a reputation for putting on surprise gigs by famous acts. Previously it's hosted the Arctic Monkeys, Lily Allen and the Young Knives.

One of the most amusing pop videos of recent years sees Jarvis Cocker playing the London cab driver from hell, as he heads to Bethnal Green, in 2006's *Don't Let Him Waste Your Time*. En route he tells his passenger to dump her boyfriend as he nonchalantly bumps into pavements and street furniture, while pedestrians and cyclists dash for their lives. The 1995 video for *Common People*, the best-known song by Cocker's indie band Pulp, used the groovy 1970s-style dance floor of Stepney's Nightclub, next to The George Tavern, on the Commercial Road, currently derelict and boarded up. The video saw Cocker pushed around in a shopping trolley by actress Sadie Frost.

Fleetwood Mac's troubled guitar genius Peter Green was born in Bethnal Green in 1946 and grew up at 18 Antenna House, Old Bethnal Green Road. He formed Fleetwood Mac in 1967 after he left John Mayall's Bluesbreakers, where he had replaced Eric Clapton. He left Fleetwood Mac in 1970, giving away a lot his earnings. For much of his life he battled with drug-induced schizophrenia, but is much-heralded by other guitar greats. Blues giant BB King said of Green: "the sweetest tone I ever heard. He's the only one who gave me the cold sweats".

The Libertines' 2000 debut album *Up the Bracket* was written when Pete Doherty and Carl Barât lived in a Bethnal Green squat they christened The Albion Rooms. The album referenced London cultural icons such as The Clash, the Small Faces, Tony Hancock and Chas & Dave. Bucks Fizz singer Cheryl Baker was also born in Bethnal Green.

BOW
LONDON E3

Born Dylan Mills in nearby Bow, in 1985, Dizzee Rascal was raised by his mother on a council estate. He was expelled from four schools and, at the fifth, barred from every lesson except music, where a music teacher recognised his talent. How prophetic that was. Dizzee Rascal would go on to enjoy major commercial acclaim and success with his 2003 *Boy in da Corner* album, which also won the Mercury Music Prize. Rascal, along with Wiley, were both members of Roll Deep, one of the first acts to bring the new genre known as grime to the nation's attention. One of the most exciting new musical genres to emerge from the capital in recent years grime is a uniquely London sound, a distillation of UK Garage, dancehall and hip hop. From its humble beginnings in Bow in the early noughties, via pirate radio stations such as Rinse FM, Freeze 92.7 and MajorFM.com, grime has grown in popularity to such an extent that several of its main players, notably Dizzee Rascal, Tinchy Stryder and Lady Sovereign, are seen as part of the mainstream. Dizzee Rascal even appeared on Jools Holland's *New Year Hootenany* in 2009/10.

HACKNEY
LONDON E8/E9

They did things differently in the 1970s: casual racism, sexism and homophobia were rife. Rock Against Racism was formed amid an atmosphere of rising racial tension and a few choice comments by some pop superstars in the mid-1970s: David Bowie's apparent Nazi salute at Victoria Station (which he later blamed on his drug usage) and Eric Clapton pledging his support for Enoch Powell, ranting about "a foreigner" pinching his wife's bottom at a concert in Birmingham. In response

to these and the rise of the far-right National Front, Rock Against Racism mobilised themselves. Bands staged a series of concerts, preceded by marches, in areas where the National Front had support. The largest and most famous event was in Victoria Park, Hackney, in April 1978. A crowd of 100,000 (including a young Billy Bragg) watched RAR-supporting acts The Clash, X-Ray Spex, Tom Robinson Band and Steel Pulse.

Nowadays Victoria Park hosts the annual High Voltage heavy metal festival in July and the Underage Festival in August for 14-18-year olds (inclusive). Revellers have to take their ID to prove they're young enough to get in. A decent line-up of bands ensures it's a proper rock festival, but without grown-ups and alcohol.

Above: The Clash play at Rock Against Racism, Victoria Park, in 1978.
Right: Bow's Dizzee Rascal.

Agitpop (protest songs)

SOMETIMES saying 'I love you' is not enough and it's the same in song. Pop and politics don't always mean an invite to Number 10. Rock music is about rebellion and some of the best pop songs have sought change.

We Love You, **The Rolling Stones (1967)**
This song was a statement about the British justice system after the Redlands drug bust and a 'thank you' to fans who supported them.

Glad to Be Gay, **Tom Robinson Band (1978)**
Well ahead of its time, pioneering Tom Robinson's scathing attack on homophobia is blended with dry wit. "The buggers are legal now, what more are they after?" he sings.

Biko, **Peter Gabriel (1980)**
Peter Gabriel's haunting tribute to murdered black South African activist Steve Biko samples funeral drums and became an anthem of the anti-apartheid movement.

America Is Not the World, **Morrissey (2004)**
Mozzer's broadside at his adopted homeland included the lyric: "The president is never black, female or gay." With the inauguration of President Obama in January 2009 he was only two-thirds right.

Two Tribes, **Frankie Goes to Hollywood (1984)**
Air raid sirens and voice-of-doom actor Patrick Allen reading extracts from the nuclear war Protect and Survive manual played their part. But better still, the video featured actors playing Cold War stalwarts Ronald Reagan and Konstantin Chernenko fighting each other in a pit, surrounded by a baying mob laying down bets.

Oliver's Army, **Elvis Costello (1979)**
Costello wrote this scathing attack on the Northern Ireland situation after a 1978 visit to Belfast. Many young school kids sang along to the jolly tune oblivious to the subject matter.

Gimme Some Truth, **John Lennon (1971)**
Former American president Richard Nixon was targeted by Lennon's poison pen: "No short-haired, yellow-bellied son of Tricky Dicky's gonna Mother Hubbard soft-sap me".

Free Nelson Mandela, **The Special AKA (1984)**
Elvis Costello produced this 2-Tone single recorded by members of The Specials and The Beat demanding the release of South African freedom fighter Nelson Mandela. It reached number nine in the UK charts and raised global awareness of apartheid.

Hear also:
White Riot, The Clash (1977); *There Is Power In A Union*, Billy Bragg (1986); *Do They Know It's Christmas?*, Band Aid (1984); *Meat is Murder*, The Smiths (1985); *God Save The Queen*, Sex Pistols (1977); *Real Great Britain*, Asian Dub Foundation (2000); *Give Peace A Chance* and *Imagine*, John Lennon (1969,1971).

Before glam-rock demigod Marc Bolan threw himself headfirst into mid-1960s London clubland and went from a mod to a hippy, his regular orbit was the streets of Hackney. He was born in September 1947 in Hackney Hospital and, from his birth until 1962, he lived with his parents and brother Harry at 25 Stoke Newington Common. Bolan – then little Marc Feld – attended Northwold Primary School, in Northwold Road, before enrolling at the William Wordsworth Secondary Modern School, Wordsworth Road, Shacklewell, in 1958.

Hackney also played an important role in the formation of the Sex Pistols. In 1971, the young teenager Sid Vicious and his mother relocated here from Tunbridge Wells, moving into a council tower block on Queensbridge Road in Haggerston. He would meet John Lydon at Hackney Technical College and later bassist Jah Wobble (Lydon's future bandmate in Public Image Limited).

Hackney might have been the inspiration for the fictional east London area of Squatney where spoof heavy metal band Spinal Tap spent their formative years in the 1960s as The Thamesmen. What is certainly in Hackney is Throbbing Gristle's studio, The Death Factory, at 10 Martello Street. The band lived and recorded their pioneering industrial music and mechanical noise here between the mid-1970s and early-'80s. Local girl Leona Lewis lives around the corner from her parents' place in Hackney. "Paparazzi don't come to Hackney – it's only when we go to Islington," she says on her website.

Below: Marc Bolan began life in Hackney.
Opposite page: The Small Faces' Itchycoo Park was the first song in the UK to be banned for overt references to drugs.

East End chappies Ronnie Lane, Kenney Jones and Steve Marriott formed the Small Faces in Manor Park, part of Newham. It's been said that Marriott's dad, Bill, ran a jellied eels stall outside the Ruskin Arms in High Street North, a pub venue with an impressive roster of acts, including an early gig for Iron Maiden back in 1976 (Maiden's founder and bassist Steve Harris comes from Leyton). The Small Faces started out as genuine East End mods but would soon be sharp-dressed Carnaby Street mods. Conveniently their first manager Don Arden (the late estranged father of Sharon

Osbourne) operated out of offices at 52-55 Carnaby Street, above John Stephen's legendary mod clothing store.

As a 12-year-old Steve Marriott played the Artful Dodger in Lionel Bart's production of Oliver before enrolling at The Italia Conti Academy of Theatre Arts. A few years later he discovered the blues of Jimmy Reed and Muddy Waters and in 1963 Marriott cut a single for Decca, though it was never released. After a stint with The Moments was short-lived he settled for a job at the J60 music shop, in Manor Park High Street. In 1964 he met future songwriting partner Ronnie Lane and drummer Kenney Jones. They were in a band and needed a singer and guitarist, because Lane was keen to change to bass – the reason for their visit. Shop assistant

Marriott jammed with his two new friends all day, under the pretence Lane was looking for a bass. Marriott did sell Lane a bass, but at such a discounted rate that when Marriot's boss found out he was sacked, and the Small Faces were born.

One of the band's best-known songs, 1967's psychedelic-mod number *Itchycoo Park* is thought to be inspired by a place in Manor Park called Little Ilford Park. Released on Andrew Loog Oldham's pioneering Immediate label, the song was the first in the UK to be banned for overt references to drug use.

Along with 1970s heart-throb David Essex, one of the Small Faces' two Ronnies, singer-songwriter Ronnie Lane was born in Plaistow on April Fools' Day in 1946. The place was immortalised in Ian Dury's *Plaistow Patricia*, featuring one of the most memorable opening lines in pop history (unrepeatable here, in case your granny is reading over your shoulder).

DOCKLANDS
LONDON E14

Claustrophobia was the byword in The Specials' *Ghost Town* video, as the band crammed into an old 1960s Vauxhall Cresta and drove through a deserted Blackwall Tunnel and east London's empty streets. The video was filmed one Saturday night in June 1981 after the band had performed an afternoon gig in Rotherham. Shooting began at nine in the evening and lasted until eight the following morning. No wonder the band appear in such sombre mood. The band spent all night going under the Thames and back through the Tunnel, with a car in front filming everything. When dawn rose on the Sunday they headed towards an eerily-deserted City of London financial district. The video's parting shots see Coventry's finest throwing stones into the Thames.

After Liverpool band The La's split, bassist John Power formed Britpop band Cast and the band are pictured at the Royal Exchange in the City of London on the cover of their 1995 album, *All Change*. The same year, Radiohead's *Just* video, in which half the city join a man lying down in the street, was shot near Liverpool Street station.

WALTHAMSTOW
LONDON E17

Pictures on Blur's 1994 *Parklife* sleeve, including the close-up of a pair of greyhounds in mid-race action, were snapped at the now defunct Walthamstow Stadium dog track, in Chingford Road (the stadium closed in 2008). Blur frontman Damon Albarn may be more into world music and hip hop nowadays, but *Parklife*'s laddish charm captured Britain in the mid-'90s and helped the resurgence of British pop culture. Albarn lived in Leytonstone while his father taught at Walthamstow Art College. Ian Dury was a student here, as was Peter Blake, the pop artist who created The Beatles' *Sgt Pepper's Lonely Hearts Club Band* album cover.

Growing up, The Bonzo Dog Doo-Dah Band's Vivian Stanshall lived in Walthamstow's Grove Road and in recent years, East 17 have flown the flag for the area (no prizes of guessing where the group took their name from). Bizarrely, East 17 singer Brian Harvey once famously ran over himself. In 2005, he fell from the driver's door of his Mercedes convertible as he leaned out of the window while reversing onto a main road. He sustained two broken legs, a punctured lung and was lucky to survive.

Above: Ian Dury was a student at Walthamstow Art College.

RAIN GREY TOWN, KNOWN FOR ITS SOUND:

LONDON FROM ABROAD

LONDON HAS LONG ATTRACTED THE ATTENTION
OF SONGWRITERS THE WORLD OVER.

"I am lonely in London without fear / I'm wandering round and round here nowhere to go." So sung Brazil's answer to Bob Dylan, Caetano Veloso, in his ode to the capital, *London London*, when a military dictatorship forced Veloso and fellow musician Gilberto Gil (Brazil's former minister of culture) into exile in London between 1969 and 1972. The song captures the emotions of a homesick outsider living in a large foreign city, similar sentiments echoed by the Aussie band The Waifs on *London Still*: "Today I dream of home and not of London anymore / I'm in London still."

With a psychedelic, spiralling guitar sound and the opening line "Eight miles high and when you touch down, you'll find that it's stranger than known," the BBC and most American radio stations refused to play *Eight Miles High* by the American folk-rock band The Byrds. They viewed it as a drug song. As a result it quickly fell off the charts, even though the band claimed the inspiration was their first visit to London in 1965 and the subsequent concert tour of England. The song's original title was Six Miles High – a transatlantic airliner's cruising height – but was later changed because

'eight' was deemed more poetic, plus it was in honour of The Beatles' song, *Eight Days A Week*. Another lyric astutely characterises London as a "rain grey town, known for its sound". Ironically, the band's Gene Clark left the band partly due to a fear of flying, which made touring impossible.

Years earlier, in 1948, the SS Empire Windrush brought the first wave of Caribbean music to Britain. In his song, *London Is The Place For Me*, Trinidadian singer and songwriter Aldwyn Roberts – better known as calypso star Lord Kitchener – encapsulates the optimism of a new life in the UK for the Windrush generation of West Indian immigrants. Composed en route to England, Kitchener happily performed the song aboard the Windrush to waiting news crews when the ship docked at Tilbury (see box, page 132).

Another of Trinidad's great calypsonians, Lord Beginner, was also on board. In the next decade, 'Kitch' enjoyed a large following amongst West Indian immigrants with his songs about the Caribbean lifestyle they had left behind. Songs such as *Sweet Jamaica* warned West Indians back home of the difficulties of immigrating to London and

the frosty reception they should expect in England. Kitchener stayed in the UK until 1962 when he returned to his newly-independent Trinidad and Tobago.

The Camera Eye, an epic 1981 song by cult Canadian rockers Rush, highlighted the cultural differences between London and New York. The 11-minute song begins with the sounds of New York traffic, then crosses the Atlantic for a poetic look at the capital. Rush lyricist and drummer Neil Peart is widely regarded amongst rock fans, critics and fellow musicians as one of the greatest rock drummers of all time. The bells at the end are not part of his drum-kit, rather the tolling of Big Ben.

'Wistful and weathered/
The pride still prevails/
Alive in the streets of the city'

Hear also:
Werewolves Of London, Warren Zevon (1978); *English House*, Fleet Foxes (2008); *Fans*, Kings of Leon (2007); *P.25 London*, The Black Crowes (1994); *Emit Remmus*, Red Hot Chili Peppers (1999).

South London

CLAPHAM
LONDON SW4/SW9/SW12

Anorak alert: Squeeze's much-loved 1979 south London kitchen sink drama *Up the Junction* has more in common with Roxy Music's *Virginia Plain* than you might think. Both songs are unusual in that there's no chorus and the last lyrics sung are the actual title (and they were both top five hits in the UK). Songwriter Chris Difford was a continent away when he wrote the song that mentions Clapham Common; homesick on a bus on the band's first American tour just outside of New Orleans. In the US in the early 1980s some music journalists touted Difford and Tilbrook as 'the new Lennon and McCartney'. Clapham Common also gets a shout in the Morrissey song *Mute Witness*. In June 1986, thousands of people attended an Artists Against Apartheid concert on Clapham Common, organised by The Special AKA's Jerry Dammers. The concert lost money but was ultimately successful in that it led directly to two huge international follow-up concerts at Wembley Stadium – the first two years later to celebrate Nelson Mandela's 70th birthday and call for his release from jail, and then two years after that to celebrate his freedom.

BALHAM
LONDON SW12

My Back Pages, in Balham's Station Road, is one of the few independent bookshops left in London, and is named after the 1964 Bob Dylan song on *Another Side of Bob Dylan*. Acoustic folk-pop duo Turin Brakes hail from here while *Bongos Over Balham* was the name of a 1974 album by pub rockers Chilli Willi & the Red Hot Peppers.

BATTERSEA
LONDON SW11

The first time hard rockers Free played together was as teenagers in a room above the Nag's Head pub in Battersea, in 1968. They were signed to Island Records later that year aided by British blues pioneer Alexis Korner who gave them their name and introduced bassist Andy Fraser to the band. Korner had previously had a band called Free At Last but the young rockers liked the idea of just Free. The Clash, featuring a barking Joe Strummer, performed in the rain at dusk at Battersea Pier on the video for The Clash's 1979 doom-laden vision of the capital *London Calling*. The video was directed by the band's old friend Don Letts. The film-maker worked with The Clash on several other projects, including the documentary *Westway to the World*. He was also a founding member of Big Audio Dynamite.

Self-righteous hypocrites, greedy money-grabbers and their mindless followers. No, not Pink Floyd themselves but the pigs, dogs and sheep portrayed in the lyrics of *Animals*, the band's 1977 album inspired by George Orwell's political allegory, *Animal Farm*. Punk rock was sweeping the land and rock dinosaurs like Pink Floyd were on the wane but that didn't stop the Floyd's Roger Waters floating a giant inflatable pig over Battersea Power Station to symbolise capitalism, greed and the corruption of power. In early December 1976, scores of photographers were assembled to record the flight of the helium-filled 40-foot pig, but due to strong winds capitalism was soon flying out of control (an accurate analogy for today's financial shenanigans, in more ways than one). The porcine prop soon broke free from its moorings and into the flight path of aeroplanes. Airline captains across the south of England reported seeing a UFO – an Unidentified Flying Oink. Additional attempts to re-shoot didn't work out and eventually a photograph of the pig was superimposed onto a shot of the Power Station. The pig finally crashed to the ground and was recovered in Kent.

You'll also spot it in The Beatles' film *Help!* Battersea Power Station that is, not the pig. The Who recorded *Quadrophenia* a stone's throw away from Battersea Power Station at their Ramport Studios in Thessaly Road, a former church they had converted. Pete Doherty's Babyshambles recorded a song called *From Bollywood to Battersea*, while garage act So Solid Crew hailed from Battersea's tough Winstanley estate. The Maccabees named their 2007 song *Latchmere*, on their debut *Colour It In* in honour the band's swimming baths of choice – Battersea's Latchmere Leisure Centre in Burns Road:

> 'No bombing and no heavy petting/
> So just stay in your lanes/
> Verruca socks and not forgetting to/
> Just stay in your lanes.'

Critics called The Stranglers sexist and misogynist and, in 1978, the band lived up to their reputation as the dirty of men of punk. At a concert in Battersea Park in September no-one was watching Jean-Jacques Burnel's bass-playing. During a performance of *Nice 'n' Sleazy* the band were assisted by a coterie of French strippers. It's impossible to imagine anything like that happening now.

WIMBLEDON
LONDON SW19/SW20

It was a scantily-clad time in London's musical history. In the same month rock giants Queen rented Wimbledon Stadium for a day to promote their double A-side single *Bicycle Race / Fat Bottomed Girls*. For the *Bicycle Race* video, 65 naked women cyclists were filmed peddling around the racetrack. Special effects protected the models modesty. The publicity photographs that accompanied the double A-side release featured scores of the naked models on bikes, hired to stage a nude bicycle race. Afterwards, bicycle suppliers Halfords refused to take the saddles back and insisted the band pay for replacements.

Fairport Convention's late lead singer Sandy Denny helped introduce traditional folk music into the band's repertoire. The sleeve of their 1969 album *Unhalfbricking* was taken outside the Wimbledon home of Denny's parents in Arthur Road. The couple in the photo are Denny's parents, Edna and Neil. However, look closely and you'll see the band in the garden half-hidden behind a trellis fence. Folk legend Denny was born in nearby Worple Road, and was one of Led Zeppelin

frontman, Robert Plant's favourite singers. Hers was the only voice apart from Plant's ever to be heard on a Led Zeppelin track, singing on the haunting duet with Plant *The Battle of Evermore*. She served her apprenticeship singing folk at the

Top: The Stranglers controversial use of French strippers at a concert in Battersea Park.
Above: The flying pig from Pink Floyd's *Animals*.

Troubadour but it was as a member of Fairport Convention that she made her name. Leader Richard Thompson was impressed by her grasp of songwriting. Wimbledon Common was, of course, home to the environmentally-friendly Wombles, who appeared in novels, a TV series and, come the mid-1970s, a series of successful novelty hit singles. The man behind the civic-minded furry creatures, singer/songwriter and producer, Mike Batt, also wrote the TV series theme tune.

In stark contrast, Wimbledon's Jamie Treays – aka Jamie T – burst onto the music scene in 2007 with Mercury Prize nominated *Panic Prevention*, a vivid portrait of late-teenage life in Noughties Britain. Treays was born and raised in Wimbledon and was schooled at the exclusive Reed's School in Cobham, Surrey.

BRIXTON
LONDON SW2/SW5/SW9

The Windmill in Blenheim Gardens is a small, bohemian Brixton pub venue that showcases new and emerging bands on their way up. A dig directed at hip indie crowds, The Cribs' first top 30 single, 2005's *Hey Scenesters!* was inspired by the Windmill. *The Guns of Brixton* was The Clash's strong reggae-influenced number on *London Calling*, written and sung by bassist Paul Simonon. Brixton's Coldharbour Lane is honoured on 1997's *Exile on Coldharbour Lane*, the debut album by Brixton's Alabama 3. The album title is a clear pun on The Rolling Stones' *Exile On Main Street*. The band are probably not short of a few royalties; a track from the *Coldharbour Lane* album, *Woke Up This Morning*, was the theme tune to hit US TV series, *The Sopranos*. Brixton can also claim X-Ray Spex singer Poly Styrene, synth-pop duo La Roux (Tintin and Tilda Swinton doppelganger Elly Jackson and Ben Langmead) and 1970s rock chameleon David Bowie

as its own; Ziggy's alter ego was born and spent his early childhood at 40 Stansfield Road and later went to Stockwell Infants School on Stockwell Road. Brixton beatmasters Basement Jaxx – Felix Buxton and Simon Ratcliffe – started out here in 1994, where they hosted a regular night club called Rooty, which they also called their second album.

OVAL
LONDON SW8/SE11

Ian Dury and Chaz Jankel wrote 1977's *New Boots And Panties!!* together at Dury's flat next to the Cricketers pub – a £3-a-week bedsit that overlooked the Oval Cricket Ground. The block of flats near the Oval were called Oval Mansions but with typical wit, Dury renamed them Catshit Mansions.

BARNES
LONDON SW13

A happier musical milestone associated with leafy Barnes is the phenomenally successfully Olympic Studios in Church Road which claims a host of firsts and a stunning array of acts. Opening in 1963, The Rolling Stones were one of the first bands to arrive, recording their first official session there in May 1963 and later, in 1968, Led Zeppelin recorded their first album in the same studios.

And the first few tracks of Jimi Hendrix's *Electric Ladyland* were recorded here before production travelled to New York. The stellar roll call of albums recorded here includes The Verve's *Urban Hymns*.

WATERLOO
LONDON SE1

The first album cover shoot for style and fashion photographer Janette Beckman, whose early work graced the pages of *Melody Maker* and *The Face*, was The Police's 1978 debut *Outlandos D'Amour*, shot in a dark tunnel near Waterloo. Songs and albums that mention Waterloo include, of course, The Kinks' immortal *Waterloo Sunset*; *Waterloo to Anywhere*, the debut album by Carl Barât's group Dirty Pretty

Above: Robert Plant and the legendary folk singer Sandy Denny.

Things (basically The Libertines without Pete Doherty); and a song by a Swedish band you may have heard of called Abba. Sadly, their famous 1974 Eurovision Song Contest-winning ditty (see Brighton, page 83), is not about the station at all but a metaphor for relationships.

KENNINGTON
LONDON SE11

For the cover sleeve of her 2007 album, *Overpowered*, Irish singer, Róisín Murphy, formerly of Moloko, is pictured stirring her cappucchino in a marvellously outlandish outfit. The café she is sat in is the popular Parma Cafe, at 412 Kennington Road.

LAMBETH
LONDON SE1/SE11

A small bronze sculpture on display at the Imperial War Museum formed the cover image of The Jam's 1979 release *Setting Sons*. Cast in 1919 after the First World War, *The St John's Ambulance Bearers* is by the late sculptor, Benjamin Clemens. Sadly, the piece has not been on display for several years and remains in storage as part of the museum's permanent collection.

TOWER BRIDGE
LONDON SE1

Several acts have sought inspiration from Tower Bridge as a backdrop for their album artwork. In 1978, Paul McCartney appears with his wife Linda and Denny Laine in front of the bridge on the sleeve of Wings' *London Town*. The album featured the hit *With A Little Luck* and the huge smash Mull of Kintyre, not on the original album but a bonus track on the 1990s reissue. The bridge can also be seen on the cover of *Handsome*, the 1975 debut of Ian Dury's pub rock band Kilburn and the High Roads. And once again on the sleeve of Iron Maiden's 2000 release *Brave New World*, with vocalist Bruce Dickinson back as frontman. The futuristic cover shows Tower Bridge in the foreground with The Thames and something evil lurking in the clouds above.

20th century boy: Marc Bolan – from mod to glam rocker

LESS than a month after Elvis Presley died, rock 'n' roll fans were mourning another loss; Marc Bolan was killed instantly when his purple Mini GT went out of control on a humpback bridge and smashed into a tree near Barnes Common. It was just before five am on September 16, 1977, and Bolan was on his way home from a nightclub in Berkeley Square when his car went out of control on a humpback bridge on Queen's Ride. It was being driven by his American girlfriend Gloria Jones, mother of his son, Rolan Bolan.

The Hackney mod-turned-mystical folkie-turned glam rocker was two weeks away from his 30th birthday. "There were times when Marc asked me to take pictures of him behind the wheels of the car because he had this premonition he was going to die in a car crash," Bolan's photographer, the late Keith Morris, recalled in 2001.

The crash site is now a place of pilgrimage with a commemorative stone but it's the personal messages from fans pinned to the tree that make the shrine special. If you want to visit the site it's best to approach via Gipsy Lane. A bust of Bolan was unveiled by his son Rolan in 2002 but the clear highlight here are the touching messages from fans for whom he clearly means an awful lot still today. The Gipsy Lane site is also well attended on the annual anniversary of Bolan's death, with fans meeting up for an all-night vigil. "It's a combination of his lyrics and his music which draws people to Marc," says Sue Garvock, Chair of the Official Marc Bolan Fan Club. "That's not saying he appeals to everyone, because he doesn't, but for those who *get* Marc, they recognise something special. Perhaps there's also something about the tragic way he died which makes him an idol. He will never age and his music will last forever fresh in our hearts. He had that androgynous look that made everyone swoon! What a cheeky grin too." That fateful September night Bolan was travelling home to what would turn out to be his last home, at 142 Upper Richmond Road in East Sheen, painfully close to the accident site.

WOOLWICH
LONDON SE18

Heavy metal music is not the first thing you think of in Woolwich but, in July 1981, a concert at the Woolwich Odeon by new wave heavy metal band Diamond Head would unwittingly change the genre. In the audience was an enthusiastic 17-year-old American-Danish teenager on a pilgrimage. Wannabe drummer Lars Ulrich had saved all his pocket money and flown from California to see his favourite band in concert. Such was his enthusiasm for the Stourbridge band he not only ended up backstage but hanging out

Boys keep swinging: a short history of glam rock

THE early 1970s was a time of industrial strikes, deep-seated racist attitudes, homophobia, violence on the football terraces and in town centres, and hard-drinking blokes who didn't mind telling the new piece of skirt in the office that she was well tasty and could you get us another cuppa, love? Yet, amidst the fug of stale beer and testosterone there developed a music genre and fashion that was often androgynous, even camp, with men sporting platform-soled boots, outrageous hairstyles and – whisper it – make-up.

Glam rock grew out of the psychedelic and art rock scenes of the late 1960s and soon divided into two main camps: at one end of the spectrum were the more serious bands such as T.Rex, Roxy Music and David Bowie's alter ego, Ziggy Stardust; while at the other end were the fun-loving, chart-busting pop sensations, namely Slade, Sweet, Mud, Alvin Stardust, Roy Wood's Wizzard, Suzi Quatro and, ahem, Gary Glitter, who used to be better known for his over-the-top performances on *Top of the Pops*.

Some, most notably Mark Bolan and T.Rex, managed to keep a platform boot in both camps, with a string of top 10 hits. In fact, it could be argued that Bolan started it all off with his appearance on *Top of the Pops* in 1971, performing *Hot Love* (his first number one) wearing a satin suit and glitter.

Between 1972 and '76, these glam rock acts dominated the UK singles charts, but though hugely successful on their own shores, they made little impact in the US, with the exception of Bowie, who went on to become a major superstar, influencing artists such as Lou Reed, Iggy Pop and the New York Dolls.

Glam was effectively killed off by punk rock in 1976, but its flamboyance and narcissism were adopted by the emerging New Romantics in the '80s, especially Adam and the Ants and Flock of Seagulls, and its more androgynous aspects were developed further by Culture Club, Bronski Beat and Frankie Goes to Hollywood. It also had a direct influence on US rock band Kiss and west coast 'hair metal' acts like Twisted Sister and Mötley Crüe. It must be in their make-up.

with the band and sleeping on the couch of Diamond Head guitarist Brian Tatler's house for a bit. He returned to Los Angeles and a year later wrote to the band to say he'd formed his own band called Metallica. The band originally performed Diamond Head covers.

NEW CROSS
LONDON SE14

Goldsmiths College on Lewisham Way is where it all began for Blur. In 1988, students Graham Coxon and Damon Albarn were introduced to Alex James and formed a band called Seymour. To complete the four piece they enlisted an old friend from Colchester, Dave Rowntree, to play drums. Albarn, Coxon and Rowntree (now there's a firm of solicitors for you) all grew up in the Essex army town. After a dozen or so gigs in and around London, the band ditched Seymour and renamed themselves Blur in 1989. One of their first gigs with their new moniker was the 1989 degree show in which Damien Hirst and other young British exhibited. Several other rock 'n' roll players have attended Goldsmiths: Velvet Underground's only British-born member John Cale, Brian Molko of Placebo, Steve Mackey of Pulp; and two sociology graduates, Dire Straits bassist John Illsley and dub poet Linton Kwesi Johnson. Punk svengali Malcolm McLaren left the college in 1971 without completing his degree. The Bonzo Dog Doo-Dah Band formed here in 1965; they produced four great albums during the 1960s as well as the hit single *I'm The Urban Spaceman*.

The Only Living Boy in New Cross was a 1992 song by indie band Carter The Unstoppable Sex Machine, a pun on Paul Simon's *The Only Living Boy In New York*. Hatcham Social are a New Cross indie four piece who formed in 2006. They named themselves after Hatcham, an ancient name for New Cross.

BLACKHEATH
LONDON SE3

Squeeze's Chris Difford wrote the lyrics to the 1981 single *Tempted* (sung mostly by singer/songwriter Paul Carrack) on the back of a cigarette packet in a taxi cab en route to

Left: Marc Bolan and T.Rex.
Opposite page top: The Crystal Palace Bowl.
Opposite page bottom: AC/DC and Bon Scott, who died aged just 33.

Heathrow Airport. Some of the lyrics refer to the journey and in particular places he saw while travelling through Blackheath Village: "Passed the church and the steeple, the laundry on the hill". Pianist, bandleader and TV presenter Jools Holland was born in Blackheath and formed Squeeze with Difford and Glenn Tilbrook at the age of 15; they toured the pubs and clubs of southeast London.

LEE
LONDON SE12

The Stranglers were photographed inside the Manor House library in Old Road in Lee, near Blackheath, for the cover of 1977's *Rattus Norvegicus*. Built in 1772 as a Georgian country house, the mansion house became a public library in 1902.

BROCKLEY
LONDON SE4

1982's *Hilly Fields (1892)*, a 1982 psychedelic rock song by nick nicely (Nickolas Laurien), puts Brockley firmly on London's musical map. It was written in honour of Brockley's grassy hill of the same name which reaches 175 feet high and has great views north to the City and south to the South Downs.

UPPER NORWOOD
LONDON SE19

Not many outdoor venues are blessed with a pond in front of the stage but at the Crystal Palace Bowl bands perform on the other side of one. The Bowl is a great venue on warm summer evenings; a natural slope allows great views of the stage as the sun goes down and drunk fans attempt to swim to the stage. When Pink Floyd performed their epic *Echoes* here in the early 1970s the band's sound equipment was blamed for killing all the fish in the pond. The morning after the gig several hundred fish were found floating on the surface and Floyd were presented with a bill for them.

HERNE HILL
LONDON SE24

In 1980, Island Records boss Chris Blackwell travelled to see an up and coming Irish band called U2 at the Half Moon pub in Herne Hill. Blackwell wasn't that impressed with the band's live performance but liked them as individuals. Island signed the band and their debut album *Boy* was released in October.

DULWICH & DENMARK HILL
LONDON SE21/SE5

As you pass Dulwich's famous private school Alleyn's, in Townley Road, keep an ear cocked for music coming from open windows. You may just hear future a star in the making. Alleyn's impressive musical alumni includes some of the leading talent in British pop today: Ed Simons of The Chemical Brothers; Felix White of The Maccabees; singer/songwriter Jack Peñate whose grandfather was *Gormenghast* author Melvyn Peake; and Florence Welch of Florence and the Machine, dubbed the new queen of British pop in 2009.

The AC/DC single *Touch Too Much* proved a touch too prophetic for original frontman Bon Scott. In February 1980,

the 33-year-old Scott choked to death on his own vomit after a drinking spree and died of alcohol poisoning outside 67 Overhill Road, East Dulwich. He had been left in a car outside to sleep off the effects of a night at the Camden Town Music Machine spent with a friend and neighbour Alistair Kinnear, watching a Protex gig. Kinnear discovered Scott's body curled around the gearstick and rushed him to Kings College Hospital in Denmark Hill, where he was declared dead on arrival. The coroner's report cited acute alcohol poisoning. Scott was flown to Australia and cremated and AC/DC more than survived the singer's death. They recruited a new singer, Brian Johnson (see Gateshead, page 292), and soon recorded the groundbreaking *Back in Black* album. The band went on to sell more than 80 million records.

The revered Irish blues guitarist and songwriter Rory Gallagher (no relation to the Oasis brothers) also passed away in Kings College Hospital in 1995. But for every exit in this world there's an entry, and Paul and Linda McCartney's fashion designer daughter Stella was born here in 1971. It was a double birth of sorts; the ex-Beatle also came up with a name of his new band – Wings – while waiting in a hospital wing during Stella's difficult birth. McCartney was inspired by the image of angel wings that kept coming back to him. Wings was a definite improvement on the band's prototype name – Turpentine. Ruskin Park, opposite the Kings College Hospital, was where Pink Floyd's first official photo session took place in 1967. Florence Welch also attended Camberwell College of Art between 2006-2007, long after acid casualty Syd Barrett studied there in the mid-1960s before forming Pink Floyd.

GREENWICH
LONDON SE10

There had been rumours of a Led Zeppelin reunion concert for years but it took the 2006 death of Atlantic Records boss Ahmet Ertegun for the band to reform for one night. The venue was the 22,000- capacity O2 Arena in Greenwich, the giant spiked dome formerly known as Millennium Dome. Constructed in 1999 during the honeymoon period of Labour Prime Minister Tony Blair's first term, it was the band's first full live set since 1980. The O2 is now London's premier large-sized concert venue, hosting all the top names. Since its opening in 2007, many other top gigs have taken place here but it's the Led Zeppellin show that has already attained legendary status. A staggering 20 million people worldwide applied for tickets

in an online lottery for the one-off concert in December 2007, which was billed as a tribute to Ahmet Ertegun, the co-founder of Atlantic Records, who signed the band in 1968. Jason Bonham, son of the band's original drummer John, stood in for his late father. Ertegun was as universally admired as any music executive could be. His patient rearing of bands like Led Zeppelin is cited by artists as evidence of the kind of nurturing absent at major labels nowadays. "No band gets the chance to be shit anymore before you get good," Doves frontman Jimi Goodwin told the music press in 2010.

Blur's memorable comic video to accompany their 1994 *Parklife* single starred frontman Damon Albarn and actor Phil Daniels on the road as double-glazing salesmen. The Parklife roadsign says NW6 but it was filmed south of the river in pre-Millennium Dome-Greenwich in August 1994. Most of the action takes place in River Way, although Ordnance Crescent and the Sun-in-the-Sands roundabout are also visible. Sadly the old street and surrounding area were demolished in construction on the Dome.

CHARLTON
LONDON SE7

The famous concert footage of The Who's guitarist Pete Townshend sliding in rainwater across the stage on his knees was at a gig at The Valley, Charlton Athletic's ground, in May 1976. Considered to be one of the band's greatest shows, it was also the loudest ever gig up until then, and the band entered the Guinness Book of Records. The noise was measured at 120 decibels from 50 metres away, precisely the volume the World Health Organisation describes as the pain threshold.

The Stranglers 1978 single *Old Codger*, off their third album *Black and White* featured an old fan of the band, the late jazz singer George Melly, on guest vocals. Frontman Hugh Cornwell wrote the song with Melly in mind. The video was shot in Charlton's Maryon Park, the same park used in the 1960s film *Blowup*, starring David Hemmings and Vanessa Redgrave.

DEPTFORD
LONDON SE8

Squeeze's roots lie in Deptford and Greenwich, where the band cut its teeth in local pubs and venues. The illustrious songwriting partnership of Chris Difford and Glenn Tilbrook was forged when they met in the spring of 1973. They first performed a year or so later at the long-gone Northover pub, located between Catford and Downham. Other early venues included The Deptford Arms, The Bell – in Greenwich behind the church – and Greenwich Borough Halls on Royal Hill. In March 2010, Difford and Tilbrook returned here to unveil a Performing Rights Society plaque in their honour, at the site of one of their first concerts in 1975. Chris Difford's songs like *Slap And Tickle* and *Cool For Cats* were inspired by dodgy Deptford geezers and southeast London's criminal underbelly.

Dire Straits were also linked to Deptford when they started out. Initially known as Cafe Racers, their first gig took place outside a flat in the Crossfield Estate in Deptford Church Street, in 1977. A commemorative plaque was unveiled there in 2009 to mark the spot, attended by guitarist and singer/songwriters Mark Knopfler and bassist John Illsley. A few gigs later, at The Albany in Douglas Way, supporting Squeeze, was where the band changed their name to Dire Straits. Their new name reflected their awful financial situation. Deptford guitar virtuoso Gordon Giltrap's first instrument was a plastic ukelele. He was part of the 1960s London folk club scene alongside the likes of Bert Jansch and John Renbourn. Deptford also claims indie quartet Athlete and former Cockney Rebel, Steve Harley.

PECKHAM
LONDON SE15

While studying at St Martins College in Charing Cross Road, Pulp frontman Jarvis Cocker lived near Holly Grove in Peckham. He later wrote a 1993 Pulp song – *59 Lyndhurst Grove* –after going a party at a house at that address and being thrown out by the owner:

> 'There's a picture by his first wife on the wall/
> Stripped floor-boards in the kitchen and the hall/
> A stain from last week's party on the stairs/No one knows who made it or how it ever got there.'

Peckham is name-checked in Carter The Unstoppable Sex Machine's (Carter USM) *The Taking of Peckham 123*, on their debut *101 Damnations* album, released in 1989.

ELTHAM
LONDON SE9/SE12

Both Squeeze's Glenn Tilbrook and Boy George were expelled from Eltham Green Secondary School in Middle Park Avenue – but for very different reasons. Tilbrook was booted out for refusing to get his hair cut while Boy George – then just George O'Dowd – was thrown out because he refused to be caned for bunking off. Anarchist punks Conflict hailed from Eltham.

THAMESMEAD
LONDON SE2/SE28

Aphex Twin's nightmarish 1997 video *Come to Daddy* was shot around Thamesmead's now-demolished Tavy Bridge Shopping centre.

Above: Squeeze, local boys of Deptford
Opposite page: Dire Straits settled on their name after a gig supporting Squeeze.

West London

EARLS COURT
LONDON SW5/SW10

The yacht-filled watery backdrop that adorns the cover photograph of Led Zeppelin's 1976's *Presence* was a makeshift marina installed inside the 1975 London Boat Show at the Earls Court Exhibition Centre. The family sat around the table cheerfully staring at a mysterious black object were photographed separately in a studio. Earls Court has also traditionally been the venue for the annual Brit Awards, which usually provides a few colourful moments to fill newspapers for weeks. None have topped Jarvis Cocker's 1996 upstaging of Michael Jackson with his very English take on Jackson's moondance. During a performance of the king of pop's *Earth Song*, Cocker leapt up on stage and wiggled his backside. "My actions were a form of protest," Cocker later said. Although many loathed what he did, for many others Cocker became a national hero.

Unlike the 1960s central London folk club Les Cousins, The Troubadour is still around today. The famous coffee bar on the Old Brompton Road opened in 1955, and by the early 1960s hosted live folk music in its small basement venue. It was also an intellectual and artistic hub of London in the 1950s and 1960s, with the Afro-American revolutionaries the Black Panthers meeting here when they left Paris after the 1968 riots. Musically, this was the first venue where a young Bob Dylan performed in London in 1962. The Rolling Stones drummer Charlie Watts got a lucky break there when he met blues impresario Alexis Korner, who invited him to play at the Marquee Club. Led Zeppelin jammed there after their famous Earls Court gigs and Tom Robinson and Elvis Costello used to play there too. American singer/songwriter Paul Simon and Jimi Hendrix played there in its 1960s heyday. Remaining true to its roots, The Troubadour still hosts emerging talent. "It's an interesting place, and has a nice feel of history to it," says Nick Roberts, drummer with upcoming band Felix Fables.

A photograph of Syd Barrett crouching in the bedroom of his flat in Wetherby Mansions, Earls Court Square, made the cover of *The Madcap Laughs* in 1968. It is now a studio belonging to Syd's former flatmate, pop artist Duggie Fields. The singer previously lived in a large pharmaceutical-friendly townhouse at 101 Cromwell Road that was divided into flats.

FULHAM BROADWAY
LONDON SW6

An Ian Dury song, *What A Waste*, a top ten hit single in 1978 for him and the Blockheads, Dury recalls that he could have been the "ticket man at Fulham Broadway station". It was written by Dury and songwriting partner Rod Melvin decades before London Underground introduced its Oystercard system which would have made a ticket man redundant. A few hundred yards left out the station and its shopping centre is the home of Chelsea Football Club. On the cover of his 2000 album *Sing When You're Winning*, Port Vale fan Robbie Williams is pictured at Stamford Bridge stadium in a series of celebratory poses. A football's kick away from Fulham Broadway is a shop front featured on the sleeve of folk-rockers Mumford & Sons 2009 debut album, *Sigh No More*. The band appear in the window of a shop, at 596 Kings Road – the antique dealers Pimpernel & Partners. Mumford & Sons rose from the same London nu-folk scene as Laura Marling and Noah and the Whale, congregating for country hoedowns at the Bosun's Locker, underneath Markham House, 138a King's Road, until it closed in 2008. Upstairs, in the 1960s, stood Mary Quant's Bazaar boutique where she invented the mini skirt.

PUTNEY
LONDON SW15

Is this the real school of rock? Electro-poppers Hot Chip founders, Alexis Taylor and Joe Goddard met at the Elliott School, the southwest London comprehensive in Putney, a veritable musical wellspring that has also produced 2010 Mercury Award-winning The xx, dubstep producer Burial and Peter Green of Fleetwood Mac. "I don't want to give them too much credit because technically they just neglected us," The xx frontman Oliver Sim told the BBC about the school after scooping the top prize. "There was so much time to do our own thing and they gave us a room to hang out in during break time and gave us time to figure things out for ourselves, which worked quite well for us because I always find it hard being taught something creative."

Putney's famous Half Moon boasts live music seven days a week, hosting unsigned acts as well as well-known names up for an intimate, unpretentious venue – just a large back room of a decent boozer. It opened as a haven for folk music in 1963 with acts like John Martyn, Bert Jansch, and Ralph McTell, and American blues men like Bo Diddley and Champion Jack Dupree. The pub venue hosted early performances from The Rolling Stones and The Who; k.d.lang's first UK performance; U2's first sell-out gig in 1980; Kate Bush's debut performance and residences from both Elvis Costello and Steve Marriott. The pub was also the venue of Marriott's last ever UK gig.

Above: The incomparable Freddie Mercury.
Opposite page: The album artwork for Led Zeppelin's *Presence*.

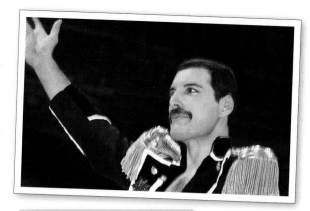

KENSINGTON
LONDON W8

The former home of one of England's greatest performers was at 1 Logan Place, just off the Cromwell Road, Kensington. This was the house of the late Freddie Mercury, lead singer of Queen. It is surrounded by a high wall which used to be covered in graffiti and messages scrawled by Queen fans from around the world, particularly from Japan. Before moving to Logan Place, Mercury lived at 12 Stafford Terrace in Kensington, in the mid '80s.

Nearby Lexham Gardens has two T.Rex connections: Marc Bolan used to reside at number 81, while number 108 was producer Tony Visconti's flat where T.Rex recorded demos for their snappily-titled 1968 debut album *My People Were Fair and Had Sky in Their Hair… But Now They're Content to Wear Stars on Their Brows.*

Before Queen made the big time, Freddie Mercury ran a stall at the three-storey indoor clothes emporium, Kensington Market, one of London's fashion landmarks. The market, a labyrinth of lock-up stalls, opened in 1969 and attracted sartorially curious Londoners and shoppers from all over the world. The 120 stallholders would sell one-off designs and played a key role in adorning rock 'n' roll stars of yesteryear; from hippies in the 1960s, to punks in the 1970s through to goths in the 1980s. Demolished in 2001, at least the market lives on in a 1989 song, *Salvador Dali's Garden Party* by Dan Treacy's band Television Personalities:

> 'I wore by brand new paisley shirt/
> I bought last week from Kensington Market/
> And I wore my brand new Chelsea boots/
> I rode there on my scooter but there wasn't
> anywhere to park it'.

In a past life the Famous Three Kings pub, in North End Road next to West Kensington tube, was the near-legendary music venue The Nashville Rooms. Originally a country and western venue (hence the name), in 1977 it became a punk and new wave hotspot, with early appearances by the Sex Pistols, supporting Joe Strummer's The 101ers – before too long the line-up would be reversed. The Sex Pistols inspired Strummer to quit his group and form a new band, The Clash. It was at The Nashville that the final line-up of The Damned was decided, when drummer Rat Scabies and bassist Captain Sensible met vocalist Dave Vanian. Years later, Elvis Costello, who made his live debut at the venue in May 1977, would pop off to the real Nashville in Tennessee to record his country music-inspired album, *Almost Blue*.

You will often see people carriers out front and guitar cases in the lobby of the K West hotel, Kensington House in Richmond Way. Just two clues that these former BBC offices are now London's premier rock 'n' roll hotel. Touring bands make up a quarter of the hotel's business. In fact, the glass-fronted K West is so loved by today's rock stars the hotel even employs a music and entertainment sales director to pamper them and look after their every whim. It has a late check-out facility and blacked-out curtains so musicians can sleep during the day.

PADDINGTON
LONDON W2

In the late 1970s, Paddington-based Stiff Records was seen as the coolest record label in Britain, if not the world. The nerve centre was their offices at 32 Alexander Street, near Paddington Station. Stiff was run by the management team of Irish businessmen and former manager of Brinsley Schwarz, Dave Robinson and Jake Riviera, who once managed Essex R&B pub rockers Dr Feelgood. Stiff acts to follow included Ian Dury, Elvis Costello, Dr Feelgood and Nick Lowe. A bit like a musical mincer, Stiff swallowed up many pub rock acts and regurgitated them as punk and new waves bands. They had initially launched the label in August 1976 from a tiny office in Notting Hill, with a £400 loan from the late Dr Feelgood frontman Lee Brilleaux.

BAYSWATER
LONDON W2

In 2006, the late king of pop Michael Jackson booked nearly all the rooms of the trendy Hempel Hotel in Bayswater in exchange for a performance. He also requested that an 18-foot wall be erected on the first floor to ensure his privacy. Eleven years earlier, when Manic Street Preachers guitarist Richey Edwards checked out of the Embassy Hotel at 150 Bayswater Road (now the Ramada London Hyde Park hotel), on 1 February, 1995, he and the hotel entered the realms of pop legend. Unlike the 213-room building that overlooks Kensington Gardens, Edwards was never seen again (see Gloucestershire, page 193). Until Kensington's K West Hotel appeared on the scene in 2001 pretty much every touring rock band stayed at The Columbia, Britain's most famous rock 'n 'roll hotel, at 95-99 Lancaster Gate, near Hyde Park.

WARWICK AVENUE
LONDON W9

Warwick Avenue, the 2008 melancholic ballad by Welsh soul singer and chanteuse Duffy, has put this well-to-do neighbourhood of Victorian houses well and truly on the musical map. Tourists and Londoners have been meeting each other "by the entrance of the tube" ever since, some to start relationships, others to end them, like in the song. The video starts with a brief shot of Warwick Avenue tube station before concentrating on a tearful, reflective Duffy sitting in the back of a taxi as it drives away. The taxi scene was originally only supposed to be just one part of the video.

Now that this area is so gentrified it's hard to think it was ever full of squats, but back in the boiling hot summer of 1976 the four-storey 42 Orsett Terrace near Royal Oak was one of punk's most famous squats. Back then it was occupied by The Clash frontman Joe Strummer (who wrote *London's Burning* here) and his girlfriend Palmolive (the stage name of Spanish-born drummer Paloma Romero). Sid Vicious also resided here and joined The Flowers of Romance, rehearsing in a claustrophobic basement with Keith Levene (later to be John Lydon's guitarist in Public Image Limited), Palmolive and Viv Albertine, who would become The Slits, with Ari Up. The living conditions at Orsett Terrace basement inspired the early Clash song *How Can I Understand The Flies?* The London punk scene was more than a little incestuous with Strummer dating Palmolive, Mick Jones going out with Viv Albertine and John Lydon later marrying Ari Up's mother, Nora.

HOLLAND PARK & NOTTING HILL
LONDON W8

The leafy milieu that Canterbury prog rockers Caravan are surrounded by on the sleeve of their second album is not the Kent countryside but Holland Park. The 1970 album was called *If I Could Do It All Over Again, I'd Do It All Over You*, a line taken from The Goon Show.

In the 1970 film *Performance*, Mick Jagger plays rock star recluse Turner in his Notting Hill hideaway – at 25 Powis Square – who is joined by James Fox's gangster character Chas. Some of the dialogue from the film was sampled in Big Audio Dynamite's *E=MC²* released in 1986. Local band Quintessence had the lyric, "Things look great in Notting Hill Gate, we all sit round and meditate."

Songs inspired by the Portobello Road area include the Blur song *Blue Jeans* on 1993's *Modern Life is Rubbish* and *Portobello Man* by The Bevis Frond. Honest Jon's Records has sold reggae, African classics, rare R&B and diverse sounds from its Portobello Road store since 1974. In 2000, Damon Albarn approached the shop about starting a record label that reflected classic American soul, African music and Jamaican reggae. It's called Honest Jon's.

LADBROKE GROVE
LONDON W10

The Jam may have posed for an album here but this part of west London undeniably belongs to The Clash. The Elgin pub at 96 Ladbroke Grove is widely thought of as the birthplace of the band. Joe Strummer used to play here with his first band the 101ers – named after the squat they lived in at 101 Walterton Road in Maida Vale. The 101ers played a residency here as part of London's then thriving pub rock scene. They cemented their ties to the area with the band's only album, *Elgin Avenue Breakdown*.

The Clash's Mick Jones used to peer down onto the Westway from his grandmother's flat on the 18th floor of Wilmcote House on the Warwick Estate. The Westway (A40) has also featured on numerous album covers; Bloc Party's *A Weekend In The City* shows a night photograph of the Westway/A3220 West Cross Route interchange, as well as The Clash's live compilation, *From Here to Eternity*. But even more sleeves have been shot underneath the Westway. In 1998, model Lucy Joplin was photographed at a football pitch under the Westway by Scarlet Page, daughter of legendary Led Zeppelin guitarist Jimmy Page. The image ended up as the cover of the Stereophonics second album, *Performance and Cocktails*. Six months after the success of *In The City* The Jam released another album in 1977, *This Is the Modern World*. The sleeve pictured the Woking trio under the Westway flyover roundabout at the end of Latimer Road. Blur's *For Tomorrow* mentions the Westway, as does The Clash's *London's Burning*:

> 'Up and down the Westway and I'm looking for a flat/ This block leads to that block, this block leads to that.'

In 1993, All Saints named themselves after the All Saints Road in Ladbroke Grove, where they met. Before recording

Above: The Clash.
Opposite page: The Damned outside Stiff Records.

IT and Friends were based nearby. IT's editor, John 'Hoppy' Hopkins, along with political activist Michael X, set up the London Free School, a radical education programme that arranged the first Notting Hill Carnival.

In February 1976, a few months before punk exploded, Cambridge graduate Geoff Travis opened a record shop off Ladbroke Grove, at 202 Kensington Park Road. Called Rough Trade, it became a hub for punk's salvos on mainstream music.

The shop became a veritable mecca for imports, indie and the latest reggae and punk releases but Travis's brainchild was to establish an alternative distribution network. Anyone who had a few hundred pounds was able get their record into shops up and down the country. Rough Trade may have started as a small record shop but it defined a revolution in independent music.

SHEPHERD'S BUSH
LONDON W12

Now a rather charming mainstay of the O2 Academy group, the Shepherd's Bush Empire has been one of London's top music and entertainment venues ever since it opened as a music hall in 1903. It staged variety performances and revues until the early 1950s when the venue was bought by the BBC and turned into a television theatre. Shows like *Hancock's Half-Hour*, *That's Life!*, *Crackerjack*, *The Old Grey Whistle Test* and *Jim'll Fix It* were broadcast from here, and from 1985, the theatre was used exclusively for the *Wogan* chat show three nights a week. The Beeb left in 1991, and after a £2 million refit, the Empire re-opened as a 2,000-capacity music venue in March 1994 with a gig by Seattle grunge rockers, Soundgarden. It's proved to be a popular rock and pop venue ever since, hosting small gigs by leading international acts such as David Bowie, The Rolling Stones, The Who, Oasis, Bon Jovi and Blur. In March 2003, during a Dixie Chicks concert, lead singer Natalie Maines criticised the imminent invasion of Iraq and told fans the band were ashamed that the president of the United States, George W Bush, was from their home state of Texas. The comments angered many Americans who protested by cancelling ticket sales in the US and boycotting their music.

together Shaznay Lewis and Melanie Blatt started their singing careers as backing vocalists at Sarm West Studios, Trevor Horn's ZTT recording studios in Basing Street in Ladbroke Grove. Before Horn moved in the studios were a converted church owned by Island Records. Many Island artists used the studio but it was also hired out to other bands. Led Zeppelin recorded *Stairway To Heaven* here in 1970, while Bob Geldof and Midge Ure assembled an all-star line-up for the Band Aid single *Do They Know It's Christmas?* recorded here in 1984. Ladbroke Grove also gets a name-check on Van Morrison's *Astral Weeks*.

Before investment bankers and trustafarians gentrified the area, rebellion was more than turning up the collar on one's Hackett polo-shirt. From the late 1960s onwards Ladbroke Grove was the hub of the London underground, producing psych-rock bands like Hawkwind and The Pink Fairies. Edgar Broughton Band, Quintessence and Steamhammer were also local. Ladbroke Grove was the nerve centre of British counterculture: there was a Hell's Angel commune on Powis Square, the Black Panthers would meet at the Mangrove restaurant on All Saints Road, while underground magazines

Top left: Hawkwind.

Bottom left: Rough Trade Records, 1977.

Opposite page: The last performance from Ziggy Stardust was at the Hammersmith Odeon.

Singer-guitarist Gavin Rossdale's band named themselves Bush because they all used to live in Shepherd's Bush, but the most famous band attached to this west London neighbourhood is The Who. They exploded onto the music scene in the 1960s with their potent mix of youthful energy and manic aggression, exploding drum kits and smashing guitars, and even Pete Townshend telling American political activist Abbie Hoffman to "f*** off" his stage at the Woodstock festival. From early ground-breaking songs like *My Generation* and *I Can't Explain* to songs from their rock operas *Tommy* and *Quadrophenia*, they have often been dubbed the best rock 'n' roll band in the world. A label most warranted when fans witnessed their explosive live performances at venues like Charlton Athletic's football ground, Leeds University and Woodstock are taken into account. During their first months together in the early 1960s The Who used to play at the Goldhawk Social Club, at 205 Goldhawk Road. Across the road was Townhouse Studios, where The Jam recorded *Setting Sons*, Peter Gabriel recorded *Games Without Frontiers* in 1979 and Phil Collins recorded the explosive drum burst for *In the Air Tonight* a year later. The studios were built by Virgin Records supremo Richard Branson in the late 1970s before being absorbed by the EMI/Virgin Studio Group. Townhouse closed in 2008.

HAMMERSMITH
LONDON W6

File under: gone but not forgotten. The sorely-missed Hammersmith Palais at 242 Shepherd's Bush Road was immortalised in song, on The Clash's *(White Man) In Hammersmith Palais*, Joe Strummer's tale of being the only white person at an all-night reggae gig at the venue. After he name-checks the line-up, including Dillinger, Leroy Smart and Delroy Wilson, Strummer sings: "Turning rebellion into money", which may well have been a swipe at the punk movement. Ian Dury mentioned the venue in his 1979 hit *Reasons To Be Cheerful, Part 3*, while Elton John famously held his extravagant 50th birthday party here in 1997. The Hammersmith Palais began life as the Palais de Danse in 1919 and quickly became noted for its giant ballroom, stylish decor and the quality of its live acts. Early on it featured jazz concerts and a residency by the Joe Loss Orchestra, featuring Elvis Costello's father Ross MacManus as singer. It closed in April 2007 to make way for offices and

a restaurant. The last band to play there were Manchester's The Fall captured on a DVD called *Last Night At The Palais*.

Hammersmith's other stellar venue is still going strong. Formerly known as the Hammersmith Odeon, The HMV Hammersmith Apollo in Queen Caroline Street was for many years the spiritual home of British rock. A large venue that still manages somehow to feel intimate, it's hosted all the big names in rock. David Bowie famously killed off his alter ego Ziggy Stardust here at the end of his UK tour in 1973 and more recently the Super Furry Animals saw off their alter egos, The Yetis. At a gig in the early 1980s a disgruntled Marc Almond encouraged jeering male members of the audience to go and play with their "insignificant little penises".

The Hammersmith Gorillas (later just The Gorillas), led by rock 'n' roll veteran Jesse Hector, formed here in 1973. The 1980s musical genre psychobilly (punk-tinged rockabilly music) centred around Hammersmith, and in particular the Klub Foot, a sticky, cramped basement club at the once-posh Clarendon Hotel. Pioneered by The Meteors in 1980, a fellow psychobilly band were King Kurt and rather aptly their 1986 album *Big Cock* was released on Stiff Records.

CHISWICK
LONDON W4

One of the promo films used to promote The Beatles' 1966 *Paperback Writer/Rain* single was filmed in the grounds of Chiswick House, an 18th century Palladian villa in Burlington Lane. The Fabs travelled here in May 1966 and under the direction of Michael Lindsay-Hogg mimed to the song walking in and around the conservatory, sitting on a bench and in the

statue garden. One of the first-ever pop promos, the full colour video was first shown on *Top of the Pops* two weeks later. The upshot of these short films, of course, was the band no longer had to appear live on TV to promote their singles.

Metropolis Studios, located at The Power House, 70 Chiswick High Road, have been used by a myriad of musicians, with recordings by the likes of Michael Jackson, Iron Maiden, The Clash, Amy Winehouse, Beyonce, Led Zeppelin, The Who and Lily Allen. The studios are named after the futuristic Fritz Lang film.

Tony Green of Turnham Green was a character in Ian Dury's *This Is What We Find* from *Do It Yourself*.

ACTON
LONDON W8

In what would turn out to be one of his last-ever live performances, on 15 November, 2002, Joe Strummer and his band, The Mescaleros, played a benefit gig at Acton Town Hall in aid of the families of striking firemen. During the performance, Strummer was unexpectedly joined on stage by ex-Clash guitarist Mick Jones to play old Clash tunes, including *Bankrobber*, *White Riot* and, naturally, *London's Burning*. It was the first time the two men had shared a stage since Jones was booted out of The Clash 19 years earlier. Just five weeks later Strummer was dead (see Taunton, Somerset, page 181).

The earliest origins of rock giants The Who can be traced to Acton. Frontman Roger Daltrey grew up in Acton's Bollo Lane and, except for drummer Keith Moon, the rest of the band attended Acton County Grammar School (now Acton High School). In the summer of 1962, Daltrey bumped into his old schoolmate John Entwistle walking down Acton High Street with a bass guitar slung over his shoulder and promptly invited Entwistle to join his five-piece, The Detours. A few weeks later on, at Entwistle's suggestion, Pete Townshend joined the band on rhythm guitar.

One of Britain's earliest pop stars, Terry Nelhams – later renamed Adam Faith – was born at 4 Churchfield Road, in 1940. Faith grew up in an Acton Vale council block and attended John Perryn Junior School. Influenced by Lonnie Donegan, he joined a skiffle group.

Acton has provided inspiration for at least two songs: Elvis Costello's *I'm Not Angry*, from his 1977 debut *My Aim Is True*, in which he portrays the former Elizabeth Arden cosmetics factory in Wales Farm Road as the "vanity factory". Struggling to make ends meet as a musician, Costello worked here during the day as a data entry clerk. The premises, at 140 Wales Farm Road, has been converted into a business centre, aptly known as The Perfume Factory, with a number of office suites. The Manic Street Preachers song *Askew Road* (B-side of 2004 single *The Love of Richard Nixon*) is named after the Acton street where the band would stay with their late publicist and co-manager, Philip Hall, who died in December 1993.

EALING
LONDON W8

Art schools have long been a finishing school for rock and pop stars and a musician delivery service. The Ealing campus of Thames Valley University, in St Mary's Road, was once Ealing Art College where Pete Townshend, Freddie Mercury and Ronnie Wood all attended during the 1960s. One of

Townshend's lecturers here was Gustav Metzger, whose concept of auto-destructive art inspired Townshend's guitar-smashing routine.

Neil Tennant and Chris Lowe originally called their pop duo West End but changed it to Pet Shop Boys after a couple of mates who worked in a pet shop at the top of Springbridge Road, a hundred yards away from the club where The Rolling Stones were born. Brian Jones was performing as Elmo Lewis at The Ealing Club, 42a the Broadway, one night in April 1962 when he met Mick Jagger and Keith Richards for the first time. When it opened in 1959 as a jazz dive it was immediately nicknamed the 'Moist Hoist' because of its position in a leaky basement at the foot of some steep outside steps. Condensation poured down the walls and dripped incessantly from the ceiling when the club was full, threatening to electrocute musicians and audience alike. In March 1962, guitarist Alexis Korner, who was hugely influential in the spread of blues in England, opened his Ealing Club and it soon attracted every budding guitarist and harmonica player for miles. The venue still exists but as a nightclub called The Red Room, and previously as Club Azur (nicknamed Club Are You Sure? by locals).

The late Jimi Hendrix Experience's Mitch Mitchell was born and grew up in Ealing. Before he played the drums he was a child actor who played the Bisto Kid and an Ovalteenie in TV commercials. The funk group and acid jazz pioneers, The Brand New Heavies also hail from here, as does Fleetwood Mac's John McVie. Indie band The Magic Numbers, made up of a double set of brothers and sisters (Romeo Stodart and his sister Michele and Sean Gannon and his sister Angela), and possibly the most hirsute four-piece not in metal, are from here too. Ealing also claims the late soul diva Dusty Springfield (born Mary O'Brien; see also Henley-on-Thames, page 166) and easy-listening crooner Matt Monro. Born in East London as Terry Parsons, Munro spent most of his life in Ealing. Originally he was a bus driver who sang in his spare time but was plucked from obscurity by one of Elton John's musical heroes, Winifred Atwell.

PERIVALE
LONDON UB6

Those that loathe prog rock look away now: keyboard supremo Rick Wakeman was born in Perivale in 1949. The wizard hats and capes were only a tiny sum of his parts.

Before he joined Yes in 1971 Wakeman worked as a session musician playing piano on songs such as Cat Stevens's *Morning Has Broken* and David Bowie songs such as *Changes*, *Oh! You Pretty Things* and *Life on Mars*. Oh, and as for the Mellotron on Bowie's *Space Oddity*, that was Wakeman too.

Perivale's art deco marvel, The Hoover Building, made even more glorious at night when the building is illuminated with fluorescent green light, was lionised in Elvis Costello's 1980 song *Hoover Factory*:

> 'Five miles out of London on the Western Avenue/
> Must have been a wonder when it was brand new/
> Talkin''bout the splendour of the Hoover factory/
> I know that you'd agree if you had seen it too'.

Bottom: Mitch Mitchell (centre) with Noel Redding and Jimi Hendrix.
Below: The name Pet Shop Boys comes from Ealing.
Opposite page: Three out of four of The Who grew up in Acton.

The Southeast

Kent
East Sussex
West Sussex
Surrey
Middlesex

2

Kent

Tunbridge Wells ⟩

The phrase 'Disgusted of Tunbridge Wells' entered the lexicon when an editor of the local newspaper in the 1950s instructed staff to concoct letters for publication because the paper wasn't receiving many genuine ones. One reporter signed his, "Disgusted, Tunbridge Wells," and, ever since, the town has been an imagined vanguard of conservatism, inhabited by easily offended Middle Englanders. Such mythical residents would surely be appalled to learn their parish produced two punk prodigies.

The troubled guttersnipe and incarnation of punk itself, Sid Vicious, spent some of the most secure years of his childhood in Tunbridge Wells. Born Simon John Ritchie in London in 1957, he later attended Sandown Court School, a rough secondary modern in the Kent town. For four years he lived with his mother in rented accommodation at 43 Lime Hill Road, an Edwardian townhouse subdivided into apartments.

Later, punk band the Anti-Nowhere League would also hail from Tunbridge Wells, with their first gig taking place in 1980 at St Mark's Hall. Their first single the following year was a lively re-working of the Ralph McTell classic *Streets of London*, but it was the B-side that got the Metropolitan Police working overtime, seizing copies of the single on the grounds of obscenity. *So What* is an action-packed tour of southeast England that brags of drug use, sex with farmyard animals and the attainment of a sexual disease (which was later covered by the biggest heavy metal band in the world, Metallica). The lyrics are based on a real character the band encountered. Singer Nick 'Animal' Culmer said the jovial little number was written to ridicule a gobby local gangster they overheard in a pub boasting about his exploits and travels:

> 'Well, I've been to Hastings/
> And I've been to Brighton/
> I've been to Eastbourne too/
> So What, So What/
> And I've been here/
> And I've been there/
> And I've been every f***ing where/
> So What, So What/
> So What, So What, you boring little c***'

Considering the town's stuffy image, it's perhaps surprising another Tunbridge Wells native is singer-songwriter and poet Shane MacGowan of The Pogues. He was born here in 1957 before moving to County Tipperary with his family at an early age.

Before they became Brinsley Schwarz, the leading lights of the pub rock scene existed as the Tunbridge Wells-based guitar group Kippington Lodge. They included bassist and singer Nick Lowe and eponymous guitarist Brinsley Schwarz. They released five singles on Parlophone in the mid-1960s to little response.

The video for Marillion's third single, *Garden Party*, was filmed on the grounds of Groombridge Place, a manor house with moat, vineyards and formal gardens near Tunbridge Wells. (It's on YouTube, but don't worry, you can always turn the sound down.)

Left: Sid Vicious, hell-raising child of Tunbridge Wells.
Opposite: Siouxsie Sioux with the Banshees at the Belle Vue, Manchester, in 1977.

Paddock Wood

The annual Hop Farm Festival is held at the Hop Farm Country Park in early July. The inaugural festival in 2008 meant the crowded summer festival season had a new kid on the block, and it was deemed a huge success, due to a headline set by Neil Young. In 2010, it scored the only UK live appearance by Bob Dylan, still on his Never Ending Tour (there's a long-running unofficial competition where you try to guess what song Dylan is singing before it finishes). The festival is billed as a back-to-basics weekend all about the music and fans, meaning no sponsorship, branding or VIPs.

Chislehurst

Chislehurst Caves, at Old Hill, are a tangle of man-made caverns and passages that snake over 20 miles underneath southeast London suburbia. Originally made to mine chalk and flint, the caves were used as a hiding place for Royalists during the English Civil War and as an air raid shelter during World War II. Liverpool's famous Cavern was not the only cavernous venue to entertain 1960s gig-goers. The Caves were a popular live music venue, attracting groups like Jimi Hendrix, Pink Floyd, The Rolling Stones and local boy David Bowie, who all played alongside prehistoric fossils on a stage barely bigger than a double bed. The hand-carved caves are over 8,000 years old and were used by druids, Romans and Saxons. The caves also appeared in the 1959 Adam Faith film *Beat Girl* and the 2008 video of *Honey and Sulphur* by thrash metal band Cradle of Filth.

Punk icon Siouxsie Sioux, the enigmatic singer of Siouxsie and the Banshees, grew up as plain Susan Dallion in Chislehurst. As part of the Bromley Contingent (see Bromley, below), Siouxsie was thrust into the public consciousness on the infamous *Today* show with ITV's grump-in-chief Bill Grundy in December 1976. In fact, it was Grundy's misjudged effort to get it on with Siouxsie ("we'll meet afterwards shall we?") that set in flow punk's decisive moment, the foul-mouthed flare-up with the Sex Pistols that outraged the nation, or at least a tabloid press baying for their blood.

The Siouxsie and the Banshees song, *Hong Kong Garden*, is a tribute to a local Chinese takeaway of the same name on Chislehurst High Street, written in response to some

skinheads bullying the Chinese people who worked there. "I remember wishing that I could be like Emma Peel from The Avengers and kick all the skinheads' heads in," Siouxsie told *Uncut* magazine many years later. "Because they used to mercilessly torment these people for being foreigners. It made me feel so helpless, hopeless and ill."

Fans first experienced the band's individual style and freshness when they debuted at the 100 Club Punk Rock Festival in 1976. The band's boundlessly influential sound would clock them some 30 hits. Furthermore, Siouxsie's look – black leather and lace, ghost-white face, blood-red lips and midnight black hair – inspired a whole generation of Goths.

Bromley & Beckenham

In the summer of 1976 a group of outrageously dressed London teenagers and followers of the Sex Pistols bound together by music and attitude were dubbed the 'Bromley Contingent' by *Melody Maker* writer Caroline Coon. Amongst the in-crowd of the entourage (not a million miles from Andy Warhol's Factory hangouts) were Siouxsie Sioux, Steve Severin, Simon Barker, Jordan, Soo Catwoman and William Broad, aka Billy Idol. These cult suburban anti-heroes would travel from Bromley to West End clubs and gay discos such as Louise's, a lesbian club at 61 Poland Street in Soho. They chose gay clubs like this because their attendance at straight venues at that time would provoke antagonism. Some of these first fans of the Sex Pistols went on to become musical

Let all the children boogie

Perhaps the most iconic 1970s *Top of the Pops* performance, which beguiled viewers and influenced future singer-songwriters, was David Bowie's *Starman*. Artists like Echo & The Bunnymen's Ian McCulloch, Madness's Suggs and Spandau Ballet's Gary Kemp have all cited Bowie's 1972 TV performance as the spark that ignited their desire to follow a pop career.

Dressed in a colourful jumpsuit, strumming a bright blue acoustic guitar with a camp arm draped around guitarist Mick Ronson's shoulder, redhead Bowie references Marc Bolan: "Some cat was laying down some *get-it-on* rock 'n' roll." The performance helped *Starman* rocket up the charts and into the top 10 two weeks later. More importantly, even hardened teenage boys started to wear make-up and camp it up.

The archetypal rock chameleon, Bowie was pop's ch-ch-ch-ch-changing man. As a master of reinvention; Bowie absorbed influences and then re-mastered them. In the space of a few years he killed off Ziggy Stardust, the transgender space pirate who becomes a rock 'n' roll star, and his Aladdin Sane persona – complete with lightning flash across his face – and morphed into a bequiffed blue-eyed soul boy for his 1975 soul album, *Young Americans*. Before long he had changed again into the Thin White Duke persona, and then reflected the bleakness of pre-unified Germany in his Berlin Trilogy, including *Low*, widely regarded as a classic.

Bowie spent his earliest formative years in Brixton, before his family moved to Bromley, to 23 Clarence Road and then 106 Canon Road. When he was 10, his parents moved to 4 Plaistow Grove, Sundridge Park. In late 1967, he changed his name from David Jones to Bowie, after the knife, to avoid being mistaken for Monkees singer, Davy Jones.

After a few years living in central London and South Kensington, he returned to live in Beckenham in 1968, at the rented gothic mansion, Haddon Hall, 42 Southend Road (now converted into a block of flats). Bowie lived here with his American wife, Angie, and posed for the cover of *The Man Who Sold The World* here in a dress. Around the corner, Bowie ran the Beckenham Arts Lab folk club every Sunday night in a back room of the Three Tuns pub on the High Street (now a branch of the Zizzi restaurant chain).

stars themselves: Billy Idol joined Chelsea and later formed Generation X. And, a couple of years later, Siouxsie Sioux and Steve Severin mutated into Siouxsie and the Banshees; the band that sprang from the heart of the Contingent transcended the Sex Pistols themselves.

Another woman who hailed from Bromley and made punk sound so fresh was X-Ray Spex singer Poly Styrene. Long before she belted out songs that rallied against consumerism, she was born Marianne Elliott to a British mother and a Somali former aristocrat father. She later grew up in 1960s Brixton and attended Stockwell Manor School, where her Maths teacher was none other than astronomer and Queen guitar virtuoso, Brian May. He was a supply teacher there for a while before the lure of guitar strings proved too powerful. Polly and her school friends used to tease May about the holes in his shoes and his long hair.

This leafy suburb also spawned Fatboy Slim (born Quentin Norman Cook) and The Clash's drummer Topper Headon, but Bromley's most famous former resident is David Bowie (see box). Bowie was a pupil at Bromley Technical High School (now Ravensbourne School) in Oakley Road. Guitarist and singer Peter Frampton also attended the school and his father was one of Bowie's schoolteachers.

Frampton was born in nearby Beckenham in 1950 and first tasted success as singer in the 1960s pop group The Herd, then in Humble Pie with Steve Marriott, later of the Small Faces. His global breakthrough in the mid-1970s with his huge-selling *Frampton Comes Alive!*, with its talk box guitar which Frampton could control the sound of by changing the shape of his mouth.

Other Beckenham boys are Haircut 100's Nick Heyward and David Batt, better known as David Sylvian, singer-songwriter of Japan, who went solo and worked with Robert Fripp and Ryuichi Sakamoto.

There's another legendary band with Beckenham roots; one that, regardless of prevailing trends, has pretty much kept to its original principles and the same three guitar chords: Status Quo. The band, who were nearly called The Queers, started gigging in Beckenham in the early 1960s and went through a number of name changes before Status Quo became the status quo. The band's part-time gas plumber manager suggested The Queers and Muhammad Ali. They were The Scorpions, then The Spectres, then Traffic for a week, then Traffic Jam. Finally their manager reckoned on Status Quo, even though frontman Francis Rossi didn't have a clue what it meant.

Sidcup

Multi-instrumentalist and producer John Baldwin – better known as Led Zeppelin bassist John Paul Jones – was born in Sidcup in 1946 into a family of musicians. His father was a big band arranger and pianist who started to teach his son the piano when he was six. Jones was an old friend of Jimmy Page and a top London session musician before he joined Zeppelin.

The Rolling Stones and The Pretty Things had a lot more in common than their Dartford origins (see page 74): Keith Richards went to the same art school, Sidcup Art College, as Pretty Things frontman Phil May and guitarist Dick Taylor. Taylor was even a Rolling Stone for a few months in 1962.

Biggin Hill

The front sleeve of Pink Floyd's *Ummagumma* was shot near Cambridge (see Cambridgeshire) but the back cover, showing all the band's sound gear and equipment spread out, was photographed on the runway at Biggin Hill airport. Also pictured were the band's roadie, Alan Stiles, and road manager, Peter Watts, father of the actress Naomi Watts.

The White Bear pub in Fickleshole, near Biggin Hill (but actually in Surrey), was the setting at sunrise for the cover photograph of Grand Drive's 2002 album, *See the Morning In*. The country-rockers were photographed in a field opposite the pub. The album was produced by Jim Cregan, who laid down the memorable acoustic guitar solo on *Make Me Smile (Come Up and See Me)* by Steve Harley & Cockney Rebel. Grand Drive were named after a road between Raynes Park and Sutton, the southwest London suburb where the band's brothers Julian and Danny Wilson grew up.

Chatham

He was the one-time beau of Tracey Emin and the godfather of homemade punk and rhythm and blues. Chatham's favourite son is the multi-faceted Billy Childish, a prolific painter, publisher, poet, writer and musician. Inspired by punk, Childish produced a series of fanzines, including

Chatham's Burning, and formed a teenage punk band, The Pop Rivets, in 1977. When New Romantic music was all the rage ("the worst form of music ever"), he formed a rock 'n' roll band called The Milkshakes, who once released four albums on the same day. Every five years or so Childish disbands his groups and starts again from scratch. Subsequent groups were called Thee Mighty Caesars, Thee Headcoats (who released a single called *We Hate the F***in' NME*), and The Buff Medways, who drew heavily on his local Kent roots, like on the band's 2005 album, *Medway Wheelers*, named after the old cycling club Childish's mother belonged to in the 1950s. There is footage of Mrs Childish riding through Whitstable on the title track video.

Above: Billy Childish performing in July 2009.

Progressive Rock
Close to the (Technical) Edge

NEXT time you watch *The X Factor*, try to imagine a complicated 20-minute song about wizards, jesters and topographic oceans, performed by a band wearing capes and spangly costumes. Nowadays they wouldn't make it past security. But in the late 1960s and early 1970s this sort of performance was all the rage amongst UK rock audiences.

Progressive rock – 'prog rock' or just 'prog' – was an ambitious home-grown genre of rock music. Blues-influenced mainstream rock was replaced by diverse arrangements drawn from jazz, classical, folk and experimental influences.

Prog was the Essex of musical genres, arguably the most-maligned rock form of them all. Its detractors dismissed prog as 'up-its-own-arse music' that could only conceivably appeal to rather strange, or estranged, males. Its critics were unforgiving and ignored its often sumptuous melodies and astounding musicianship. Instead they spurned the entire category outright, citing its silly costumes, fanciful themes and meandering, tuneless soloing.

Two resonant images perfectly capture the overblown nature of the golden age of prog: Yes's Rick Wakeman lurking behind his keyboards in a wizard hat, and overhead shots of huge articulated lorries transporting Emerson Lake & Palmer's stage equipment.

Sure, prog *was* pompous and self-indulgent but it reflected the tendency of the time to produce complex music that drew upon ever more divergent sources, requiring a technical expertise that went up to 11. It also reflected the changing tastes of radio listeners as short pop songs on AM radio had changed to longer FM-oriented styles.

Simplicity took a back seat in prog rock. As band members were virtuoso musicians who could play a bit, performances could be seen as a showcase of technical ability. They experimented with tempo changes and ever-changing time signatures and ventured beyond pop's typical verse-chorus-bridge structure in favour of the improvisational traditions of jazz and psychedelic rock. This meant lengthy musical interludes and extended instrumental solo passages – sometimes a guitar solo went on so long guitarists were forced to sit down, if they weren't sitting down already. As a result, prog songs – sometimes called movements or suites – tended to last up to 20 minutes. Or, in some cases, as long as one half of a football match. Prog tracks went on so long if you downloaded them today you could probably only fit a couple on an iPod. Prog giants Jethro Tull's classic 1972 album, *Thick As A Brick* – which sent-up the concept album – consisted of one extended track clocking in at 43 minutes. (The band's guitarist had the suitably proggy name of Martin Lancelot Barre.)

The concept album was another all-important element of progressive rock, bringing together epic, elaborate narratives, or a collection of songs related to an overall theme. Prog's free-range rhythmic approach

augmented the standard rock apparatus of guitar, bass, drums and organ with flutes, violins, keyboards and saxophone, instruments often more associated with folk and jazz. And, of course, no self-respecting prog band was complete without a wall of synthesisers and electronic musical instruments. The Mellotron and Moog synth became as synonymous with the genre as capes and dry ice.

The genre's chief prog-tagonists were Yes, Genesis, King Crimson, Jethro Tull, and its first supergroup, Emerson, Lake & Palmer, who came together in 1970 from the members of The Nice, King Crimson and The Crazy World of Arthur Brown. Their lyrics reflected progressive rock's higher musical yearnings; catchy three-minute love songs were out in favour of lofty concepts and themes. Prog bands ignored reality piling up outside the studio doors in favour of fantasy, folklore and mythical worlds. Who cared about social issues or dancing with your baby when you could 'stand on hills of long forgotten

yesterdays', or 'summon back the fire witch to the court of the Crimson King'?

Live shows meant intricate theatrics and elaborate lighting with giant mirrors and lasers that synchronised with the sound. Yes's futuristic stage antics featured large spaceship props; Jethro Tull released rabbits on stage whilst the band's enigmatic singer-songwriter Ian Anderson mastered the art of flute playing while standing on one leg. Emerson, Lake & Palmer's flying piano was a Steinway grand spun from a crane, and Genesis frontman Peter Gabriel made several flamboyant costume changes in order to act out song narratives.

One more important prog staple was the artistic album sleeve. A photograph of the band just wouldn't do. The mystical landscapes of graphic artist Roger Dean graced the expansive, gatefold sleeves of albums by prog rockers Uriah Heep and Yes.

But all good things must come to an end and come the mid-1970s the exalted music of

progressive rock became a soft target for pub rockers and punks. To them prog was remote and pompous; it was time to slay rock's dinosaurs and return to simpler music and three-minute songs of youthful bluster.

It's likely that Manchester prog rockers Van der Graaf Generator were only spared savagery by the punks because Sex Pistol John Lydon had been a fan. Robert Fripp soon called time on King Crimson; musicians in Yes and Emerson, Lake & Palmer pursued solo work, as did Peter Gabriel.

In Don Letts' film about The Clash, *Westway To The World*, bassist Paul Simonon recalls the moment he discovered his brother listening to Yes. When he removed his headphones Simonon heard the sounds of tweeting birds. "God! What are you listening to?" he asked incredulously.

Above: Rick Wakeman of Yes. Gold cape and all.

Over the years he has released 120-plus albums, many of which are inspired by Kent people and places. For his latest band incarnation, Wild Billy Childish & The Musicians of the British Empire, he recorded an autobiographical song called *Back Amongst The Medway Losers* in 2008. The cover of the album, *Thatcher's Children*, was designed by legendary Sex Pistols cover artist, Jamie Reid. Kent's poet of the Medway Towns refuses to leave his home-town of Chatham and lives just a short walk from the River Medway, which inspires many of his paintings.

Billy Childish's fellow Chatham resident and Medway troubadour is Pete Molinari. The singer-songwriter's 2007 debut album, *Walking Off the Map*, was made in one day in Childish's kitchen and recorded live on Childish's old Revox tape machine.

Chatham's Tap 'N' Tin pub in Railway Street was the first venue The Libertines played following the release of singer Pete Doherty from Wandsworth prison in October 2003. Doherty reunited with his band for the 'Freedom Gig' just a few hours after being released from jail. A photo from the evening made it onto the cover of 2004's imaginatively titled album, *The Libertines*.

Canterbury ⟫

The city's St Dunstan's Street, near Canterbury's imposing West Gate, is portrayed on the cover of 1976's *Blind Dog at St Dunstans* (sic) by local prog-rockers Caravan. St Dunstan was a 10th century Archbishop of Canterbury and patron saint of the blind; a neighbourhood west of the city centre is named after him. The album title was inspired by Noël Coward answering a child who had asked why one dog had mounted another: it was blind and was pushing him all the way to St Dunstan's. The names of shops on the cover have canine puns like the Mongrel Travel Agency and Barkleys Bank. Local buses are just able to squeeze through the West Gate, which has stood for six centuries, guarding the road from London, and is the only one of the city's seven gates to survive.

The late John Peel was a big fan of the dub-reggae-folk fusion of Dreadzone. *A Canterbury Tale* was a gorgeous chilled-out track on their 1995 album, *Second Light*. It evokes pastoral England and heavily samples the violin motif from *The Lark Ascending* by Ralph Vaughan Williams. *Canterbury* was also the title track and name of an album by Midlands

heavy metal band Diamond Head, who did much to inspire the formation of Metallica. Vinyl pressing plant problems ensured this 1983 album was a flop.

Conventional wisdom suggests that a fat, balding white man might struggle to forge a successful reggae recording career but Kent-born Alexander Hughes thought otherwise. As the English ska and reggae star Judge Dread, he took his name from Prince Buster, who he once worked for as a bodyguard. The first white artist to have a reggae hit in Jamaica died on stage at Canterbury's Penny Theatre in 1998 at the end of a gig. Just as he urged the audience to applaud his band, he walked offstage and suffered a fatal heart attack. He grew up in a West Indian household in Brixton where his bulky frame helped him carve out an early career as a bouncer at Brixton's Ram Jam club, and as a debt collector for Trojan Records, the label set up by Island's Chris Blackwell in 1968 to showcase the best Jamaican sounds.

Attracting thousands of festival-goers each year, the annual Lounge On The Farm has taken place at Merton Farm near Canterbury every July since 2006. The festival's byword is local, with all food and drink sold being produced within 20 miles of the festival site; the cider is from nearby Pawley Farm, the beer from Kentish brewery Hopdaemon. The festival's keep-it-local ethic extends to the music, with bands from the Kent area playing, as well others from further afield.

Herne Bay ⟫

Some of the musicians associated with the two leading bands of the Canterbury scene (see page 70) – Richard Coughlan and David Sinclair of prog rockers Caravan and Kevin Ayers of Soft Machine – were born in this seaside town a few miles northeast of Canterbury. One of England's most imaginative and eccentric songwriters, Ayers was brought up

Right: Squeeze: (l-r) John Bentley, Chris Difford, Gilson Lavis, Jools Holland, Glenn Tilbrook.

in Malaysia but returned to Kent as a guitar-playing teenager. He helped found The Wilde Flowers in the mid 1960s but never cut any records.

An unlikely rock figure who grew up in Herne Bay was broadcaster and former *Blockbuster* presenter Bob Holness. For many years it was believed that Holness had played the famous sax solo on Gerry Rafferty's *Baker Street*. Although there was no truth in the story, Holness played along and even embellished it, saying he'd also played guitar on the classic *Layla* by Derek and the Dominos. The *Baker Street* myth was a madcap ruse created by witty writer and broadcaster Stuart Maconie when he wrote the 'Believe It Or Not' section of the *NME*, passing nonsense off as facts. He also memorably informed readers that David Bowie invented the game Connect Four. Maconie also coined the phrase 'Britpop' – and that's not a myth.

Margate

The seaside town of Margate was Britain's Benidorm until the advent of cheap holidays to the Costa del Sol. As early as 1805 there were four-wheeled canvas-covered bathing machines on its sandy beaches, concealing changing bathers from public view. The opening of the railway in 1844 made Margate a popular attraction for working class Londoners. It has been immortalised in TS Eliot's *The Waste Land* and later by Chas & Dave in 1982's *Down to Margate*: 'Down to Margate / We'll have a pill of jellied eels at the cockle stall.'

South Londoners Squeeze took their witty lyricism to the British seaside on *Pulling Mussels (From the Shell)*, a song inspired by a childhood holiday when Chris Difford stayed

in a caravan at a Margate holiday camp. The second single from Squeeze's 1980 album *Argybargy*, it perfectly captures holidaymakers at an English seaside town:

> 'Two fat ladies window shop/
> Something for the mantelpiece/
> In for bingo all the nines/
> A panda for sweet little niece'

Talking of argy-bargy, in common with other British seaside resorts, Margate was no stranger to outbreaks of cross-cultural antagonism between mods and rockers in the 1960s and mods and skinheads two decades later. Clashes at Clacton at Easter 1963 soon spread to Margate and other resorts over the next few weeks. In the absence of any Johnny Foreigner to fight in a corner of a foreign field, England's youth went to war with themselves over important stuff like clothes, lifestyle and how they did their hair.

Since opening in 1911, Margate's Winter Gardens has been a stalwart on its weather-beaten seafront. While its entertainment programme is more panto than Pinter, it still puts on enough gigs to sustain its pop prestige, founded in the 1960s when artists like Helen Shapiro, Billy J Kramer and the Dakotas and The Beatles played. In July 1963, the Fab Four played twice-nightly gigs for a week.

Dover

The white cliffs of Dover are one of Britain's most iconic images. The towering cliffs have great symbolic significance amongst the English and were the inspiration for the popular World War II song *(There'll Be Bluebirds Over) The White Cliffs of Dover*. Made famous by Dame Vera Lynn by way of bolstering the Allies' spirits, the lyrics were written by an American who never set foot in the UK. So don't expect to see too many bluebirds flying around the Kent coast – the bird's natural habitat is the US and Central America. In 2009, Dame Vera Lynn took on the right-wing British National Party after it used the song on a fund-raising compilation album without her approval. A version by early Simon Cowell charges, Robson and Jerome, hit the top spot in June 1995 in a medley with *Unchained Melody*.

The coastline was also immortalised by the appropriately named reggae legend Jimmy Cliff, in his 1969 anthem *Many Rivers to Cross*:

FOR centuries the only noise emanating from the home of English Christianity, where King Henry II's troublesome priest Thomas Becket was murdered, was the peeling of its cathedral bells. All that changed in the late 1960s and early 1970s when Canterbury became the centre of a very English take on post-psychedelic pop that produced progressive rock and jazz fusion.

The Canterbury Scene was a collection of musicians based in or associated with the cathedral city, notably Soft Machine, Caravan, Gong, Hatfield and the North, Egg and Henry Cow. Over the years, the term Canterbury Scene has become known as a musical sub-genre in itself. This sprouting of progressive music stemmed from the mid-'60s band The Wilde Flowers.

Named in honour of Oscar Wilde, they were a loose collection of artistically minded young musician friends who played soul and R&B-infused pop. During their three-year life The Wilde Flowers included most of the musicians who later formed Canterbury Scene's prime movers Caravan (former choirboy Richard Sinclair and Pye Hastings) and British psychedelia pioneers Soft Machine (Robert Wyatt, Kevin Ayers). Soft Machine became regulars on the psychedelic/ underground scene alongside Pink Floyd at the UFO Club on London's Tottenham Court Road in the spring of 1967.

Another leading light of the Canterbury Scene was Australian beatnik guitarist Daevid Allen, a founding member of Soft Machine, who contacted cult American author William S Burroughs to get approval to name the band after his novel. Allen later went on to launch Gong into space from Paris when he was denied re-entry to the UK. Years earlier

after only one album with the band and fresh from an American tour supporting Jimi Hendrix, Kevin Ayers had left to embark on a solo career when his penchant for pop clashed with the jazz-rock leanings of his colleagues. Soft Machine later added a quartet of horn players, before slimming down to just one, saxophonist Elton Dean.

They became true prog rock pioneers in 1970 when they played at the BBC Proms at the Royal Albert Hall. By then they had moved away from psychedelia, towards a jazzy form of progressive rock, rich in instrumental and improvisation with a firm nod towards jazz and avant garde music.

Above: Kevin Ayers, Robert Wyatt, Mike Routledge and Daevid Allen as Soft Machine.

'Many rivers to cross/
But I can't seem to find my way over/
Wandering I am lost/
As I travel along the white cliffs of Dover'

A huge many artists have covered the song, including Joe Cocker, Elvis Costello and UB40, but, arguably, none have bettered the original. Dover's white cliffs are also mentioned in *Clover Over Dover*, a song by Blur on their *Parklife* album.

A couple of years before he opened his chain of record stores, Virgin Records, a young Richard Branson had set up a record mail-order business. An event at Dover in 1971 nearly landed the young businessman with a record he was unfamiliar with: a criminal one. The Virgin Records boss was arrested and spent the night in a Dover prison cell, charged with not having paid the duty on 10,000 records. Branson had discovered a scheme in which Virgin could export records without actually doing so, therefore avoiding purchase tax. Everything was going well until Customs & Excise officials learnt of the scam and had all the records Virgin bought for export marked with an invisible letter E. Branson avoided a criminal record but had to repay £60,000 to Customs & Excise in an out-of-court settlement.

In April 1967 Gong's Daevid Allen was refused re-entry into the UK by customs officials at Dover because he'd overstayed his work visa on his previous visit.

Rolvenden

An old walled garden in Great Maytham Hall near Rolvenden inspired children's author Frances Hodgson Burnett to write her famous book, *The Secret Garden*. But Ian Dury preferred the luxurious Toad Hall in Rolvenden and moved there in July 1978. Dury was joined by keyboardist and co-songwriter Chaz Jankel and the rest of The Blockheads to work on songs for *New Boots and Panties!!*

Amongst the songs Dury and Jankel perfected here was *Hit Me With Your Rhythm Stick*. Jankel spent long hours over his keyboard in Toad Hall's garage working on the melody, while Dury conjured up the words, or rather pretended to; he'd had the lyrics up his sleeve for several years. When they'd finished writing the song, Chaz Jankel telephoned his mother and told her he had just written his first number one. He had too; it topped the UK singles chart the following January.

Oh England, her lionheart

Scattered evenly up and down England is a whole generation of people, now in their early and mid-40s, who were schoolchildren the first time they encountered Kate Bush. For them, seeing her perform her first single *Wuthering Heights* on *Top of the Pops* in 1978 was little less than a revelation, and a vision possibly still imprinted on their minds.

It was the only source of conversation in the playground the next day; the bike-shed fumblings and ritual abuse of dinner ladies were temporarily suspended to discuss her remarkable performance. Many teenage schoolboys fell instantly and hopelessly in love with her, while schoolgirls immediately signed up for dance and singing classes. And it's an infatuation that remains today. To many, Bush is still a national treasure, one of England's most cherished musical eccentrics. You could argue *Wuthering Heights* was a triumph of English artist and audience: such a startlingly original musician met by such a wholly English response as the public took an unconventional song so readily to their hearts. It went to number one in the UK, where it stayed for four weeks.

Bush, a GP's daughter, was born in Bexleyheath in July 1958, and grew up at a 350-year-old farmhouse in Welling. She started writing songs at the age of 11, was discovered by Pink Floyd's Dave Gilmour aged 15 and signed to EMI at 16. She asserted her creative control early on when she pressed for *Wuthering Heights* to be released as a single against the wishes of record label executives. Since then her eight studio albums, her haunting vocals and escapist, otherworldly songs have continued to enthral listeners. Her catalogue of songs won her an Ivor Novello Award for Outstanding Contribution to British Music in 2002.

Essentially English, genuinely original, an eclectic child prodigy turned popular music legend… call Kate Bush what you will, she remains one of the most influential artists in pop who continues to work on her own terms – and to her own timetable; her 2005 release, *Aerial*, was her first album in 12 years.

Dungeness ⟩

There's a desolate, end-of-the-world feel to bleak and beautiful Dungeness on Kent's southernmost tip. Whether it's the splendid isolation or the dazzling light – there are no trees, hills or other shelter to shield the sun here – Dungeness is surely one of the most extraordinary corners of Kent, or even England, for that matter. Even the houses have an otherworldly feel: a seemingly random selection of tarred timber shacks, some starting life as old railway coaches. And the *Mad Max*, post-apocalyptic feel to the place is only enhanced by the looming spectre of the nearby Dungeness A nuclear power station.

As you might expect, such a barren landscape is a popular location for TV drama and advertising shoots and, notably, some album covers and music videos. The sleeve of the Pink Floyd compilation, *A Collection Of Great Dance Songs* – which features two roped dancers – was shot here. Likewise, Dublin indie rockers The Thrills travelled to Dungeness for the cover of their debut album, *So Much for the City*, as did that well-known rock 'n' roller Aled Jones for his imaginatively-titled album, *Aled*.

Rather than a village, Dungeness is more a scattering of isolated houses, the most famous of which is Prospect Cottage, the former residence of the late artist and film-maker Derek Jarman. His 1978 film *Jubilee*, in which a time-travelling Queen Elizabeth I is transported forward to a 1977 London clad in safety pins, was arguably the first punk movie. The film features various punk groups and personalities, including future pop stars Toyah Wilcox and Adam Ant, and songs from Chelsea, Adam and the Ants, Wayne County and Siouxsie and the Banshees.

A jolly, almost sing-a-long number about the place, *Dungeness*, appears on southeast London band Athlete's album, *Vehicles & Animals*, nominated for the 2003 Mercury Music Prize. Dungeness's vast shingle beach – home to over 600 species of plant, including gorse and sea kale – featured on the cover of the Howard Jones album, *Cross That Line*. In 2006, a Kent-based punk band called November Coming Fire released an album called *Dungeness* that included the song, *Powerstation*, about the nearby nuclear power station. The sound of waves crashing on the beach can be heard towards the end of the track.

Among the most bizarre sights to grace the south of England coastline are the three concrete acoustic mirrors at Denge, a former RAF site near Dungeness. As a precursor of radar, a series of these listening ears were built along England's south and northeast coasts in the 1920s to provide an early warning system for incoming enemy aircraft. Located between Greatstone-on-Sea and Lydd airfield, they resemble giant obsolete tombstones and still make for strong visuals.

The south London Indie band Turin Brakes certainly thought so. Olly Knights and Gale Paridjanian sit amongst the Denge sound mirrors for the cover of their second album, *Ether Song*, which includes the catchy top-five hit, *Painkiller*. The video for *Invaders Must Die* by The Prodigy, released as a free digital download in November 2008, was filmed here and features the acoustic mirrors prominently.

Far left: Artist and film director Derek Jarman at home in Dungeness.
Left: The Dungeness power station.

LONG before anyone thought of the concept of pop videos, The Beatles travelled to Sevenoaks in early 1967 to film sequences for their pioneering promo videos for *Strawberry Fields Forever* and *Penny Lane*. The hugely influential promos are now widely seen as the first ever pop music videos and were filmed on the grounds of the large deer park, Knole Park.

The surreal video for *Strawberry Fields Forever* was shot around a dead oak tree behind the birdhouse of the 15th-century Knole House, owned by The National Trust. The memorable scene in which McCartney jumps into the tree was, not surprisingly, filmed in reverse. He climbed a ladder, clung to a branch then dropped to the grass as the ladder was removed. He then ran back backwards to the piano and started to play. The video also features stop motion animation and jump-cuts from day to night. The former Beatles road manager Tony Bramwell spent two days dressing the tree to make it look like a piano and harp combined with strings.

The horse riding and candelabra scenes for their *Penny Lane* video were also filmed at Knole Park. Dressed in red hunting jackets, the Fab Four ride their horses through an arch in a ruined wall by the birdhouse, and later dismount to sit around a table beside two ponds. The video's street scenes were shot in east London' in Angel Lane, Stratford, near the Theatre Royal, most of which was flattened to make way for the Stratford Centre. Of course, filming also took place in Liverpool's Penny Lane, although the Fabs weren't present during filming there.

Later the same year, in September 1967, The Beatles went deeper into Kent, near Maidstone, to shoot their TV film, *Magical Mystery Tour* at West Malling. They used the town's High Street for the title sequence as well as a former RAF airfield, a fighter station during World War Two. The aerodrome was the band's second choice location; they originally wanted to shoot the film at Shepperton Film Studios in Middlesex but it was booked out. *Magical Mystery Tour* was The Beatles first film since *Help!* and it followed a bus full of eccentrics on a magic journey through the English countryside: a pretty thin plot but a good excuse to promote various songs from the *Magical Mystery Tour* album, including *The Fool on the Hill*, *Your Mother Should Know*, *I Am the Walrus* and, of course, the title track.

The opening shot of the film's best-known *I Am The Walrus* sequence was shot through a large round hole in one of the airfield's concrete anti-blast walls through which refuelling pipes linked tanker to aeroplane. These large structures, seen throughout the video, were demolished in the 1990s. It was also here the Fab Four donned their bizarre animal outfits: Ringo was a chicken, George a rabbit, Paul a hippo and, yes, John was the walrus. Meanwhile the film's finale, *Your Mother Should Know*, was filmed inside the airfield's main hangar, which had been transformed into a large sound stage.

The Bonzo Dog Doo-Dah Band also appear in the film, in a strip club performing *Death Cab for Cutie*, the song that gave the US alt-rockers from Washington state their name.

A decade later, in 1977, some more rock satirists, The Rutles, travelled to West Malling to film their *Tragical History Tour* TV special, as part of their *All You Need Is Cash* Beatles spoof. Elsewhere, *Magical Mystery Tour* later part-inspired The Style Council's cringe-making 30-minute film *Jerusalem*, with Paul Weller as King Canute.

There's little die-hard Beatles fans would find magical around West Malling today. The airfield is now Kings Hill, a mixed housing development and business park, with not a pornographic priestess nor walrus in sight.

SEE HOW THEY FLY – THE BEATLES IN KENT

The Dartford Delta...
The Rolling Stones and
The Pretty Things

ENGLISH history is peppered with successful collaborative partnerships, spanning various fields of human endeavour: Marks & Spencer; Tate & Lyle; Torvill & Dean; Brian Clough and Peter Taylor; Peter Cook and Dudley Moore; Dalziel and Pascoe. Musically it's the same: Gilbert and Sullivan; Flanders and Swann; Elton John and Bernie Taupin; Lennon and McCartney; Difford & Tilbrook; Robson & Jerome… ok, maybe not on that last one. Of course, one of the most enduring of these songwriting partnerships is Mick Jagger and Keith Richards, two rhythm and blues fans who travelled to the crossroads via Dartford and created one of the most successful and longest-running rock bands in the world.

They were even born in the same hospital, Dartford's Livingstone Hospital on East Hill, just five months apart in 1943. Grammar school-educated Jagger was a basketball-playing, middle class son of a PE teacher, while unruly Richards hailed from a working class family and doted upon his jazz band leader grandfather, Gus Dupree. He was expelled from his technical school for truancy. Richards spent his early years at 33 Chastilian Road, just a few streets away from Jagger's childhood home at 39 Denver Road. Mick 'n' Keef first met in the playground of Wentworth County Primary School when Jagger asked

Left: Mick Jagger and Keith Richards at a press conference in New York, 1965.
Below: The Pretty Things, 1964.

Richards what he wanted to be when he grew up. The young Keith replied: a cowboy, like Roy Rogers, and a guitarist.

Their initial friendship was short-lived because Richards and his family moved to a small semi-detached house at 6 Spielman Road on Temple Hill, a new council estate on the other side of Dartford. There, Richards would sit at the top of the stairs, strumming the guitar his mother Doris had bought him from her wages at a baker's shop. He would play American songs he'd heard on the Embassy label. "I always sat on the top stair to practise," Richards told Stones biographer Philip Norman. "You could get the best echo that way – or standing in the bath."

Jagger and Richards famously met again in their teens, one morning in 1961 when they boarded the same London-bound train at Dartford station. Jagger, en route to a lecture at the London School of Economics, bumped into Richards, on his way to Sidcup Art College. They vaguely recognised each other from their primary school days but the meeting might not have amounted to anything had Jagger not been carrying some American import R&B albums under his arm. Richards spotted the sacred names of Chuck Berry and Little Walter, and asked Jagger (then known as Mike) if he liked that kind of music. The train full of commuters that morning were oblivious to this momentous meeting of musical minds. A shared passion for R&B was forged and would bond them together for the next 50 years.

As they chatted they learned they had a mutual friend in Dick Taylor, Jagger's guitarist friend in Little Boy Blue and the Blue Boys. By the time the train pulled into Sidcup station, Richards had arranged to rehearse with Jagger's band. It would not be long before they met Brian Jones and keyboardist Ian Stewart and formed the band that would go on to become the world-conquering Stones.

In 2000, Jagger returned to his unloved old grammar school to open a performing arts centre that bears his name. The Stones frontman part-funded the £2.25 million centre, which includes two fully equipped venues, a recording and video studio and rehearsal rooms. At the centre's opening the school band played *Brown Sugar* and, as Jagger reminded pupils and teachers, it used to be the school assembly hall: "Where each morning we would sing our hymns and either be praised or damned for our behaviour."

In 2008, Dartford Council announced it would honour its local heroes with road names inspired by Stones songs. Several streets on Dartford's new 1,500-home Bridge development will be named after classic Rolling Stones hits. The roads, chosen by Dartford Borough Council members, will be named Sympathy Street after *Sympathy for the Devil*, and Little Red Walk after *Little Red Rooster*, the blues classic the band covered in their early days. Other roads will be called Dandelion Row, Cloud Close, Ruby Tuesday Drive, Satisfaction Street and the not terribly imaginative Stones Avenue. But Fighting Man Street, Cocksucker Close and Gimme Shelter Mews didn't make it past the brainstorming stage.

There was another R&B five-piece from Dartford with three words in their name: The Pretty Things. They went from R&B punks to psychedelic forerunners and even trumped their Kent contemporaries in the non-conformity stakes, making The Rolling Stones look like choirboys by comparison.

The roots of The Pretty Things go back to Sidcup Art College, where guitarists Dick Taylor and fellow student Keith Richards shared a love for blues and R&B. The Rolling Stones were formed when Brian Jones joined as guitarist, pushing Taylor from guitar to bass and Taylor decided to concentrate on his studies rather than play a secondary role in the Stones. The following year Taylor was playing his preferred guitar again alongside another Sidcup art student, harmonica player and singer, Phil May.

A dead ringer for Kasabian frontman, Tom Meighan, May was also an early hero of David Bowie, who covered two of their songs on his album, *Pin Ups*. The Pretty Things name was a homage to 1950s Bo Diddley song and an ironic dig at those who couldn't see beyond their unkempt look. Early newspaper articles about them dwelt on their shabby clothing and their lengthy coiffures. "Phil May must have the longest hair on the long-haired current pop scene," was the striking observation of one publication.

The band debuted at Dartford's Station Hotel in 1963 before playing some college dates in the city. They were soon playing London's 100 Club and being described as one of the hottest new acts on the London scene. Their wildness wasn't for everyone. During their first tour of Holland in 1965, a concert was broadcast live on Dutch TV, but was terminated halfway through the band's third song, when outraged viewers called to complain. New Zealand even gave the Dartford quintet a life ban.

Their energetic drummer Viv Prince often out-Mooned The Who's Keith Moon with his anarchic on-stage antics. He jumped on balloons and waved a king-size sword around the stage. Backstage, he broke chairs, lit fires and abused officials. He even swigged whisky from his shoe and joked it was methylated spirits. Away from the stage, Prince carried a dead crayfish around with him for several days, and it was Prince who accompanied Paul McCartney on his first acid trip.

Many of their R&B numbers were written from personal experience, their autobiographical lyrics joining blues structures, as in *Long Haired Blues*. Due to their appearance, the band often received the cold shoulder: taxi drivers stuck their hired sign up as soon as they saw the band, and restaurants closed when they walked in. "It was a pity because we need food to keep our hair growing!" Dick Taylor once said.

They also wrote songs about London, including the folky *13 Chester Street*, about the Belgravia pad they shared with Brian Jones, and *Death of A Socialite*, which, like The Beatles' *A Day In The Life*, was about the 1966 car crash which killed Guinness heir Tara Browne.

Where The Pretty Things differed from their 1960s R&B contemporaries was in their successful transition to psychedelia. Released within weeks of *Beggars Banquet* and *The White Album*, their 1968 album *SF Sorrow* was one rock's first concept albums and, arguably of the first rock opera, released five months before The Who's *Tommy*. The album, following the eponymous Mr Sorrow through his life, features backwards guitars, sitars and lyrics about flying to the moon on the back of a spoon. It failed to make the charts upon its release but during the intervening years has become a classic British psychedelic album.

East Sussex

Beachy Head

Seabirds and hang-gliders head to the chalky escarpment of Beachy Head to ride the air currents. Other visitors come to walk the mile-long grassy clifftop nature trail, but others, sadly, travel to the windswept headland to end it all.

Bands or artists who've been dropped by their record label may feel inclined to head to England's most infamous suicide spot just southwest of Eastbourne, where a sheer 500-foot drop to a wave-lapped lighthouse awaits below. Industrial music pioneers Throbbing Gristle did just that, but used the location to pose for an album sleeve shoot.

The ironic cover of their 1979 album, *20 Jazz Funk Greats*, shows the band smiling and looking upbeat, standing along cliffs overlooking the beautiful expanse of the ocean below. On the album's rear sleeve the cause of their merriment becomes clear. It shows the same front cover image but in black and white, with a nude corpse lying amongst the flowers, a far bleaker picture and one rather more characteristic of the band. Formed in 1975, Throbbing Gristle were as much about conceptual art as rock 'n' roll and were one of electronic music's most significant bands. There's even an ambient track on the album called *Beachy Head*, which features the sound of seagulls. To some this

Left: Genesis P-Orrigde of Throbbing Gristle.
Above: The Cure at the 1991 Brit Awards, at which they won Best British Band.
Opposite: Cotchford Farm, scene of the death of Brian Jones in July 1969.

album was the peak of Throbbing Gristle's output: a musically experimental industrial album that was also accessible to the casual ear. Some wag once suggested a 20-strong jazz-funk band should cover this album and call it 'Four Industrial Hits'. Recreate this album cover with some friends at your peril.

Crawley's finest, The Cure, went a bit further and off the edge of Beachy Head – at least viewers were made to believe as much – in their ever-popular 1985 video, *Close To Me*. The memorable video features the band crammed inside a wardrobe that tumbles over the edge of the cliff into the sea. In true English fashion the band continues to sing and play their instruments as the wardrobe slowly fills with water.

A few years earlier in 1982, Ultravox were filmed atop Beachy Head dressed as fighter pilots for the video of *Reap the Wild Wind*.

Quadrophenia spoiler alert: the white cliffs, off which Mod anti-hero Jimmy Cooper drives his former hero's snazzy scooter are, of course, Beachy Head as well.

Hartfield

Cotchford Farm, near Hartford, and the neighbouring Ashdown Forest is an area forever linked with childhood due to its association with author AA Milne. It was owned by the writer in the 1920s and was the setting for his famous books, *Winnie-the-Pooh* and *The House at Pooh Corner*. A nearby bridge over a stream was where Pooh and Christopher Robin invented their Poohsticks game. But the 16th-century Sussex farmhouse has a darker alliance with water.

The farm is a mythical site in rock history thanks to Rolling Stone Brian Jones, who mysteriously drowned in his heated swimming pool shortly after he was sacked from the Stones. The local coroner recorded "death by misadventure"; the asthmatic 27-year-old Jones had drowned under an influence of drugs and alcohol.

A few weeks earlier Mick Jagger, Keith Richards and Charlie Watts had driven to Sussex to tell Jones he was out of the band, a decision they had put off for a year. His sacking was caused by his paranoia and erratic attendance at recording sessions, but the Stones agreed to tell the world they had split due to musical differences. Scepticism about Jones' death and conspiracy theories have existed pretty much since his body was hauled from the pool on a warm July night in 1969.

On fan sites, intricate details of Jones' death are pored over obsessively and alternative theories offered. One popular thesis is that Brian Jones was murdered at the request of the Stones. Some sites even offer blue ceramic tiles – at £130 each – from the Cotchford Farm pool that Jones bought just six months before his death.

Rye

Sir Paul McCartney has owned a 933-acre estate at Woodlands Farm in Peasmarsh, near Rye, since the 1970s. It is Macca's home in the south of England, where he stays when he's not in London. A few miles away in Icklesham is The Mill, McCartney's recording studio, a restored windmill on Hogs Hill.

ATP may mean tennis in Eastbourne but in this corner of Sussex it used to stand for All Tomorrow's Parties. The annual festival, named after a Velvet Underground song, took over the abandoned Pontin's on nearby Camber Sands in 1999. The former holiday camp was the original home of the festival, a hedonistic alternative to big country field festivals like Glastonbury and Reading. It has since moved to the Butlins at Minehead in Somerset.

Camber Sands is name-checked by West Sussex's Suede in their song, *Europe Is Our Playground*:

> 'Run with me baby, let's make a stand/
> From peepshow to disco, from Spain to Camber Sands'

It is also mentioned in the first line of Squeeze's *Pulling Mussels (From the Shell)*. Elsewhere, guitar virtuoso Gordon Giltrap recorded a song called *On Camber Sands* on 1998's *Troubadour*, and Fatboy Slim called a 2002 EP *Camber Sands*.

Rye is also the location for Chris Difford's Helioscentric Studios where Keane, Supergrass, Pet Shop Boys and Paul Weller have all recorded. Meanwhile *Too-Rye-Ay*, the second album by Dexys Midnight Runners, was *not* a tribute to the Sussex town.

Hastings

Hastings Pier enjoyed a strong pull as a rock venue for over four decades. From the 1960s to as late as the 1990s, the Pier Ballroom hosted many legendary bands including The Jimi Hendrix Experience, Genesis, The Rolling Stones, The Who, and the Sex Pistols. In 1968, Syd Barrett appeared on stage with Pink Floyd for the last time here.

One of England's most influential folk singers, Shirley Collins, was born in Hastings in 1935. Her collaboration with guitarist Davy Graham on the album *Folk Roots, New Routes* is still seen as one of the seminal moments of the English folk revival.

Singer-songwriter Billy Bragg has heaped praise on Collins, calling her "one of England's greatest cultural treasures."

Although firmly associated with Camden Town and north London, Madness frontman Suggs (Graham McPherson) actually hails from Hastings (born 1961).

Hastings' beach provided the backdrop to David Bowie's *Ashes to Ashes* video. The extras consisted of Steve Strange and New Romantic friends from Covent Garden's Blitz club… except, of course, for the elderly lady who walks the beach with Bowie at the end; she was an old romantic.

Battle

It wasn't just gangs of mods and rockers who met on the English coast to settle their cultural differences. Back in the 11th century rival hordes tooled-up here for an almighty punch-up, albeit with a larger bounty. A few miles inland from Hastings, the small town of Battle is where the Normans saw off King Harold's men in a running battle in 1066, resulting in the decisive Battle of Hastings. More importantly, all three

members of piano-driven pop-rockers Keane grew up in Battle, in the shadow of the castle where King Harold was killed.

Singer Tom Chaplin, piano-playing songwriter Tim Rice-Oxley and drummer Richard Hughes were childhood friends who started making music together as teenagers in a sleepy corner of East Sussex, before forming the band in 1997. Class issues still hold a pervasive influence over the English sense of identity, and this doesn't exclude popular music.

There are few bigger crimes in rock than being middle class, so it's little surprise that some bands choose to conceal their comfortable backgrounds, drop their aitches and assume a faux identity. Keane were up against it from the start. They were loathed and their validity questioned when they were outed as ex-public schoolboys, who had attended the fee-paying Tonbridge School in Kent.

Their lack of rock 'n' roll credentials escalated: their main songwriter had a double-barrelled surname, and they recorded an album without any guitars. Oasis frontman Liam Gallagher dismissed Keane singer Chaplin as a "posh lightweight", and the band were further harmed by claims that a PR company was branding them, although in reality it only created the band's website.

In truth, Keane's guitar-free sound was not planned; their original guitarist departed the band. Some critics scorned them as Coldplay-lite, but the trio had the last laugh, winning through with Rice-Oxley's catchy melodies and Chaplin's powerful voice. Their chart-topping debut album, *Hopes And Fears*, sold five million in 2004 and Rice-Oxley won an Ivor Novello Award. "People look down their noses at us," he told the *Independent*. "I don't think you know any less about humanity and the world because you're from a small town. All the dramas and tragedies and victories of life are more potent because you actually know the people they're happening to."

Their early breakthrough hit, *Somewhere Only We Know*, is based on the fields and woods around Battle where the band played when they were growing up:

> 'I came across a fallen tree/
> I felt the branches of it looking at me/
> Is this the place we used to love?/
> Is this the place that I've been dreaming of?'

The band's name derives from a friend of Chaplin's mother who they knew as children, called Cherry Keane. She encouraged them and listened to their songs when they started out. The band were originally called Cherry Keane in her honour but later shortened it to Keane. As their success continued, singer Chaplin struggled with alcohol and cocaine problems and cancelled a tour to enter the Priory. Now, surely, you don't get more rock 'n' roll than that?

Robertsbridge 〉

The well-preserved picture-postcard Bodiam Castle, near Robertsbridge – complete with portcullis, battlements, rounded corner towers and wide moat – appears on the cover of the American release of Donovan's single, *Wear Your Love Like Heaven*. An infra-red photograph shows Donovan sitting in a boat in the moat in front of the 14th-century fortress. The castle had even more toilets than Michael Winner's Holland Park mansion: 28 in all, which drain directly into the moat. No wonder the castle has never been attacked. Bodiam Castle also appeared in a real slice of 1980s pop: Adam and the Ants' *Ant Rap* video, with the dazzling Mr Ant as a knight in shining armour.

Opposite: Battle-born Keane perform live in 2004.

Crowborough 〉

The grand old Tudor Luxford House was once the home of legendary rock manager Tony Stratton-Smith, boss of the Charisma record label. In the late sixties, Stratton-Smith managed acts like The Nice and The Bonzo Dog Doo-Dah Band. The in-house recording studio hosted artists such as Neil Diamond, Lindisfarne, Leonard Cohen, Bert Jansch, Mike Nesmith and Van Der Graaf Generator, whose 1971 album, *Pawn Hearts*, featured a photo of the house in the centre sleeve.

Luxford is an important landmark in the career of another of Stratton-Smith's bands, Genesis. Although the band had formed in 1967, four years later the original group of Peter Gabriel, Tony Banks and Mike Rutherford were joined by drummer Phil Collins and guitarist Steve Hackett. Genesis moved into Luxford House in 1971 and stayed for most of the summer. They learned to play together here, and to write and rehearse the songs that would end up on their *Nursery Cryme* album. It was the first time that the band had written without founding member Anthony Phillips.

In 1985, Stratton-Smith sold Charisma Records to Virgin Records and moved to the Canary Islands but died a couple of years later.

North Chailey 〉

Chailey Heritage Craft School for disabled children was the former workhouse where the nine-year-old Ian Dury was sent in 1951 after being struck down with polio two years earlier. *Laughter*, Dury's 1980 album with The Blockheads, reflected on his experiences at Chailey. The result doesn't always make easy listening, with harrowing lyrics about institutionalisation and people born with deformities, as in *Hey, Hey, Take Me Away*:

> 'Hey, hey, take me away/
> From the ones that go mad every night/
> They're crazy and dangerous one-legged sods/
> Who have to sit down when they bite/
> One-legged Peter who knows bloody well/
> He's got worse ever since he came in/
> This other poor c***, he was born back-to-front/
> And he's always got stuff on his chin'

Plumpton ⟩

In the early 1970s, when Led Zeppelin guitarist Jimmy Page wasn't furthering his studies into the occult at Aleister Crowley's Boleskine House near Loch Ness, he resided at Plumpton Place in Ditchling Road. Bought in 1972, this 18th-century riverside mansion near Plumpton Racecourse came with a moat and lakes, and Page installed a recording studio. A devilishly red-eyed Page can be seen playing a hurdy-gurdy on the manor grounds at the start of the Led Zeppelin film, *The Song Remains the Same*, when he is informed of the dates of the band's American tour. In September 1977, Page jammed at the Half Moon Pub next door with Ronnie Wood, as well as Arms & Legs – a band led by the then unknown Joe Jackson. Much earlier, Plumpton had been owned by Edward Hudson – owner of *Country Life* magazine and Lindisfarne Castle – and it belonged to Page until 1985. Today it is owned by the American venture capitalist Tom Perkins, who helped finance the set-up of Google, and is a non-executive director of Rupert Murdoch's News Corporation.

Brighton ⟩

The bohemian outpost of Brighton prides itself on being different. Not only did they elect Britain's first-ever Green MP at the 2010 general election, but the south coast resort revels in alternative lifestyles, free spirits and misfits: gay, straight or just warped. Brighton is the last chance saloon for non-conformists and free-thinkers to function and flourish. It's where stressed-out Londoners move to when they hanker for a gentler pace of life.

Brighton emerged as a Victorian health resort in the 18th century, when sea bathing rather than Fatboy Slim beach concerts was all the rage. It received royal approval in the 1770s when Prince Regent (the future King George IV) started visiting with his mistress, thus inspiring thousands of proles and mere mortals to follow suit with their own response: the dirty weekend. Today it is the city's eclectic cultural mix that entices visitors, although not the total exclusion of more amorous-minded trippers.

A statue in the Imperial War Museum appears on the front of The Jam's *Setting Sons* (see London, page 47), but

Brighton's famous shingle beachfront is honoured on the album's back cover, with a cracking photograph of a boxer dog guarding a lone Union Jack deckchair. A British bulldog was the original dog of choice for the photoshoot but was delayed at Barking…

Local Brighton punk-cum-oi! band, Peter and the Test Tube Babies, was pictured on Brighton's nudist beach on the sleeve of 1982's defiantly titled *Pissed and Proud*. The live debut album included two tracks not likely to be covered by Celine Dion: *Up Yer Bum* and *Shit Stirrer*. Are they bottles of merlot or shiraz that two of the band are holding on the cover? Of course not, it's the band's favourite tipple, Merrydown cider.

Bat For Lashes – aka Natasha Khan – adopted Brighton as her hometown after a childhood spent in Pakistan and Hertfordshire with her English mother and Pakistani father, part of the squash-playing Khan dynasty. In 2000, she enrolled for a degree in music and visual arts at the University of Brighton, where she started to write songs, but didn't start Bat for Lashes until 2004. Khan built up a local following and, in 2006, was singed to the small Echo label and then to EMI subsidiary, Parlophone, the following year.

She later moved to the US, to Brooklyn's Puerto Rican quarter, Williamsburg, but soon found the hedonistic party lifestyle isolating and lonely. She became homesick and moved back to Brighton to reconnect with the sea and natural landscape of the south coast.

Inevitably she's been compared to other female pop-eccentrics, like Kate Bush and Björk. She designs her stage

Brighton Music Festivals

THE south coast's city by the sea can lay claim to being one of Britain's festival capitals. Here are some of Brighton's musical offerings:

Beachdown Festival
Four days and nights of music, film and comedy on private farmland near Devil's Dyke in the South Downs, a couple of miles north of Brighton, over the August Bank Holiday weekend. The first year's festival in 2008 attracted 10,000 people but the following year's event had to be cancelled.

Brighton Live
A music festival designed for cash-strapped music lovers, held over five days in October when all the other summer festivals have ended and your Glastonbury clothes have finally dried out. Brighton Live sees new and emerging Brighton bands perform across a variety of venues in the city, all free of charge. There are also free music industry seminars, workshops and master classes providing advice and inspiration.

The Brighton Loop Festival
Starting in 2007, the Loop Festival is an annual festival dedicated to showcasing new talent, from the hottest electronic dance music through to experimental music and relaxing folk. It takes place in selected venues across the city such as the Brighton Dome, the Corn Exchange, Komedia and an open-air stage in Victoria Gardens.

The Great Escape
Europe's leading festival of new music has been dubbed the UK's answer to the South by Southwest festival in Austin, Texas. Held over three nights each May across dozens of venues in the city, it's an annual showcase for rising talent and up-and-coming acts, featuring the best local and international artists.

The Soundwaves Festival
This is Brighton's changing of the avant-garde: an experimental festival featuring cutting-edge new music by bands that also promises participatory audio experiences.

Left: Lovefoxxx of CSS performing on stage at the 2007 Great Escape festival.

costumes and sets herself and, in 2007, transformed the stage of London's Koko venue into an enchanted wood.

Fatboy Slim's links with Brighton started when he attended Brighton Polytechnic to study a BA in English, Politics and Sociology at the age of 18. The former Norman Cook immersed himself in Brighton's thriving 1980s' club and hip hop scene until 1985, when old friend Paul Heaton invited him to move to Hull and join lefty-rockers The Housemartins – their bassist had quit on the eve of their first national tour.

When the band split in 1988, Heaton and drummer Dave Hemingway formed The Beautiful South, and Cook returned to the city he loved to pursue big beat electronic dance music, with Beats International and Freak Power. His first recordings as Fatboy Slim were released in 1996. A song called *You're Not From Brighton* appears on his 1998 album, *You've Come a Long Way, Baby*.

In July 2002, as Fatboy Slim, his free concert on Brighton beach called the Big Beach Boutique, billed as 'Europe's biggest free beach party', brought chaos to the city. Organisers expected a crowd of around 60,000 people, but five times that many partygoers filled the promenade and beach between Brighton's piers. Amid safety concerns and overcrowding local police pulled the plug on the event early.

Another song that immortalises the city by the sea is Queen's *Brighton Rock*, the opener on 1974's *Sheer Heart Attack*, which aptly kicks off with the sound of a fairground whirl. The track, about a doomed beach holiday romance, was originally intended to be a duet. But Queen frontman Freddie Mercury ended up singing both the male and female vocal parts of the two lovers.

Talking of quicksilver, Mercury-nominated quartet British Sea Power are local heroes. Three-quarters of the band originate from Kendal in the Lake District but they moved to Brighton to find a more vibrant music scene and soon garnered a large local following.

They set up their own monthly Club Sea Power night at venues like The Freebutt, featuring support bands, 1930s fashion shows and film-making. The Brighton-based pastoral pop stars are keen birdwatchers and ramblers and pay tribute to the tiny South Downs hamlet of Lullington, near Alfriston, in their 2003 song, *The Smallest Church in Sussex*. The song was an early release after they were spotted by Rough Trade boss Geoff Travis, who signed them to his label:

> 'How the rill may rest there/
> Down through the mist there/
> Toward the Seven Sisters/
> Toward those white cliffs there'

The song explains that the church used to be larger, silencing any local ecclesiastical pedants who say it's not really a church but just a chancel of a dilapidated old building. The band enjoys a reputation for inventive live gigs at unusual venues. They launched their debut album, 2003's *The Decline of British Sea Power*, with a gig at the 500-year-old Ram Inn in the historic village of Firle at the foot of the South Downs, near Lewes. One tour starting in Brighton saw the band sail along the south coast, arriving at venues by boat. Another tour included stops at a seaside cafe in nearby Saltdean and at Britain's highest pub, the Tan Hill Inn, atop North Yorkshire's Pennine Way.

Taking their name from a song on David Bowie's *Hunky Dory* album, indie band The Kooks formed in 2004 while students at the south coast's rock school, Brighton Institute of Modern Music.

Politically charged folk rockers The Levellers formed in Brighton in 1988 and launched their own Metway Studios in an abandoned Brighton warehouse a few years later. They now even have their own annual festival, Beautiful Days (see Devon, page 199).

Brighton also boasts troubadour Ed Harcourt and soul singer Alice Russell, who collaborated with Brighton's Fatboy Slim (and David Byrne) on their 2010 Imelda Marcos concept album, *Here Lies Love*.

Left: British Sea Power performing at the End of the Road Festival in 2006.
Opposite page: Murals of The Who and Abba in Brighton's Music Tunnel.

And, Brighton, of course, was where it all kicked off for ABBA. The Swedish pop royals will always have the seaside resort to thank for launching them to global success when *Waterloo* won the 1974 Eurovision Song Contest held at the Brighton Dome.

ABBA are one of the artists linked with the city's musical history depicted in the Brighton Music Tunnel, a former pedestrian subway that's been transformed into a mural of famous music faces. The 80-foot artwork runs between Brighton's Marine Parade and Sea Life Centre, a building that used to house The Florida Rooms. This top 1960s Brighton venue was one of the country's first R&B clubs. Mods full of pills used to pick up girls and deposit them in the sea here, as you do. Other legendary artists who took to the Florida stage included blues legends John Mayall and Alexis Korner, and bands like The Animals and Manfred Mann.

The Music Tunnel was opened in May 2010 by Roger Daltrey of The Who, who used to play a Wednesday night residency at the club in the mid-1960s. The tunnel joins a Hollywood-style Walk of Fame at Brighton Marina, where 100 specially carved plaques bear the names of stars, including Norman Cook, The Levellers, Dusty Springfield, Annie Nightingale, Leo Sayer, Kevin Rowland, Gaz Coombes and

Love Affair's Steve Ellis, all current or previous Brighton residents. Both exhibits were the idea of Brighton singer-songwriter and record producer David Courtney, who wrote international hits with Adam Faith and Leo Sayer.

Current Brighton music venues include the Concorde 2 club in Madeira Drive, a sizeable live venue that mixes club nights with big-name gigs each month, and the city's top multi-purpose venue, the Brighton Centre.

You don't have to be on a dirty weekend to stay at the Hotel Pelirocco, a rock 'n' roll-themed hotel located on Brighton's seafront in Regency Square. While some rooms are dedicated to sex symbols like Diana Dors and Betty Page, most are inspired by music. There's the Skint room, designed by the pioneering local Big Beat record label; a Rough Trade Rough Nite room dedicated to west London's original indie record shop; Pressure Sounds, a reggae and Jamaican-style dub room, complete with Lee Scratch Perry wallpaper; and Jamie Reid's Magic Room, designed by the renegade artist who created punk's defining image when he stuck a safety pin through the Queen's nose on a Cecil Beaton portrait of the monarch. And, this being Brighton, there's a tribute to mods: a pop-art style Modrophenia room that comes complete with a scooter mirror.

QUADROPHENIA

WE SHALL FIGHT THEM ON THE BEACHES

INSPIRED by The Who's 1973 concept album, Franc Roddam's celebrated 1979 cult coming-of-age film, *Quadrophenia*, recreates the bitter running battles between mods and rockers in 1964 Brighton. A celebration of youth culture, it captures the generation of sharp-dressed, scooter-riding, working-class teenagers who rebelled against post-war austerity Britain.

Phil Daniels is on top form as London mod, Jimmy Cooper, who lives for pill-filled all-nighters with his mates and seeks excitement away from his dead-end job and dull parents. Sting plays his Vespa-riding supermod hero, Ace, and Toyah Wilcox is the modette, Monkey. A young Ray Winstone is Jimmy's old friend Kevin, who worryingly has become a Rocker since they last met.

Director Roddam originally had Sex Pistol John Lydon down for the role of Jimmy, and the mods and rockers who appeared in the riot scenes were real – the producers put an advert in a local newspaper requesting the two youth factions to get involved.

Quadrophenia is a seminal Brighton film, shot on location around the centre of the city: East Street, a narrow road down to the seafront was where the biggest clash between the rival gangs and the police takes place. One of the film's most famous scenes – in which Phil Daniels and Leslie Ash discuss quantum physics – is a narrow passageway that links East Street with Little East Street, now known to most people as 'Quadrophenia Alley'. Rival mod and rocker gangs congregate by the Palace Pier, and opposite the pier entrance is the exterior of the dance hall, now aptly the Sea Life Centre, site of the 1960s mod magnet The Florida Rooms (where The Who played).

The dance hall interior where Jimmy leaps from the balcony was actually shot in north London. The hotel, where Jimmy is disappointed to see Ace working as a bellboy, is the Victorian De Vere Grand, King's Road, the target of an IRA bomb in October 1984 during the Conservative Party Conference.

A selection of other rock films:

Control (2007)
Sam Riley was stunning as the tortured Joy Division singer Ian Curtis. He was no stranger to Curtis, having played The Fall's Mark E Smith in *24 Hour Party People* (2002) about the late Tony Wilson and the rise and fall of Factory Records.

Expresso Bongo (1959)
A training video for cut-throat pop managers everywhere? Johnny Jackson (Laurence Harvey) transforms a young funfair employee Bert Rudge (Cliff Richard) into the wonderfully named teenage heartthrob Bongo Herbert. A gritty scrutiny of the Soho rock 'n' roll scene in the 1950s, in which the legendary 2i's coffee bar makes an appearance.

Pink Floyd The Wall (1982)
A pre-knighthood Bob Geldof in his first starring role in Alan Parker's adaptation of Roger Waters' life story, with Waters supplying the screenplay. Geldof reputedly couldn't bear Pink Floyd's music.

Stardust (1974)
Dubbed the Sunset Boulevard of rock films, this sequel to *That'll Be the Day* catches up with 1960's pop star Jim MacLaine (David Essex) and his spiral into sex and drugs.

Tommy (1975)
Pete Townshend's 1969 rock opera about the loss of post-World War II innocence is tackled by Ken Russell. Memorable scenes include Elton John as the Pinball Wizard and Ann-Margret rolling around in baked beans, an image that helped a whole generation of males get through their adolescence. Also starring The Who, Eric Clapton and Tina Turner.

West Sussex

East Grinstead ⟩

Singer-songwriter and local boy Robyn Hitchcock (born in East Grinstead in 1952) name-drops his home-town in a song he recorded with his band The Egyptians, *Listening To The Higsons*:

'The Higsons come from Norwich/
And they eat a lot of porridge/
But I prefer East Grinstead/
I'm running out of living'

Sheffield Park station near Fletching was the location for the sepia-tinted sleeve of Elton John's country music-themed *Tumbleweed Connection* album, released in 1970. The station is part of the Bluebell Railway heritage line, with steam trains panting the five-mile route between Sheffield Park and Horsted Keynes.

Several pop videos have utilised the period railway station, including our old favourites Robson & Jerome, Tracey Ullman, the Pet Shop Boys and Sheena Easton's *9 to 5 (Morning Train)*. Shot here in 1980, it's a pre-feminist tale of a woman waiting all day for her man to return home from work. In his absence, dressed in a 1980s semi-*Star Trek* outfit, she flirts with a steam locomotive, rolling stock and the Sheffield Park signal box.

The late 18th-century country house, Hammerwood Park, near East Grinstead was owned by Led Zeppelin in the 1970s. It was the first building designed by Benjamin Latrobe, the architect who would later create the White House and the US Capitol in Washington DC.

Led Zeppelin had plans to use the place as a recording studio and as somewhere the band and their families could live, but these never materialised due to touring commitments and burgeoning dry-rot problems at the house. However, Hammerwood does appear at the beginning of the band's concert movie, The Song Remains

the Same, in the early gangster-style shoot-out scene. You can see the original columns at the doorway.

Led Zeppelin's formidable manager, Peter Grant – a former bouncer, wrestler and sometime actor – and road manager, Richard Cole, played the sharp-dressed hit-men driving the vintage luxury car (Grant was the cigar-smoking Demis Roussos look-a-like). The band's old friend, Roy Harper, also makes a brief appearance as one of the greedy businessmen.

Guided tours of the country house are available, and you can also stay in a Victorian bedroom with a four-poster bed. The house with a moat in the film's opening scene was Peter Grant's 15th-century home, Horselunges Manor in Hellingly, near Hailsham, north of Eastbourne. After his death from a heart attack, Grant was buried at Hellingly Cemetery. His funeral was held on 4 December, 1995; quite by chance this was exactly 15 years to the day since Led Zeppelin had announced to the world they would not continue the band without drummer John Bonham.

Created by Eric Idle and Neil Innes, *All You Need is Cash* was the 1978 spoof rockumentary that charted the rise to fame of Dirk, Nasty, Stig and Barry – aka The Rutles – from their start in Liverpool and early days in Hamburg's Rat Keller club to worldwide success. A parody of Beatlemania and documentaries made about the group, the film also sends up the meeting between the Fab Four and the leader of the Spiritual Regeneration Movement, Maharishi Mahesh Yogi, who is portrayed in the film as Arthur Sultan, the Surrey Mystic. During the 1967 Summer of Love, The Prefab Four travel to the Sultan's Bognor retreat where he fails to pick up Stig's wife.

Many hardcore Genesis fans consider 1971's *Nursery Cryme* to be the band's first great album. The subject of the short song with an unexpectedly dark ending, *Harold the Barrel*, is the owner of a Bognor Regis restaurant who serves his diners his amputated toes, before killing himself.

Genesis, the biblical story rather than the band, is parodied in Frank Zappa's song *Once Upon a Time* and Bognor also clocks a mention:

> 'And sure enough/
> Boards of oak appeared throughout the emptiness as far as vision permits/
> Stretching all the way from Belfast to Bognor Regis'

Bognor Regis was the name of an instrumental jam by Zappa.

Chichester

Antony Hegarty of Antony and the Johnsons was born in the cathedral city in 1971. He spent a "nondescript childhood" in West Sussex before moving with his engineer father and photographer mother to Amsterdam and California. He finally moved to New York at the age of 19. His second album, *I Am A Bird Now*, won the Mercury Prize in 2005.

The long-serving manager of Pink Floyd, Steve O'Rourke, dealt with the band's duelling egos after Syd Barrett's departure in the late 1960s, until his death from a stroke at the end of October 2003. At his funeral service at Chichester

Right: Antony Hegarty of Antony and the Johnsons.
Opposite page: Classic Led Zeppelin.

Unlikely heroes of English rock

Sir John Mortimer
Freedom of speech champion, closet Sex Pistols fan, or both? The late writer and QC Sir John Mortimer was renowned as a champion of liberalism and free speech. He successfully defended publishers John Calder and Marion Boyars in their 1968 appeal against their conviction for publishing Hubert Selby, Jr's *Last Exit to Brooklyn*. He also helped the Sex Pistols retain the name of their album, *Never Mind the Bollocks*. Mortimer successfully defended Virgin Records in the 1977 obscenity trial over the use of the word 'bollocks' in the album title, meaning the manager of the Nottingham branch of Virgin Records was also found not guilty for displaying the record in his shop window.

Lord William Rees-Mogg
In response to sentences passed out to Mick Jagger and Keith Richards for drug offences, an improbable source of support came from the then editor of *The Times* and Conservative Party candidate William Rees-Mogg. He penned a now legendary editorial with a title that quoted Alexander Pope: "Who breaks a butterfly on a wheel?" Rees-Mogg argued Jagger's sentence was a miscarriage of justice and that the Stones were being persecuted for their fame rather than their crime. His views were soon being repeated throughout the media, and questions on the subject were raised in Parliament. Within weeks, Richards' conviction had been quashed and Jagger's punishment reduced to a conditional discharge.

Cathedral a fortnight later, his coffin was given a send off by David Gilmour, Nick Mason and Rick Wright, who played *The Great Gig in the Sky*. It was the first time the band had performed together in public since October 1994.

The photograph on the cover of the band's 2001 compilation *Echoes: The Best Of Pink Floyd* was taken at Manor Farm, near Singleton. Designed by Floyd's long-time sleeve designer Storm Thorgerson, the artwork was an amalgam of numerous images from previous Floyd album covers.

West Wittering

Since 1966, Rolling Stones guitarist Keith Richards has owned a thatched and moated Tudor manor house called Redlands on the West Sussex coast, a few miles south of Chichester. For devotees of sixties rock 'n' roll mythology, it's a holy grail, the site of the most famous police drugs bust in musical history.

At Redlands one evening in February 1967, Richards and some friends, including Mick Jagger and Marianne Faithfull, were tripping on acid when the police came-a-knockin'. Police found nothing on either Jagger or Richards, but four amphetamine tablets, belonging to Faithfull, were discovered inside Jagger's coat. It was then, so the story goes, that police found Faithfull in a compromising position with a Mars bar, and a long-running myth started (see box on page 164). 'Mick 'n' Keef' were arrested on drugs charges: Jagger with illegal possession of amphetamines, Richards with allowing his property to be used for illegal drug consumption. To the establishment it was a landmark case, time for the judges to punish these oversexed, drug-addled upstarts for good. However, by the time of the trial several months later, the tide of public opinion had shifted in favour of the Stones, and even that most conservative of newspapers, *The Times*, was on their side (see box on previous page).

Richards has been on trial on drug-related charges five times but only the Redlands bust resulted in a prison term. He received a 12-month sentence in Wormwood Scrubs, while Jagger was sentenced to three months in Brixton Prison, but both were bailed the next day pending appeal.

Although Richards spends most of his time in the US nowadays, he still sees himself as a local and regards his West Wittering pad as home. After The Rolling Stones' huge

Bridges to Babylon tour finished in 1998, Richards returned to Redlands for rest and recovery. He even calls his West Wittering home "God's little acre." "I love that village," he once told the *Independent*. "They've always been smooth with me." Richards has joined villagers in a fight to preserve a local wood from development. And as for the day Richards donated £30,000 to renovate and repaint his local village hall, well, that's become local folklore too.

In 1967, Pink Floyd travelled to West Sussex to record a short black-and-white music video for their debut single about a man "with a strange hobby", *Arnold Layne*. Syd Barrett's lyrics about the arrest and jailing of a ladies' underwear fetishist was hardly usual subject matter for a first single. The video featured the band dressing up a mannequin before playing with it on the sandy Wittering Beach.

Where would English rock music be without its musical wellspring of new towns, places like Crawley and Haywards Heath, in the heart of the suburban drag that lies between London and the south coast? The seeds of those mascara-ed chroniclers of adolescent alienation, The Cure, were planted in Crawley, when Robert Smith and Lol Tolhurst attended primary school together. Smith's family lived next door to Tolhurst's grandmother. Later, they met guitarist Michael Dempsey at the Notre Dame Middle School where, at lunchtimes, they were exiled in the music room playing their electric guitars. They really started to hit it off when they realised they were the only pupils into Jimi Hendrix at their comprehensive, St Wilfrid's Catholic School. (More recently St Wilfrid's has spawned three of the band The Feeling: guitarist Kevin Jeremiah, keyboardist Ciaran Jeremiah and drummer Paul Stewart.)

Whilst there in the mid-1970s, Smith, Tolhurst and Dempsey formed a band called The Obelisk; changed the name to Malice as punk took off, then Easy Cure and finally The Cure. They rehearsed and drank at Smith's parents house – Smith's dad had had an extension built to cater for the increase in noise.

The band's breakthrough came when they were invited to play at The Rocket, the epicentre of Crawley's youth culture. Later, they applied the brakes to their early spiky post-punk sound in favour of gloomier tone, and released 1982's *Pornography*, a seminal goth album. The Cure have been through numerous line-up changes yet Robert Smith remains a constant.

Located near London's Gatwick Airport, Crawley is also home to the head offices of Virgin Atlantic Airways, half-owned by Sir Richard Branson's Virgin Group. Composer Mike Oldfield has been honoured with first-class Virgin flights for life, thanks to his *Tubular Bells* album, which helped establish the Virgin Records label. At the time of writing, the airline still has a Boeing 747 in service called Tubular Belle.

Isabella Rossellini look-a-like Brett Anderson, best-known as the lead vocalist of Britpop band Suede, was born in 1967 to an artist mother and classical music-obsessed father. He grew up poor in a small council estate in Lindfield, near Haywards Heath, where, if the family wanted something, they had to make it for themselves.

Anderson experienced all the frustrations of a young person living in a suburban town. He used to look up the train tracks to London and dream of escaping to the big city. His father force-fed him classical music but, when Anderson couldn't access music he was interested in, he decided to make it himself. He formed Suede in 1989 with guitarist Bernard Butler, his girlfriend of the time Justine Frischmann and bassist Mat Osman.

Like Blur, Suede's songs were an English reaction to American grunge music. Their debut album *Suede* won the Mercury Prize and was the fastest-selling UK first release since Frankie Goes to Hollywood's *Welcome To the Pleasure Dome*.

Anderson went from the dole queue to UK number one with Suede in 1993, although his songwriting partner Butler left the band the following year during the recording of their second album, *Dog Man Star*. Anderson's addiction to crack and heroin put the band on hold in the late 1990s. Anderson and Butler reunited briefly in 2004, re-emerging with a project named The Tears and a debut album, *Here Come The Tears*. Anderson has also made three solo albums.

Above: Suede circa 1993. Brett Anderson grew up in Haywards Heath.
Opposite page: Mick Jagger and Keith Richards at Redlands after being sentenced for drug violations in 1967.

Surrey

Ripley

Paul Weller's working space is a rural converted barn, Black Barn studios, in Ripley, a few miles outside his home-town of Woking. Weller's *22 Dreams*, a 2008 concept album that reflects the changing of the seasons, was recorded here over a period of a year with Steve Cradock, Weller's regular guitarist on his solo albums. Clocking in at 70 minutes, Weller said the album was designed to be listened to in one sitting, like *Sgt. Pepper's Lonely Hearts Club Band* and *Pet Sounds*. Some tracks featured Robert Wyatt on trumpet and Noel Gallagher on bass and piano. For the album artwork hundreds of photographs were taken around Black Barn studios over a period of a year and amassed together.

More conclusive proof that some good comes from suburban Surrey is Ripley's most famous son, Eric Clapton – or just 'God' to his legions of fans – who was born in the village in March 1945. His birthplace and childhood home was his grandparent's house at 1, The Green. After hearing the electric blues of Muddy Waters, BB King, Buddy Guy, Freddie King and others in the early 1960s, his grandparents helped him buy a Gibson ES-335 clone guitar and Clapton started to explore American blues music. In the summertime he used to sit on Ripley's village green and play Big Bill Broonzy tunes and learn the riffs.

Years later, soon after the short-lived supergroup Cream's farewell performances at the Royal Albert Hall in 1968, Clapton moved a few miles south to be near the Surrey village where he had spent his childhood. He bought Hurtwood Edge, an Italian villa near Ewhurst, surrounded by woodland, for £30,000. He moved here to get away from London and, moreover, to escape from the clutches of notorious Detective Sergeant Norman Pilcher of the Drug Squad, whose professional hobby was busting famous rock stars. Pilcher led raids on The Beatles and The Rolling Stones but was later convicted of conspiracy to pervert the course of justice and jailed for corruption. Cream drummer Ginger Baker tipped off Clapton that he was a target but that the copper would turn a blind eye if Clapton left town.

In the early 1970s, Clapton sunk into several years of heroin addiction and self-imposed seclusion, rarely emerging from his Surrey estate. His telephone went unanswered and Clapton avoided even his oldest friends. Some would come to visit him periodically but soon leave when there was no reply. Once, Ginger Baker turned up, planning to drive Clapton to the Sahara Desert in a Land Rover. Baker's logic was that it would be one place where Clapton would not be able to score any heroin.

Woking

Woking has been responsible for musical heroes other than Paul Weller and The Jam (see box on next page). Status Quo's Rick Parfitt was born in the town in 1948 and is nostalgic about the place he grew up. When he returns to his home-town, he sits outside the house where he lived until the age of nine. "I sit there and reminisce. I look at the paving stones; I remember doing hopscotch. I look at a spot where my Dad's first car was parked," Parfitt told *The Times*. As well as a reputation for only playing three chords, Status Quo are known as Britain's hardest-working rock band and have sold 118 million albums.

Woking was a focal point in the tragic story of Badfinger. Touted as replacements for The Beatles when they first appeared in the late 1960s, their connections with the Fab Four didn't end there. They recorded most of their albums for The Beatles' label, Apple, and they got their name from The Beatles' original road manager and 'fifth Beatle' Neil Aspinall, who suggested Badfinger, from *Bad Finger Boogie*, the original title for *With a Little Help From My Friends*. They also recorded Paul McCartney's *Come And Get It* and later played on John Lennon's *Imagine* as well as George Harrison's *All Things Must Pass*.

The band's Pete Ham and Tom Evans wrote one of the most successful singles of all time: the power ballad *Without You*. Harry Nilsson added a lavish string arrangement and topped the charts with it in 1972, as did Mariah Carey a couple of decades later. But by 1975 Badfinger were broke.

The band's American manager, Stan Polley, had gained complete control of Badfinger's finances, all income went via his accounts and the band had to settle for modest salaries. Later, racked by personal and money problems and just a month before the birth of his first child, Badfinger's guitarist and songwriter Pete Ham hanged himself in his Woking garage, aged just 27. A suicide note blamed Stan Polley for his death. In a tragic mirror of Ham's death, his Badfinger bandmate Tom Evans also took his own life at the end of 1983, hanging himself from a willow tree in his back garden. He was besieged by money problems and depression over Ham's death.

Woking can also claim some responsibility – or, if you're an unabashed music snob, blame – for the Spice Girls, who kicked off their careers at a Knaphill-based studio in 1994 after being picked from hundreds of hopeful competitors in an audition.

Epsom

In ruptured, post-war England, many towns in Surrey seemed idyllic: a safe and secure environment for parents to raise their children into respectable solicitors, bankers or end-of-Empire administrators. They were never supposed to become guitar gods and rock 'n' roll icons. Not accounting for the fact that children become rebellious teenagers, the Surrey towns of Wallington, Ripley and Epsom spawned England's great triumvirate of guitarists: Jeff Beck, Eric Clapton and Jimmy Page.

Led Zeppelin guitarist Page spent many of his formative years in Epsom, his family having moved to Miles Road when he was eight. In an almost occultist happening, it was in this house that Page discovered his first guitar. Page commented later that the guitar was just there and he didn't know if it had been left behind by the previous family, or by a friend.

Maybe the dance-rock five-piece EMF, best-known for their international smash *Unbelievable*, thought so too. Despite hailing from the Gloucestershire town of Cinderford over 100 miles to the west, their name was nothing to do with the physics term, electromotive force, but an acronym of Epsom Mad Funkers.

The Clash frontman Joe Strummer spent several years of his childhood in Upper Warlingham, near Epsom. When his roving

WOKING CLASS HERO
PAUL WELLER & THE JAM

The Modfather, His Royal Modness, The Changing Man… call Paul Weller what you like, he remains one of the most respected and inventive songwriters in English pop music. Before his resurgent solo career, he emerged out of punk with The Jam, among the most successful British bands of the late 1970s and early 1980s.

Aged 14, Paul Weller got together with some friends from Sheerwater Secondary School (now the Bishop David Brown School) to form a band that became The Jam. Inspired by The Who, The Kinks and the Small Faces, they would squeeze into Weller's bedroom at his parents' house to practise. They played their first-ever gig just around the corner from Stanley Road at the Working Man's Club in Walton Road. When they started out Weller's father booked the band gigs in pubs and clubs in the Woking area, where they played Chuck Berry, The Beatles and early Motown covers.

By the time Weller left school at 16, Bruce Foxton had auditioned to join him, drummer Rick Buckler and rhythm guitarist Steve Brookes and they continued as a four-piece.

1972

1958

1976

Born in the Surrey town of Woking in May 1958, Weller grew up in a modest Victorian terraced council house at 8 Stanley Road, with no heating or hot water and an outside toilet. His late father, John, would later become his manager for almost 30 years until ill-health forced him to retire in 2006. His mother, Ann, was a cleaner at Woking's 19th-century mosque, one of the first to be built in Britain. His parents bought Weller his first electric guitar when he was 12 years old and encouraged their son's obsession with pop music. Later, as manager, John Weller followed his son on the road, and Ann Weller ran The Jam fan club, ensuring fans received T-shirts, photographs and other band memorabilia.

The breakthrough for The Jam came when Weller attended a gig by the Sex Pistols in 1976. Inspired by their lyrics and attitude and those of punk's other leading lights, The Clash, Weller started to write about contemporary issues and themes that affected him. His sentiments expressed in his lyrics about disaffected youth were recognised by youngsters trapped in suburbs up and down the land.

Although The Jam were inspired by punk and emerged from the same era, they were never punks, distancing themselves from the genre with their smart mod revivalist attire, and the fact they'd been gigging for several years and hadn't formed the band in a flash. Nor did they share the Year Zero-like punk ethos that rejected all pop music that had gone before them. But what they shared with punk was the desire to break down the barriers between performers and audience, inviting fans to watch their soundchecks and join the band backstage after shows.

Weller was 18 years old when The Jam released their first single, *In the City*, in 1977. With their sharp, perceptive lyrics, many of the hits that Weller wrote for The Jam captured the zeitgeist and made him a spokesperson for a generation. When Weller baited the privileged in *The Eton Rifles* (see page 152) the song confirmed The Jam as one of the UK's biggest and most influential bands. Weller's portrait of Britain on 1982's *Town Called Malice* caught the social turbulence of Thatcherism's early days: the disturbing effect of

unemployment and of the break-up of suburban working class communities. It was written about Weller's home-town of Woking but could have been about any suburban English town. (For more songs influenced by Thatcherism see The Margaret Thatcher Songbook, page 242.)

For most of the 1980s, Weller courted the Labour Party, endorsing Red Wedge, a collection of left-leaning rock musicians who toured the UK by bus touting their support for Labour. In 1984, his then band, The Style Council, released the record *Soul Deep*, which helped raise money for striking coal miners. But by the time Tony Blair was elected Prime Minister in 1997, Weller was disillusioned with politics and he refused to let Labour use his song *The Changingman* in the run-up to the election. And his snubbing of Blair didn't end there. He tried to discourage his good friend

Noel Gallagher from accepting Tony Blair's invitation to Downing Street and later turned down the offer of a CBE in 2006 because he didn't want his photograph taken with Blair, who he dubbed "a war criminal".

For all Weller's suburban disquiet and disaffection, his acute eye for the details of everyday British life and his romantic vision of England has bracketed him alongside the likes of Ray Davies of The Kinks. The Jam song, *Tales From the Riverbank*, celebrated water meadows, pastoral fields and golden countryside near Woking, where he used to play as a child:

'Paradise found down by the still waters /
Joined in the race to the rainbow's end/
No fears no worries just a golden country/
Woke at sunrise, went home at sunset'

1977

1982

A change of musical direction (and hairstyle) came in 1982 when Weller famously split up The Jam at the height of their success to form soul-jazz pop collective, The Style Council, with keyboardist Mick Talbot. But his new sound (not to mention a new look of brightly-coloured sweaters tied around the neck) alienated many Jam fans.

They released albums throughout the 1980s until they disbanded at the end of the decade when their label Polydor refused to release their fifth album. With no recording deal Weller's career appeared to be over, until he embarked on a remarkable solo career in the 1990s.

1995

Early in the decade Weller went back on the road and returned to a rougher guitar-led sound on his second solo album, 1993's *Wild Wood*, which received critical acclaim and returned Weller to the top of the charts. Inspired by the North Downs countryside, the title was taken from the name of a local country house.

Then came his 1995s home-coming album, *Stanley Road*, in which Weller revisited his Woking roots. The album had a working title of *Shit Or Bust* but was renamed in honour of the road where Weller grew up. His former house has since been demolished and the road is now lined with a large office block on one side and a block of flats opposite.

This album went to number one and became one of the best-selling albums of his career. Suddenly Weller was fêted again as one of Britain's finest songwriters and cited by the Britpop bands, Oasis and Blur, as a seminal influence. He was also given a Lifetime Achievement Award at the 2006 Brit Awards.

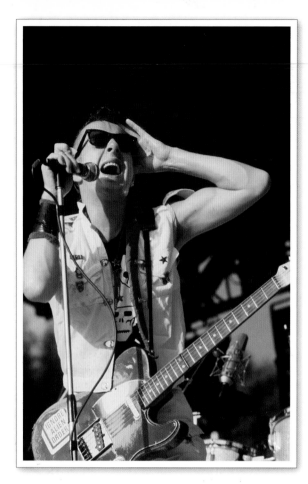

The Stranglers were punk outsiders, the odd-men-out of the genre. Rock critics loathed them and not just because keyboards, saxophones and moustaches were far from *de rigueur*. Formed in September 1974 in Guildford, once a resting place for medieval pilgrims travelling to and from Canterbury, the band were originally known as the The Guildford Stranglers, even though none of the band came from Guildford. But Surrey's county town became their early base. Only bassist, Jean Jaques Burnel, grew up locally. He and his French parents moved to nearby Godalming in his early teens and he attended Guildford's Royal Grammar School.

The band was formed when frontman Hugh Cornwell advertised for a drummer for his band Johnny Sox in *Melody Maker* and Jet Black (born Brian Duffy in Ilford) turned up. When Black mentioned he had accommodation above his Guildford off-licence *The Jackpot*, Cornwell left his squat opposite the Roundhouse in Camden Town. A successful local businessman, Black also owned a fleet of ice-cream vans, which they soon employed to tour pubs and working men's clubs in their early days.

In 1978, when The Stranglers played at Guildford's University of Surrey on BBC 2's *Rock Goes to College*, Messrs Cornwell, Burnel, Black and Dave Greenfield quit the stage after only a few numbers because non-university students had not been allowed in. The band called the audience "a bunch of elitist c***s."

The University of Surrey was also the venue for the first performance by Led Zeppelin under their new name, in 1968. In 2008 Led Zeppelin guitarist Jimmy Page was given an honorary doctorate by the university for services to the music industry.

And lest we forget, one-hit wonders The Vapors, formed in Guildford in 1979 and reached number

diplomat father, Ron, was assigned a long spell in Whitehall in 1959 he moved the family to a small 1930s hillside bungalow perched Swiss chalet-style at 15 Court Farm Road, Upper Warlingham. Strummer later dismissed the home as a "bungalow in south Croydon". Strummer's father decorated the new house with artefacts gathered from his foreign, postings like a Persian leather ottoman footstool and bongo drums, as well more usual domestic items like a radio similar to the one depicted later on the *London Calling* single sleeve. Strummer – known then by his real name, John Mellor – was sent to the local state Whyteleafe Primary School nearby and then, aged 10, to a public school a few miles to the southwest, the City of London Freemen's School in Ashtead.

The recurring childhood dream portrayed in *Pink Floyd The Wall* – where Pink runs endlessly across a rugby field – was filmed on Epsom Downs.

Left: Joe Strummer of The Clash.
Right: The Stranglers.
Opposite page: Peter Gabriel at his outrageous best dressed in his famous flower costume while performing live with Genesis, 1973.

three in the UK singles chart the following year with *Turning Japanese*. They were discovered by The Jam's Bruce Foxton and supported the mod gods on a nationwide tour.

Singer-songwriter Robyn Hitchcock sung about Guildford and Jenner Road in particular on *No, I Don't Remember Guildford* on his 1999 album, *Jewels For Sophia*:

> 'But no, I don't remember Jenner Road /
> Even though we lived there/
> And things came through the letterbox thick and fast'

Guilfest each July at Stoke Park, Guildford, is an annual three-day festival renowned for its huge variety of live acts that straddle rock, pop, blues and folk. Not all music festivals are suitable for children or older folk but Guilfest sees itself as a family festival, jam-packed with fun for the little darlings alongside the music: stuff like stilt-walking, face-painting and balloon-modelling.

There's a good chance that the cheery young folk you see walking around Guildford carrying guitars and instrument cases are students at the town's Academy of Contemporary Music (ACM), located on Bridge Street, near Guildford station. Founded in 1997, the academy focuses on rock and pop music and attempts to secure its students careers in the music industry. The place helps you progress as a musician and gives you the tools, confidence and inspiration to take your musical talent to a professional level," says professional percussionist and ACM graduate, Nick Roberts, now drummer in a band called Felix Fables, who formed at the academy.

Graduates include crimson-dreadlocked singer-songwriter Newton Faulkner, Amelle Berrabah of Sugababes fame and session drummer Toby Couling who has toured with Mercury Award-winner Speech Debelle. From 2009 the academy has also offered a course on how to be a roadie.

Several years before she became the face of L'Oreal, an *X-Factor* judge and the nation's latest Princess Diana surrogate, Girls Aloud's Cheryl Cole was involved in a nasty incident in a Guildford nightclub. In January 2003, shortly after the band's debut single, *Sound of the Underground*, hit number one she was charged with racially aggravated assault of lavatory attendant Sophie Amogbokpa. The artist formerly known as Cheryl Tweedy was found guilty of actual bodily harm but acquitted of the racial charge. She didn't deny calling Amogbokpa "a f***ing bitch," or of hitting her, which she claimed was self-defence. The judge criticised Cole for expressing no remorse and ordered her to pay her victim £500 compensation and carry out 120

hours of community service. Cole spent this time picking up litter around Newcastle and sandpapering benches at the amateur football club Newcastle Blue Star. At the time of the assault the nightclub was imaginatively called The Drink, but now trades as The Casino.

Godalming ⟩

At various points in the 1970s, Genesis former frontman Peter Gabriel took to the stage wearing elaborate costumes featuring bat wings, daffodils sprouting from his head and a monstrous walking deformity called the Slipperman, with an inflatable phallus. He also shaved a large chunk of hair from the front of his head, and wore his wife's red Ossie Clark dress and a fox head. Their 1974 rock opera *The Lamb Lies Down on Broadway* was the improbable tale of teenage Puerto Rican graffiti artist Rael from New York who encounters underground goblins on a spiritual quest. Punk arrived to dethrone Genesis and the overblown theatrics of bands like them, but England's most famous public schoolboy rockers outlasted all their detractors to become rock legends. And not one of them succumbed to the excesses that saw many of their peers fall by the wayside.

It all started at the 400-year-old Charterhouse, the famous boarding school near Godalming, where keyboardist Tony Banks, guitarist Mike Rutherford and singer Peter Gabriel were all privately educated in the 1960s. Fellow founder member Anthony Phillips quit the group early on because of stage fright. Their breakthrough came when the band sent a demo tape to another Charterhouse graduate, Jonathan King.

The now-disgraced pop

impresario christened them Genesis and secured a deal with Decca Records. Later, Genesis would be joined by a young drummer named Phil Collins. The former child actor had once played the Artful Dodger in a stage production of *Oliver!* and was an extra in both The Beatles' film *A Hard Day's Night* and *Chitty Chitty Bang Bang*. When Gabriel left, they auditioned for another singer but finally promoted from within, choosing Collins to front the band. The band's flamboyant songs about mythical beasts and giant hogweeds were replaced by shorter, more commercial fare. These new, radio-friendly numbers divided earlier Genesis fans and some decided the band's new direction was not for them.

Other former musical Carthusians are a mixed bag: Led Zeppelin manager Peter Grant, Karl Wallinger of World Party fame and composer Ralph Vaughan Williams, who, like Genesis, created characteristically English music.

Every Genesis album since 1981's *Abacab* has been recorded at the band's studio, The Farm, in the small nearby village of Chiddingfold. The Stranglers' founder and drummer Jet Black rented a house here to get the band into shape before embarking on their punk career.

The video for *Over My Shoulder*, a number 12 in 1995 for Mike Rutherford's off-shoot venture, Mike & the Mechanics, was filmed on Chiddingfold's village green. It was written by Rutherford and singer-songwriter and keyboardist Paul Carrack two decades on from his classic Ace song, *How Long?*

Dorking ❯

Bow Wow Wow were Malcolm McLaren's early-1980s, post-Sex Pistols project, featuring 14-year-old singer Annabella Lwin and ex-Adam And The Ants members Matthew Ashman, Dave Barbarossa and Leigh Gorman. The late punk svengali chose a recreation of Édouard Manet's 1863 painting *Le Déjeuner sur l'Herbe* (The Lunch on the Grass) for the cover of the 1981 album, *See Jungle! See Jungle! Go Join Your Gang Yeah! City All Over! Go Ape Crazy*. The title was taken from a lyric McLaren wrote about spending a night in the woods as a child.

The cover shoot did not take place in France but near Dorking. Photographer Andy Earl drove up and down river banks searching for a place that looked similar to the painting and that didn't have a housing estate in shot. He

found it by a pond in the shadow of Box Hill, a popular viewpoint since Charles II's reign and named after the box trees that grew there.

Lwin didn't know about the cover until she turned up and a mischievous McLaren convinced her it was imperative she take her clothes off for the shoot. When Lwin's mother found out, she reported McLaren to the police, who nabbed most of the negatives. Plans for the sleeve were dropped, Lwin was hauled off to an aunt's house on Dartmoor and told she'd never see her bandmates or manager again. When the furore died down, Lwin rejoined the band, and her mother later changed her mind about the image, which was finally used on the cover of a 1982 EP.

Weybridge & Walton-on-Thames ❯

John Lennon and Ringo Starr were near neighbours on Weybridge's exclusive St George's Hill estate in the mid-1960s. Lennon lived in 27-room, mock-Tudor Kenwood from 1964 until 1968, when he sold it following his divorce from Cynthia.

Do you want to come in for a coffee, or perhaps we could make an album? One night in 1968, when Cynthia was away, Lennon invited Yoko Ono back to Kenwood for an all-night session of musical experimentation in an upstairs home studio. The recordings ended up as their *Two Virgins* album. After making the recording, the two got it together.

Above: Anabella Lwin was a controversial member of 1980s outfit Bow Wow Wow who themselves were discovered by Malcolm McLaren.

In 1965, Starr followed in Lennon's mock Tudor footsteps and bought Sunny Heights, less than a kilometre away from Kenwood. Lennon later moved in here with Ono after his divorce, until his move to Tittenhurst Park the following year.

According to author Mark Lewisohn, possibly the world's leading authority on The Beatles, the *Rubber Soul* album cover wasn't shot in Lennon's garden at Kenwood, but near Cobham in autumn 1965. Photographer Robert Freeman took the sleeve photo of the band in front of some rhododendron bushes in the woods near Lake Bolder Mere and the disused Wisley Airfield.

Both singer-songwriter and producer Nick Lowe and actress and singer Dame Julie Andrews were born in Walton-on-Thames.

Walton-on-Thames is also associated with several disgraced pop personalities. The town was the venue of the notorious Walton Hop, a teenage disco run by Deniz Corday, friend of the 'king of hits' Jonathan King. The former pop impresario was a regular at the club, as were the late Bay City Rollers manager Tam Paton and former Radio 1 DJ Chris Denning. All have been convicted of child sex offences as a result of Surrey Police's Operation Arundel, which targeted sex offenders at the club. In November 2001, Jonathan King was charged with three child sex offences, dating back over three decades. Following publicity surrounding his arrest, a dozen other victims told police that King had abused them during the 1970s and 1980s. Some claimed King had picked them up at the Walton Hop, which closed in 1990.

Bagshot

By 1979, much of suburban Surrey was pogo-ing to the sounds of punk. The Members hailed from Bagshot, and their top 20 hit, *The Sound of the Suburbs*, was a clear mission statement and anthem of suburban alienation.

Hersham

More suburban punks came courtesy of the working class community of Hersham. Sham 69 took their name from some graffiti the band's founding frontman Jimmy Pursey spotted on a wall. 'Walton and Hersham '69' celebrated a local football team's victorious 1969 season, but half of it had disappeared so it read, 'sham '69'. While some punks concealed their comfortable middle class origins, Sham 69 were proud, proletarian Cockney Cowboys who wore their working class roots as a badge of honour. Their third album, 1979's *The Adventures of the Hersham Boys*, name-checked their home-town, as did the rousing, anthemic song, *Hersham Boys*. The sing-a-long track was a near music hall foot-stomper that celebrated working class communities surrounded by wealthier suburbs, and a more essentially English song it would be hard to find:

> 'It's down to the hop for the local girls/
> They're not beauty queens but they're our pearls/
> But when you go to bed tonight?
> Don't worry about us, we're alright!'

A hilarious earlier line sees Pursey imitate his haughty, patronising neighbours: 'Stop being naughty take our advice'. Sham 69 were never as trendy as The Clash or the Sex Pistols. Despite the fact that their first single, *I Don't Wanna*, was produced by The

Above: The Beatles' classic Rubber Soul album sleeve.
Right: Sham 69 at the London's punk club The Roxy in 1977.

Velvet Underground's John Cale, fashionable, art-school punks still ignored them. However, they attracted a loyal following and performed regularly at the infamous yet short-lived London punk club, The Roxy.

Just as many of the first wave of UK punk bands were on the wane, Sham 69's popularity grew, and they influenced the later street punk and Oi! movements. They returned to the UK top 10 in June 2006 with *Hurry Up England*, a reworking of their 1978 hit *Hurry Up Harry*, which provided an anthem for England football fans during the 2006 World Cup in Germany.

New Malden

Although raised in Glasgow, the influential singer-songwriter and guitarist John Martyn was born Iain David McGeachy in New Malden in 1948. The only son of two Glaswegian light opera singers, he taught himself to play the guitar aged 15 and would become one of the most revered acoustic guitarists of his generation.

After leaving school, he appeared regularly at the famous Soho folk club Les Cousins. In 1968, he was the first white artist signed to Chris Blackwell's Island label, recording his first album, *London Conversation*. Always keen to take his guitar playing into the unknown, he experimented with electronic effects, in particular a tape device known as the Echoplex, which enabled him to play on top of guitar loops. Introduced on his second album, 1970's *Stormbringer!*, it became his signature sound.

Martyn spent a lot of his career dependent on drugs and alcohol. At one concert in Spain he was so drunk he fell off the stage – but still received three encores. In 2003, his right leg was amputated below the knee due to a burst cyst but he continued to perform from a wheelchair. He died in January 2009, aged 60, but left a strong legacy as an innovative singer-songwriter. His music, a fusion of folk, blues and funk, influenced many artists, including Portishead, Eric Clapton and U2. Many of his albums, in particular 1973's *Solid Air*, are seen as timeless classics.

Richmond

In 2002, an interactive musical bench was created in Richmond Park as a memorial to the late Ian Dury. Located in Poet's Corner, near Pembroke Lodge, a favourite spot of Dury's, the solar-powered bench has a socket that allows visitors to plug in their own headphones and hear some of his songs. The bench also has the song title *Reasons To Be Cheerful* carved into the wood. Dury loved Richmond Park and he used to bring his children here.

The cover of The Verve's 1997 multi-million selling *Urban Hymns* features the band in the not particularly urban location of Richmond Park. The cover was produced by sleeve designer Brian Cannon, best known for his work with Oasis.

Instead of the park, Aussie indie rockers The Go-Betweens travelled to Richmond Green for the cover of their 1984 album, *Spring Hill Fair*. The sleeve showed the band glaring from a balcony inside Richmond Theatre, which dates back to 1899. The theatre's exterior also appeared in *The Krays*, starring Spandau Ballet's Martin and Gary Kemp, as the East End gangsters' nightclub.

The Georgian mansion The Wick on Richmond Hill was for many years the family home of the late actor Sir John Mills. His grandson, by his actress daughter Hayley, is Kula Shaker frontman Crispian Mills. Rolling Stone guitarist Ronnie Wood bought the house in 1972 and made it his home for most of the 1970s. The cover of his debut solo album, *I've Got My Own Album To Do*, in 1974, pictured Wood in his oval drawing room, and featured Rod Stewart and Ian McLagan from The Faces as well as the aptly-named Chanter Sisters on backing vocals. The album was recorded in the home basement studio Wood built and featured 'Mick 'n' Keef' from the Stones. A jam between Jagger and Richards here formed the basic track for the Stones' 1974 song, *It's Only Rock 'n' Roll (But I like It)*, also recorded at Wood's home studio. Whenever Keith Richards sought escape from police raids on his Cheyne Walk pad, he stayed in the coach house at the end of the garden.

Richmond and the British Blues Explosion

N Britain in the early 1960s you could hear the distant rumblings of the Mississippi Delta. Not everyone was enamoured with Tin Pan Alley pop music. There was a sizeable amount of English blues fans and musicians who rejected pop in favour of authentic black folk music from the American south: the blues.

As performed by artists such as Howlin' Wolf, Little Walter, Memphis Slim, Muddy Waters and Bo Diddley, this music went largely unheeded in the US, where white Americans ignored it and urban blacks preferred uplifting soul music. In Britain, it was the traditional jazz and folk revival movements that paved the way for British blues music. Its chief architects were folk like jazz bandleader Chris Barber, who in the late 1950s brought over blues and gospel legends like Sister Rosetta Tharpe, Muddy Waters, Howlin' Wolf and Sonny Boy Williamson.

By the early 1960s British blues fanatics had their own scene, centring on Blues Incorporated, a band formed by two blues musicians, guitarist Alexis Korner and harmonica-player Cyril Davies. Waiting in the wings were John Mayall's Bluesbreakers from which emerged two future legendary blues guitarists Eric Clapton and Peter Green. But the British blues scene really took off at the end of 1963, thanks to five young blues musicians called The Rolling Stones.

Fans connected with them because their raw, new sound was something you could dance to. They were also as young as their audience, unlike other blues players who were much older and still associated with jazz. While the Stones spearheaded the scene, they were followed by the likes of The Animals, The

Yardbirds and Manfred Mann. By the following year, the British take on the blues could be heard at every venue in the country.

Musicians interpreted the music for themselves but ensured their audience were aware who originated the music: be it Robert Johnson, Freddie King or Muddy Waters. Later, when R&B bands toured the US, they reintroduced Americans to part of their own musical heritage. In effect, the 1960s British invasion sold a repackaged, disregarded music back to white America. Ironically, it took the British blues explosion to raise the profile of blues music back in the US.

Compared with the Mississippi Delta, the outskirts of London may seem rather insignificant in the history of blues music but London suburbs like Dartford, Ealing and Richmond were instrumental in the 1960s British blues explosion. As the R&B scene took off, it spawned legendary venues like Richmond's Station Hotel, which housed the Crawdaddy Club (now The Bull) directly opposite Richmond railway station. The venue was a jazz club before its founder, Russian immigrant Giorgio Gomelsky, started a rhythm and blues club in 1962. The Crawdaddy has gone down in pop music history as the venue where The Rolling Stones performed as house band at the start of their career.

Their Sunday night residency at the club was a defining moment in the band's career even though it had an inauspicious start. At their first gig in February 1963, there were only three people in the audience – half as many as there were on stage. But each week the number swelled and soon there were several hundred fans keen to catch the young

home-grown R&B sound. To accommodate the hordes of Stones fans, the venue moved to new premises in the clubhouse of the nearby Richmond Athletic Ground.

In mid-April 1963, The Beatles dropped by to check out the competition, and George Harrison recommended the band to Dick Rowe at the Decca label, who had famously turned down the Fab Four. He did not make the same mistake twice and signed the Stones to a recording contract.

The Crawdaddy audience was awash with young musicians who would soon have R&B bands of their own: Pete Townshend of The Who, Rod Stewart and Ian McLagan of the Small Faces and Phil May and Dick Taylor of The Pretty Things. Also in the audience were a group of guys who would launch themselves onto the world and replace the Stones at the club six month later: The Yardbirds.

Top: Keith Relf of The Yardbirds.
Above: The Rolling Stones in their early years, 1963.
Opposite page: Ronnie Wood at his Richmond home, The Wick, in 1974.

Since the late seventies, the house has been owned by another rock legend, Pete Townshend. The panoramic view from the top of Richmond Hill – the bend in the Thames, royal parks and palaces – has long inspired writers and artists. JMW Turner's watercolour, *View From Richmond Hill*, created in around 1790, was painted at the late 18th-century Wick House, home of painter Sir Joshua Reynolds; it is next door to what is now Townshend's house. Steve Cradock, guitarist with Ocean Colour Scene and Paul Weller, celebrated the view in his song, *Beware of Falling Rocks*, on his 2009 debut album, *The Kundalini Target*:

> 'As in view from Richmond Hill we know/
> Through Turner's eyes it's kinda set in stone'

The annual Reading Festival started life as the National Jazz and Blues Festival in Richmond before it moved up the Thames (see Reading).

Carshalton

Carshalton's largest contribution to music was the wonderfully untrendy and unpretentious glam rockers, Mud, founded by lead singer Les Gray, who died in 2004, aged 57. When they teamed up with songwriting team Nicky Chinn and Mike Chapman in the early 1970s, they scored a string of hits, including three number ones: *Tiger Feet, Lonely This Christmas* and *Oh Boy*. Guitarist Rob Davis later enjoyed huge success as a songwriter, composing (with Cathy Dennis) Kylie Minogue's mega hit *Can't Get You Out of My Head*, which also won an Ivor Novello award.

Merton

One-hit wonders The Merton Parkas were a parka-wearing late-1970s mod-revival band formed in Merton (see what they did there, with their name?). Their keyboardist Mick Talbot (later of Dexys Midnight Runners and The Style Council) was born in nearby Wimbledon.

Right: Captain Sensible (far left) and The Damned play live in 1977.
Opposite page: Ozzy Osbourne, 1981.

Rock enrol

Its premises may look more like offices on an industrial estate, but it has been nurturing future pop stars since 1991. Selhurst, near Croydon, is the location of the performing arts college, BRIT School, or to give its full name, The BRIT School for Performing Arts and Technology. Noisettes' energetic, bouncy singer Shingai Shoniwa and guitarist Dan Smith met and formed the band in 1996 whilst at the school. Two members of The Feeling met as BRIT School students: lead singer and songwriter Dan Gillespie Sells and bassist Richard Jones. The BRIT School also helped cultivate the talents of Kate Nash, Leona Lewis, Amy Winehouse, Adele (Adkins), Imogen Heap and Polly Scattergood. The school also spawned Luke Pritchard, lead singer of The Kooks. He dated fellow student Katie Melua, about whom he subsequently wrote most of the band's first album.

Croydon

Late singer-songwriter Kirsty MacColl hailed from Croydon, and the title of her anthology, *From Croydon to Cuba*, acknowledges her origins and her end. She was tragically killed by a speedboat off the coast of Mexico in 2000. The daughter of folk singer Ewan MacColl, she teamed-up with Shane MacGowan (*Fairytale of New York*) and Johnny Marr (*Walking Down Madison*) and reworked Billy Bragg's *A New England*. She also penned some fun pop songs of her own, such as her 1981 single, *There's A Guy Works Down The Chip Shop Swears He's Elvis*.

The Damned's Captain Sensible (Ray Burns) grew up in Croydon and went to Stanley Technical School (now the

Harris Academy) in nearby South Norwood. Early on in his music career he played guitar in a covers band called Oasis, no less. The foundations of punk band The Damned were laid when he worked alongside his old drummer friend Christopher Millar (aka Rat Scabies) at the Fairfield Halls (see Crap jobs box). Miller was re-named Rat Scabies after he contracted the skin infection, but their name changes also meant they could keep signing on for the dole.

Indie pop trio Saint Etienne, fronted by singer Sarah Cracknell, formed in Croydon in 1990, where two of the band grew up: songwriter, music journalist and DJ Bob Stanley, and keyboardist and DJ Pete Wiggs. There's nothing remotely Tasmanian about their 1993 single *Hobart Paving* – the title comes from the name of a local building company. Bob Stanley once described central Croydon as, "like a *Captain Scarlet* set, all very clean, with flyovers and underpasses."

Since opening in 1962, the Fairfield Halls has hosted famous names from Pink Floyd to The Beatles and early UK gigs by legendary bluesmen like Muddy Waters, Howlin' Wolf and Sonny Boy Williamson. Several live albums have been recorded here too. Family recorded one side of their album, *Anyway*, in the Halls in 1970, and the live album *Five Bridges* by Keith Emerson's band, The Nice. The following year saw the turn of Traffic, who recorded *Welcome to the Canteen* here and the album cover was shot in the venue's canteen.

Tangerine Dream played here in 1975 but the concert wasn't as eventful as an infamous PJ Proby gig a decade earlier, when the American singer's blue skin-tight velvet trousers split along the seam on stage. He explained the ripped clothing was an accident due to the weak velvet material, but the same thing happened again at another concert two days later. His audience loved it but the establishment was less impressed. A frantic popular press pilloried Proby and he was banned from all theatres and from performing on TV.

Former top Croydon venues included The Greyhound in Park Lane and The Cartoon in West Croydon, but a popular current venue is the Black Sheep on the High Street, an oasis of individuality amongst chain pubs. Swapping between indie and rock nights, drum and bass and hip-hop, it also provides a home for Croydon's dubstep scene, which fuses UK garage music, dub music nod drum and bass.

crap jobs

THE path to rock and pop stardom is not always paved with gold. In some cases it's the opposite…

- Rat Scabies, drummer of The Damned, was once employed at the Fairfield Halls in Croydon. He worked with his friend Ray Burns (Captain Sensible) as a porter; their duties included cleaning the toilets.

- Vince Clarke, of Depeche Mode, Yazoo and Erasure fame, was once employed at Southend Airport emptying the chemical toilets on aeroplanes, filling up buckets of… A tough job, but at least it gave him money to buy records.

- The Damned's frontman Dave Vanian was a gravedigger at Heath Lane Cemetery in Hemel Hempstead.

- The first job is the creepiest. Rod Stewart was also a gravedigger and abandoned his dreams of playing pro football to dig graves at London's Highgate Cemetery. He downed his shovel after a few weeks.

- Ozzy Osbourne worked a number of bum jobs before his music career with Black Sabbath took off. He tested car horns and was even a burglar for a short period of time (if that can be classed as a job). But it's his days in an abattoir that Ozzy remembers most warmly. He had to slice open cow carcasses and remove the contents of their stomachs. "I used to vomit every day; the smell was something else," he reveals in his autobiography, *I Am Ozzy*.

- Carl Barât of The Libertines was once a salad tosser and worked in a centre for drug addicts, but not necessarily at the same time.

- The Jarman brothers (from The Cribs) all worked in a toilet paper and serviette factory. Gary Jarman would later claim that he and his brothers were the sole manufacturers of napkins in the UK.

Middlesex

Heathrow Airport

As mythical as some English rock stars are, none have developed the ability to walk on water or indeed fly. As a result, they have to catch aeroplanes like the rest of us great unwashed. Over the decades Heathrow has got used to the sight of hordes of screaming and weeping fans amassing at London's main airport to meet or wave goodbye to their musical heroes.

In late February 1964, over 3,000 excited fans greeted The Beatles returning home from their triumphant first US tour. Over 400 girls camped overnight to assure prime spots on the roof of the Queens Building viewing platform, one of London's most visited attractions back in the 1950s

In November 1972, the roof was crowded again as hundreds of young girls bunked off school to bid farewell to their heart-throbs, The Osmonds. The 500th episode of *Top of the Pops*, broadcast in October 1973, featured another fresh-faced US heart-throb, David Cassidy. For the hour-long

special he flew over especially from the US on his private jet to perform his song, *Daydreamer*, on the Heathrow tarmac. Then he flew straight back to Los Angeles.

Another American, Peter Buck, lead guitarist of US rock band REM, didn't receive such a warm welcome. He was arrested at Heathrow in April 2001, following an alleged air rage attack on two members of British Airways cabin crew on a flight from Seattle. The usually laid-back Buck allegedly became abusive to staff as soon as his flight took off, and it worsened to such an extent that the captain radioed ahead and requested police to meet the plane at Heathrow. Among other rock 'n' roll antics, Buck was said to have thrown a carton of yoghurt at a stewardess across the first class cabin.

Five years later, in 2006, US gangsta rapper Snoop Dogg and five members of his entourage were arrested at the airport following a mass brawl. Fighting broke out after some members of the entourage were refused entry to British Airways' first class lounge – they only had economy class tickets. Rappers fought with security, hurled bottles of duty free drink around and smashed display cabinets as travellers in the departure lounge, including singer Ronan Keating, looked on in disbelief. Seven policemen were injured and a witness said one police officer was hurled across the room "like a rag doll" by a seven-foot member of Tha Doggfather's posse.

In February 2003, Hole lead singer and Kurt Cobain's widow, Courtney Love, was arrested at Heathrow on suspicion of disruptive behaviour and endangering an aircraft on

Far left: Delirious crowds meet The Beatles on their return from the USA at Heathrow Airport in 1964.
Left: The 'Doggfather' Snoop Dogg leaves Heathrow airport after being arrested in the airport's VIP lounge.
Opposite page: Dedicated fans of the punk outfit, The Ruts.

a Virgin Atlantic flight from Los Angeles. She was accused of abusing cabin crew and refusing to put on her seatbelt. After landing, Love emerged from the aircraft wearing sunglasses and bright red lipstick and was escorted across the tarmac and bundled into a waiting police van. Ever the performer, when a policewoman tried to put a jacket over her head to stop photographers taking pictures, Love threw it off and waved at assembled snappers. "She was very drunk," recalls one of the photographers.

Heathrow police arrested pop legend Diana Ross in September 1999, after a female airport security officer complained the singer assaulted her. A routine security check turned into a shouty confrontation when Ross accused the security officer of touching her up. Ross was detained for nearly five hours before she was cautioned but released without charge.

An early Heathrow incident occurred in May 1958, when enthusiastic English music fans looked forward to the arrival of 22-year-old legend Jerry Lee Lewis in what promised to be the biggest tour to date by an American rock 'n' roll star. *Whole Lotta Shakin' Goin' On* and *Great Balls Of Fire* had been huge hits in the UK, and demand for tickets had been so great that 27 concerts were organised. Newly married for the third time, Lewis arrived at Heathrow with his new bride, Myra Gale Brown, in tow. Nothing unusual happened until reporters started asking questions about the singer's new wife. When it emerged she was his first cousin and only 13 years old, it caused uproar, and the tour was cancelled after only three concerts. Lewis left the UK less than a week later.

Heathrow is mentioned in Squeeze's everlasting *Cool For Cats*, in which the police nab "a gang of villains in a shed up at Heathrow", while Level 42 recorded an instrumental jazz funk track called *Heathrow* on their 1981 debut album. The cover photograph of the late Robert Palmer's 1974 first solo album, *Sneakin' Sally Through the Alley*, was taken in Heathrow's famous tunnel. Pictured running with Palmer in the subway is 1970s model Josephine Florent who later married Palmer's long-term manager, David Harper. Even though they were photographed in the wee small hours, the shoot still cost Palmer's label Island Records around £1,000 – a princely sum in 1974 – because the Heathrow tunnel had to be closed to traffic.

 Hayes

Nineteen eighty was a bad year for lead singers. Just a few months after Joy Division's Ian Curtis hanged himself, Malcolm Owen, frontman of rude boy rockers, The Ruts, was found dead in the bath at his mother's house in Hayes. He died from a heroin overdose, aged 25, soon after he had recorded a John Peel session with ska legend Laurel Aitken.

Formed in Hayes in 1977, The Ruts made their live debut at The Target pub, now a large branch of McDonald's, at the Target Roundabout. With songs that mixed punk and reggae with streetwise lyrics and political activism, The Ruts were seen by many as the natural successors to The Clash. Their 1979 dub reggae single, *Jah War*, was written in response to that year's violence at an Anti-Nazi League protest against the right-wing National Front, in the heavily Asian-populated Southall nearby. One demonstrator, Blair Peach, was knocked unconscious by a police baton and died the following day from head injuries. The lyric: 'Hot heads came in uniform / Thunder and lightning in a violent form' refers to the Special Patrol Group (SPG), the Metropolitan Police's infamous public disorder unit whose overzealous tactics came to prominence when they also ruffed-up picket line protestors at the famous 1970s Grunwick dispute. Another Ruts song, *S.U.S*, protested against the Sus laws (short for Suspicion of Committing a Crime), which gave police controversial stop-and-search powers. After Owen's death, his bandmates continued, aptly as Ruts DC (*da capo*, or back to the start). Ironically, some of The Ruts' songs rallied prophetically against heroin use, including *H-Eyes* and *Love in Vain*: 'Don't want you in my arms no more.'

Many of The Beatles' movies were filmed in the Twickenham area. The scene in *Help!* in which the Fab Four arrive at an ordinary-looking street in a Rolls Royce and disappear into some terraced houses was shot at Ailsa Avenue, St Margarets, between Richmond and Twickenham. Ringo enters number five, John seven, Paul nine and George 11. But don't bother knocking at any of these houses for a nose around. Although the interior made it seem as though all four houses had been knocked into one huge room, it was a Twickenham Film Studios set.

In *A Hard Day's Night*, Ringo downs a pint in The Turk's Head pub at 28 Winchester Road. Feel free to do the same but this place is best avoided before rugby internationals at nearby Twickenham Stadium. In recent years the stadium has transformed itself into a rock venue, hosting stadium rockers who don't need the money like The Eagles, The Police, Iron Maiden, U2, Bon Jovi and The Rolling Stones. In common with many large venues, unless you're near the front your favourite band may appear as dots on the horizon,

and it's back to entry-level physics again. As sound travels slower than light and the stage is so far away the music can be out of sync with the band on the huge video screens.

Elsewhere in Twickenham, Rod Stewart was discovered one night in early 1964 on the railway station platform by Blues legend Long John Baldry. The 19-year-old Stewart was just starting out on his monumental five-decade career and had been to see The Cyril Davies All Stars, featuring Baldry, at the Eel Pie venue. Stewart wasn't singing *Downtown Train* in his distinctive husky, rough-edged tones (Stewart's cover of the Tom Waits song came much later) but the classic Howlin' Wolf song, *Smokestack Lightning*, on his harmonica. Today he'd probably get slapped with an ASBO but they struck up a conversation as both the blues singer and his soon-to-be young protégé waited for the last train back to London. When Stewart told Baldry he was a singer too, he offered Stewart a job as second vocalist at £35 a week and invited him to play at the Marquee Club the following week. When British blues legend Cyril Davies died of leukaemia soon afterwards, Baldry became the band leader and renamed them the Hoochie Coochie Men. As well as music, railways have loomed large in Stewart's life for years. He also lays down tracks as a keen railway modeller, and once said that appearing on the cover of a *British Railway Modelling* magazine would mean more to him than being on the cover of *Rolling Stone*. Stewart is not alone in being a rock 'n' railer: Eric Clapton, Phil Collins and pop tycoon Pete Waterman are all model railway enthusiasts.

A respectful nod towards Isleworth, hardly the rock 'n' roll capital of the world but birthplace of two unsung heroes of English pop. Born in 1938, session bassist Herbie Flowers wrote Clive Dunn's *Grandad*, a number one for the *Dad's Army* star in 1971. He was a member of the supergroup Sky, with classical guitarist John

Above: Rod Stewart began his long career after being discovered in Twickenham in 1964.
Left: Vince Taylor.
Opposite page: Elton John (left) with long term songwriting partner Bernie Taupin.

Williams, and was in another band called Oasis long before the world had heard of the Gallagher brothers. As a session musician, his bass lines have graced many songs, notably Elton John's *Madman Across The Water* and David Bowie's *Space Oddity*.

His involvement with Bowie led to him working on Lou Reed's *Transformer* album, for which he created one of the most memorable bass lines in pop history on *Walk on the Wild Side*. The famous bass line is actually a mix of two: Flowers played upright acoustic bass on one track then overdubbed it with an electric bass. He once said he thought doubling up gave the track more character – it also enabled him to earn twice as much money.

Isleworth was also the birthplace of rocker Vince Taylor whose rise and fall was the inspiration for David Bowie's Ziggy Stardust character. The name came from a London tailor's called Ziggy's that Bowie saw from a train one day. The black leather-clad Taylor's attempts at stardom in Britain and the US failed, but he enjoyed cult hero status in France in the early 1960s where he was dubbed 'the French Elvis'. His name also lives on because of his classic 1959 British rock 'n' roll song, *Brand New Cadillac*, later covered by The Clash on *London Calling*.

Brentford ❯

Syon House in Syon Park has been home of the Duke and Duchess of Northumberland for over four centuries and is open to the general public. It's a popular location for film and TV. Syon House's Great Conservatory played a starring role in the video of The Cure's *The Caterpillar*, made in 1984 by their regular video director, Tim Pope.

Syon House itself was the location for the cover shoot of the 1973 Paul McCartney & Wings album, *Band on the Run*. The sleeve shows Macca and the band caught in a prison spotlight and joined by several more escaped convicts, all played by top 1970s celebrities: legendary chat-show host and journalist Michael Parkinson, singer and comedian Kenny Lynch, actor James Coburn, raconteur and gourmet chef Clement Freud, actor Christopher Lee and boxer John Conteh.

Pinner ❯

Rock royalty Sir Elton John started out life as a pudgy-faced only child formerly known as Reginald Dwight in this northwest London commuter suburb. Born in March 1947, his childhood heroes, Liberace and boogie-woogie pianist Winifred Atwell, gave a clue as to the direction he would head in.

Until he was five he lived with his mother Sheila Dwight in a semi-detached council house at 55 Pinner Hill Road. He attended Pinner County Grammar School (now Heathfield School), where he immediately eyed up the school's resident Steinway grand. Soon enough the young Reg's music teacher recommended him for the Royal Academy of Music's junior scholarship programme. He later moved with his mother and her partner into a ground floor flat at 30 Frome Court, Pinner Road (he returned some years later with lyricist, Bernie Taupin, to write many of their early numbers, including *Your Song*).

Known at the time as Reggie, the 15-year-old Elton John started playing professionally on the often ignoble pub circuit. In 1962, he secured a regular slot as pub pianist at the nearby mock-Tudor Northwood Hills Hotel (now the Namaste Lounge with the Los Angeles-sounding address of Joel Street, Northwood Hills). He learned early on how to win over the crowds, playing a range of popular standards by Chuck Berry, Jerry Lee Lewis, Jim Reeves and Ray Charles.

EEL PIE ISLAND

ONE of Greater London's legendary music venues was located on a raised mudbank in the middle of the Thames at Twickenham. Sandwiched between a nature reserve at each end, tiny Eel Pie Island is little more than a third of a mile long and home to several dozen houses, some boat-houses and a working boatyard. Some curious visitors keen to follow in the bare footsteps of stoned hippies and visit this counter-cultural haven are distraught to learn no trace of the Eel Pie Island Hotel remains. A modern block of flats called Aquarius now occupies the site of the venue which rocked to the early sounds of The Rolling Stones, The Who and Rod Stewart.

But long before the island secured its invincible rock heritage, it was a resort for day-trippers. In 1830 the first pub on the island was replaced by the grand hotel, complete with a large bar. With the creation of the hotel's ballroom with a sprung floor in 1898, tea dances became all the rage. Londoners who couldn't afford the seaside would travel up the Thames on steamboats to spend a day relaxing in the hotel's grounds. The island has enjoyed a long association with music, with Charles Dickens mentioning the place in *Nicholas Nickleby*: "Unto the Eel-Pie Island at Twickenham, there to make merry upon a cold collation, bottled beer, shrub, and shrimps, and to dance in the open air to the music of a locomotive band."

From the 1950s onwards the hotel's dancehall would become a microcosm of the burgeoning British music scene, first as a jazz club hosting influential New Orleans-style British trad jazz acts like Ken Colyer, Acker Bilk and Chris Barber. It then responded to the boom in British R&B with leading blues players like Alexis Korner and Cyril Davies. The trad jazz crowd were replaced by young mods and rock 'n' rollers, including Ian McLagan, soon to become the keyboardist for the Small Faces. The Rolling Stones had a weekly slot on Eel Pie Island, and McLagan secured a gig for his band The Muleskinners after he helped the band shift their equipment across the bridge one night. He also first met Rod Stewart here, when he played with Long John Baldry, and saw Memphis Slim with the Tridents, with Jeff Beck on guitar.

The Eel Pie crowd was full of the budding musicians and art school students who would soon become so influential on the British music scene. The venue was also an early platform for John Mayall's Bluesbreakers, featuring Eric Clapton, as well as David Jones (later Bowie), Pink Floyd (with Syd Barrett and their bubble light-show) and The Who. Pete Townshend was so enamoured with the island venue he later named his music company after it. Revellers at the club were issued with little Eel Pie passports as membership cards.

The venue's driving force was Arthur Chisnall, not a music promoter but a social researcher and local junk shop dealer. He started his own jazz club as a personal project and social experiment to give the young post-war generation a voice and an environment where they could be themselves. Such a venue may sound dreamy compared with today's huge corporate amphitheatres like nearby Twickenham Stadium but, in reality, it was a shabby, crumbling place. There were massive holes in the roof and the dilapidated floorboards were in the advanced stages of decay. The house piano at the side of the stage had seen better days; punters poured drinks into it and bits of broken glass lurked among the hammers. Bands in the tiny dressing room above the stage could see everything going on underneath them. A young Ronnie Wood once relieved himself in a bucket upstairs but it leaked onto the stage where his brother Art, and his band, The Artwoods, played.

In 1957, a connecting footbridge linked Eel Pie Island to Twickenham. But in its early days musicians and punters were reliant on an old chain barge. "In those days you got to the island by boat, you had to pull yourself across on a rope, it was fairly primitive and you could hear jazz playing in the distance," recalled the late George Melly who often performed there. Awaiting visitors on the other side were two local old ladies ready to collect a tuppence toll fee. Bands still had to trawl their instruments and amps onto the island themselves until an enterprising local offered to transport their equipment across the bridge on a Mini Moke for a small charge.

With hundreds of revellers attending the place at weekends, the venue caught the attention of the police who viewed it as a beatnik-infested vice den. The club closed in 1967 because the owner could not meet the huge repair costs and was fined for allowing unregistered fans into the club. It briefly reopened in 1969 and enjoyed a renaissance as a progressive rock venue called Colonel Barefoot's Rock Garden, where Pink Floyd and Black Sabbath played. This club lasted until the following year when squatters moved in.

According to Canadian poet Chris Faiers in his memoir, *Eel Pie Dharma*, these squatters consisted of "200 dossers, hippies, runaway school kids, drug dealers, petty thieves, heroin addicts, artists, poets, bikers, American hippy tourists, au pair girls and Zen philosophers from all over the world," whose focus was orgies and consuming large quantities of LSD.

Almost two decades after the hotel was burnt down in 1971 in a mysterious fire, it was immortalised by George Harrison in *Cockamamie Business* (a previously unreleased track) on his 1989 compilation, *The Best of Dark Horse*:

'Bust my back on the Levy/
Broke my strings on the BBC/
Found my chops on Eel Pie Island/
Paid my dues at the Marquee'

The indie five-piece Mystery Jets were formerly based on Eel Pie Island. Their surroundings influenced their music and they even sampled the sound of drills from the boatyard. Today, the tiny Thames island of boat-houses and picket-fenced gardens is almost entirely residential. When one resident tried to put on a gig in a hall over a boatyard a few years ago, neighbours complained about the noise. Suburbia may have triumphed over bohemia but the island still enjoys a reputation as an outpost of eccentrics, artists and free spirits.

Another musical connection is its most famous resident, inventor Trevor Baylis, a former club reveller who ended up living there. It was on Eel Pie Island that Baylis devised the first wind-up radio.

His name change from Reggie to Elton John derived from two bandmates he toured with in the 1960s R&B group, Bluesology: saxophonist Elton Dean and singer Long John Baldry. But his early talents as a musician and showman flourished alongside his songwriting soulmate Bernie Taupin. They both answered an advert in the *NME* placed by Liberty Records A&R man Ray Williams, before joining the Tin Pan Alley production line for publisher Dick James Music.

Some music critics have suggested that some of Elton John's 1970s albums written with Bernie Taupin, notably *Goodbye Yellow Brick Road*, *Captain Fantastic and the Brown Dirt Cowboy*, *Tumbleweed Connection* and *Honky Château*, will endure for as long as people listen to pop music. The Pinner piano man's reworking of *Candle in the Wind*, recorded at the 1997 funeral service of Diana, Princess of Wales, remains the best-selling record of all time (since charts began), shifting 33 million copies. It originally appeared on Elton John's fêted 1973 album *Goodbye Yellow Brick Road*; Taupin's original lyrics were a tribute to another vulnerable, deceased blonde woman with a string of men friends, Marilyn Monroe.

Duran Duran's Simon Le Bon attended West Lodge Infant and Primary schools, sang in the choir at Pinner Parish Church and later went to Pinner County Grammar School, the same institution as Elton had attended a few years earlier.

Harrow ➤

The Who's first-ever gig took place at the former Railway Tavern pub by Harrow and Wealdstone tube station. One momentous evening in September 1964 they were discovered playing there by their future manager Kit Lambert; quite by chance, it was the same night guitarist Pete Townshend originated his trademark guitar-smashing routine. During the performance Townshend accidentally cracked the head of his Rickenbacker guitar on the venue's low ceiling, then smashed the remainder of the guitar out of frustration. Then, in true rock'n'roll, the-show-must-go-on fashion, he simply picked up another Rickenbacker and carried on.

Townshend said later he expected everybody to be amazed that he had broken his guitar. "But nobody

did anything, which made me kind of angry in a way." Determined to get the event noticed by the audience, he proceeded to make a big thing of breaking the rest of the guitar. "I bounced all over the stage with it and I threw the bits on the stage and I picked up my spare guitar and carried on as though I really had meant to do it."

A week later an even larger crowd turned up for their next gig at the Railway, expecting Townshend to smash another guitar. But he declined. Instead, as an act of solidarity, Keith Moon, happily stepped in and wrecked his drum-kit, and their auto-destructive stage antics became an essential part of The Who's live performance for years. *Rolling Stone* magazine listed Townshend's guitar-smashing incident at the Railway Tavern as one of its '50 Moments That Changed the History of Rock 'n' Roll' (albeit alongside the birth of Rick Astley). A photograph of the Railway Tavern appears on the inside of the gatefold sleeve of The Who's 1971

Right: Pete Townshend's now legendary destruction of his guitar during gigs began at the Railway Tavern pub in 1964.

Opposite page: Ross Philips, Kai Stephens, Richard Archer and Steve Kemp of Hard-Fi.

compilation *Meaty, Beaty, Big and Bouncy*. By the 1990s the venue was derelict, and in 2002, it was destroyed by fire and replaced by a block of flats.

Rolling Stones drummer Charlie Watts studied graphic design at Harrow Art School, at Brookshill, Harrow Weald, in 1961. The late Sex Pistols manager Malcolm McLaren attended briefly in 1963 and met fellow punk legend Vivienne Westwood. They became partners, later forming the King's Road boutique that spawned the Sex Pistols.

The late Rick Wright, keyboardist and songwriter with Pink Floyd, was born and grew up in nearby Hatch End. He met his future bandmates Roger Waters and Nick Mason as an architecture student at the Regent Street Polytechnic in 1962. Along with Waters' childhood friend from Cambridge, Roger 'Syd' Barrett, they would form The Pink Floyd Sound, but the name was soon shortened.

Ruislip

In the summer of 1959 The Shadows were not yet the legendary group they would become. In fact they were called The Drifters and had been asked by a similarly named US soul group to change their moniker. With legal action threatened, they temporarily called themselves The Four Jets. One day that July bassist Jet Harris and guitarist Hank Marvin were relaxing at the Ruislip Lido and nearby Six Bells pub when Harris conjured up their new name, The Shadows.

The band, with Cliff Richard in tow, returned to Ruislip Lido a few years later, in 1961, to film the box office smash, *The Young Ones*.

Staines

Suburbs may be largely identical, anonymous and invisible but they have long been an important wellspring of English popular music. By placing their suburban roots firmly at the centre of their songs, indie rockers Hard-Fi have put their home town of Staines on the English musical map.

The band's first album in 2004 was recorded for no money in a converted mini-cab office, with its limited 1,000 copies selling out. They re-recorded the album the following year as *Stars of CCTV*, when they secured a licensing deal with

Atlantic Records. It sold 800,000 copies, was nominated for the Mercury Prize, reached number one and helped them sell out five nights at the Brixton Academy.

Feltham is Singing Out, from their first album, is about the Feltham Young Offenders Institution, a few miles east of Staines, where a friend of bassist Kai Stephens was imprisoned. For their second album, 2007's *Once Upon a Time in the West*, the band were offered the chance to record at Abbey Road but instead chose their Cherry Lips studio, the same old cab office as their debut (although it was mixed elsewhere).

Amusing working titles for the album punned on two 1970s classic albums, *Bat Out of Staines* and *Songs in the Key of Staines*. The album's first single, *Suburban Knights*, championed life in Staines and other non-descript suburbs. To many, *Tonight*, another track on the album, transposed Bruce Springsteen's Asbury Park to Staines, with its dreams of breaking out of suburbia via the Great West Road (the famous road that heads west out of London). Hard-Fi frontman Richard Archer has said the band's songs are about basic human emotions, but using the backdrop of a town like Staines.

Feltham

Best known for its Young Offenders Institution, Feltham is unlikely to top any tourist destination hot-list. But it played a part in the development in one of the country's most enduring musical stars: the artist formerly known as Farrokh Bulsara.

Feltham was Queen frontman Freddie Mercury's first home in England and the place where he began to explore his musical future. Feltham may not sound as exotic as Zanzibar but this is where his parents moved to, when they arrived in England in 1964. Mercury's father worked in Zanzibar as a court cashier under the British Government, but fled after political upheaval. (Zanzibar was a British protectorate until 1963 when it was granted independence.)

Between 1964 and 1968 the late Queen frontman studied art at Isleworth Polytechnic (now West Thames College) and lived in Gladstone Avenue, just down the road from Brian May, who was born in Hampton but also grew up in Feltham. As kids, May used to go round to Freddie's house and they listened to Jimi Hendrix records together.

In November 2009, Mercury's time in the borough was honoured on the 18th anniversary of his death with the unveiling of a Hollywood-style star plaque in the shopping centre on Feltham High Street. The plaque was unveiled by May, alongside Mercury's sister Kash Cooke and mother Jer Bulsara who told assembled fans: "[Freddie] grew up to be a man with a big appetite for life and an even bigger talent for music. These things were there in him even as a boy and coming to England gave him the opportunity to develop his talent and ambition."

The video for Oasis's *Stand By Me* was filmed in Feltham shopping centre in 1997. While the song borrowed a chord sequence from David Bowie's *All the Young Dudes*, the video was heavily inspired by an award-winning TV advert for the *Guardian* newspaper, in which people seen to be carrying out criminal acts are in fact helping people in trouble.

Heston

Without Jimmy Page, Heston would only be famous for its motorway service station. The legendary Led Zeppelin guitarist was born here in January 1944 and his early guitar playing reflected a time of British devotion to American blues music. Later he branched out and soaked up the influence of acoustic English folk guitarists like John Renbourn and Bert Jansch.

Another fabled guitarist, Ritchie Blackmore, most famously of Deep Purple, was born in the West Country but moved to Heston aged two. He attended the former Heston Secondary School in Heston Road.

Wembley

Wembley Stadium's famous twin towers were levelled in February 2003 in order to make way for a new stadium. The old stadium held a special place in many English hearts as the venue where the England football team won the 1966 World Cup. But Wembley has never been solely about staging sport.

Since 1972's revivalist The London Rock 'n' Roll Show, featuring Little Richard, Chuck Berry and Jerry Lee Lewis, the stadium has hosted major concerts. Amongst the 50,000-strong crowd in the stadium that August was a young Malcolm McLaren; the boss of King's Road Teddy Boys clothing store, Let It Rock, was selling his trademark *Vive Le Rock* T-shirts.

Many of the pop world's biggest names have entertained crowds here, and some have even assembled together on the same day for tribute concerts in honour of Freddie Mercury and Nelson Mandela's 70th birthday in 1988. Most famously, the British section of the Live Aid concert took place here in July 1985, a one-day Woodstock for the yuppie generation. Soon-to-be-knighted Bob Geldof pricked our consciousness, and it was the post-hippy generation's turn to think it could change the world. A Channel 4 poll two decades later ranked Queen's performance at Live Aid as the best live performance in history.

The nearby indoor arena that resembles an aircraft hangar is Wembley Arena (known as the Empire Pool until 1978), a leading London concert venue since the 1950s. Beatlemania was replaced by equally hysterical T.Rextasy when Marc Bolan and T.Rex played two sell-out shows here in March 1972. Beatles drummer Ringo Starr was amongst the 10,000 screaming fans each night, capturing it for posterity in his *Born to Boogie* film.

Wembley's most famous musical sons both became legendary drummers. The late Keith Moon grew up at 134 Chaplin Road, Wembley, and attended the nearby Alperton Secondary School. Bandleader, artist and Rolling Stones drummer Charlie Watts grew up near Wembley Stadium; Mick Jagger sometimes introduced him as "The Wembley Whammer" during gigs. Jagger has not always been so respectful towards Watts, once referring to him as "my drummer". An unhappy Watts has since made the assertion that The Rolling Stones frontman is "my singer".

Shepperton

Before their flamboyant and catchy rock songs launched them onto the global stage, Queen played regular gigs in the pubs around Shepperton. They returned there in November 1983 to record the video for *Radio Ga Ga* at Shepperton Film Studios, a homage to Fritz Lang's 1926 film *Metropolis*. It cost more than £110,000, making it one of the most expensive Queen videos. Directed by David Mallet, it features footage from the original film mixed with images of the song's writer Roger Taylor driving his bandmates through Metropolis in a flying car. The band also performed the song in front of the city's workers, 500 extras and Queen fans drafted in at short notice to stand before their heroes and perform the distinctive double clap in the chorus.

The Who's 1979 rock documentary biopic, *The Kids Are Alright*, features concert performances, rare clips and

Above: One of the most iconic performances of the last 30 years saw Freddie Mercury's Queen play to a global audience from Wembley stadium.
Right: Live Aid organisers Midge Ure and Bob Geldoff on stage at Wembley in 1985. They brought together the biggest acts of the time to create a marathon of music.

interviews with the band. It also shows the last live appearance of drummer Keith Moon, performing in front of an invited audience at Shepperton Studios in late May 1978, four months before his death. The film's performance of *Won't Get Fooled Again* was the last song the original line-up of The Who ever performed together.

East Anglia

Cambridgeshire
Norfolk
Suffolk
Essex

3

Cambridgeshire

Cambridge ▷

Now well over a century old, legendary Cambridge venue The Corn Exchange, in Wheeler Street in the centre of Cambridge, is still going strong. Despite being a modest-sized venue, with a 1,849 standing capacity, some bands make detours to play here. Over the years, legends like The Beatles, David Bowie, Queen, Oasis, The Smiths, even Take That and, of course, local heroes, Pink Floyd, have taken to its stage. Once a working corn exchange (there's a hint in the name), it opened as a venue way back in 1875. The inaugural night, when a local choir and the Coldstream Guards played, was literally a riot; public disorder ensued when a mistake was made during the National Anthem and a mob attacked the Mayor's house. The audience were no less rowdy a century later when a crowd of hundreds rioted after US R&B legends The Drifters failed to turn up for a 1974 gig. The Corn Exchange is now a multi-purpose arts centre staging musicals, classical concerts, comedy shows and even productions by the Chinese State Circus (not all at the same time). But there's still plenty of rock 'n' roll here to get excited about. In recent years it has hosted The Kooks, The Horrors and The Feeling.

Muse's Matt Bellamy was born in Cambridge, before moving to Devon. Likewise *Grease* star Olivia Newton-John, who lived in the city until the age of five, when she emigrated to Australia with her family. Before being offered a teaching post in New South Wales, her father, Brinley, was headmaster of Cambridge and County High School for Boys, a couple of decades before Pink Floyd's founding members Roger Waters and Syd Barrett were young students there. He was also an MI5 officer during World War Two, working on the Enigma code-cracking project at Bletchley Park and taking Hitler's deputy, Rudolph Hess, into custody.

In 2008, unsigned Cambridge indie-pop trio Hamfatter chose a radical new way to raise funds for their band. They appeared on the BBC2 business investment programme *Dragons' Den*, where they performed an extract from their song, *Sziget (We Get Wrecked),* in an attempt to secure a £75,000 investment. The band received offers from all but one of the five potential investors and agreed a deal with business entrepreneur Peter Jones.

Other important Cambridge bands include new wave group The Soft Boys, whose record label Raw Records was one of the first UK indie labels to emerge from the punk movement. The label, started by Lee Wood, grew from a humble record stall at a market, graduated to the Remember Those Oldies record shop (48 King Street, Cambridge) and grew into a record label to help out unsigned local band The Users. The Soft Boys featured two Cambridge musicians: the wonderfully eccentric and witty singer-songwriter Robyn Hitchcock and guitarist Kimberley Rew, who later founded The Waves before revamping them as Katrina and the Waves in the mid-1980s and going on to win the 1997 Eurovision Song Contest.

Cambridge also spawned avant-garde rockers Henry Cow, The Broken Family Band and Boo Hewerdine. Hewerdine's 1980s indie band The Bible released two critically acclaimed albums and garnered a cult following, though major commercial success eluded them. Hewerdine has contributed to several film scores; his old friend the novelist Nick Hornby asked him to contribute to the soundtrack to the film treatment of his novel, *High Fidelity*, about working in a record shop. This was a subject close to Hewerdine's heart, having worked in a Cambridge record shop in the mid-1980s around the time he formed The Bible.

New wave trio Dolly Mixture were part of a thriving Cambridge punk scene in the late 1970s, with film director Julien Temple regularly spotted at gigs. Dolly Mixture supported The Undertones on one of their first UK tours

Above: The Soft Boys, 1978.
Left: The Cambridge Corn Exchange.

Duxford ➤

and were even once supported by U2.

The annual Secret Garden Party is an independent arts and music festival that takes place over four days at the end of July. It's unlike most festivals; revellers aren't told the precise location until they've bought a ticket and there's a different fancy-dress theme every year: one year 'Babylon and Eden', the next 'Fact or Fiction'. There are no corporate sponsors, and revellers are encouraged to participate rather than just stand back and listen to the music. Plus, with a capacity of around 6,000, it's small enough to make new friends. The combination of art, music and playfulness has seen it triumph twice as the Best Small Festival at the UK Festival Awards. It's also a previous winner of BBC Radio 1's Best British Music Festival award. (Go soon before the secret gets out.)

A Broken Frame was Depeche Mode's second album and the first written solely by Martin Gore, after Vince Clarke left the band to form Yazoo with Alison Moyet. Released in 1982, the album's striking cover image of a woman reaping a cornfield is Cambridgeshire made to look like Stalin's Russia. It was taken in a field south of Duxford near the RAF Museum. The month was September, the end of the corn season, and the crew spent many hours searching the countryside for the right spot. Photographer Brian Griffin was a fan of Russian art, especially socialist realism in Stalinist Russia, so the lone figure in the landscape was made to look like a Russian peasant reaping corn with a scythe. His vision fitted well with the synth-pop four-piece, who were keen to shed their wimpy image. The day of the shoot brought thunderstorms and torrential rain, but when the dark Cambridgeshire clouds parted to reveal bright sunlight, Griffin and his team were blessed with the perfect moment.

Ely

One-hit wonders The Look, from Ely, named themselves in honour of English 1960s model and Swinging London icon Jean Shrimpton, one of the world's first supermodels. They had a hit in 1980 with *I Am The Beat*, arguably only memorable for a unique aspect at the end of the record where the run-out groove would endlessly repeat the last line. It would continue to do so until you took the needle off the vinyl – or, more likely, threw your record player across the room. Frontman of hard-hitting Goth rockers Sisters of Mercy, Andrew Eldritch, also hails from Ely. He wrote a piano ballad for their 1987 album, *Floodland*, called *1959*, the year he was born, it begins with the lyric: "Living as angel in the place that I was born."

Huntingdon

This was the birthplace of singer Terry Reid, dubbed 'the unluckiest man in rock'. In 1968, Reid turned down an invitation to join Jimmy Page's New Yardbirds – soon to be Led Zeppelin – as frontman. He benevolently suggested Robert Plant might be the man instead. Soon afterwards Reid also declined an offer to join Deep Purple.

Whittlesey

At first glance it looks as though *The Wicker Man* has invaded the suburbs. The sleeve of Oxford-based trio The Young Knives' 2006 debut album, *Voices of Animals and Men*, features a figure made of straw and a chaperone. It is actually a homage to Whittlesey's annual Straw Bear Festival, where one lucky local dons a 70lb straw costume and parades around the ancient Fenland market town, six miles east of Peterborough. He accepts gifts of food or drink before he is burned. Luckily for the local inside the straw garb, there's no sinister Wicker Man-style finale to this procession – he is baled out first.

CAMBRIDGE FOLK FESTIVAL

EVERY summer since 1965, the 36-acre Cherry Hinton Hall, just south of Cambridge, has hosted the annual Cambridge Folk Festival. You can forget the hackneyed folk stereotypes of beards and real ale bores; it's a boy band and thrash metal-free zone but other than that, anything goes. Local fireman and political activist Ken Woollard got the festival rolling back in 1964, when he was approached by Cherry Hinton's owners, Cambridge City Council, to stage a music festival the following summer. Woollard, a regular at the newly formed Cambridge Folk Club, was inspired by *Jazz On A Summer's Day*, a documentary film about the 1958 Newport Jazz Festival. He organised acts for the first year from a telephone at Cambridge Fire Station in Parkside, booking bands including the young, unknown Paul Simon, who had just put out *I Am A Rock*. The first festival sold 1,400 tickets and almost broke even.

Today the festival enjoys a reputation for showcasing an eclectic mix of music, with top traditional folk artists alongside the finest American country and blues artists in an effortless blending of old and new. Each year it serves up a treasure-trove of rootsy diversity; you're just as likely to hear cajun, gospel and bluegrass as zydeco, jazz, world and ceilidh. The festival throws together line-ups of artists as diverse as R&B legends Booker T and the MGs, American alt-country queen Lucinda Williams, English singer-songwriter Joan Armatrading, legendary New Orleans composer Allen Toussaint or Bassekou Kouyate from Mali. With such musical diversity, inevitably, Cambridge Folk attracts serious music fans. It seems all kinds of roots musicians are welcome, just as long as the music comes from the heart.

PINK FLOYD'S CAMBRIDGE

CAMBRIDGE has never enjoyed the popular musical pedigree of Liverpool, Manchester or London, but three locals who named their band after two American blues musicians saved it from relative rock obscurity. Cambridge figures large in the origins of the key members of Pink Floyd. Syd Barrett, Roger Waters and David Gilmour were all born in the city or grew up here from an early age. The band's long-time sleeve designer, Storm Thorgerson, also grew up in Cambridge and knew Barrett and Waters from school.

Founder members Syd Barrett, who was born in the city, and Roger Waters, who grew up in Cambridge after moving from Surrey at an early age, went to school together. But when Barrett, Floyd's singer, songwriter and guitarist, became rock's most famous acid casualty and departed the band, Waters enlisted old Cambridge friend Gilmour as his replacement. After Barrett's demise, Waters became the band's creative engine.

Cambridge probably has more churches and bicycles per square mile than anywhere else in England. As for the thousands of bikes you see chained up around the city, well, thanks to Floyd's 1967 song, *Bike*, written by Cambridge's favourite psychedelic son, you wonder how many of them are borrowed. And you can't help but scan them for the following:

'A basket, a bell that rings/
And things to make it look good.'

Kings College, Cambridge

The lawn in front of Europe's finest Gothic buildings and Cambridge's biggest tourist attractions, King's College Chapel, inspired Roger Waters' lyrics on *Brain Damage* from *Dark Side of the Moon*. The song features the line: "The lunatic is on the grass."

Grantchester Meadows, Grantchester

Number 109 was the birthplace of Floyd guitarist David Gilmour. The rugged fenland around the city and, in particular Grantchester Meadows, was remembered in the song, *Ummagumma*, from the 1969 album of the same name. "I spent many, many happy hours fishing for roach with a bamboo rod and a piece of bread in that bit of the river Cam," Gilmour said in 2003. "I have powerful memories of the warmth of summer mud oozing up between my toes. That time turned out to be creatively important for me – my work is coloured to a certain extent by the sound of natural history."

Great Shelford, near Cambridge

The cover of *Ummagumma* was designed by their sleeve guru Storm Thorgerson. The photograph was taken at a house in Great Shelford, near Cambridge, owned by the parents of Thorgerson's girlfriend, Libby January. For years Floyd fans have wondered if there was any significance to the *Gigi* soundtrack leaning against the wall. In 2008 Thorgerson squashed their hopes, saying it has no hidden meaning – it was included to deliberately cause such debates.

Cambridge Corn Exchange, Cambridge

The legendary Wheeler Street venue hosted Syd Barrett's last live appearance in February 1972 with his new but short-lived post-Floyd band, Stars, when they supported legendary American punk trailblazers the MC5.

60 Glisson Road, Cambridge

This was the birthplace of the late Syd Barrett – on 6 January, 1946. Aged four, Syd and his family moved a mile or so away to a large semi-detached Cambridge villa at 183 Hills Road.

The Anchor, Silver Street, Cambridge

This pub in the heart of Cambridge, located next to the river Cam, was where young local student Roger Barrett decided to change his name. He adopted a new name in honour of local jazz bassist Sid Barrett but changed the spelling to Syd to distinguish himself from the jazzman.

Hills Road Sixth Form College

Formerly the Cambridge and County School For Boys, this was the second school Roger Waters attended with Syd, having earlier attended Morley Memorial Junior School on Blinco Grove. David Gilmour attended Perse School on the same road. Waters' miserable experiences would heavily inspire the songs on *The Wall* and, in particular, *The Happiest Days of Our Lives*, which evokes the sadism of some of his teachers. A former pupil described the place to music journalist Mark Blake in his Floyd biography *Pigs Might Fly* as: "A grammar school that thought it was a public school, with masters, mortar boards and sadism." Such images are familiar to anyone au fait with *The Wall*, or who has seen Gerald Scarfe's accompanying visuals.

6 St Margaret's Square, Cambridge

His deteriorating mental health forced Syd Barrett to withdraw from the spotlight and, in 1978, he returned to Cambridge, turning up on the doorstep of his sister, Rosemary Breen, having walked all the way from London. He moved into his mother's modest 1930s semi-detached in St Margaret's Square, where he lived until his death. Here he gardened, studied art, painted and was friendly with his neighbours, but received nobody except his immediate family. He became a mythical figure and, on occasions, had to dodge fanatical fans, curious cranks and newspaper reporters who wanted to know what had happened to the good-looking, hugely talented pop star. He died in July 2006, aged 60, from pancreatic cancer and was cremated. On his death certificate his occupation stated: retired musician. His St Margaret's Square home was put on the market and attracted considerable interest, mostly from nosey Floyd fans. Finally it was sold to a couple that claimed they knew nothing about Barrett.

Arnold Layne, Cambridge

Not the name of a street in the city (although savvy Cambridge council or tourism officials might like to rename a road in its honour) but a real landmark of English psychedelic pop. *Arnold Layne* was a 1967 Floyd single: a true-life tale about a local man who stole women's underwear from washing lines in Cambridge.

Gog Magog Hills, outside Cambridge

Floyd's second single, *See Emily Play*, released in 1967, was inspired by the Gog Magog Hills, just south of Cambridge, where the band hung out. "I was sleeping in the woods one night after a gig somewhere, when I saw this girl appear before me. That girl was Emily," Barrett once said. The hills were also where Barrett's first magic mushroom trip was captured on film by student friend and Cambridge scenester Nigel Gordon. This infamous footage has become known as *Syd's First Trip*, recorded for generations of Floyd fans, some of whom describe the footage as exploitative.

Ely Cathedral, north of Cambridge

Ely's 12th-century cathedral appears on the cover of the Floyd's last studio outing, 1994's *The Division Bell*. The artwork, once again by long-time Floyd collaborator Storm Thorgerson, was composed so that the Norman cathedral appears between the open mouths of two huge metal face sculptures. Weighing 1,500 kg, the large Easter Island-style structures were lifted and placed in a field in Cambridgeshire on the Stuntney side of the small cathedral city. They were then photographed during different weather and light conditions over a two-week period. Early reports suggested the structures were more than 80 feet high but in reality were only around nine feet. The lights seen through the sculptures' mouths are actually car headlights erected on poles; fanatical Floyd fans are only too pleased to tell you the lights don't appear on the US release. The sculptures are long gone and now reside in the Rock and Roll Hall of Fame in Cleveland, Ohio. Upon its release, Floyd fans started to inspect the sleeve in the same way they'd done with *Ummagumma*. Were the structures' two faces looking at each other, or is it merely a single face looking out?

Norfolk

Norwich ⟩

Delia Smith, joint majority shareholder at Norwich City Football Club and the UK's best-selling cookery author, has more rock 'n' roll cred than her mumsy image portrays. No, she wasn't a Hawkwind groupie, nor '60s hippy chef Psychedelia Smith, who served acid-laced blancmange, magic mushroom crumble and hash brownies with a difference. It's a more traditional-looking bake that grants her a rock 'n' roll pedigree. Long before she showed the nation how to boil an egg, Delia made the famous birthday cake that appears on the cover of the 1969 Rolling Stones album, *Let It Bleed*.

The arched doorways and alcoves of buildings on Norwich's Colegate, north of the River Wensum, appear on

the montage sleeve of *What's this For!*, the second album by post-punk band Killing Joke, released in 1981.

Before he became a TV comedy actor and writer, Charlie Higson was a colourful student at Norwich's University of East Anglia, even sporting a blue mohican haircut for a while. In 1980 he formed a band and called himself Switch. At first they were The Higson 5, then The Higson Brothers and The Higson Experience, before deciding on The Higsons. By now, their quirky debut single, *I Don't Want To Live With Monkeys*, had been released on the indie Romans In Britain label.

John Peel gave it extensive airplay and the song reached number two in the indie chart. This led to periods with the record labels Waap, 2Tone and Upright Records. Their first album, *The Curse of The Higsons*, featured the wonderfully titled, *Where Have All The Club-A-Go-Gos Went Went?*. Robyn Hitchcock acknowledged them in his song, *Listening to the Higsons*, which includes the line:

> 'The Higsons come from Norwich/
> And they eat a lot of porridge'

Another line in the song refers to The Higsons' track, *Got To Let This Heat Out*:

> 'I thought I heard them singing/
> Gotta let this hen out'

Hitchcock and his band The Egyptians later used this for the title of their 1985 live album, *Gotta Let This Hen Out!*

The first venue in the UK to ban the Sex Pistols was Norwich's premier music venue, the 1,550-capacity LCR (Lower Common Room), situated within the University of East Anglia. It attracts the best live acts and can get pretty cramped for sold-out gigs (there are steps down to the moshpit so most can get a good view if they hang back). The Waterfront (another venue owned by the Union of University of East Anglia Students) is Norwich's top alternative venue, and The Marquee in Rose Lane is the place to check out new bands.

Norwich Arts Centre, located in St Benedicts Street in the converted St Swithin's Church complete with tombstones, has been a leading light of the city's live music scene since 1980. It was at this venue, after a gig in May 1991, that iconic Manic Street Preachers guitarist and lyricist Richey Edwards made an artistic statement with a difference. He carved the words '4REAL' into his forearm with a razor blade. The troubled Manic was interviewed after a set by the then *NME* journalist Steve Lamacq, who questioned the Manics' authenticity, asking whether the band were for real. The answer was an emphatic, yes, as Edwards performed this gruesome act of self-harm. Lamacq was shocked and called an ambulance.

Until he was released in August 2009 on compassionate grounds, Ronnie Biggs was an inmate at Her Majesty's Prison Norwich, on Mousehold Heath. The Great Train Robber and one-time recording artist with the Sex Pistols sung on two songs in Julien Temple's Sex Pistols film, *The Great Rock 'n' Roll Swindle*. Both *No One Is Innocent* and *Belsen Was A Gas* were recorded at a studio in Biggs' exiled home country of Brazil, with Pistols guitarist Steve Jones and drummer Paul Cook.

In 2001, Biggs returned to the UK voluntarily and was promptly arrested. He spent several years in high-security Belmarsh Prison but, with his health rapidly declining, he was moved to Norwich prison. Labour Home Secretary Jack Straw finally freed Biggs on compassionate grounds in 2009, the day before his 80th birthday.

East Dereham

On 29 July, 1967, Pink Floyd had two gigs booked. Before they headed down to London for a high-profile show at the Alexandra Palace they had arranged a gig at East Dereham's Wellington Club. Restive locals welcomed them by chanting abuse, and, just moments into their light show, empty pint glasses started to sail through the air into Nick Mason's drum kit. They teased out a shortened version of *Interstellar Overdrive* before grabbing their guitars, shaking broken glass and beer off Mason's drum kit and throwing the lot into a van and racing to London in the band's Bentley. "I'll never forget that night," Roger Waters later said. "We played to a roomful of about 500 gypsies, hurling abuse and fighting, and then we did the Ally Pally."

Brit Award-winning singer-songwriter Beth Orton hails from East Dereham. It would have been hard for her to attend the Floyd gig because she was born three years later, in 1970. She lived locally before moving to east London aged 14.

Aylsham

The headless ghost of Anne Boleyn supposedly haunts Blickling Hall, near Aylsham; Henry VIII's unfortunate second wife was born here. More recently, in an episode of *I'm Alan Partridge*, everyone's favourite Radio Norwich DJ takes his Ukrainian girlfriend to Blickling Hall, telling her it's Bono's house and that he's a close friend of the U2 frontman.

Most years, Blickling Hall, owned by the National Trust, opens its grounds in the summer for a series of weekend outdoor concerts, with capacity for 6,000 people. Acts like Van Morrison, Bryan Ferry, Simply Red and Jools Holland have appeared here.

Great Yarmouth

Madness were another band who quickly excelled at making pop videos, specialising in witty three-minute mini-movies. The promo for the 1982 single, *House of Fun*, told the tale of an awkward teenager's visit to a chemist on his 16th birthday to buy some condoms. Most of the video was shot in London, but scenes of the north London Nutty Boys riding a rollercoaster were filmed at Great Yarmouth Pleasure Beach, including the finale of the band doing the 360-degree rollercoaster loop.

Mean, moody-looking and attired in traditional black costume, The Stranglers stood on seaweed-strewn boulders on Hunstanton Beach at low tide for the cover of their acclaimed 2004 album *Norfolk Coast*. Some 14 years after their original lead singer Hugh Cornwell left the band, it was their first album featuring Baz Warne as the band's guitarist and singer, with the three remaining original members: drummer Jet Black, bassist Jean-Jacques Burnel and organist Dave Greenfield.

Singer-songwriter David Gray says he finds inspiration for his songs on the beautiful north Norfolk coast, where he owns a seaside home in Holme-next-the-Sea, near Hunstanton. Since buying the property in the mid-noughties he has rekindled a childhood love of nature and bird-watching. "When I made some money, the first thing to do was get a cottage up here," Gray told BBC Norfolk in 2008.

He enjoys the Wensum Valley between Norwich and Fakenham, one of Norfolk's most diverse natural areas, and the open marshes and bird reserves of north Norfolk. When he first went to Blakeney, about 10 miles east of Hunstanton, he says he was "blown away" (not literally, we must presume) looking out over the marshes. You don't often see barn owls and marsh harriers in Crouch End, north London, where Gray has his recording studio.

Parts of the video for *Pure Shores* by All Saints were filmed at nearby Holkham Beach. The song was penned for the soundtrack of the 2000 film, *The Beach*, starring Leonardo DiCaprio. The other beaches in the video are pre-tsunami Phi Phi Islands in Thailand.

Roger Taylor, drummer of Queen – not Duran Duran's drummer of the same name – was born in Dersingham, just south of Hunstanton.

Two seaside halls along the coast between Sheringham and Cromer put rural Norfolk on the rock 'n' roll map. The hugely popular West Runton Pavilion and Cromer Royal Links Pavilion – often called 'the Links' – were the Jagger and Richards of Norfolk music venues.

From the 1960s to the 1980s, the Cromer Links and West Runton Pavilions were regular stop-off venues for bands on mid-size UK tours. For years, bands travelled to this rock 'n' roll backwater for a warm-up gig before national tours, keen to test their acts out in the sticks, away from the critical eyes of the city-based music papers.

The venues responded to the trends of the day. Instead of waltzes and ballroom dancing, along came pop and rock legends, glam rockers, through to splenetic punk bands like The Damned, The Buzzcocks and The Clash. One hardy regular used to cycle from Norwich to West Runton in full Teddy Boy costume.

Opening in 1973, the Pavilion audience would crowd the beer-soaked floors each week, whatever band was on, leaving a few hours later usually deafened and hungover for a week. A West Runton Pavilion crowd were stunned by the Sex Pistols' first visit in 1976; and the Pistols played their penultimate UK gig at the Cromer Links on Christmas Eve the following year. The Clash appeared at a Rock Against Racism concert at the Pavilion in 1979.

It was also a popular venue with a new wave of British heavy metal outfits like Iron Maiden, Magnum and Saxon – the inspiration for cult spoof rock film *Spinal Tap*. They flattered one audience with the semi-legendary: "West Runton, you're the rock 'n' roll capital of the world!"

Motörhead played the last gig at the Pavilion in 1983 as a thank you to a venue that welcomed them when others didn't. They brought their *Bomber* stage-set and equipment, which was designed for much larger venues like London's Hammersmith Odeon. If locals appear deaf when you ask for directions, it's probably because their ears are still ringing today.

Opening nearly a decade earlier in 1964, the Cromer Links was put on the map by The Who in 1967, when they smashed up their gear at the end of the gig in front of a rowdy crowd. A local hotel was asked to keep their restaurant open for the band after the show but was less than impressed when all they ordered was a glass of milk.

Another night, drunken blues legend Long John Baldry was driven to his Cromer hotel but instead of retiring for the night, he ran into the sea wearing his suit and shoes. A bomb hoax at a Slade gig in 1972 saw singer Noddy Holder offering a £50 reward to anyone who would identify the prankster.

The Links burned down in April 1978, and the Pavilion was demolished in February 1987, but both live on in the hearts of many. The Village Inn pub in West Runton commemorates the old venue with a blue plaque celebrating some of the legends that played there: Chuck Berry, T-Rex, Black Sabbath, Sex Pistols and The Clash.

Above and opposite page: West Runton's Pavillion hosted many a heavy metal gig. Among those to play were Saxon (opposite) who were later to become the inspiration for the cult spoof rock band *Spinal Tap*, and Motörhead.

Suffolk

Southwold

The term, boutique festival, is applied to any music festival that doesn't sell out within three minutes. One of these is Latitude, held each July on the Henham Park estate near Southwold on the Suffolk coast. Voted Best Music Festival by BBC 6 Music listeners in its first year, 2006, when the headline acts were The Zutons and Snow Patrol, it's since been described as a more laid-back Glastonbury with smaller crowds. As well as live music from top-name mainstream bands, Latitude offers poetry, literary events, cabaret, comedy and theatre performances, spread across four stages.

Stowmarket

The untimely death of BBC Radio 1 DJ John Peel in 2004 robbed the nation of a much-loved musical hero, credited with propelling hundreds of bands to fame. The DJ is buried in the graveyard of Great Finborough, the village where he lived for 33 years, a few miles southwest of Stowmarket. "Teenage dreams, so hard to beat," a line from his favourite song, *Teenage Kicks* by The Undertones, appears on his gravestone, a song he famously promoted on his show. And the Liver Bird, the emblem of Peel's other passion, Liverpool FC, sits above it.

Peel moved to the village in the 1970s with his family, into a thatched cottage which he named Peel Acres, and broadcast many of his shows from his house studio. Peel was Radio 1's longest-serving DJ when he died in October 2004, aged 65. It took three DJs to replace him and no natural successor

for him has been found. As the unrivalled champion of new British music for nearly four decades on his late-night show, he discovered some of the most influential bands of recent history, including Pulp and The Smiths.

Some 3,000 mourners attended his funeral on 12 November, 2004 at St Edmundsbury cathedral, Bury St Edmunds, including many of the artists he championed. Peel's coffin, garlanded with red flowers in honour of his beloved Liverpool, was carried out of the church to a recording of *You'll Never Walk Alone* before it segued into *Teenage Kicks*.

Right: The irreplaceable John Peel.
Opposite page: The Darkness, entertaining performers from Lowestoft.

In 2010, Peel's son Tom Ravenscroft followed in his father's footsteps, landing his own weekly show on the BBC digital station, 6 Music. Evidently a chip off the old block, he too is a champion of new artists.

Lowestoft

The seaside resort of Lowestoft claims three very different contributions to English music. First, legendary composer Benjamin Britten was born there in 1913 and began composing prolifically at the age of seven.

Lowestoft's other contributions to music would not be welcome at the Aldeburgh classical music festival, which Britten founded in 1948 – they are much too rock'n'roll for that. In fact, they heralded an unashamed return to fist-raising rock, throwbacks to a time when long-haired rock dinosaurs ruled the world. Glam-rock revivalists The Darkness hail from Oulton Broad, just outside Lowestoft, and first got it together on Millennium Eve, 1999, at The Gillingham Swan, near Beccles, a traditional English pub owned by their aunt.

Singer Justin Hawkins and his brother Dan were sitting drinking at the bar when *Bohemian Rhapsody* came on the jukebox. Immediately, Justin Hawkins jumped off his seat and started performing to the song. His guitarist brother instantly saw him as frontman material and they formed The Darkness on the spot.

Some of their songs were inspired by Lowestoft and the surrounding north Suffolk countryside, like *Black Shuck*, the opener on their debut album, *Permission to Land*. The song is the tale of an apocryphal black dog that haunts the East Anglia coastline. In the 16th century a dog caused mayhem in the village church at Blythburgh near Southwold, killing two of the congregation and causing the collapse of the church tower:

> 'In a town in the east/
> The parishioners were visited upon/
> By a curious beast/
> And his eyes numbered but one and shone like the sun/
> And a glance beckoned the immediate loss/
> Of a cherished one.'

Three of The Darkness (the Hawkins brothers and drummer Ed Graham) were schooled at Lowestoft's Kirkley Community High School. Rather aptly, the comprehensive was the

location for the second series of Channel 4's *Rock School*, filmed in 2005, where Kiss legend Gene Simmons attempted to transform some Lowestoft teenagers into a rock band.

The undoubted star of the series was a rock singer with the rap name Chris Hardman, or Lil'Chris, who, at four feet 11 inches, was the shortest boy in the school. He was signed to the Sony label, RCA Records. Gene Simmons was full of praise for the diminutive singer but not the seaside town. "He's a David in a Goliath world," said Simmons. "He has the heart of a lion, charisma and delusional self-confidence despite living in Lowestoft, which is the most depressing place I have seen."

Ipswich

Jarvis Cocker immortalised Suffolk's county town in *Auschwitz to Ipswich* on 2006's *Jarvis*, written and performed by the ex-Pulp frontman. The song was inspired by someone he met, whose relative was interned in a Second World War prisoner-of-war camp near Ipswich. The phrase came to Cocker and he couldn't resist using it:

> 'It's the same from Auschwitz to Ipswich/
> Evil comes/
> I know from not where/
> But if you take a look inside yourself/
> Maybe you'll find some in there.'

Football is not the only thing played at Ipswich Town Football Club's 30,000-seat ground, Portman Road. The stadium has hosted some major gigs in recent years, including REM, Dire Straits and Rod Stewart.

"Ipswich? Where's Ipswich?" Red Hot Chili Peppers singer Anthony Kiedis asked the Portman Road crowd on the first night of the Los Angeles band's UK tour in July 2006. It was a refreshing take on the standard touring rock band greeting of: "Hello [insert location name]. How you doin'?"

Woodbridge

Composer, performer and producer, Brian Peter George St John le Baptiste de la Salle Eno – better known as Brian Eno – was born in the Suffolk town of Woodbridge in 1948. His proximity to American air bases, coffee bars and GIs while he was growing up meant he was exposed to American R&B and doo-wop music from an early age. He started as a drummer in his teenage rock'n'roll band The Black Aces in Woodbridge, back in 1964. A little later he was the feather boa-clad one in Roxy Music but left after their second album, *For Your Pleasure*, in 1973.

Influential and innovative, he pioneered the whole thread of ambient music, production techniques and was an early exponent of sampling on the 1981 album he made with David Byrne, *My Life in the Bush of Ghosts*. One of his compositions, the title track of *Another Green World*, was the theme tune to the BBC's long-running arts programme, *Arena*. And, as for the six-second start-up sounds of the Windows 95 operating system, yep, that was Eno too. He has collaborated with David Bowie, Talking Heads, Coldplay and U2. Bono famously said of Eno: "A lot of English rock'n'roll bands went to art school. We went to Brian."

Eno hails from a long line of Suffolk postmen and, as a child, he was a keen fossil collector who used to cycle to places like Butley Crag and nearby beaches. He drew inspiration from the Suffolk landscape of his childhood in later compositions, most notably on 1982's *Ambient 4: On Land*. Several pieces on the album are about places where he grew up: Dunwich Beach (see Four Seasons box), Lantern Marsh near Orford and Leeks Hills, a little wood located between Woodbridge and Melton.

Woodbridge's other musical luminary is Charlie Simpson from Busted.

Left: Brian Eno, born in Woodbridge and relentlessly creative.

The Four Seasons (alternate take): AUTUMN

Autumn Almanac, The Kinks

An obvious choice, but this 1967 music hall-style classic by The Kinks had to be here. It's pop poet laureate Ray Davies at his very best: closely-observed imagery and a celebration of the English and their little eccentricities:

'Breeze blows leaves over, mostly coloured yellow/
So I sweep them in my sack/
Yes, yes, yes, it's my autumn almanac.'

Dunwich Beach, Autumn 1960, Brian Eno

This is the closing track on 1982's *Ambient 4: On Land*, Eno's first collaboration with co-producer and multi-instrumentalist Daniel Lanois. To some, it is pretentious twaddle and the best cure for insomnia since the House of Commons was first televised. To others, it is breathtaking music of astounding beauty.

Harvest Festival, XTC

Perfect pastoral English pop from 1999's *Apple Venus Volume 1*. Andy Partridge's wistful and wonderful evocation of first love is set amid a stuffy school hall at harvest time:

'See the children with baskets/
See their hair cut like corn neatly combed in their rows.'

Take The Glory, Badly Drawn Boy

Strictly speaking this is a song about summer ending and winter starting, so it probably qualifies. From the Dave Lee Travis look-a-like's 2004 album of personal songs, *One Plus One Is One*.

'Summer feels like its over/
Winter is on the way/
Summer takes all the glory
Blue skies are turning to grey.'

Also hear:

Harvest Breed by Nick Drake, *Autumn Leaves* by Coldcut and, of course, anything on the now-defunct Harvest Records, launched by EMI in 1969, where Deep Purple and Pink Floyd found a home.

Essex

Epping Forest

Deep in the heart of Essex, the ancient woodland of Epping Forest was once a large royal hunting forest reserved for the likes of Elizabeth I and Henry VIII. Now it's a place of refuge for anyone.

In 1665, Londoners decamped here in the hope the greenery would shield them from the Great Plague. Centuries later, during World War II, Londoners once again turned to Epping Forest for sanctuary, evacuating there away from the air raids.

A few decades later, in the 1970s, no self-respecting prog rock group released an album without a gatefold sleeve, providing bands with a larger canvas for their ideas, artwork and concepts too big for a standard cover. For many fans it probably just provided additional space on which to roll a crafty number.

An Epping Forest blanketed with autumn leaves appears on the inside gatefold sleeve of prog rockers Emerson Lake & Palmer's 1972's *Trilogy*, featuring a photomontage of several images of the band.

A year later fellow prog rockers Genesis wrote about the place on their album, *Selling England By The Pound*. Clocking in at a suitably proggy 11 minutes and 49 seconds, *The Battle of Epping Forest* recounts the story of a turf war between two rival East End gangs.

Another Genesis – Genesis P-Orridge and his industrial experimental band Throbbing Gristle – recorded a track called *Epping Forest* on their 1982 album, *Assume Power Focus*. The young P-Orridge (born plain Neil Megson and often dubbed 'the sickest man in Britain') once lived in Loughton on the edge of Epping Forest.

Welsh rockers Feeder can be seen prancing around Epping Forest in the video for their 1996 single, *Stereo World*, while *Famous Groupies*, a song on Wings' 1977 album, *London Town*, tells the tale of a lead guitarist from Epping Forest.

In 1967, a young artist called Jeremy Ratter changed his name to Penny Rimbaud and moved into Dial House, a tumbledown cottage near Epping, with Dagenham-born artist friend Gee Vaucher. Over the next four decades the

Right: Genesis P-Orridge of experiemental outfit, Throbbing Gristle.
Opposite page: Emerson Lake & Palmer's *Trilogy* album artwork featured Epping Forest.

open-house bohemian community hosted artists, musicians, writers and outsiders. Out of it emerged a series of radical cultural, artistic and political projects.

The best-known of these was the anarchist-punk band Crass, formed in 1977, arguably the most extreme band, musically and politically, to emerge from the punk movement. While other punk bands preached anarchy, Crass lived it. They advocated self-sufficiency as a way of living and working outside what they saw as a straitjacket system of conventional employment.

They used punk's do-it-yourself ethos to get their message across, rallying against a society obsessed with consumerism, war and religion, and found a hungry audience amongst those who felt alienated by Thatcherism.

Aided by a cheap pricing policy, their records topped the indie charts for weeks. Crass gigs were often in small venues, such as scout huts and church halls, and ticket sales often benefited CND, Rape Crisis and other causes.

The band ran everything themselves at their Epping commune, away from the music industry machine. They set up their own record label and created their own stencilled polemical sleeves with a Gestetner duplicating machine.

Typed lyric sheets were often useful to decipher what was being shouted alongside a racket of dissonant guitars. The free-thinking radicals also sent their fans self-produced leaflets on topics ranging from nuclear disarmament to vegetarianism and environmental issues, long before such things were fashionable or as urgent.

Crass were hugely influential, inspiring many bands and encouraging emerging artists. The Crass label put out early music by Chumbawamba, Björk, when she led the Icelandic punk band Kukl, and Flux of Pink Indians, who released their first single on the Crass label in 1981.

The band split in 1984 and retreated to artists' studios and organic gardens. Penny Rimbaud and Gee Vaucher bought the house at auction, saving it from property developers who wanted to build on the last remaining green belt around London. It is now run as an arts centre, hosting weekend workshops and debates.

Banned by the Beeb

Celebrate The Bullet, The Selecter
Despite it's anti-violence message, the title track of The Selecter's second album, a portentous mid-tempo reggae number about gun culture, was banned by the BBC in 1981. Its release coincided with the assassination attempt on US President Ronald Reagan by John Hinckley Jr.

Fairytale of New York, The Pogues and Kirsty MacColl
Was this political correctness gone mad? The week before Christmas 2007, BBC Radio 1 edited out the words 'slut' and 'faggot' from the song for fear of causing offence, but later reversed the decision following criticism from listeners, The Pogues and MacColl's mother, Jean Newlove.

God Save the Queen, Sex Pistols
'They made you a moron/
A potential H-bomb'

Having recently been dropped by EMI but quickly scooped up by Virgin, Sex Pistols manager Malcolm McLaren was keen to promote his protégés' new single. So, while a country waved Union flags in honour of the Queen's Silver Jubilee, McLaren hired a river boat – called none other than the Queen Elizabeth – to sail along the Thames whilst the band played. Despite a nationwide ban on the band already in force, *God Save The Queen* stormed into the official UK Singles Chart at number two, dubiously kept off the top spot by Rod Stewart's *I Don't Want To Talk About It*.

Relax, Frankie Goes to Hollywood
January 1984. Nearly two decades after the furore of the Sex Pistols, it was the turn of Liverpool's Frankie Goes to Hollywood to become public enemy number one, in the BBC's eyes anyway. In a move with strong echoes of 1976, the Beeb banned *Relax*, enabling it to rocket to the number one slot and, of course, attain legendary status. Halfway through playing the song on his peak-time morning show, Radio 1 DJ Mike Read suddenly announced the lyrics were 'obscene' and refused to play it again. The rest of the BBC followed suit and banned the song, due to its reference to gay sex acts. The song had been steadily climbing the charts, but within a fortnight of Read's intervention, the song was number one, where it stayed for four weeks.

Spasticus Autisticus, Ian Dury and the Blockheads
Written in 1981 as a disdainful "war cry" in response to that year's International Year of Disabled Persons, Dury's song was banned by the BBC for its use of the word 'spastic'. Dury, himself left crippled by childhood polio, commented later: "So, that means in 1982 everyone was going to be all right? I thought it was a load of bollo', so I wrote a song about it." The title is inspired by the end of Stanley Kubrick's film, *Spartacus*, where the protective Roman gladiators all chant "I'm Spartacus!" when ordered to identify their leader.

Also banned
Arnold Layne by Pink Floyd, *(We Don't Need This) Fascist Groove Thang* by Heaven 17, *Smack My Bitch Up* by The Prodigy, *We Call It Acieeed* by D Mob and *A Day In The Life* by The Beatles.

Barking

Apart from forces' sweetheart Dame Vera Lynn, Barking has produced Billy Bragg, now universally known as 'the Bard of Barking' (see box). A cover of his song, *A New England*, was a hit for Kirsty MacColl who is connected to the area by her legendary folk singer father, Ewan MacColl (one of the founders of the Theatre Workshop with his wife, Joan Littlewood).

Barking's other unlikely local boy is U2's guitarist The Edge – real name David Evans – who was born here in 1961, although he and his family moved back to Dublin soon after.

It's easy to visualise Canadian rock legend Neil Young singing about prairie winds while strumming Hank Williams's old guitar; not so easy to picture him lying in a bed provided by Barking Council. This was the case during the recording session for *A Man Needs a Maid* and *There's a World* with the London Symphony Orchestra for his classic album, *Harvest*, released in 1972. Young chose Barking Town Hall as the venue to record these two tracks whilst bed-bound with a back injury.

Dagenham

Ok, so it's not quite Motown, but Dagenham has a musical legacy many towns would crash a car for. It was built up around the Ford factory (in an ideal world 1970s pub-rockers The Motors should have come from here).

Dagenham has been the inspiration for two songs, both called *Dagenham Dave*. Morrissey's 1995 single was about an archetypal Essex wide boy, while the other by The Stranglers on *No More Heroes*, told the story of a passionate fan of the band who threw himself off Tower Bridge in February 1977. Although he came from Manchester, Stranglers frontman Hugh Cornwell nicknamed him Dagenham Dave because he had worked at the town's Ford plant.

After she left school, local Dagenham girl Sandra Goodrich worked at the Ford plant until she resigned one day, telling factory floor colleagues she was going to be a singing star. She found early success singing in a local talent competition and was soon spotted by Adam Faith. Within a few months she had a new name, Sandie Shaw, and was appearing on *Top of the Pops* with her first number one, the Bacharach and David song, *(There's) Always Something There To Remind Me*.

Three years later she won the 1967 Eurovision Song Contest for the UK with *Puppet on a String*. Many years later, in 1984, she appeared on *Top of the Pops* again, performing *Hand in Glove* with The Smiths. It was a memorable appearance, with the Swinging Sixties icon rolling around in a black leather dress. Few pop stars in recent years have looked like they're having so much fun.

Depeche Mode's Martin Gore spent the first three years of his life in Dagenham, where both his parents worked at the Ford car factory.

Also hailing from Dagenham is Brian Poole, lead singer of 1960s group Brian Poole and The Tremeloes. Formed in Dagenham in 1958, they have gone down in history as the band Decca signed at the expense of The Beatles. On New Year's Day in 1962, the label was on the prowl for a 'Beat' group and auditioned two promising new bands, The Tremeloes and four young mop-tops from Liverpool. Decca preferred The Tremeloes, believing their sound was more marketable and that guitar bands were on the way out. (The Tremeloes are still going today.)

Brian Poole's daughters are Shelly and Karen Poole, better known as pop duo, Alisha's Attic, while the son of Tremeloes bassist Len 'Chip' Hawkes, is Chesney, best-known for his 1991 one-and-only chart-topper.

The Dagenham Roundhouse, also known as the Village Blues Club, in Lodge Avenue was a legendary rock venue at the turn of the 1960s and 1970s. Many acts from Led

Above: Dagenham's very own Sandie Shaw in 1968.

Tilbury was the port for me

EVER since a large number of West Indian immigrants settled in England after the Second World War, their influence on the music scene has been immense.

When the decaying troopship, the *SS Empire Windrush*, docked at Tilbury in June 1948, its passengers were the first wave of post-war Caribbean immigrants to reach the UK. On board the *Windrush*, seeking a new life in the UK, were two of Trinidad's most famous calypso singers, Aldwyn 'Lord Kitchener' Roberts and Egbert 'Lord Beginner' Moore.

Shortly after their arrival, calypso music – songs and lyrics associated with the Trinidad Carnival – was performed in small clubs and dance halls. The songs told of the new immigrants' experiences in their adopted land: from specific events like the victory of the West Indies cricket team at Lords in 1950 to the Queen's Coronation two years later. There were observations about strange aspects of English daily life: the drab weather, interfering landladies and travelling on the Underground.

In his book, *Bass Culture*, author Lloyd Bradley says the calypso music became "the official soundtrack of black Britain" in the 1950s and early 1960s.

Nowadays it's impossible to envisage what England would be like had the *Windrush* never docked at Tilbury. Certainly there would be no annual Notting Hill Carnival, no sound systems, reggae or bluebeat. There would also be no jungle music, rap, techno, house and ska, which would in turn mean no Steel Pulse, The Specials, The Selecter, Tinchy Stryder, Sting and The Police, no Lily Allen and probably only half of The Clash.

Northern Whale, a track by Damon Albarn and Paul Simonon's supergroup, The Good The Bad & the Queen, mentions Tilbury docks:

'It pulls you further out to sea/
Under the lights at Tilbury/
Life still love/
Your melody.'

Zeppelin to Black Sabbath performed here. Just around the corner, near Mayesbrook Park, is Bragg Close, a local road named in honour of local hero Billy Bragg.

The late comedian and musician Dudley Moore used to play the organ at Becontree's St Thomas church.

Billlericay

'Had a love affair with Nina, in the back of my Cortina/
A seasoned up hyena could not have been obscener.'

Imagine one of William Cobbett's 19th-century rural rides undertaken by a modern-day Essex swaggerer. Using double entendres and his rhyming genius, Ian Dury put the Essex commuter town of Billericay on the map with his memorable send-up of an Essex wide-boy, *Billericay Dickie* from 1977's *New Boots and Panties!!*.

This masterful meeting of music hall bawdiness and rock 'n' roll chronicles the exploits of the eponymous mouthy brickie and his conquests, which include the aforementioned Nina, plus Janet and Sandy. Many lesser-known Essex towns are name-checked in the song, such as Shoeburyness, the Isle of Thanet and Burnham-on-Crouch. *Billericay Dickie* is an Essex travelogue, the likes of which you won't see in the travel pages.

It has been stated that Billericay was Dury's home-town. It wasn't. He was born in Harrow, Middlesex, but sometimes claimed he was from Upminster (see Ian Dury box).

Harlow

The massive banks of synthesisers and electronic equipment that dominate a Chemical Brothers set are a throwback to the heady days of progressive rock but they couldn't sound more different. Tom Rowlands and Ed Simons, aka the Chemical Brothers, are not from Harlow but they chose the new Essex town for the sleeve of their 1998 collection of remixes, *Brothers Gonna Work It Out*. The cover features the modern Catholic church, Our Lady of Fatima in Howard Way.

The church hall is available for hire and hosts dance classes but Britain's biggest dance act are now probably a tad too successful to DJ here.

BASILDON TO THE FUTURE

N March 2010, Basildon erected its own five-foot Hollywood-style sign, welcoming visitors to the Essex new town as part of a marketing project. The sign was originally meant to read: 'Basildon, Home of Depeche Mode and Not Much Else' but the extra signage cost too much.

Joking aside, Depeche Mode's Andy Fletcher once memorably described his home-town as the town that went wrong. "One reason the band are still around today, he says, is that their work ethic stems from the fact none of them want to go back there.

Built to accommodate the burgeoning post-war population from London's East End, Basildon won't win any beauty awards, nor top any pop pilgrimage lists. In fact, the mere mention of Basildon evokes self-satisfied smiles of snobbery amongst England's middle classes. Knowing looks dismiss the town as a soulless urban sprawl from which nothing good ever comes. But that's clearly not true. Basildon has produced one of England's most successful bands.

No members of the chart-topping 1980s synth-pop band Depeche Mode were actually born in Basildon, but they all grew up there from an early age. Despite vitriolic criticism from the music press – including a savage mauling by a young (Steven) Morrissey in *Record Mirror* – Depeche Mode went on to massive mainstream success in Europe and the US. In 2009, they packed out Paris's Stade de France to 100,000 fans.

Before they played the London clubs as part of the New Romantic, scene they would headline their local disco, Croc's Glamour Club in nearby Rayleigh on Saturday nights.

Croc's is now the Pink Toothbrush, above the concrete shopping mall in the High Street. Depeche Mode's origins go back to the late 1970s, when Vince Clarke and schoolmate Andy Fletcher formed the band No Romance in China, while at Basildon's Nicholas Comprehensive. In 1979, they renamed themselves French Look, then Composition of Sound and,

when Martin Gore joined, they ditched their guitars in favour of synthesisers. Finally, in 1980, with new recruit Dave Gahan on board, they adopted the name Depeche Mode, the title of a French fashion magazine.

In the 1970s, as factories closed down and unemployment grew, Basildon was a volatile place to be. Martin Gore hated his late teenage years in Basildon and recalls it as a violent place with nothing to do. Singer Gahan was sometimes beaten up because he dressed unusually, and Gore would be ridiculed for wearing black nail varnish.

At the end of the 1970s, mainstream record labels were ignoring electronic bands. Enter Daniel Miller, musician and founder of Britain's first electronic indie label, Mute Records, initially just an outlet for Miller's own post-punk outfits The Normal and Silicon Teens. He discovered the Basildon band that would swell the Mute labels coffers one night in November 1980, when they supported Mute act Fad Gadget in a Canning Town pub better known for Oi! bands, the now-demolished Bridge House in Barking Road. The quartet played four mono-synths balanced on beer crates and were immediately offered a record contract. Miller introduced them to sequencers, and they soon evolved into his real-life Silicon Teens, becoming a huge hit-making pop act.

The band were initially dismissed as lightweight pretty-boy teeny-boppers, but they helped transform the synthesiser from geeky exploratory device used by beardy soundtrack composers to every budding pop star's instrument of choice. When synth-pop reigned for a few years in the early 1980s, the instrument replaced guitars as the preferred pop tool of the time.

After their first album, songwriter Vince Clarke unexpectedly left his childhood mates in 1981 to form the groundbreaking synth-pop duo Yazoo, fronted by the R&B voice of Alison Moyet, another Basildon native. (Strictly speaking she was born in Billericay but grew up in Basildon, where

she was a singer in Basildon punk band The Vandals.) They'd first met aged 11 at the same Basildon Saturday morning music school. Yazoo also signed to Mute Records, but after 18 months the pair split. Clarke set up Erasure and Moyet went on to have a successful solo career.

Under the new direction of the band's main songwriter and guitarist Martin Gore, Depeche Mode got increasingly darker, moving away from synth pop and towards goth rock. Gore took to wearing leather skirts, their sound became heavier, their songs edgier and more socially aware, dealing with politics, mass consumerism and sadomasochism. Despite often releasing albums with titles that sound like brands of condom (*Ultra, Exciter, Violator*), and despite frontman Gahan battling serious heroin addiction, the band have proved they are Essex boys with serious staying power.

Britpop's Pioneers

To many listeners, Britpop pioneers Blur were natural heirs to Ray Davies and The Kinks' tradition of English suburban songwriting that sees magic in the mundane. Furthermore, Blur's music spoke to their peers in a way that only a rare breed of British rock groups have managed. Many of their songs, in particular on *Modern Life Is Rubbish*, *Parklife* and *The Great Escape*, captured the zeitgeist, reflecting the cultural shifts happening in Britain.

Blur frontman Damon Albarn's early years were spent living in multicultural east London, but his family moved to the outskirts of all-white Colchester when he was nine. He later described the place as "a small country town with Thatcherite aspirations: the worst combination."

Blur really started way back in 1980 when Albarn met guitarist Graham Coxon at Colchester's Stanway Comprehensive School where they sang in the same choir. Albarn's father, Keith, had been involved in the late-1960s psychedelic rock movement, managing The Soft Machine. Coxon and Albarn started performing with drummer Dave Rowntree who worked for Colchester Council programming computers. Alex James first met Coxon and then the rest of the band in the late 1980s, as a student at Goldsmiths College in south London.

Under the very un-rock 'n' roll name Seymour, they gigged around London before sensibly renaming themselves Blur in 1989, and signing to Food Records later that year.

When Albarn moved to Colchester, the area was still largely countryside but, in the early '80s, he saw property developers transform fields into estates, what Albarn called "Barrett House white suburbia." He saw these developments as symptomatic of the creeping Americanisation of English life, and started to write songs.

Their second album, 1993's *Modern Life Is Rubbish*, set the benchmark for the genre "what is known as" Britpop. The album's satire of modern suburban life and celebration of Englishness was a backlash against America. Songs like *Sunday Sunday* evoked Sunday newspapers, the traditional roast lunch and snoozing in front of *Songs of Praise* on TV. Blur also unleashed the first of Albarn's unhinged Essex characters, the "modern retard" *Colin Zeal*.

The following year's *Parklife* further celebrated the sometimes comical eccentricities of English life, and thrust Blur firmly into the mainstream. Albarn intended the album's songs as a sketch of British life in the mid-'90s, with firm nods to psychedelia, punk, synth pop and the long-standing wellspring of British pop, music hall. The album that ignited Britpop featured sing-a-long anthems like *Girls & Boys* and the title track, a modern mod classic voiced by *Quadrophenia* star Phil Daniels. Listeners were introduced to another of Albarn's desperate Essex characters, *Tracy Jacks*, a golf-loving civil servant who buckles under the pressures of modern life. He escapes to Walton-on-the-Naze, on the Essex border near Clacton, and decides to demolish his house.

Parklife reached number one in April 1994 and won the band four Brit Awards in 1995. The next release, *The Great Escape*, shot straight into the UK album charts at number one, selling over one million copies.

Their fifth album, the self-titled *Blur*, released in 1997, featured further portrayals of Essex life, most memorably on *Essex Dogs*: from the idyllic "watching dogs somersault through sprinklers on tiny lawns" to a menacing violent undercurrent of "terminal pubs."

In 2002, Coxon's alcohol problems meant he was asked to leave the band after not showing for the first session for the *Think Tank* album. The band members spent many years apart, in which Albarn worked with Malian musicians, scored an Anglo-Chinese opera and launched his cartoon-fronted Gorillaz, and James made more cheese than music at his Oxfordshire farm.

Blur didn't play again until re-forming for an emotional headline performance at Glastonbury 2009 and for two concerts in London's Hyde Park. However, a fortnight before Glastonbury, they played a small comeback concert, their first show for nine years at a restored goods shed at the East Anglian Railway Museum at Chappel and Wakes Colne railway station near Colchester, using a vintage carriage as a dressing room. This was the site of their first-ever public appearance in 1988, and a plaque commemorating the band has been erected there in their honour.

Right: Keith Flint, immediately recognisable mentalist from The Prodigy.
Left: Blur's *Modern Life is Rubbish*.

Braintree

Braintree's The Prodigy were arguably the Sex Pistols for the rave generation. They came together at all-nighters in a Braintree acid house club called The Barn. Liam Howlett, a talented pianist who grew up in Chelmsford then Braintree, and dancers Keith Flint and Leeroy Thornhill were regulars there.

Howlett had previously released a hip-hop song as part of an act called Cut 2 Kill. When Flint asked him to make him a dance compilation tape, Howlett responded with some dance tunes and some break-beat-driven tracks he'd created in his home studio.

The Prodigy emerged in 1990 and their single, *Charly*, reached number three the following year, becoming a huge rave anthem.

The band's lively, leering vocalist, Braintree-born and -raised Flint, once modestly described himself as a stage diver who crashed the stage and never got chucked off.

Their second album, 1994's *Music For The Jilted Generation*, firmly planted politics on the dancefloor, delivering a damning verdict on the government's Criminal Justice Bill, which targeted rave parties and, in effect, rave culture itself. A line on the track, *Their Law*, is uncompromising:

> 'Crack down at sundown/
> F*** 'em and their law'

In the early 1970s, a few years before Steve Harley hit the number one spot with *Make Me Smile (Come Up and See Me)* in 1975, he was a reporter on the local newspaper the *Braintree and Witham Times*.

Is it a place or person? Romford residents know Harold Hill as a post-war new town, but to many others it sounds more like the name of everyone's favourite friendly elderly neighbour who clings to his wife's arm en route to the post office and sprays digestive biscuit crumbs over you when he stops for a chat. Rhyming virtuoso Ian Dury's Harold Hill was more into DIY and self-harm in a memorable verse of *This Is What We Find*, from Dury's 1979, album *Do It Yourself*:

> 'Home improvement expert Harold Hill from Harold Hill/
> Of do it yourself dexterity and double glazing skill/
> Came home to find another gentlemen's kippers in the grill/
> So he sanded off his winkle with his Black & Decker drill'.

Romford's South Street, near the railway station, is name-checked in Ian Dury's tale of teenage shoplifting and soft-porn, *Razzle In My Pocket*.

Singer-songwriter Imogen Heap hails from Romford, born there in 1977. Her popularity and sales were boosted by the use of her music on the US TV series *The OC*.

Southend-on-Sea ⟩

Formerly thriving English seaside resorts like Southend could easily be the model for Morrissey's *Everyday Is Like Sunday*: once vibrant but now faded and living on past glories. Once popular with day-trippers, Southend used to

Above: The Kursaal Flyers at the Kursaal amusement arcade in Southend-on-Sea, 1975.

boast the biggest fairground in the south of England. In the 1950s it proved such a draw that visitors slept on the beach, unable to find hotel rooms.

The town is immortalised by that most English of bands, The Kinks, in their 1968 song, *Picture Book*, which recalls, "A holiday in August, outside a bed and breakfast in sunny Southend."

The Kursaal Flyers named themselves after the Kursaal theme park on Southend's Eastern Esplanade. They made their debut in February 1974 at Southend's Blue Boar pub and had a hit in late 1976 with *Little Does She Know*, produced by Mike Batt of The Wombles fame.

Kursaals drummer Will Birch later became a music journalist, writing a book about the pub rock scene and an Ian Dury biography.

Built at the start of the 20th century, the ballroom of the Kursaal (a spa, or cure-hall in German) had a fine dancefloor and was visited by famous bands and orchestras: Ted Heath and his orchestra, Johnny Dankworth and Cleo Laine all graced the stage. Vera Lynn also began her singing career here, with resident bandleader Howard Baker.

Southend was the closest coastal resort to London's East End and a popular day-trip destination. The Kursaal attracted hordes of mods and teddy boys who visited Southend at weekends and bank holidays. They would get drunk in pubs near the station before heading to the park to ride the dodgems and pick fights with punch-bag machines.

The Kursaal closed in the 1970s with much of the land sold for housing development, but its listed entrance hall remains and has been reopened as an entertainment complex.

Southend enjoyed a thriving 1960s coffee bar scene, with outlets with evocative names like Shades, Capri, Zanzibar and Panda. Shades was a seafront coffee bar popular with mods, owned and run by the parents of guitarist Robin Trower, who grew up in Southend. Trower formed local band The Paramounts with his co-Southend High School pupil and friend, Gary Brooker. They would go on to form Procol Harum.

Cliffs Pavilion, in nearby Westcliff-on-Sea, was the venue of a momentous Oasis gig in 1995, when they performed *Live Forever*, *Good to Be Free*, *Supersonic*, *Some Might Say* and a cover of The Beatles, *I Am the Walrus*. The concert was later released as a DVD package called *Live By The Sea*.

Southend's top live venue is Chinnerys on Marine Parade, hosting major signed acts and local bands.

Weirdness, eccentricity and the desire – and courage – to be different have long been the wellspring of English culture. The wonderfully singular Vivian Stanshall grew up

The Bard of Barking

GUITAR over his shoulder, politics on his sleeve, singer-songwriter Billy Bragg is a custodian of the long rock music tradition of dissent and protest. He's an artist who has always put content before style in a business that often worships image. He was arrested in 1983 during an anti-apartheid sit-in outside South Africa House; he backed the miners' strike and staged benefit concerts in support of the sacked Liverpool dockers. He also campaigned fiercely for Labour's Red Wedge in the 1980s to appeal to younger voters. And, in the 2010, election he rallied against the British National Party in Barking and Dagenham. He's also done his own Johnny Cash-style prison gigs, at Liverpool Prison in Walton; his Jail Guitar Doors project (named after the 1978 song by The Clash), provides musical instruments for serving inmates. He even wrote a book, *The Progressive Patriot*, claiming English socialists can wrestle patriotism back from the far right. During all his activism somehow he also found time to write some songs: bittersweet love songs, rooted in Englishness, as often as not with serious polemical content.

Born in 1957, Bragg's political consciousness was pricked when he saw the National Front campaigning outside his school gates at Barking Abbey Comprehensive. His musical career started in 1977, in the punk band Riff Raff, and when they fizzled out, he joined the Queen's Royal Irish Hussars tank regiment for a few years, before returning to music, and striking out as a solo artist

One night, the unsigned Bragg famously rushed to the Radio 1 studios, armed with a copy of his record and an Indian takeaway, after DJ John Peel had announced on air that he was hungry. Peel played some of Bragg's song and, not for first time, launched a career.

Thanks to his amenably blokish manner, no one was surprised when he called his 1996 album *William Bloke* and his backing band, The Blokes; it included keyboardist Ian McLagan, a boyhood hero from the Small Faces. Bragg has collaborated with REM, Johnny Marr, Kirsty MacColl, Kate Nash, Natalie Merchant and Wilco (that's America's alt-country rockers, not Canvey Island's Wilko Johnson). In late 1998 and 2000 he collaborated with the Chicago band to release two albums of Woody Guthrie's unrecorded lyrics set to his own music.

Bragg's song, *A13 Trunk Road To The Sea*, was an ingenious re-working of the Bobby Troup classic, *(Get Your Kicks On) Route 66*, made famous by Chuck Berry and The Rolling Stones, but relocated to his home county:

> 'It starts down in Wapping/
> There ain't no stopping/
> By-pass Barking and straight through Dagenham.'

Bragg told London's *Time Out* magazine that if Bruce Springsteen could romanticise New Jersey, he didn't see why he couldn't do the same for Essex. "I was sick of hearing people sing songs about America. How did we know that Amarillo, New Mexico, wasn't as dreary as Dagenham?"

Bragg now lives in Dorset, overlooking the sea, but his mother, Marie – named after music hall queen Marie Lloyd – still lives in the same Barking house her son grew up in the 1950s and '60s.

in Southend as an awkward child with little in common with his family. Aged 13, he had already decided to swap his Essex accent for a Noël Coward lilt and to dress like a dandy. Within a few years he would meet another conceptualist art student Neil Innes and form The Bonzo Dog Doo-Dah Band (originally called The Bonzo Dog *Dada* Band).

Southend's Eddie and the Hot Rods started life in 1975, when four local teenagers formed a band and started playing their own manic style of R&B. None of them was called Eddie; instead they were fronted by the energetic Barrie Masters.

Their early gigs were in Southend pubs but they were soon an instant success on the London pub rock scene, signing to Island Records. Their bluesy harmonica player Lew Lewis was in the band for the release of their first two singles, before he was sacked from the Hot Rods.

In a bizarre scene worthy of *Monty Python's Flying*

Right: The Bonzo Dog Doo-Dah Band in 1967, the conceptual group of Vivian Stanshall and Neil Innes.
Below: From Southend pubs to big concerts – Eddie And The Hot Rods in 1977.

Circus, Lewis was sentenced to seven years in prison in 1987 for holding up a post office in the suburb of Westcliff on-Sea with a fake pistol, in a costume and riding on a shopping bike. The bungled robbery emanated from years of drug addiction and undiagnosed mental health problems.

Southend four-piece These New Puritans, led by singer-songwriter Jack Barnett and his twin brother drummer George, grew up in nearby Leigh-on-Sea. Their acclaimed second album, *Hidden*, which utilises a wide variety of instruments and sounds, from bassoons to synthesised drums, draws inspiration from the marshy landscapes of the Thames Estuary.

"And the Thames flows between the grass," a line from *We Want War*, emerged when Jack Barnett was travelling on a train to London. "It feels like the Thames is flowing underneath the ground, because the land looks like waves, you see the water coming up and it's not quite one or the other," he told the *Independent*.

These New Puritans were one of the local bands who revolved around the Junk club, opened in 2002, in the basement of the seafront Royal Hotel. Like most cultural forms, popular music is prey to the cult of the 'next big thing;' Southend got its day when the *NME* put another local gothic-garage band The Horrors on its cover. Suddenly, from nowhere, there was a 'Southend scene'.

Leigh-on-Sea's answer to Glastonbury is the annual Leigh Folk Festival at the end of June. It is Britain's largest free folk festival, with gigs taking place in the town's halls and pubs. The fun includes sacred harp singing, introductory drumming workshops, Scottish ceilidhs and an open-mike competition, in search of the next Ewan MacColl.

Saffron Waldon

The nearby village of Arkesden, near the Essex border with Cambridgeshire and Hertfordshire, was the last home of the Small Faces frontman Steve Marriott. He was killed in April 1991, when a house fire, thought to have been caused by a cigarette, swept through his 16th-century thatched cottage. Marriott was on the verge of a comeback when he died, aged 44. He was a huge influence on today's top songwriters like Paul Weller and Noel Gallagher.

Lord Upminster

THE story of Ian Dury is one of the most improbable in popular music: a disabled art teacher emerges from the pub rock and punk movements to top the charts and become a world-class lyricist.

Drury mixed vaudeville and a love of music hall with punk and funk to produce that pop rarity: unforgettable lyrics that make you laugh. He wrote humorously about everyday life in his own parlance, enjoying a bit of Coward up his Betjeman. He was from Essex, in case you couldn't tell. Actually, he wasn't, strictly speaking, but it didn't matter as he became an honorary Essex man.

Dury was born in 1942 in the next parish along from Elton John, in Harrow, Middlesex. He would always say he was born in Upminster, where he grew up with his mother and aunt, and it's a place ingrained in his lyrics. His teenage years were evoked in songs like *Upminster Kid* – a 1975 Kilburn and the High Roads song – and in the 1981 album (with the Blockheads) called *Lord Upminster*, which included the controversial *Spasticus Artisticus* (see Banned by the Beeb box on page 130).

Aged seven, Dury was left partly crippled, after contracting polio in a Southend swimming pool on a hot afternoon in August 1949. He spent time in institutions for disabled children, including Braintree's Black Notley Hospital and the Chailey Heritage Craft School in Sussex. He later wrote a song about the place, *Hey, Hey, Take Me Away*, on 1980's *Laughter*.

Aged 16, Dury left school to study at Walthamstow Art School, where his art tutor was pop artist Sir Peter Blake, who became a life-long friend. He went to London's Royal College of Art. An interest in jazz led him to go and see blind American virtuoso Rahsaan Roland Kirk, renowned for being able to play several saxophones simultaneously.

The death of Gene Vincent in 1971 inspired Dury to get a band together and write songs; his early lyrics were simply scenarios that made him laugh. While teaching at Canterbury School of Art, he dreamed up a band, Kilburn and the High Roads, recruiting some art students, including bassist Humphrey Ocean and guitarist Keith Lucas.

Dury was soon sacked from Canterbury and had already turned 30 when the Kilburns began to play the art school circuit in 1971. They stood out from the pub rock crowd and not just because of their polio-stricken frontman and crippled drummer who walked with the aid of crutches. Instead, it was largely because of their music: a mix of 1950s rock 'n' roll fused with jazz, reggae and anything else that suited them. After several long and hard years on the pre-punk pub circuit, they recorded only one album, *Handsome*, but spilt soon afterwards.

Towards the end of the Kilburns, songwriter Chas Jankel joined the band, and Dury found a writing partner. Signed to Stiff Records, they formed the Blockheads and created two of the most popular albums of the late 1970s: the massively successful *New Boots And Panties!!* and *Do It Yourself*, which also helped keep Stiff Records solvent.

Dury wrote *My Old Man*, a touching song on that first album about his father, William, who drove buses for London Transport. For a further glimpse of Dury's extraordinary talents as lyricist you need look no further than another song inspired by his Dad, *The Bus Driver's Prayer*, which gives *The Lord's Prayer* a Greater London slant:

'Our Father/
Who art in Hendon/
Harrow Road be Thy name/
Thy Kingston come/
Thy Wimbledon/
In Erith as it is in Hendon.'

Punk's poet laureate succumbed to cancer in 2000, aged 57. Shortly before his death Dury said he didn't care if he was remembered. Fat chance he won't be; he remains one of England's best-loved songwriters who influenced the next generation of shrewd wordsmiths, from Madness to Lily Allen, and countless others.

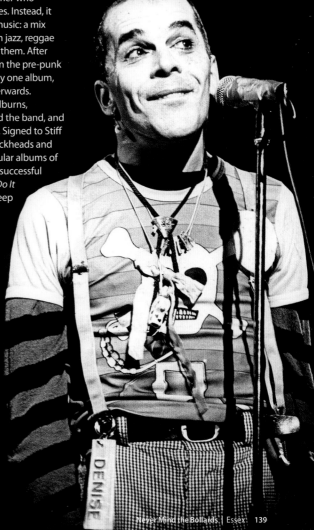

Chelmsford

The star-studded annual V Festival has taken place at Hylands Park, two miles outside Chelmsford, in mid-August since 1996. The event is twinned with a simultaneous festival in Staffordshire's Weston Park, with both events sharing the same artists although clearly not at the same time. Acts perform in Essex on Saturday and then head to the West Midlands on the Sunday and vice versa.

As prison gigs go, it doesn't quite rank up there with Johnny Cash's *At Folsom Prison*. When the Sex Pistols played to 500 inmates at Chelmsford Prison in September 1976, there was jeering scuffles and the sound of breaking glass. Between songs, Lydon even called for the prisoners to riot. The gig was recorded for a bootleg, *Live at Chelmsford Top Security Prison*, and released as a live album in 1990. But was it a great rock 'n' roll swindle? In *England's Dreaming*, punk chronicler Jon Savage revealed that early Sex Pistols sound man Dave Goodman doctored the original recording, hiring a Johnny Rotten impersonator who can be heard inciting inmates to riot.

Clacton-on-Sea

Seaside towns have always been a great place for social interaction, especially at weekends and on bank holidays. For years, coastal resorts like Clacton hosted an activity as integral to English seaside town tradition as kiss-me-quick hats, striped deck chairs and candyfloss. Bored with discussing Wittgenstein, on Easter weekend, 1964, mods and rockers indulged in a spot of subcultural argy-bargy, a new national sport that originated at English seaside resorts in the early 1960s. Rival youth gangs descended upon Clacton, fighting each other and vandalising streets and shops.

Singer-songwriter, composer and record producer Helen Folasade Adu, better known as Sade, spent most of her childhood in the seaside resort of Clacton. Born in Nigeria in 1959 to a Nigerian academic and an English nurse, she moved to England with her mother when she was four, after her parents split. She is the most successful female solo artist in British history, with more than 50 million albums sold.

The video for the Pet Shop Boys' cover of the famous American country song, *Always On My Mind*, was filmed in Clacton. They utilised the seafront and the amusement arcades in Pier Avenue. Clacton was also the setting for *It Couldn't Happen Here*, the band's 1987 musical journey across England.

Colchester

Colchester's most famous contribution to music is Blur (see box on page 134), but it doesn't end there. The Essex university town has also been the location for a couple of album sleeves. When it was known as the Bakers Arms, the Beer House in Magdalen Street was the local British boozer depicted on the cover of Marillion's album, *Clutching At Straws*.

The cover is almost a reworking of Edward Hopper's famous painting, *Nighthawks*, but set in a typical English boozer, featuring the likes of Dylan Thomas, Truman Capote and Lenny Bruce.

Essex University was where the sleeve of Fairport Convention's *What We Did On Our Holidays* was created. The band sketched the picture of the band performing on a blackboard given to them in a changing room before a gig at the university.

Harwich

At Easter, 1964, Radio Caroline started broadcasting aboard a ship in the North Sea, off the coast of Harwich. The first song played was *Not Fade Away* by The Rolling Stones. But it did; it was shut down in the summer of 1968.

Also, the port of Harwich sometimes leads to Amsterdam and therefore to a regular flow of mood-improving chemicals, which helped clubbers party at a frenetic pace during England's 1990s rave culture, and beyond.

"F*** all this pop stuff, let's play rhythm and blues!" was the rallying cry of guitarist Wilko Johnson of cult Canvey Island R&B heroes Dr Feelgood, who helped kill off the hippies and give the green light to punk. Their glory days were the mid-'70s pub-rock scene, just before punk, when they won a loyal following of fans with their energetic no-nonsense sound and raucous live sets.

They played loud, tight and fast: gruff-voiced frontman Lee Brilleaux belted out screeching harmonica and vocals, while manic guitarist Wilko Johnson strutted around the stage like the crazy-eyed local nutter you'd expect to see pushing a crocodile of supermarket trolleys around the town centre, for fun. Dr Feelgood started out as a 1950s-style rock'n'roll band, before switching to a rawer, more aggressive sound that helped launch what would soon be known as punk rock – once Joe Strummer had seen them and gone off and formed his own band.

Canvey is a marshy, muddy and unlikely rock'n'roll outpost of the Thames Estuary, between Tilbury and Southend-on-Sea, which Feelgood fans affectionately call the Canvey Delta. Separated from the Essex mainland by a series of creeks, its flat, reclaimed marshland lies below sea level and is susceptible to flooding at high tides. It's studded with wooden seaside shacks and pubs, leftovers from its previous incarnation as a Cockney holiday resort. There are shell-sand beaches and huge estuary views that include huge vast refinery pipes; Wilko Johnson didn't nickname his home town Oil City for nothing.

All of Dr Feelgood – Johnson, Brilleaux, bassist John B Sparks and drummer The Big Figure (born John Martin) – were Canvey-born-and-bred. They grew up as neighbours, just a few roads from each other, and had childhood memories of the devastating 1953 floods that claimed over 50 lives. Brilleaux, the band's late frontman

who died in 1994, grew up playing games on the creeks and making pirate dens on the marshes. His ashes were scattered on nearby Long Horse Island.

It was a £400 loan from Brilleaux to Stiff Records co-founder Jake Riviera that helped launch the label. The first venue they played was the Railway Hotel in Pitsea, and incredibly energetic live shows soon made them favourites on London's pub rock circuit.

Sadly, in 1977, the band's original line-up fell victim to the pressures of fame. Personality clashes and squabbling led to Wilko Johnson being fired from the band he had founded. A revamped Dr Feelgood limped on, while Johnson joined Ian Dury's Blockheads before embarking on a solo career.

Loyal to their roots, the Feelgoods naturally chose a location in their home-town for their album sleeves. The debut album, 1975's *Down By The Jetty*, was shot exactly where it said on the tin: down by a jetty, on Canvey Island's pier head. The Admiral Jellicoe pub on the High Street features on 1977's *Be Seeing You*, which pictured the band (minus Wilko, replaced by new guitarist Gypie Mayo) inside their favourite watering hole. Inevitably, since the cover photograph was taken, the pub has been refurbished and enjoys a different decor inside.

The Oysterfleet Hotel in Knightswick Road saw many great Feelgood gigs during the 1970s, as well as hosting Eddie and the Hot Rods and The Kursaal Flyers. And 1994's *Down At the Doctors*, a live album of Lee Brilleaux's last-ever gig was recorded here, shortly before he died of lymphoma cancer. The hotel now hosts an annual Lee Brilleaux Memorial gig on the weekend nearest his birthday, 10 May. Fans, plus former and current members of the Feelgoods, celebrate the band's music and raise money for charity in honour of the late singer.

The South

Hampshire
Berkshire
Buckinghamshire
Bedfordshire
Hertfordshire
Oxfordshire

Hampshire

Petersfield

Posh and progressive Bedales, in Petersfield, is one of the UK's most expensive private schools. The fashionable £9,605-a-term school is a popular choice with the rich and famous. Rock stars Sting and Mick Jagger sent their children there, and Jazz Mellor, daughter of The Clash frontman Joe Strummer, was also a pupil. Other ex-students include pop star Lily Allen; Luke Pritchard, lead singer of The Kooks; Jamie West-Oram, guitarist with The Fixx; and Teddy Thompson, the singer-songwriter son of British folk royalty Richard and Linda Thompson. He spent his teenage years at Bedales, playing "half-arsed white blues" in a school band. The American lyricist Alan Jay Lerner was also a pupil, albeit much earlier in the 20th century. Bedales, known for its liberalism, was founded in 1893 in reaction to restrictive Victorian public schools.

Winchester

At the start of the recording of *Physical Graffiti* in late 1973, John Paul Jones told Led Zeppelin manager Peter Grant he was seriously thinking about quitting the band to become the choirmaster at Winchester Cathedral. But after a few weeks off he changed his mind and rejoined the band to record at Headley Grange.

Grant had previously managed the novelty group The New Vaudeville Band. They enjoyed chart success on both sides of the Atlantic in the mid-1960s with a playful music hall-style number called *Winchester Cathedral*. It was a US number one and reached number four in the UK singles chart.

A former student of Winchester College, singer-songwriter Robyn Hitchcock paid tribute to the city in a song simply called *Winchester*, from his 1986 album, *Element of Light*.

Winchester School of Art's most famous ex-student is ambient music pioneer and record producer, Brian Eno, who studied fine art here in the late 1960s. Aaron Fletcher of the Mercury Prize-nominated Isle of Wight indie band The Bees studied printmaking here three decades later.

During 1969, Fairport Convention penned and rehearsed the songs for their classic *Liege & Lief* album at the Queen Anne mansion in the nearby parish of Farley Chamberlayne. They rented the house to recuperate from a motorway crash in May of that year which killed drummer Martin Lamble and their friend, Jeannie Franklyn. Several other members of the band were injured when their van crashed on the M1 travelling home from a gig in Birmingham. *Liege & Lief* was named 'Most Influential Folk Album of All Time' at the BBC Radio 2 Folk Awards in 2006.

The archaeologically rich rolling hills of Twyford Down, near Winchester, became a byword for dissent in the early 1990s when people protested at the construction of a new motorway extension. Protestors lost their battle, however, and the M3 drove through the Down like an earthquake fault-line slicing through the landscape. *Twyford Down* was the standout track on the 1994 album, *The Plot Thickens*, by the London-based acid-jazzers Galliano, the first band signed to Eddie Piller and Gilles Peterson's Talkin' Loud label. The start of the song provides a tour guide's potted history of the Down, before it segues into the sound of protest. The album also features a funked-up version of the Crosby, Stills and Nash song *Long Time Gone*.

Cathedral, a Graham Nash song on 1977's *CSN* album, was based on an acid trip and crisis of faith he experienced in Winchester Cathedral on his 32nd birthday.

Blissfields Festival, at Bradley Farm in Alresford, about seven miles from Winchester, started in 2001 as a summer party for 70 people and now attracts several thousand revellers each year. Like Glastonbury, it is held on a dairy farm but, unlike Glastonbury, Blissfields is an uncommercial, intimate

family festival, which avoids sponsorship and concentrates on unsigned bands (even if it attracts some big name headliners).

Nearby, General Dwight D Eisenhower addressed US troops prior to the D-Day Landings in 1944 at the Matterley Bowl, a natural amphitheatre in Winchester. This is the new home of the annual electronic dance music jamboree, the Glade Festival. Glade originally existed as just a dance stage at Glastonbury each June before becoming an independent festival in its own right.

Beaulieu

A young Rod Stewart lost his virginity to an older woman at the Beaulieu Jazz Festival, an experience that provided the inspiration for his first solo hit, *Maggie May*, in 1971.

Top: The Fairport Convention, 1969.
Above: Acker Bilk and his jazz band at Lord Montagu of Beaulieu's jazz festival, 1960.

Presumably she was a blonde: 'The morning sun when it's in your face really shows your age / But that don't worry me none in my eyes you're everything.'

In the late 1950s Lord Montague's Beaulieu estate hosted the annual Beaulieu Jazz Festival, one of Britain's first pop festivals, each summer, until the early 1960s when rival fans fought each other in the 'Battle of Beaulieu'.

Portsmouth, Southsea and *Tommy*

KEN Russell's 1975 cinematic take on Pete Townshend's 1969 rock opera, *Tommy*, was largely shot at locations in and around Portsmouth. The ballroom scenes were shot at the old Gaiety Theatre on Southsea's South Parade Pier, which survived heavy bombardment during the Second World War but not a mid-1970s movie crew. It burned down in June 1974, during the filming of *Tommy*. The fire is believed to have started when a spotlight set light to some drapes. The flames were soon out of control and several hundred actors, extras and crew were evacuated from the scene. Footage of the burning pier appears at the end of the film. The pavilion was rebuilt but it's a pale imitation of the original. One of the highlights of the film, the iconic *Pinball Wizard* sequence, featuring Elton John in huge cherry red Dr. Martens bovver boots and Roger Daltrey's chilling blank stare, was filmed inside Southsea's Kings Theatre.

Another Southsea musical landmark is the 400-capacity Wedgewood Rooms, a popular venue famous for putting on up-and-coming bands. There's also the Edge Of The Wedge bar alongside the venue, which hosts local acts and DJs.

Aldershot

Aldershot was the birthplace of Michael Hayes – better known as Mickie Most – one of the most influential record producers of his generation. He discovered The Animals (and produced *The House of the Rising Sun*) and Suzi Quatro and moulded the careers of Donovan and Lulu. He produced hits for Herman's Hermits and Jeff Beck and managed The Yardbirds, before they evolved into Led Zeppelin and his business partner Peter Grant took hold of the reins. He signed Hot Chocolate, who gave RAK Records, the label he formed in 1969, a long run of chart hits. The company was also home to unpretentious and unforgettable 1970s pop acts with one-word names like Mud, Smokie, Kenny and Racey.

Mickie Most was the Simon Cowell of his day, appearing as a tough, no-nonsense panellist on ITV's *New Faces*. In the 1980s, Most signed Johnny Hates Jazz, which featured his son Calvin Hayes on keyboards. Calvin was a former partner of Kim Wilde, another of his father's discoveries. Most was diagnosed with cancer in 2000 and died in 2003, aged 64.

The Beatles played their first gig in the south of England in December 1961 at Aldershot's Queens Road Palais Ballroom in front of an 18-strong audience.

Andover

Until they recorded *Wild Thing*, The Troggs were largely viewed as little more than a bunch of inconsequential hicks from the sticks. Jimi Hendrix's performance of their legendary song at the 1967 Monterey Pop Festival, when he set his guitar alight with lighter fuel before smashing it, became an iconic performance in rock history.

Before The Troggs (originally called The Troglodytes) formed in Andover in 1964, lead singer Reg Presley was a local bricklayer called Reggie Ball. He adopted his new last name on the advice of manager, Larry Page, who thought it might bring the band some Elvis-related action. Their original rehearsal room was situated above the Copper Kettle café at 12 High Street, now the site of beauty salon, above a bookmaker.

In the early 1990s, The Troggs travelled to Georgia in the US to collaborate with lifelong Troggs fans REM on the album *Athens Andover*, which links the band's two hometowns. By the time Wet Wet Wet's version of The Troggs' *Love Is All Around*

Left: Pete Staples, Reg Presley and Ronnie Bond of the Troggs, 1960.
Below: Led Zeppelin IV album cover.
Opposite page: Pinball Wizard, from The Who's rock opera *Tommy*.

(featured in *Four Weddings and a Funeral*) spent 15 weeks at number one in 1994, Presley had developed a keen interest in another strange phenomenon: crop circles.

His interest was sparked one day in 1990 when he discovered a crop formation at Alton Barnes in Marlborough. He used royalties earned from the Wet Wet Wet cover to finance research into the subject and later published his findings in a 2002 book, *Wild Things They Don't Tell Us*.

As well as Wild Thing, the now infamous Troggs Tapes of the band arguing during a recording session for the mid-1970s song *Tranquility* have become the stuff of rock history, inspiring scenes in *This Is Spinal Tap*.

Headley ❯

Headley, close to Hampshire's border with Surrey, enjoys a rich musical legacy as the place where Led Zeppelin wrote and recorded much of their material in the early 1970s, from *Led Zeppelin III* to *Physical Graffiti*. After initial sessions in London at Island Studios, the band decamped to Headley Grange, a three-storey former Victorian workhouse in the Hampshire countryside. The majority of Led Zeppelin's untitled fourth album – now generally known as Led Zeppelin IV – was recorded in 1971 within its stone halls. The band was one of the first to use the emerging Rolling Stones mobile studio, which was parked outside the 18th-century building that once housed the infirm and orphaned.

Much of the monolithic *Stairway To Heaven* was written here by frontman Robert Plant. Meanwhile despite Jimmy Page's interest in the occultist Aleister Crowley, *Black Dog*

was actually inspired by a stray black labrador retriever that hung around during recording. Instead fans speculated on the runic symbolism on the album's cover.

The unusual noises at the beginning of *Black Dog* are the sweet sound of guitars warming up. The colossal drum sound on *When the Levee Breaks* (frequently sampled in rock songs and dance music) was achieved by John Bonham playing drums in the huge main hallway, with a stereo microphone hanging from the central stairwell. "We always wanted the drums to sound like real drums but that hall made them sound like super cannons," Jimmy Page told *Mojo* magazine.

You can get a glimpse inside Headley Grange in the 2009 documentary *It Might Get Loud*, in which Page returns there to discuss the recording of Led Zeppelin IV with U2's The Edge and Jack White of The White Stripes. Headley Grange is now a privately owned house but a firm stop on the Zeppelin heritage trail. Most fans keep a respectful distance but one relieved the owners of their gates (with Headley Grange written on them) prior to Led Zeppelin's O2 reunion concert in 2007.

Other bands to record and live at Headley Grange included Bad Company, Peter Frampton, The Pretty Things and Genesis. By the time the latter had arrived here to live together and write 1974's *The Lamb Lies Down on Broadway* the place had fallen into disrepair with rats scurrying across the floors.

Led Zeppelin had rented Headley Grange on the recommendation of Fleetwood Mac, themselves no strangers to the manor house, or indeed the area. Before they left for Los Angeles and global stardom in 1974, Fleetwood Mac got it together in the country, living communally at Benifold, a large Victorian mansion on Headley Hill Road. Immediately before the band bought it for £23,000 in 1970 it had been another retreat: an ecumenical house of prayer and healing.

Basingstoke

William Shakespeare (in *Henry IV Part II*) and Gilbert and Sullivan (in *Ruddigore*) made early jokes about Basingstoke, setting in motion something of a national sport. Its town centre is a much-loathed eyesore that was once described as resembling New York's Ground Zero on 12 September, 2001. Such snipes almost make you rally to its defence.

Since 2007, the annual free, two-day Basingstoke Live festival has taken place every July at the War Memorial Park, featuring music and dance from local, national and international bands.

Carl Barât from The Libertines and Dirty Pretty Things was born in Basingstoke to an armaments factory worker father and a CND activist mother. He once dismissed his home-town with the one-liner: "Have you seen *The Office*?"

Singer-songwriter Tanita Tikaram spent her early teenage years in the Hampshire industrial town, while Robyn Hitchcock recalled a train journey through Basingstoke on the title track of 1984's *I Often Dream of Trains*:

> 'And there in the buffet car/
> I wait for eternity/
> Or Basingstoke'

The New Forest

Some country pubs have such low ceilings it's advisable to walk in wearing a crash helmet. One such boozer located on the edge of the New Forest is the East End Arms in Lymington, which serves drinks and tasty nosh with a rock 'n' roll twist. It is owned by John Illsley, a founder member and bassist of Dire Straits.

The Decision, a 2006 single by The Young Knives, describes horses in the New Forest "running in their Sunday best".

Eversley

Mercury Prize-nominated folky singer-songwriter Laura Marling hails from the small village of Eversley on Hampshire's border with Berkshire. She moved to London and became part of London's nu-folk scene in 2007 as a member of the original line-up of indie folk band Noah and the Whale. She has since been lauded as one of country's most original and talented young songwriters. The song *Goodbye England (Covered in Snow)*, the first single from her 2010 album *I Speak Because I Can*, is a hymn to her home village and was inspired by a walk she took with her father when she was a child around Eversley village.

Southampton

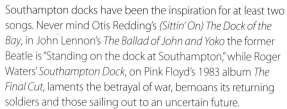

Southampton docks have been the inspiration for at least two songs. Never mind Otis Redding's *(Sittin' On) The Dock of the Bay*, in John Lennon's *The Ballad of John and Yoko* the former Beatle is "Standing on the dock at Southampton," while Roger Waters' *Southampton Dock*, on Pink Floyd's 1983 album *The Final Cut*, laments the betrayal of war, bemoans its returning soldiers and those sailing out to an uncertain future.

In February 1957, the 32-year-old Bill Haley stepped off the *Queen Elizabeth* at Southampton as the first American rock 'n' roll star to tour Britain; some 5,000 fans were there to welcome Haley and his Comets. Meanwhile hard-living singer Bon Scott's last ever gig with AC/DC was at Southampton's Gaumont Theatre (now the Mayflower Theatre) in January 1980.

Top Southampton music venues include the 600-capacity The Brook, which puts on new, established and tribute acts, and the Joiners Arms, which opened back in 1968 and continues to give a platform for up-and-coming bands as well as hosting top names.

R&B singer-songwriter Craig David was born in Holyrood, Southampton, where he grew up on a council estate. His musical education started early when he watched his father play bass in reggae band Ebony Rockers. When he wasn't playing football in Hoglands Park, he joined his father at local dance clubs, where he learned to DJ. Aged 19, he was the youngest solo male artist to get a debut UK number one hit, with his 2000 single, *Fill Me In*. Southampton's Solent University later bestowed him with an honorary doctorate in music: he has sold 13 million records and won a record eight Mobo Award nominations.

Southampton also claims comedian and former milkman Benny Hill as its own. He had a milk round in Eastleigh – when he wasn't chasing young women around local parks – which provided clear inspiration for his 1971 number one, *Ernie (The Fastest Milkman In The West)*.

Rock island

THE Needles are an outcrop of limestone rocks that protrude out of the sea, like pirate's teeth, on the Isle of Wight's western peninsula. But it was rock of another kind entirely that drew music fans and revellers to the island: the legendary Isle of Wight Festivals.

These started in 1968 and peaked in 1970 with one of the biggest rock concerts ever held, when half-a-million people assembled to watch The Doors, The Who, Joni Mitchell and Jimi Hendrix. Loved-up hippies wore clothes as colourful as the sandstone cliffs of Alum Bay and wafts of marijuana smoke contrasted with the island's fresh, invigorating air that had proved so popular with poet Alfred Lord Tennyson.

The three-day music festival was revived in 2002 and is now held at Seaclose Park near Newport as an alternative to Glastonbury. Each year the headliners are some of the biggest names in rock like The Who, David Bowie and The Stereophonics.

The island's other musical event is the ever-growing three-day music jamboree, Bestival, held annually at Robin Hill Country Park near Newport. It was started in 2004 by island-born BBC Radio 1 DJ Rob Da Bank and it rounds off the festival season each September. It features a line-up of top bands and DJs and is renowned for its fun fancy dress theme. Along with having a good time, festival organisers clearly enjoy a good pun: Restival is a quiet chill-out zone featuring hammocks inside Mongolian yurt tents, and Breastival is an area reserved for new and expectant mothers.

Dimbola Lodge (Freshwater Bay) is the former home of the celebrated Victorian portrait photographer, Julia Margaret Cameron. It now houses a photography museum dedicated to her memory alongside a great exhibition dedicated to the history of the original Isle of Wight Festivals, with memorabilia from the first three events. The Jimi Hendrix Memorial Garden features a life-size bronze statue of the guitarist, erected in 2006. Aptly it faces Afton Down

just down the road, where he performed at the 1970 festival, his last-ever gig, 18 days before he died. The museum's curator is poet and music writer Brian Hinton, author of rock biographies, a fine book about the US alt-country music scene and *Bold as Love*, which charts the history of the Isle of Wight Festival.

In 1960, John Lennon and Paul McCartney hitchhiked down from Liverpool for a summer holiday on the Isle of Wight, staying with McCartney's cousin who ran The Bow Bars pub in Ryde. Since the mid-'60s Beatles aficionados have debated whether the song, *Ticket to Ride*, was inspired by this trip.

The Isle of Wight has been immortalised in song, most famously by the Fab Four in *When I'm Sixty-Four*, written by Paul McCartney: "Every summer we could rent a cottage in the Isle of Wight / If it's not too dear."

The Men They Couldn't Hang's third album, 1988's *Waiting For Bonaparte*, features a song about the Isle of Wight called *Island in the Rain*, a musical and maritime travelogue that conjures up images of harbours and shorelines.

Singer-songwriter Robyn Hitchcock lived in Yarmouth in the 1980s and his favourite beach on the island, Compton Beach, along the coast road between Freshwater Bay and Brook, was the inspiration for the song *Airscape*, on 1986's *Element of Light*. The beach also appears on the album cover. The musician's father was the novelist Raymond Hitchcock who grew up in Ventnor.

Bands hailing from the Isle of Wight include poppy jazz-funksters Level 42. Bassist Mark King, famous for his distinctive slap bass lines, guitarist Boon Gould (his real name is the fantastically grand-sounding Rowland Charles Gould) and his drummer brother, Phil, all grew up on the island.

Mercury Prize-nominated six-piece indie band The Bees also come from the island and are proud of their Ventnor roots.

Right: The 1970 Isle of Wight festival, featuring Hendrix

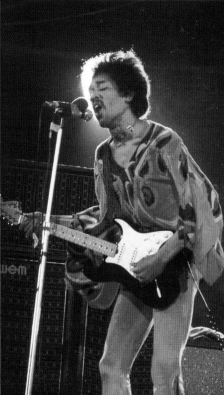

Berkshire

Reading

One of the UK's longest-running music festivals, the Reading Festival – held over the August Bank Holiday weekend – actually started life around 30 miles east in Richmond, Surrey. In 1961 the leafy suburb hosted the first event, originally known as the National Jazz and Blues Festival. The venue was Richmond Athletic Ground but stuffy locals objected to the annual invasion of herds of beatniks, worried they might bring their house prices down.

Their objections proved successful and the festival was banished to Windsor in the mid-1960s, later finding a permanent home further along the river as the legendary Reading Festival in 1971.

In the 1970s the festival focused on a mixture of prog rock, blues and heavy rock acts. Sham 69 and The Jam played in 1978 and American punks The Ramones the following year, but during the 1980s Reading became largely synonymous with heavy rock bands.

Since 1999, the Reading Festival has been twinned with a simultaneous festival in Leeds, with the same acts appearing at both festivals (obviously on different days).

From 1986 until 2006 Reading also hosted the world music festival WOMAD (World of Music Arts and Dance), pioneered by Peter Gabriel in the early 1980s. But it grew too big for its site at the Rivermead Leisure Complex and transferred to Wiltshire.

In 1953 Reading was the birthplace of Mike Oldfield – of *Tubular Bells* fame. Six-piece alt-rockers The Cooper Temple Clause hail from nearby Wokingham.

Reading is also forever linked with Led Zeppelin's triumphant, untitled, best-selling fourth album – universally known as Led Zeppelin IV. To the disquiet of other Atlantic Records executives, the late Ahmet Ertegun, who signed the band in 1968, allowed the band to release the album without a title and without any mention of their name anywhere on the cover.

Instead, the sleeve shows a 19th-century oil painting of an old Victorian woodland worker nailed to a demolished house in the West Midlands, contrasting an old rural way of life with a grim urban landscape. This picture was found in a Reading antique shop by singer Robert Plant and despite massive sales of the album worldwide – it's the fourth-biggest-selling album of all time – no one knows the name of the artist, nor indeed the old man in the painting.

The Fox and Hounds pub, Gosbrook Road, Caversham, was where John Lennon and Paul McCartney played in their pre-Beatles days. In 1960, the not-so-fab two pulled pints behind the bar during the week and then strummed their guitars on Saturday nights as The Nerk Twins. Lennon and McCartney used to hitchhike down from Liverpool during school holidays to work here.

Slough

Come Friendly Bombs (2009), by Watford punk band Gallows, takes its title from Sir John Betjeman's famous poem 'Slough' in which the poet rails against the assault on rural England by new town development. Morrissey's summoning of Armageddon to a decaying English seaside town, "Come, come, come nuclear bomb," a line from *Everyday Is Like Sunday*, is another clear reference to the poem. Talking of coastal towns, *Costa del Slough*, a song on Marillion's 1998 album, *Radiation*, envisages the Berkshire town as an English seaside resort after global warming has taken hold: "The hole in the ozone layer / Is all right by me / Make England warmer in the summer." Much-maligned, never bombed, Slough is also name-checked in The Jam's 1979 hit single, *Eton Rifles*: "There's a row going on down near Slough." (See Eton.)

Taplow

Welsh prog-rockers Man chose Taplow station, near Maidenhead, for the gatefold sleeve of their 1973 album, *Back Into The Future*, a double album divided into studio and live discs. On the cover, the band, their family and studio crew are dressed in hired period costumes, posing as Victorians on a day out to the seaside. The station is on the Wales to Paddington main line, so express train passengers may have thought they were travelling back in time.

The Buckingham Palace scenes in The Beatles' film *Help!* were actually shot at Cliveden, the famous former Astor family mansion. Owned by the National Trust, it's now an über-posh five-star von Essen hotel, with 376 acres of magnificent formal gardens and parklands that slope down to the River Thames. The mansion was the meeting place for a group of 1920s and '30s political intellectuals called the Cliveden Set and the scene of notorious parties in the 1960s from which the political scandal the Profumo Affair arose. War minister John Profumo met Christine Keeler, a call girl and mistress of an alleged Russian spy, and tainted the reputation of Harold Macmillan's Conservative government.

Windsor

The Ricky Tick, where a frustrated Jeff Beck of The Yardbirds smashes his guitar to pieces as Keith Relf sings *Stroll On* in Michelangelo Antonioni's film *Blowup*, looks like the old Marquee Club in Oxford Street (before it moved to Wardour Street). But it was actually a reconstructed set at Elstree Studios, meticulously modelled on the influential 1960s R&B venue, the Ricky Tick Club at Windsor's Star & Garter hotel. The Ricky Tick hosted legendary acts like Cream, Jimi Hendrix, The Rolling Stones (who had a residency here in 1963) and The Who – the band Antonioni originally wanted for the film, because the Italian director was intrigued by Pete Townshend's guitar-breaking routine of the time.

For the cover of his 1978 album, *A Single Man*, a sartorially elegant Elton John was photographed along the Long Walk, the 2½-mile straight avenue in Windsor Great Park that runs south from Windsor Castle. The castle's residents get a brief mention in *7&3 Is The Striker's Name*,

Above: The Libertines at the Reading Festival in 2009.

a track on Paul Weller's 2010 release, *Wake Up The Nation*, his tenth studio album: "Curse those f***ers in their castle / They're all bastards too."

On 24 September, 1980, Led Zeppelin were preparing to go on the road again after their summer Tour Over Europe. After the first day of rehearsals for a forthcoming North American tour, the band left Bray Studios near Windsor and retired to Jimmy Page's home, the Old Mill House in Mill Lane, Clewer Village – the former residence of actor Michael Caine. During the day drummer John 'Bonzo' Bonham had been drinking heavily, mixing quadruple vodkas with medication to lessen his withdrawal from heroin addiction. And Bonham continued to drink throughout the evening, downing more than 40 measures of vodka. Around midnight, Page's assistant Rick Hobbs helped Bonzo to a guest room and laid the drummer on his side. He was found the next day in a pool of vomit – he had choked several hours earlier. He was 32.

Eton

Paul Weller was 21 years old and living in a rented caravan when he penned *Eton Rifles*. A biting satire about the age-old class war, the song rails against inequality and social division in Britain. It was written in response to a TV report he'd watched about an unemployment march from Liverpool to the Houses of Parliament. Weller was incensed when he saw right-to-work marchers jeered at by Eton schoolboys as they passed the famous college. "I just thought that was a great scene. The unemployed going past this seat of learning and being jeered at by all these w**kers," Weller explained later.

In 2008, it was revealed that *The Eton Rifles* is the favourite song of ex-Eton pupil David Cameron, then humble leader of the Conservative Party. Cameron was a 12-year-old newcomer to Eton when the song was written and had just joined the cadet corps – precisely the target of Weller's ridicule:

'All that rugby puts hairs on your chest /
What chance have you got against a tie and a crest'

"Which part of it didn't he get?," Weller responded. "It wasn't intended as a f***ing jolly drinking song for the cadet corps!"

Ironically, 18 years later, Bruce Foxton, Weller's former bassist in The Jam, enrolled his son Iago as a new pupil at Eton College.

Ascot

From the summer of 1969, Tittenhurst Park, a 72-acre estate on London Road in Sunningdale near Ascot, was the home of John Lennon and Yoko Ono for two years. Lennon bought the house for £145,000. His new pad was also the setting for The Beatles' last-ever photo session on 22 August, 1969. Two photos from the session were used on the front and back covers of the *Hey Jude* compilation album, released in 1970. After a car crash in Scotland one summer, Lennon had his written-off vehicle squashed into a cube and exhibited in his mansion grounds as a work of art.

John and Yoko built their own recording studio – Ascot Sound Studios – in the grounds of their new estate, allowing them to record without booking studio time at Abbey Road or elsewhere.

It also meant John could keep his distance from other ex-Beatles and British fans who hated Yoko's inaccessible avant-garde leanings. First they recorded the two *Plastic Ono Band* albums, released simultaneously in 1970. Photographs for the album sleeves were shot on the grounds of Tittenhurst Park and were almost identical. Both have John and Yoko relaxing under a tree on a sunny day. Lennon's album sees the ex-Beatle lying against Yoko, and for her album, they simply reverse positions, with Yoko lying against Lennon's body. The following year, 1971, saw Lennon record his best-selling *Imagine*, with co-producer Phil Spector. In the *Imagine* video Lennon plays the piano in the mansion's white drawing room. In 2000 George Michael bought Lennon's piano for £1.45 million.

When Lennon moved to the US, he sold the Tittenhurst grounds and recording studio to former bandmate Ringo Starr, and the estate was home to the drummer until 1988, when he sold it for £5 million. It is now valued at around £30 million. Ringo renamed the facility Startling Studios and hired it out to musicians, while he went to live in France. Birmingham heavy metal band Judas Priest recorded their *British Steel* album at Tittenhurst, but they preferred the house to the studio and promptly moved recording equipment there. They made their own sound effects by hitting hammers against radiators, slamming doors and whipping guitar cables on flight cases – and recorded it all. Anything was game. The sound of milk bottles smashing can be heard on *Breaking the Law*, while the curious wrenching sounds on *Metal Gods* are cutlery trays from Ringo's kitchen being dropped; swooshing noises are billiard cues being swung through the air.

Left: John Bonham, drummer of Led Zeppelin, died at the Old Mill House aged just 32.
Above: Tittenhurst Park became the residence of John Lennon and Yoko Ono in 1969.

Glam rock superstar Marc Bolan was photographed at Tittenhurst Park for the cover of T. Rex's 1972 album, *The Slider*, which included the singles, *Metal Guru* and *Telegram Sam*. His producer Tony Visconti snapped the photo with Bolan's camera during the filming of *Born to Boogie*, Ringo Starr's T. Rex documentary.

The Nags Head pub, at 28 High Street, Sunningdale Village, next to Tittenhurst Mansion, was the local for Lennon and visiting musicians and producers, like George Harrison, Billy Preston and Phil Spector.

Newbury

Could there be a better name for a rock star's country mansion than Stargroves, a large Victorian House in East Woodhay, about five miles southwest of Newbury? This was Mick Jagger's country mansion in the 1970s, where, earlier, Oliver Cromwell stopped by for a cuppa after the second Battle of Newbury in 1644. Jagger lived here when he wasn't in his London pad, overlooking the Thames in his house on Chelsea's exalted Cheyne Walk. Jagger bought the estate in 1970 for £55,000 and installed The Rolling

Stones Mobile Studio, a mobile recording control room located in a custom-built truck (so the Stones could lay down recordings outside their normal studio environment). The Stones recorded there before moving to France in the spring of 1971 for tax reasons to record what many regard as their finest album, *Exile on Main Street*. The band failed to find a suitable French recording studio, so they recorded the album at Keith Richards' luxurious rented villa in Villefranche-sur-Mer, near Nice and transported the remote recording truck from England. Other bands visited Stargroves to use the mobile studio, including The Who. They recorded several songs there, including, in 1971, *Won't Get Fooled Again*, which Pete Townshend had originally written for his aborted concept album and film, *Lifehouse*. Many of the *Lifehouse* songs were resurrected for *Who's Next*, which started life as a week of demo sessions at Stargroves and were Townshend's extended synthesiser breaks emerged from those sessions. In 1972, Led Zeppelin recorded parts of the albums *Houses of the Holy* and *Physical Graffiti* at Stargroves. Deep Purple, Bob Marley and the Wailers and Iron Maiden also recorded there. In 1998, Stargroves was passed on to rock star royalty when Rod Stewart bought it for £2.5 million. However, he never lived there and put it up for sale a little while later.

Buckinghamshire

Aylesbury

Prog rockers Marillion formed in Aylesbury in 1979 and the market town's cobbled square inspired their debut single, 1982's *Market Square Heroes*. They originally called themselves Silmarillion, after JRR Tolkien's posthumous tome, but shortened their name to avoid any copyright issues. They played their first gig at Berkhamsted Civic Centre in March 1980. The band's original line-up split in 1988 but, in 2007, the square hosted a performance of the song with original singer Fish back on vocals. The surprise one-off reunion was part of the town's annual Hobble on the Cobbles one-day music festival, which takes place in late August.

Friars Club was a legendary music venue that attracted all the top bands. Over its 15-year history (1969-1984), the list of bands who played there reads like the Rock 'n' Roll Hall of Fame: Queen, David Bowie, Lou Reed, Roxy Music, Black Sabbath, King Crimson, Genesis, Fleetwood Mac, The Clash, The Jam, U2, Blondie, The Police and Mott The Hoople, who were audience favourites. The venue's first night was 2 June, 1969, at the now-demolished New Friarage Hall, a British Legion ex-servicemen's club in Walton Street. The artists appearing were blues player Mike Cooper and prog rockers Mandrake Paddle Steamer. In 1975 Friars moved to Aylesbury's Civic Centre where it hosted some of the best bands on the planet for another nine years.

When the club closed in December 1984, it had nearly 90,000 members and was regarded as one of the best live venues of its kind. Friars was held in such high regard by musicians that American artists such as Jonathan Richman would fly over to the UK, play just the Friars and a London venue and return to the US. In 2009, three special concerts marked its 40th anniversary, featuring acts which showcased the different stages of the club's history. The first gig featured

bands who'd played there in its first year, like the Edgar Broughton Band, the Groundhogs and headliners The Pretty Things, who first played Friars in June 1969, soon after the club opened. Performances by Stiff Little Fingers, Penetration – and later Kid Creole and the Coconuts and China Crisis – reflected the punk/new wave era of the early '80s.

Drummer Robert Wyatt, a founding member of legendary underground psych-rock group Soft Machine, once spent eight months recuperating in Stoke Mandeville Hospital, on the edge of Aylesbury. In June 1973, the inebriated Wyatt had fallen from a third-floor window at a party in London's Maida Vale, breaking his spine and causing paralysis from the waist down. He used his time in Stoke Mandeville to hone songs for his solo album, *Rock Bottom*, released in 1974. Without the use of his legs, his career as a drummer was limited but he returned to the music scene in a wheelchair,

Above: Aylesbury proggers, Marillion.
Opposite page: Pink Floyd's The Wall was largely filmed at the famous Pinewood Studios in Iver Heath.

and embarked on a career as a composer. Although his accident prohibited the use of his feet, he continued to play drums with his hands.

Formed in 2003, the Mercury Prize-nominated band Sweet Billy Pilgrim also hails from Aylesbury. They are named after the hero in Kurt Vonnegut's novel, *Slaughterhouse-Five*.

Buckingham ❯

Music magnate turned transport tycoon, Richard Branson, is an ex-pupil of one of England's leading private schools, the ultra-exclusive Stowe School. So is Roger Hodgson, founding member and singer of Supertramp, Crispian Mills from psych-rockers Kula Shaker (son of actress Hayley Mills and grandson of Sir John Mills), late jazz singer and writer George Melly and choral composer Howard Goodall. The school was an unusual venue for The Beatles, who played here in April 1963 at the

request of pupil and fellow Liverpudlian David Moores, heir to the Littlewoods business empire and later the chairman (now honorary life president) of Liverpool Football Club. The Fab Four were paid £100 for the gig, but the audience remained seated throughout and entirely silent.

Iver Heath ❯

Pink Floyd The Wall, Alan Parker's adaptation of the band's 1979 album, with a screenplay by Roger Waters, was filmed on set at Pinewood Studios, Iver Heath. It was also shot in various locations in England: the school riot at the disused Beckton Gasworks, East London; the Nuremberg-style rally, with sinister flags bearing Gerald Scarfe's crossed hammer symbol, used the Royal Horticultural Halls in Westminster and the mental ward was a disused cake factory in Hammersmith. The 530-acre Black Park in nearby Wexham is a popular location for many film productions, including several Carry On films. The pine trees, heathland and lake stood in for Transylvania in the Hammer horror films, which Kate Bush paid homage to in 1978 single, *Hammer Horror*, but it was the pop promo for her *Army Dreamers* that was shot here. As was the video for Bob Marley's *Buffalo Soldiers*, a metaphor for black resistance that also told of the black soldiers of the US Army's 10th Cavalry Regiment – nicknamed Buffalo Soldiers by Native American tribes they fought in the 19th century.

Burnham

"And it burns, burns, burns." Johnny Cash was inspired to write his classic song, *Ring of Fire*, after an eventful dining experience at Burnham's Taj Mahal Tandoori restaurant in 1962. Miraculously, a decade later Bryan Ferry penned

Both Ends Burning after an evening there. The restaurant burned down in 1982 after a renegade piece of flock wallpaper fell onto a regular diner's sizzling chicken shashlik. No one was seriously injured.

Marlow

Traffic drummer Jim Capaldi lived at the Old Parsonage, a medieval priory near the riverside at Marlow, until his death in January 2005 from stomach cancer, aged 60. Capaldi, who played with 1960s greats such as Jimi Hendrix, The Grateful Dead and Jefferson Airplane, bought the former rectory for £38,000 in 1969 with his new-found wealth. Born in Evesham, Worcestershire, he is best remembered as drummer with Traffic, the group he and Steve Winwood formed in 1967 with two other west Midlands musicians: guitarist and songwriter Dave Mason and flautist/saxophonist Chris Wood. At the building's heart is a capacious medieval hall with a minstrels' gallery, once the scene of 14th-century banquets. In true rock'n'roll spirit, Capaldi held some wild parties here: Jimi Hendrix, Bob Marley and Keith Moon were amongst the music legends that came to stay at the Old Parsonage, and when, John Lennon stayed, some of his previously unheard songs were privately previewed before release. Capaldi married Brazilian-born Aninha at Marlow's All Saints Church in 1975.

The late Ronnie Lane of the Small Faces once resided at Monks Corner, the house in which Jerome K Jerome, author of *Three Men In A Boat* lived in the early part of the 20th century. The house, in woods near the sleepy

Left: The Style Council.
Opposite page: Kajagoogoo, 1980s synth-popsters.

town of Marlow on the River Thames, saw visits by other members of the Small Faces, including Steve Marriott. In the 1970s, Ronnie Lane opted for the full rural existence, travelling up and down the country, living the nomadic gypsy lifestyle with a touring musical caravan he called The Passing Show.

Milton Keynes

'We used to chase dreams, now we chase the dragon/ Mine is the semi with the Union Jack on'

Come to Milton Keynes, from The Style Council's 1985 album, *Our Favourite Shop*, wasn't exactly a cheery invite to visit the town. It was more Paul Weller at his most scathing, a damning indictment of the prevailing Thatcherite beliefs of the time. Using Milton Keynes as an example, the former Jam frontman took a swipe at Middle England and its changing values six years on from Margaret Thatcher's first election victory. Weller railed against the creeping soullessness caused by a seemingly unstoppable thrust towards monetarism and selfishness. He took the song title from an advert he saw on TV with the catchphrase, "Come To Milton Keynes". The folk of Milton Keynes were outraged and ignored the fact the song was a metaphor and not directed personally at them. Predictably, it did not sit well with the town's officials, residents or indeed the local newspaper who blasted Weller on their front page. They were annoyed by his appraisal of a town he had never been to.

Perhaps Weller should have played the song live at Milton Keynes' major venue, the 65,000-capacity open-air National Bowl. Ironically, the venue opened in 1979 – the same year as Thatcher became PM – with gigs by Geno Washington and Desmond Dekker and has since enjoyed a stellar role-call including The Police, U2, Michael Jackson, Oasis, Queen, Bon Jovi and REM.

Milton Keynes' main shopping centre – now called The Centre:MK – was the location for the video for Cliff Richard's 1981 hit, *Wired For Sound*. The video is a real find if you have a Lycra fetish. Cliff, conservatively dressed in black leather and yellow T-shirt and listening to an early '80s Sony Walkman, roller skates through the city centre – around the John Lewis store and the surrounding underpasses – stalked by multi-coloured Lycra-clad groupies on roller skates. Ah, that's the 1980s for you.

Bedfordshire

Luton

Back in the day when Elton John wore hats – and tried to convince the world he was straight – Olney Headwear, at 106 Old Bedford Road, made his straw boaters.

Leighton Buzzard

Near the scene of the 1963 Great Train Robbery, which propelled sometime Sex Pistols vocalist Ronnie Biggs onto the world stage, lies Leighton Buzzard, home to 1980s synth-popsters Kajagoogoo who grew out of the indie band Art Nouveau. Best-known for their chart-topper, *Too Shy*, they were fronted by porcupine-haired singer Chris Hamill. To create his stage name, Limahl, he simply rearranged the letters of his surname.

The Leyton Buzzards' single, *Saturday Night (Beneath the Plastic Palm Trees)*, tickled the feet of the 1979 UK Singles Chart, at number 53. The pub rockers – then new wavers – weren't from Bedfordshire at all, but rather from Leyton in East London.

Leighton Buzzard is also where The Barron Knights formed in 1960. They started out as a straight pop group before recording parodies, and are still performing today despite the retirement of founding member, Butch Baker, and death of original lead singer Duke D'Mond. They parodied Supertramp, Pink Floyd and Brotherhood of Man, but their 1978 pastiche, *A Taste of Aggro*, was their biggest hit, selling over a million records.

Hertfordshire

Aldbury ❯

The Hertfordshire village of Aldbury, three miles east of Tring, is surrounded by 5,000 acres of National Trust woodland known as the Ashridge Estate. It's the quintessential, genteel, picture-postcard English village, with a backdrop of rolling green fields – it's the image of Englishness craved by American tourists dressed in tennis gear.

There are ducks on the green, crowing cocks; the village even has its very own Morris dancers, the Aldbury Morris Men. Pubs have names like The Valiant Trooper that whisk you back to a time when England owned all the pink bits on the map. There are even some old stocks and a whipping post, presumably preserved in case Rick Astley visits. But remember, this is the English countryside so nothing is ever quite as it seems. It's another stocks that bestows Aldbury its rock 'n' roll status.

Just outside the village is the large Georgian mansion, Stocks House. Built in 1773, it was once home to the American Playboy executive Victor Lownes and famous for wild parties attended by 1970s celebs. Actor Tony Curtis and other A-list stars would come down to the village pubs and enjoy a drink. The one-time girls' Catholic school was a training camp for Playboy bunnies.

After Lownes' dismissal from Playboy in 1981, the mansion became Stocks Hotel Golf and Country Club, an upmarket 18-room hotel with adjoining golf course. It caught the eye of Manchester's Oasis in 1997 as they were looking for a location for the cover of their third album, *Be Here Now*. The resulting sleeve image sees the band outside Stocks House by the swimming pool, surrounded by various props, including a Rolls Royce parked in the pool, in homage to Keith Moon, and an inflatable globe, a nod to the band's *Definitely Maybe* cover.

A decade earlier, the mansion briefly became Pop Promos-R-Us with parts in music videos for The Fun Boy Three (and their cover of George Gershwin's *Summertime*), Kajagoogoo (*Hang on Now*) and Madness (for their cover of Labi Siffre's *It Must Be Love*, in which he makes a cameo appearance as a violinist).

Stocks closed as a hotel in November 2004 and is now privately owned by retired horse-trainer and entrepreneur, Peter Harris, and lived in by his son-in-law, retired flat-racing jockey, Walter Swinburn and his family. Needless to say, it is no longer open to the public.

St Albans ❯

St Albans' most famous musical sons The Zombies – featuring breathy singer Colin Blunstone and keyboardist Rod Argent – formed in 1961 while the band members were still at their respective schools. They secured a contract with Decca Records in May 1964, after they'd won a newspaper-sponsored competition, and immediately recorded their first hit, *She's Not There*. It reached number two in the US, and Decca dispatched the band on an American tour on the back of it.

Of course, English rock 'n' roll and beat groups were hugely popular in the States in the mid-'60s and The Zombies rode the crest of the British invasion wave. They experienced a taste of Beatlemania for themselves, playing to enormous arenas and enthusiastic fans. They later signed with CBS, and adapting to the prevailing musical times, produced what is generally regarded as their masterwork, the psychedelic *Odessey and Oracle*, with most of the songs recorded at Abbey Road studios.

Upon its release in 1967, the band told the music press the misspelling of 'odyssey' was deliberate and held special and deep significance. However, Rod Argent later admitted the story was a cover-up because their sleeve designers had fouled up and there wasn't time to change it. *Beechwood Park*, a summer-drenched track on *Odessey and Oracle* was written by their Barnet-born bass player/songwriter Chris White. It refers to a place in the village of Markyate, close to the Buckinghamshire and Bedfordshire borders, where White was raised and his parents ran the village shop:

'And we would count the evening stars/
As the day grew dark/
In Beechwood Park'

Rod Argent was educated at the famous St Albans School, a private school that dates back to the 10th century, making one of the world's oldest. There he met fellow Zombies Paul Atkinson and Hugh Grundy. Multi award-winning lyricist Sir Tim Rice and Tim Hart of folk rockers Steeleye Span were also pupils there, as were Edd Gibson, Ed Macfarlane and Jack Savidge of indie band Friendly Fires, who all met at the school. There's plenty of escapism in their songs and the band say they've managed to flee St Albans through their music.

Sixties folk superstar Donovan, once dubbed 'the British Bob Dylan', was born in Glasgow but moved to Hertfordshire with his family at the age of 10. Inspired by the US folk revival, Donovan dropped out of art school and threw himself into the Hertfordshire folk scene of the 1960s, descending on local clubs and especially the small folk refuge, The Cock Inn pub in St Peters Street. There he met the leading lights of the British folk scene: Maddy Prior, Bert Jansch, John Renbourn and locals like Mac McLeod and Mick Softley who taught him new guitar techniques. Donovan also started to put pen to paper and hone his singer-songwriting craft, which before long would capture the mood of London's Swinging Sixties.

Hatfield

Rock 'n' roll history is peppered with bizarre accidents (see East London for pop idol Brian Harvey's car accident). A fracas outside Hatfield's Red Lion pub in January 1970 saw The Who drummer Keith Moon accidentally run over and kill his chauffeur, bodyguard and friend, Neil Boland (although Boland's daughter, Michelle, disputes this and says Moon's wife Kim was behind the wheel). The incident took place as Moon was opening a disco at a pub owned by some friends while fleeing from a group of locals who wereattacking his Bentley. Also in the car were Moon's wife, Kim, 'Legs' Larry Smith, drummer of The Bonzo Dog Doo-Dah Band, and his girlfriend Jean Battye. Although Moon was given an absolute discharge, he was haunted by the accident for the rest of his life and had frequent nightmares. Moon and his wife later divorced and, in 1978, she married Ian McLagan of the Small Faces, a month after Moon died. She was later killed in a car crash herself in Texas in 2006.

Early seventies Canterbury rockers Hatfield and the North took their name from a famous north London road sign that directed motorists out of the capital and onto the A1 road to Edinburgh. The sign is still there, but instead of 'Hatfield and the NORTH', it now reads, a little disappointingly, 'The NORTH, Hatfield'. The prog band recorded two albums: an eponymous debut and 1975's *The Rotters' Club*. The latter inspired a 2002 novel of the same name by Jonathan Coe about three 1970s Birmingham teenagers, one of whom starts a prog rock band called Gandalf's Pikestaff.

Freddie Mercury never lived in or rocked out Hatfield House, but another queen – Queen Elizabeth I – spent much of her childhood in the stately home. Several centuries later it was the turn of a dandy highwayman. With the introduction of MTV in 1981, bands increasingly

Left: Rod Argent, Colin Blunstone, Hugh Grundy, Paul Atkinson and Christ White, members of The Zombies.

experimented with TV-friendly visuals to promote songs. With their war paint make-up, pirate costumes and Burundi drums, Adam and the Ants made one of the first really memorable pop videos. *Stand and Deliver*, the first single from their 1981 album, *Prince Charming*, was filmed in and around Hatfield House. In the video Ant's dandy highwayman applies his make-up, robs a stagecoach and gets captured, but escapes the gallows with help from his band. In an early role, Adam Ant's then girlfriend, actress Amanda Donohoe, appears briefly at the start of the video. It was the band's most successful single, remaining at number one in the UK for five weeks; the video helped MTV break them in the US.

Below: Adam And The Ants, 1981.
Opposite page: Phil Taylor, Eddie Clarke and Lemmy, members of Motörhead, 1980.

There are more Gallows in Watford and it's unlikely you'll see this five-piece represent the UK at the Eurovision Song Contest anytime soon. Gallows are led by generously tattooed frontman, Frank Carter, who grew up in nearby Hemel Hempstead. Their 2009 album, *Grey Britain*, the second by the seriously peed-off provincial punks, chronicles a bleak and broken Britain, so grim it should have come with a free razor blade. The epic *Crucif***s* sets the tone (complete with string sections recorded at Abbey Road):

> 'Great Britain is f***ing dead/
> So cut our throats/
> End our lives/
> Let's f***ing start again'

In contrast, Watford is the birthplace of Geri Halliwell, the pop *chanteuse* formerly known as Ginger Spice. Hertfordshire claims another two Spices: Posh Spice Victoria Beckham (from Goffs Oak) and Baby Spice, aka Emma Bunton (Barnet).

Long-term Watford FC supporter, singer-songwriter Sir Elton John, stepped down as club chairman in 2002, but he retains close links with the club as Honorary Life President. The Rocket Man became chairman and director in 1976, injecting lots of money into the club. He appointed future England boss Graham Taylor as manager and the club climbed up three divisions into the top flight, where they finished runners-up in 1983 and reached the FA Cup final a year later. John still stages concerts at the Vicarage Road stadium and donates funds from ticket sales to the club.

Surrey-born singer-songwriter and producer Nick Lowe grew up in the village of Sarratt, near Watford. The future Jesus of Cool spent his teenage years as a mod, hanging around with fellow mods in the Watford shopping precinct before hotfooting it to Watford Trade Union Hall in Woodford Road for Saturday night dances, seeing bands like The Action and the High Numbers (who later morphed into The Who).

From central London to inner peace… Bhaktivedanta Manor, near Watford, is the home of the International Society for Krishna Consciousness (ISKCON), or the Hare Krishna movement. This is the mansion that George Harrison donated to the movement in 1972. Back then, interest in Hare Krishna had grown so rapidly that the existing temple in London's Bury Place near the British Museum was much too small. So Harrison asked a British devotee to locate a much larger property near to London. Piggott's Manor, a mansion in Hilfield Lane, Aldenham, near Watford, was chosen, and Harrison lived here for a while when it opened. "Because he has given shelter to Krishna by providing this temple, Krishna will surely provide shelter for him," said AC Bhaktivedanta Swami Prabhupada, founder of the Hare Krishna movement.

Rickmansworth

The front cover of Echo & The Bunnymen's 1980 debut album, *Crocodiles*, is a night-time photograph of the band in Croxley Hall Woods, near Rickmansworth. The Liverpool band originally wanted the photographs to incorporate burning stakes but decided on a lighting assistant instead because of possible associations with the American white supremacist organisation the Ku Klux Klan. Modest as ever, when head Bunny Ian McCulloch saw the finished artwork he described photographer Brian Griffin's work as "better to look at than the Mona Lisa."

Barnet

Dressed in black cowboy suits, heavy metal trio Motörhead rarely looked so mean and motherless as on the cover of their *Ace of Spades* album. It could be the parched, unforgiving Wild West landscape in which they are standing. The outlaw sleeve image was drummer Phil Taylor's idea and the band hardly had to travel at all. A sandstone quarry in sunny Barnet stood in for the Arizona desert on the first Motörhead album cover to feature images of the band, so the blue sky and clouds were 100 per cent Hertfordshire. Recorded in August and September 1980, the album was produced by the late Vic Maile at his Jackson's Studio in Rickmansworth. A 1960s Pye sound engineer turned record producer, Maile helped produce The Who's *Live At Leeds* and Motörhead's live album, *No Sleep 'til Hammersmith*.

Nearby, The Streets – aka Mike Skinner – was the proud owner of a Rolls Royce Silver Shadow on the sleeve of his 2006 album, *The Hardest Way to Make an Easy Living*. Skinner and his heavily customised black Roller with rear-hinged back doors are pictured beside the hedge that surrounds the bowling green in Barnet's Oak Hill Park.

Elstree

The video – or 'pop promo' to use the lingo of the time – for Queen's groundbreaking *Bohemian Rhapsody* was shot in November 1975 at Elstree film studios, where the band were rehearsing for a tour. The video was produced so that the band didn't have to mime such a difficult song on *Top of the Pops*. Recorded in just three hours on a budget of £3,500, the video follows the same composition as Mick Rock's cover photograph of *Queen II*. The video's success opened the floodgates for pop promos and it became commonplace for record labels to produce a video to complement a single release.

Top producer Trevor Horn's synth-pop outfit The Buggles paid tribute to the film studios with *Elstree*, a single from 1980's *The Age of Plastic*. Another single from the album, *Video Killed the Radio Star*, proved more successful, reaching the number one slot. Aptly, it was the first music video to be shown on MTV, in August 1981.

Pop svengali Simon Cowell – the man who gave the world such luminaries as Zig and Zag and Robson & Jerome – also grew up in Elstree.

Stevenage

Knebworth House is one of the UK's most famous Tudor mansions, with world-renowned gardens open to the public. Since 1974 its grounds have netted the big cats, staging world-famous open-air rock and pop concerts. Led Zeppelin held court in the 1970s and Oasis reigned supreme two decades later. Led Zeppelin played two huge shows here at the beginning of August 1979, in front of more than 250,000 fans. When they arrived by helicopter singer Robert Plant recalls seeing "this huge sea of people." Quite a contrast to his early gigs at Stourbridge Town Hall. Over 100 major artists have played there since 1974, including Pink Floyd, The Rolling Stones, Queen (their last-ever live show), Paul McCartney, Elton John, and more recently, Robbie Williams. Pop duo Tears for Fears also shot their *Mad World* video here in 1982.

Ware

Singer-cum-gardener Kim Wilde followed in her parents' musical footsteps. She moved to Hertfordshire aged nine, with her singing and dancing mum, Joyce Baker (of The Vernon Girls fame) and veteran rocker dad Marty. She was educated at Presdales secondary school for girls and, in 1980, she completed a foundation course at St Albans College of Art & Design. She kick-started her music career signing to Mickie Most's RAK Records label and, within a few months, her debut single, *Kids In America*, was number two in the UK.

In September 1996, she married Hal Fowler, her co-star in the West End musical *Tommy*, at St Giles Church in the village of Codicote – wedding guests included Sir Tim Rice. The newly-weds' honeymoon was delayed so Wilde could promote her new single, a cover of Evelyn 'Champagne' King's 1978 disco hit, *Shame*.

Standon

Each summer the village of Standon, near Puckeridge and Hertfordshire's border with Essex, hosts the annual Standon Calling festival. What started as a birthday barbecue for a few dozen people in 2001 made the leap to a live music event in 2004. Now it aims to showcase established bands and breaking acts in the intimate grounds of a 16th-century mansion. A swimming pool is available to revellers along with a range of accommodation from ship cabins to beach huts.

Cheshunt

Born in India, where his father Roger worked as catering manager who serviced Indian Railways, perennial evergreen pop star Cliff Richard grew up – and first performed – in Cheshunt. As Harry Webb, he was educated at Cheshunt County Secondary School and lived with his family at 12 Hargreaves Close, a three-bedroom council house on the Bury Green Estate. It wasn't long before he was taking the bus to London to play the legendary 2i's coffee bar and starring as Bert Rudge in *Expresso Bongo*, a biting satire of the music biz. A block of flats, Cliff Richard Court, has been named in his honour in Cheshunt High Street. Neighbours report the flats are wired for sound and full of bachelor boys who need a summer holiday, as well as a living doll and devil woman who don't talk anymore.

Hertford

When heavy rock meets a Hammond organ you get the titans of heavy rock, Deep Purple, who formed in Hertford in 1968. They were one third of a holy trinity of British heavy

Above: Ritchie Blackmore's Deep Purple on stage in the USA, 1974.
Left: Cliff Richard in a scene from the 1959 film 'Expresso Bongo'.
Oppostie page: Liam Gallagher of Oasis performs live at Knebworth, 1996.

rock groups that turned it up to 11 as the 1960s blasted into the 1970s (the other two being Led Zeppelin and Black Sabbath). Despite personality clashes, in particular singer Ian Gillan and virtuoso guitarist Ritchie Blackmore, and numerous line-up changes (eight different line-ups, 14 different musicians), Deep Purple are the only ones still going. But it is their near-mythical 1969-1973 Mk II line-up of Gillan, Blackmore, drummer Ian Paice, bassist Roger Glover and Hammond organist Jon Lord that shook the rock world to its core.

Bushey

Duran Duran frontman Simon Le Bon was born in Bushey in 1958. Wham!'s George Michael moved to Radlett in his teens with his family and met Andrew Ridgeley at Bushey Meads comprehensive in Coldharbour Lane. Wham! backing singer Shirlie Holliman – later of Pepsi & Shirlie fame and the future Mrs Martin Kemp – also hails from Bushey.

ROCK MYTHS DEBUNKED

KEITH MOON DROVE HIS ROLLS ROYCE INTO A SWIMMING POOL

No, he didn't. Sounds good, even looks good; Oasis certainly thought so, depicting a Rolls Royce floating in a swimming pool on the cover of *Be Here Now*. And, given Moon the Loon's reputation for mayhem, the incident is totally believable. After a spectacular row with his wife at his space age mansion in Chertsey in 1972, Moon drove off in his lilac Roller, announcing he was going to kill himself. He took off down the drive but soon returned to the house covered in mud. He had reversed his Rolls, not into his swimming pool but into a muddy pond at the bottom of his drive where it got stuck on the muddy fringes. The garden pond has pretty much been referred to as a swimming pool ever since.

Another version of Moon's mythic motoring incident supposedly took place on his 21st birthday party at the Holiday Inn, Flint, Michigan. Rock 'n' roll folklore says Moon drove a Lincoln Continental into the hotel swimming pool. Sadly, as much as we want it to be true, this never happened either. According to Tony Fletcher in his acclaimed biography, *Dear Boy: The Life of Keith Moon*, the drummer made the whole incident up in an interview with *Rolling Stone* journalist Jerry Hopkins in 1972, and the myth mushroomed from there. "It was a beautiful story," writes Fletcher, "superbly told and one would love to believe it. But it's not true. And impossible in a dozen ways, once one stops laughing at it long enough to study the details." Even so, The Who's Roger Daltrey still swears blue there's truth in the rumour. "The only confirmed kill I ever heard of was one or two golf buggies, which ended up in the pool in Flint after the birthday party," recalls The Who's former PR, Keith Altham.

MARIANNE FAITHFULL WAS PLEASURED WITH A MARS BAR

No, she wasn't. Everyone knows it was a Curly Wurly. Seriously, it was neither. In February 1967, newspapers reported that Mick Jagger had performed chocolate bar cunnilingus on Faithfull at a party at Keith Richards' Sussex estate. But it was just a rumour and the start of an insidious campaign to discredit her and The Rolling Stones after police found drugs during a bust. The establishment were determined to discipline such a brazen-faced pop group.

MAMA CASS CHOKED ON A HAM SANDWICH

No, she didn't. 'Mama' Cass Elliot of the 1960s Los Angeles group The Mamas & The Papas is the most famous person never to have choked on a ham sandwich. Her death at the age of 32 in 1974 at Harry Nilsson's Mayfair flat was the result of heart failure, brought on by 15 years of regular drug use – and being a bit fat.

PAUL MCCARTNEY IS DEAD

No, he isn't (not at the time of writing, anyway). Rumours have circulated for decades that the Beatle was decapitated in a moped crash in 1966 and has been residing in the big octopus's garden in the sky ever since. Rumours cite evidence of the hand above Paul's head on the *Sgt. Pepper's Lonely Hearts Club Band* sleeve (an Indian sign of death); the second part of the registration number of the white VW on *Abbey Road* is 28IF – the age Paul would've been if he'd lived, and, moreover, the *Abbey Road* cover is his funeral march. There's also Paul wearing a black carnation in *Magical Mystery Tour*, while the others wore red. Ok, so who is the chap with the dyed hair who rhymed 'keyboard' with 'oh lord' when duetting with Stevie Wonder?

Oxfordshire

Mapledurham

It's surely a candidate for the scariest album cover ever, if you exclude Kevin Rowland's *My Beauty* (which pictures the former Dexys Midnight Runners frontman clad in lingerie). The striking, eerie image on the sleeve of Black Sabbath's eponymous first album conjures up the chilling apparition in *The Innocents*, Jack Cardiff's 1961 film of Henry James's novel, *The Turn of the Screw*.

The spooky building behind the ghostly figure of a woman dressed in a black cape is the historic Mapledurham Watermill, England's last working corn and grist mill on the River Thames in Oxfordshire, close to Reading and the Berkshire border. Satan was indeed just around the bend: the album was released in February 1970 – appropriately on Friday the 13th.

Heavy metal's first album starts with the sound of pouring rain and a crackle of distant thunder before Tony Iommi's three-note leaden guitar riff laid the blueprint for a whole new musical genre that would rocket in popularity through the 1970s and beyond.

The old watermill has stood on this site for centuries, and is mentioned as far back as the 11th century in the Domesday Book, although most of the existing building dates from the 15th century. During the 17th and 18th centuries, nearby communities relied entirely on the mill. It is still operational and produces high-quality stone-ground flour and is open at weekends and Bank Holidays between Easter and the end of September. Sabbath fans can also stay at one of the Grade II-listed holiday cottages; remember to pack a black dress and a wig if you want to recreate the sleeve.

Right: George Harrison of The Beatles sits in the peaceful grounds of his Henley residence Friar Park. He lived here until his death in 2001.

Henley-on-Thames

George Harrison arrived at his Friar Park country estate and 16-track recording studio in Gravel Hill in 1970, not long after The Beatles split. He lived at the 120-room Victorian neo-Gothic mansion, a former nunnery, perched on a hill high above Henley, until his death from cancer in 2001, aged 58.

Harrison recorded music here but he was also an enthusiastic gardener, transforming himself into a modern-day Capability Brown. When he arrived at Friar Park he set about restoring the overgrown Victorian gardens that had been neglected by the previous owners, a group of Catholic nuns.

The sleeve of his 1970 triple album, *All Things Must Pass*, sees him surrounded by some of his gnomes on an immaculately manicured lawn. A song on that album, *The Ballad Of Sir Frankie Crisp (Let It Roll)*, was inspired by the estate's former owner, the 19th-century lawyer Sir Frank Crisp, who lived there between 1875 and 1919. He built spectacular gardens, complete with subterranean caverns,

an underground lake and Alpine meadows featuring a 20-foot sandstone replica of the Matterhorn.

Harrison's 1976 song, *Crackerbox Palace*, on *Thirty Three & 1/3*, was also inspired by Friar Park; he gave his mansion the unofficial moniker after visiting Lord Buckley's Los Angeles home of the same name.

Harrison penned *Blow Away*, the upbeat title song of his 1979 self-titled album during a rainstorm in a Friar Park garden shed. After John Lennon was murdered outside his New York apartment in 1980, Harrison introduced special security measures around the 34-acre estate: a 10-foot-high wall equipped with lights, video cameras and a security alarm, directly connected to the local police station 400 yards away. Despite this extra security, an intruder broke into Friar Park in December 1999 and attacked Harrison and his wife, Olivia. After grappling with the intruder, who was armed with a knife, he was left with stab wounds and head injuries. Harrison was diagnosed with cancer in 1997, and his garden continued to provide sanctuary for him until his death. *Revolver* cover designer Klaus Voormann – once rumoured to be joining The Beatles when McCartney left – used to live in a house on the estate.

Born Mary O'Brien to a music-loving Irish Roman Catholic family, Dusty Springfield told the nuns at her convent school she wanted to be a jazz singer, but she was clearly more soulful – Sir Elton John would later call her the greatest white singer there's ever been.

She sung with her brothers in The Springfields before going solo and signing to Atlantic Records, appearing on the first-ever edition of *Top of the Pops* (New Year's Day, 1964) and recording her classic *Dusty in Memphis* album (1969). She returned to the pop charts in 1987 with the Pet Shop Boys on *What Have I Done To Deserve This?*.

In 1994 she was diagnosed with breast cancer; Dusty lost her battle in March 1999, but not before being awarded an OBE. She was cremated, with her ashes scattered in County Clare, Ireland, and Henley-on-Thames, where she lived out her final years.

There's a dedication to her in the graveyard of St Mary's Church, Henley, and, each year, on the nearest Sunday to her birthday (16 April) there's an annual Dusty Day when fans celebrate her life and music. It started off in Henley, but in more recent years has been held at Finnegan's Wake pub in Ealing, the west London suburb where she grew up and, aptly, not far from a shop that gave the Pet Shop Boys their name (see West London chapter).

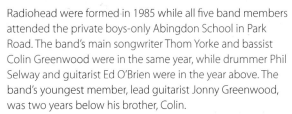

Abingdon

Radiohead were formed in 1985 while all five band members attended the private boys-only Abingdon School in Park Road. The band's main songwriter Thom Yorke and bassist Colin Greenwood were in the same year, while drummer Phil Selway and guitarist Ed O'Brien were in the year above. The band's youngest member, lead guitarist Jonny Greenwood, was two years below his brother, Colin.

The band's original name, On A Friday, referred to their weekly rehearsal in the school music room. They changed their name to Radiohead when they signed to EMI in 1991, inspired by a favourite Talking Heads track, *Radio Head*, from the 1986 album, *True Stories*. Within a few years they would emerge from the fringes of indie rock into the mainstream and be dubbed the best band in the world.

An event in July 2003 at Harrowdown Hill, a wooded area in the village of Longworth about seven miles west of Abingdon, was the inspiration for Thom Yorke's song of the same name, on his solo album, *The Eraser*. Yorke's song, about a man under unbearable pressure who is hounded to his death, was influenced by the death of Dr David Kelly. The Ministry of Defence weapons expert was found dead after appearing before a Parliamentary committee investigating British intelligence failings about the possibility of weapons of mass destruction (WMD) in Iraq. The resulting judicial Hutton Inquiry into the events leading up to his death ruled that Dr Kelly had committed suicide, but parts of the media and British public were sceptical. Kelly's evidence raised doubts about Saddam Hussein's possession of WMD – the official reason for Tony Blair's decision to invade Iraq.

The song is named after the place where Dr Kelly's body was found; Yorke has said the song is the angriest he has ever written.

In 1985, Kate Bush brought a touch of Tinseltown to Oxfordshire in her charming video for *Cloudbusting*. The song was inspired by a book Bush had read, called *A Book Of Dreams* by Peter Reich. The Vale of the White Horse, near Abingdon, was the location for the video, which starred actor Donald Sutherland as psychoanalyst Wilhelm Reich and a tomboyish Bush as his young son Peter. Like some of the best pop videos, it is like a Hollywood movie told in just few minutes, and follows Reich's arrest and imprisonment, because he has invented a cloudbusting machine that makes it rain.

The Uffington White Horse, exquisitely carved into the hillside off the A420, inspired the cover of the 1982 XTC album, *English Settlement*, which was recorded at The Manor, Oxfordshire. *Uffington Wassail* is a song on Half Man Half Biscuit's album, *Trouble Over Bridgewater*.

Oxford

Oxford has long since jettisoned its image of tweed-loving academics, dreamy spires and strange punting rituals. Nowadays the sweet sound of evensong rehearsals escaping from a chapel is far from being the only music you'll hear. Of course, being a university town Oxford, straddles the radical and the traditional, and that relates to its music too.

For a number of years, Oxford has enjoyed a musical renaissance. Most notably, of course, with Radiohead, Supergrass and turn-of-the '90s shoe-gazers, Ride, once Oxford's biggest band. But, more recently, the place has spawned Foals, Stornoway and The Young Knives (by way of Ashby-de-la-Zouch), whose bassist goes under the name House of Lords.

A key venue in Oxford's burgeoning music scene was The Zodiac, at 190 Cowley Road. Since 2006 it has been part of the O2 Academy chain, re-named accordingly and spruced up with a £2-million refurbishment. But such was the esteem that the former venue was held in that it will probably forever be known amongst locals as The Zodiac.

The venue hosted big name acts, but also made a point of being a springboard for Oxford's own bands. The video to Radiohead's 1992 single, *Creep*, was shot here, showing the future paranoid androids performing the song in the venue's dark enclaves. The Zodiac was also an early Supergrass venue; in their early days the band spent a couple of years sharing a house nearby at 345 Cowley Road.

Oxford's other top music venue The Jericho Tavern, at 56 Walton Street, first opened in 1818, when Thom Yorke was still a gleam in an ancestral eye. Showcasing up-and-coming acts on tour and local wannabes, it's likely that any Oxford band you might have heard of learned the ropes on The Jericho's stage. But one band more than any other looms large. As a rag-tag bunch of mangy students called On A Friday, Radiohead played their first gig here in late 1986 and, after several more performances, producers and record labels began to take note. In 1991, they played to two dozen A&R reps and were soon signed. Thom Yorke could leave his day job at nearby store Cult Clothing and Colin Greenwood could focus on music full-time rather than selling records at the Our Price music store.

A young Supergrass also learnt the ropes at The Jericho, playing many early gigs there, including the one in 1994 that secured them a record deal. The bands roots lie in Wheatley, a quiet, leafy Oxford suburb, five miles east of the city. The former Britpop teens grew out of The Jennifers who formed at Wheatley Park School in Holton and had to lie about their ages to get gigs. However, they soon built a reputation on the local indie scene. As Supergrass, the trio immediately set about putting their experiences as stoned youths in Wheatley into song. Their 1994 debut single, *Caught By the Fuzz*, tells of lead singer and guitarist Gaz Coombes's brush with the law: being arrested for cannabis possession.

In 1995, they were approached by Hollywood director Steven Spielberg, who had enjoyed their cheery *Alright* video – shot nowhere near Oxford but on a north Wales beach – and who proposed they collaborate on a *Monkees*-style TV show. The band turned him down, deciding to work on their next album instead. They would later write more locally influenced drug songs: *Shotover Hill*, from their 1999 self-titled album, is about the former Royal game reserve above Wheatley that once supplied the King with his venison. Today the woods and open fields are popular with walkers with great views over Oxford, but the band used to travel here to score from local travellers:

> 'Hear the sound of the wind it howls my name/
> Hear the cold light of day you can see it in my eyes
> they've changed'

Funniest Thing, from 2002's *Life on Other Planets*, refers to the band's early drug-induced hallucinations at the Gothic Revival folly nearby:

> 'Was the funniest thing that I saw/
> All these creatures were climbing the walls'

In June 2010, the band decided to call it a day after a series of farewell gigs. The reason? Yes, you've guessed it, creative differences.

Pyrton ▷

Pyrton Manor in the village of Pyrton, a few miles southeast of Wheatley, appears in the video of Blur's 1995 chart-topper *Country House*. It's not the sumptuous structure pictured at the start, or on the single's cover – that's Neuschwanstein Castle in Bavaria, which was built as a homage to German composer Richard Wagner and was later the inspiration for the castle in Walt Disney's *Sleeping Beauty*. Pyrton Manor appears as the residence of bowler-hatted businessman Keith Allen, who's trapped inside a giant version of the Ratrace board game. Directed by artist Damien Hirst, a Blur contemporary at south London's Goldsmiths College in the late 1980s, the band all appear, most notably parodying Queen's groundbreaking *Bohemian Rhapsody* video.

Shipton-on-Cherwell

In 1971, a 21-year-old entrepreneur in the mail order record business opened a London record store called Virgin. The same year he bought a 16th-century Grade II-listed stately home at Shipton-on-Cherwell, near Woodstock, and set about converting the manor house into the UK's first residential recording studio.

It was a breakthrough for the industry, meaning musicians could stay on-site and record through the night, then sleep all day – a much more rock'n'roll arrangement. Before The Manor – as the Shipton studio came to be known – bands would have to attend set sessions and go home. The first band to use Richard Branson's new studio in November 1971 was Vivian Stanshall's surreal group The Bonzo Dog Doo-Dah Band.

Stanshall was back the following year to record *Sir Henry at Rawlinson End*, his spoken word project about life in an English country house with a servant named Old Scrotum. Whilst there, he was asked to contribute to the first album on Branson's new Virgin Records label, a one-man instrumental suite in which a virtually unknown 19-year-old teenager would play *all* the instruments. Suddenly Mike Oldfield found himself in the middle of the English countryside, quite a contrast to his previous digs in a tiny room in Tottenham.

The Velvet Underground's John Cale had recently used some special bells during the recording of *The Academy in Peril*, and Oldfield asked if he could hold onto them. Stanshall acted as narrator on what would become Oldfield's ground-breaking *Tubular Bells*, introducing instruments as the record reached its climax.

The album proved an unlikely success – with its opening sequence used to chilling effect in *The Exorcist* – making a fortune for Oldfield and helping to secure Branson's Virgin empire.

Gong, Sandy Denny and Tangerine Dream all recorded at The Manor in the early 1970s, and it continued to be popular throughout the 1980s and half of the '90s too, with the likes of XTC, The Cure, Black Sabbath, The Cult and Public Image Limited all recording there. In the 1990s Radiohead recorded some of their breakthrough album, *The Bends*, at the studio; Paul Weller's *Stanley Road* was one of the last albums to be recorded there.

The studio closed in April 1995, following the takeover of Virgin by EMI, and the barn which used to house the recording studio was converted into a games room. In 2010,

The Manor went up for sale, a snip at £5.75 million, "offering every creature comfort for a large family," as the estate agent boasted in timeless prose. Branson, now of course Sir Richard Branson, owns a home in nearby Kidlington.

Banbury

Fairport Convention are folk pioneers, the first UK band to play English folk music with electric instruments. Each August the Oxfordshire village of Cropredy, near Banbury, hosts the band's annual Fairport Cropredy Convention music festival. The Cropredy Convention started as a one-day event in 1980 and now runs over three days. The festival line-up is varied but the Fairports have always traditionally closed the festival on the Saturday night. The band has been through various line-ups since forming in 1967 but still features founding member Simon Nicol and early recruit Dave Pegg. A 1973 line-up of the band is pictured on the back sleeve of their ninth album, *Nine*, outside Cropredy's 17th century village pub, The Brasenose Arms.

At the age of 16, Oxford-born folkie singer-songwriter Thea Gilmore began her musical career with work experience at Fairport Convention's Woodworm Studios in the village of Barford St Michael, just south of Banbury where the band were recording. There she was discovered by her long-time collaborator, producer and now husband, Nigel Stonier. She was raised nearby in the village of North Aston and got hooked on music via her Irish parents' record collection, which included Joni Mitchell, Bob Dylan and The Beatles. She began writing aged 15 to cope with her parents' divorce and has since released 10 albums.

Chipping Norton

Now owned by the world's largest hotel chain, Best Western, The Crown and Cushion Hotel in the High Street is a 15th-century Cotswolds coaching inn that was once owned by The Who's Keith Moon, a rock star with a penchant for not leaving hotel rooms as he found them.

He went into partnership with Ron and Yvonne Mears, his neighbours in Old Park Ridings, Winchmore Hill. Complaints from sniffy Chipping Norton residents about Moon taking over the hotel proved fruitless as it was his neighbour's name listed as landlord over the door.

Unsurprisingly, Moon's tenure attracted a younger crowd. His presence depended on The Who's touring commitments and was, therefore, erratic, but any visits provided the perfect opportunity for Moon to play the pub landlord with all-night drinking sessions. Members of Led Zeppelin and Pink Floyd, and friends like Elton John, Ringo Starr, Vivian Stanshall and 'Legs' Larry Smith from The Bonzo Dog Doo-Dah Band were regulars.

One night, Moon even funded a coach-load of regulars from Soho drinking club La Chasse to travel to the Cotswolds and return the following day after a night's free food, drink and board. When The Who bassist John Entwistle came to stay with his Scottish deerhounds in tow, Moon complained that their barking disturbed his guests. The irony of the situation was not lost on Entwistle who'd been expelled from hotels around the world thanks to Moon's unruly behaviour.

Until recently, the Crown and Cushion's website stated: "Under new ownership, it would be an understatement to say, the locals have seen a vast improvement in standards, service and attention to detail as well as a re-decorate and freshen up." Whether it was a reference to the late drummer's stewardship of the hotel is not clear.

Aston Tirrold

In 1967, Steve Winwood's new band Traffic retreated to a remote, derelict gamekeeper's cottage near the rural Oxfordshire village of Aston Tirrold, southeast of Didcot. (Back then, the area was located in Berkshire but is now in Oxfordshire thanks to 1970s boundary changes.) This is where the band famously isolated themselves from the London music scene for two years to write and rehearse songs that would end up on their debut album, *Mr Fantasy*. Taking their cue from The Grateful Dead, who had lived together in a house in San Francisco's Haight-Ashbury, Traffic moved the communal living concept a stage further. They pioneered the 1970s rock tradition of getting it together in the country: living and working together under the same roof as a collective.

Steve Winwood formed Traffic with the three friends with whom he'd played soul music back in Birmingham: drummer Jim Capaldi, saxophone and flute player Chris Wood, and guitarist and sitar player Dave Mason. Using a mixture of influences, they created a unique sound that blended folk, R&B and soul with pop psychedelia. Their rural cottage had no mains electricity, so the band ran their amps off a portable generator. They built a stage outside so they could play in the open air and just jammed until something good emerged that could be woven into a song.

The band's first audience were the local fauna: crows, rabbits and field mice. Traffic's collaborative method of songwriting and communal living initially emerged for practical reasons. They had stayed together in a London house but their neighbours complained whenever they began to play. "We wanted somewhere where we could just play whenever we wanted," Winwood said later. Set amid rolling downs, their cottage in the middle of nowhere proved inspirational, and the band found the surrounding landscape influenced their music. "We tried to absorb the country into the music somehow," Winwood said. "Embody the things we'd seen into the music, try to make instrumental passages that evoked the landscape."

> 'Day in the city/
> Oh what a pity/
> I could be in Berkshire where the poppies are so pretty'
> (*Berkshire Poppies*, Traffic).

The image on the sleeve of *Mr Fantasy* sees the band in the front room of their cottage on the downs near Aston Tirrold. The building was used once more for the cover of *The Best of Traffic*, with the band photographed outside.

Opposite page: Vivian Stanshall and the The Bonzo Dog Doo-Dah Band were the first to use The Manor recording studio in 1971.

Dear Prudence on The Beatles' *White Album* was about actress Mia Farrow's sister; Don Everly's daughter Erin was the inspiration for Guns N' Roses' *Sweet Child O' Mine*, and Lou Reed immortalised Warhol-clique transsexual Holly Woodlawn on *Walk On The Wild Side*. But what about the songs inspired by English people, well-known or otherwise?

your **SONG**

Side 1

Four Winds, The Lightning Seeds (2009)
The title track on The Lightning Seeds' 2009 album, *Four Winds*, is a tribute to frontman Ian Broudie's brother, Robert, a well-known Liverpool civil rights lawyer. Suffering from depression, he leapt to his death from the top of Liverpool Cathedral in October 2006. "I wish the four winds / Could blow you home / Back to when we could sit and find a way / To face today / But I guess you got those blues / And when you get those blues / There's nothing you can do."

Country House, Blur (1995)
The "professional cynic whose heart's not in it" and retires to an expensive house in the country to escape big city pressures was Blur's former manager, Dave Balfe, boss of Food Records between 1983 and 1994. Balfe sold Food to EMI in 1994 and moved to "a very big house in the country."

Hey Jude, The Beatles (1968)
Perhaps only Tammy Wynette's D-I-V-O-R-C-E can rival *Hey Jude* as the most famous song about a marriage break-up. Written to soothe the pain of Cynthia and John Lennon's five-year-old son, Julian, whose parents were separating, Paul McCartney changed the original title, *Hey Jules*, to Jude, because he thought it sounded better.

Orinoco Flow (Sail Away), Enya (1988)
Irish singer Enya immortalises her English record company boss Rob Dickins on her number one hit. Dickins was the head of her label, WEA Records, in the late 1980s.

She's Leaving Home, The Beatles (1967)
Inspired after Paul McCartney read a newspaper story about love-struck 17-year-old schoolgirl Melanie Coe who ran away from her north London home. "A-Level Girl Dumps Car and Vanishes," the *Daily Mail* headline read. Coe was found 10 days later living with her boyfriend, a croupier who had once been 'from the motor trade' like in the song. Unknown to McCartney he had met Coe four years earlier on the set of pop show *Ready Steady Go!* and presented her with first prize for miming to Brenda Lee's *Let's Jump The Broomstick*.

Side 2

For Your Babies, Simply Red (1991)
Mick Hucknall wrote this song on *Stars* – Britain's biggest selling album in both 1992 and 1993 – after his Simply Red managers Elliot Rashman and Andy Dodd started having children around the same time.

Lucy In The Sky With Diamonds, The Beatles (1967)
Seen as a surging ode to psychedelia upon its release, it caused controversy because of its hallucinogenic theme and veiled reference to the drug LSD. Lennon, however, always maintained the song was not a drug reference. Instead it's another *Sgt. Pepper's Lonely Hearts Club Band* song inspired by real-life events: a nursery school painting by Lennon's son, Julian. The girl with kaleidoscope eyes was four-year-old Lucy O'Donnell, a classmate of Julian's at Heath House nursery near Kenwood, the Lennon residence at St George's Hill in Weybridge. One day in 1966 Julian came home from nursery with a magical painting of a girl surrounded by sparkling stars and showed it to his father. "It's Lucy, in the sky with diamonds," Julian said and out came Lennon's notebook. Later, Lucy O'Donnell trained as a special needs nursery teacher before becoming Surbiton housewife Lucy Vodden – *Lucy in Surbiton With Husband* doesn't have the same ring somehow. She died in 2009, aged only 46, from the disease of the immune system, lupus.

Sunshine Superman, Donovan (1966)
The song was written about Donovan's future wife, Linda Lawrence, who was married to Rolling Stone Brian Jones. When Jones died in 1969, Donovan married his widow, raising Jones's son Julian, and two daughters of their own, together. Donovan's actress daughter Ione Skye came from a 1960s relationship with American girlfriend Enid Karl (née Stulberger).

Song For Guy, Elton John (1978)
Elton John's cheerful if largely instrumental song about death was inspired by morbid thoughts of his own demise and the death of Guy Burchett, a 17-year-old Rocket Records messenger boy killed in a motorcycle crash.

Something, The Beatles (1969); Layla, Derek And The Dominoes (1970); Wonderful Tonight and Old Love, Eric Clapton (1977, 1989)
Possibly only Jesus' mum has inspired more songs than model and photographer Pattie Boyd. She met her first husband, George Harrison, on the set of *A Hard Day's Night* and, a few years later, he wrote *Something* on *Abbey Road* about her. Enter Eric Clapton.

Boyd's unavailability was a magnet to him and *Layla* was Clapton's tortured declaration of love for her even though Boyd was still married to George Harrison, one of his best friends. *Layla*, recorded with Derek And The Dominoes, was based on a book by a 12th-century Persian poet Nizami about a man who's in love with an unobtainable woman.

In September 1976, now married to Boyd, Clapton wrote *Wonderful Tonight* about her while he waited for her to get ready for a party hosted by Paul and Linda McCartney. While Boyd took her time trying on dresses, Clapton sat strumming his guitar. In the time Boyd had taken to get ready he had written *Wonderful Tonight*. And in the end… in 1988, after nine years of marriage, Clapton and Boyd were divorced; *Old Love* (1989) describes the end of their relationship.

Boyd's sister Jenny was once married to Mick Fleetwood; no Fleetwood Mac songs were written about her but a former beau, Donovan, wrote *Jennifer Juniper* about her.

The Southwest

Bristol
Somerset
Wiltshire
Gloucestershire
Dorset
Devon
Cornwall

Bristol

In 2010, Bristol was voted 'Britain's most musical city'. The survey, compiled by the Performing Rights Society, which collects royalties for thousands of artists, placed Bristol ahead of London, Liverpool and Manchester. Away from Bristol's 1990s Trip Hop scene (see next page), which spawned artists such as Massive Attack and Portishead, Bristol has produced rootsy soul singer Beth Rowley, who grew up in the city from the age of two although she was born in Lima, where her parents were Baptist missionaries. Her saxophonist is Ben Castle, son of the late entertainer and trumpeter Roy Castle.

Bristol can also claim Gravenhurst (singer-songwriter Nick Talbot); synth duo F*** Buttons; Beki Bondage of punk band Vice Squad; Banarama's Sara Dallin and Keren Woodward (whose partner is Wham!'s Andrew Ridgeley); goth legend Wayne Hussey of The Mission and The Sisters of Mercy, and early 1970s prog rockers Stackridge, who are still gigging today.

Bristol's famous venue, the Colston Hall, has hosted a stellar array of rock and pop legends that reads like a Who's Who of 20th and 21st-century popular music. However, local group Massive Attack have always refused to play the 2,000-seat venue because of its historical link to the transatlantic slave trade. The hall is named after Edward Colston, the 18th-century Bristolian businessman and notorious slave trader, and the band have vowed not to play the venue so long as it retains its current name.

The Bristol Hippodrome in St Augustines Parade has also seen many famous acts and was the venue of the last gig by Eddie Cochran in 1960 (see page 187). A much-loved top Bristol venue is the Thekla, located aboard an old Baltic coaster moored in the city's East Mud Dock since the early 1980s. The ship ended up in Bristol thanks to the wonderfully eccentric late musician Vivian Stanshall. It was once his floating home and was sailed from the northeast to the Bristol docks in 1983, where Stanshall had it converted into a floating theatre and art space called The Old Profanity Showboat. Two years later the ship saw the debut of Stanshall's production, *Stinkfoot, a Comic Opera*. In the 1990s and early 2000s, Thekla became a prominent Bristol drum and bass club and many of Bristol's trip hop scene played in the Thekla's hull. It was reopened as a music venue and nightclub in 2006, thanks to a major makeover by DH Promotions, who also own several Nottingham venues including the Rescue Rooms. The top floor was refurbished and now houses a bar called Old Profanity in honour of the late Stanshall.

Between Bristol and Bath lies the town of Keynsham, also the title of the 1969 album by Stanshall's Bonzo Dog Doo-Dah Band. Other Bristol venues include the 450-capacity Fleece, in St Thomas Street. Open every night, it hosted a lot of top bands when they started out, like Muse and Oasis. Elsewhere, the former 18th-century prison Fiddlers Club, in Willway Street, and the Louisiana, in Wapping Road, are good for new and on-the-up acts.

The influential rock drummer Cozy Powell was killed in a car crash in April 1998 during bad weather near Bristol. He was driving at 104 mph when his Saab 9000 crashed into central reservation barriers on the M4. He was 50 years old.

Those strange album titles explained

Abacab, Genesis (1981)
Nothing to do with the magic circle, or the name of a Swedish taxi firm, the title simply derives from an early version of the title track's musical parts. Early on, the band labelled the three different sections of the song with letters of the alphabet, referring to them as sections A, B and C. At one point the sections spelled ABACAB. The finished song didn't follow the original structure but the band decided to keep the title anyway. The final version read more like 'ACCAABBAAC' but was not quite as easy for fans to pronounce or, more importantly, for Phil Collins to sing.

Disraeli Gears, Cream (1967)
A classic malapropism: when a Cream roadie mentioned drummer Ginger Baker's racing bicycle had 'derailleur' gears, he said 'disraeli' gears by mistake, unwittingly referencing the 19th-century prime minister, Benjamin Disraeli. The misunderstanding became an inside joke, and ended up as an album title.

Heligoland, Massive Attack (2010)
The mysterious title of Massive Attack's fifth album references an archipelago of tiny islands in the North Sea, off the coast of Germany. The album features a large cameo guest-list of artists, including Damon Albarn. His song, *Saturday Come Slow*, is about passing through Bristol and the West Country.

Maxinquaye, Tricky (1995)
Bristol's Tricky was raised by his grandmother. The title of this critically acclaimed solo debut album was inspired by his late mother, Maxine Quaye, who killed herself when he was just four years old.

Ogdens' Nut Gone Flake, Small Faces (1968)
Still seen as a classic today, the title of this music hall meets psychedelic masterpiece derives from Ogden's Nut Brown Flake, a popular brand of rolling tobacco. The distinctive circular cover was a parody of a tobacco tin and folded out to reveal pictures of the band. The original word Brown was changed to Gone, reflecting the band's frequent state of mind.

Ummagumma, Pink Floyd (1969)
The title of this 1969 album may sound like the spluttering of a new born child, but was instead a 1960s Cambridge University students' euphemism for having sex. Some band members of Pink Floyd have since said the word is meaningless and was totally made up.

Unhalfbricking, Fairport Convention (1969)
This title derives from the word-game, Ghost, in which players try not to complete an actual word. The electric folk band used to play it whilst on the road and golden-tonsilled singer Sandy Denny's contribution was the inexplicable *Unhalfbricking* (for the location of the album sleeve, see page 45). There's nothing remotely Belgian about the band's next album, *Liege & Lief*, released later in 1969. The title was simply two Middle English words: 'liege' meaning loyal and 'lief' meaning ready.

According to Paul McCartney, the title of one of The Beatles' greatest songs, *Eleanor Rigby*, was part-inspired by a shop in Bristol called Rigbys (Eleanor came from Eleanor Bron, the actress who had starred in *Help!*). In early 1966, McCartney visited girlfriend Jane Asher in Bristol where she was performing at the Old Vic. The name was also later discovered on a gravestone in St Peter's churchyard in Woolton, Liverpool.

Bristol's Dave Prowse is best known as the six-foot six-inch actor behind *Star Wars'* Darth Vader, as well as the Green Cross Code Man. But in the late noughties he took off the costumes to manage Cardiff band Losing Sun and the subsequent solo career of their drummer and multi-instrumentalist Jayce Lewis. Because of his gentle West Country accent, Prowse's *Star Wars* co-stars nicknamed him 'Darth Farmer'.

Right: Bristol's Thekla club.
Opposite page: Members of Massive Attack in 1991.

TRIP HOP
THE BRISTOL SOUND

THE ambient sounds, meditative beats and eerie vocals that characterise trip hop and the Bristol Sound have their origins in a racially diverse city that got rich on slavery. Massive Attack first came together as part of a multi-ethnic DJ collective The Wild Bunch that ruled the Bristol 'sound system' scene of the late 1980s. Formed when DJ Nellee (Nellee Hooper) met DJ Milo (Miles Johnson), they were later joined by Daddy G (Grant Marshall), Mushroom (Andrew Vowles) and graffiti artist 3D (Robert Del Naja) who used to spray the Wild Bunch's name on walls around Bristol. Indeed, the Bristol Sound was very much tied in with street art; internationally renowned Banksy – who would later design Blur's *Think Tank* album cover – started out at around the same time.

When Hooper became busy with Soul II Soul in 1989 and Miles Johnson left for New York, Mushroom, 3D and Daddy G formed Massive Attack. They enlisted the help of producer Cameron McVey and his wife, singer Neneh Cherry, who provided the trio with encouragement and financial support. McVey became their manager and Cherry let them record in her house.

Massive Attack's first single, *Any Love*, was co-produced by precursors of trip hop, duo Smith & Mighty (Rob Smith and Ray Mighty) who linked-up beat machines and sequencers to produce a laid-back groove. Their debut album, 1991's *Blue Lines*, was built around samples of old soul, funk and reggae records and included a cover of a 1970s soul hit, *Be Thankful for What You've Got*. Produced by Jonny Dollar and Cameron McVey, *Blue Lines*

was a commercial success and critics threw words like "epochal" at it, others called it album of the 1990s. It's seen now as the first trip hop album. But what exactly is trip hop?

There's some debate about the term's origins, but trip hop was probably coined by journalist Andy Pemberton in the June 1994 issue of *Mixmag*. The genre is usually characterised by a slow and relentless tempo, with big bass-lines (albeit less booming than house music), rhythm drop-outs, as in dub, and snippets of instruments, samples or noises. The tone is often sleepy, jaded-sounding, and the vocals are usually sung with a simmering intensity (by women) or rapped softly (by men). Lyrics tend to spring from the wounds of social and romantic pain.

Bristol had been quick to pick up on the new New York hip hop scene of the early '90s. Local DJs came back from the US with hip hop tapes, which were copied and spread around, becoming massively influential. Bristol's pioneering DJs put their local spin on the international phenomenon and developed hip hop into a different style. It was modified by adding a laid-back beat, or slow and heavy drum beats, creating a sound drawing on acid jazz, Jamaican and dub music. A music culture that embraced MC-ing, break-dancing and graffiti art was exploding in Bristol before it ever reached London. It became Bristol's signature sound, which would later be termed trip hop.

Around this time the Wild Bunch were playing outdoor parties in Clifton, using one deck and a hi-fi. Their reputation quickly spread and they soon had a Wednesday

night residency at the "sticky-carpeted dank cellar" that was the Dug Out bar, in Park Row: Bristol's Hacienda. This was where they mixed up reggae with soul and funk, brought it in old punk tunes and played the electronic hip hop of the day.

A few years later, the seminal *Blue Lines* would feature a number of collaborators, such as reggae legend Horace Andy and London singer Shara Nelson, notably on the track *Unfinished Sympathy*, which started out as a jam in Bristol's Coach House studio during rehearsals in the middle of 1990.

The album also featured rapper Tricky (Adrian Thaws), later employed on 1994's *Protection*. Tricky's 2008 solo album, *Knowle West Boy*, took its name from the run-down area of Bristol where he grew up. As a kid Tricky was inspired by reggae and the music of The Specials and the 2-Tone label.

At Coach House, the tape operator (and tea boy) on *Blue Lines* was a hip hop fan and breakbeat connoisseur called Geoff Barrow. When they heard his demo tapes, Massive Attack, McVey and Cherry encouraged Barrow to develop his ideas. Portishead was formed when he met Exeter-born, Bristol pub circuit blues vocalist Beth Gibbons at an Enterprise Allowance initiative meeting. The band were named after his home-town on the Severn Estuary a few miles from Bristol. Their collaboration produced *Dummy*, the startling debut album of trance-like beats and haunting melodies that scooped them the Mercury Prize in 1995.

Dummy was cut at State of Art Studios in Bristol's edgy Easton district. Portishead's bass-

and-beat pulse, as well as an instrumental sparseness and lyrical darkness, is typical of the slow bump and grind of the Bristol Sound.

Roni Size had also attended Wild Bunch parties and later, with Reprazent, would earn more kudos for Bristol, winning the Mercury prize in 1997 with drum and base album, *New Forms*.

However, predictably the Bristol Sound became bankable and trip hop was taken over by marketeers who realised it made perfect background music for restaurants and department stores, who all seemed to be suddenly playing – and still are playing – trip hop compilations. The pioneering genre became banal dinner party fodder. In response, the Bristol contingent abandoned their familiar samples, leaving slow tempos as the sole link between their work and a faceless genre they wanted nothing to do with.

Trip hop lives on, however. Post-trip hop artists include UNKLE, Morcheeba, Sneaker Pimps, Alpha and Mudville, acts who've integrated trip hop into other genres, including ambient, R&B, breakbeat, drum and bass and acid jazz. Trip hop has influenced major artists outside the genre, including Nine Inch Nails, Björk, Blur, Beth Orton and Radiohead.

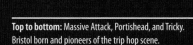

Top to bottom: Massive Attack, Portishead, and Tricky. Bristol born and pioneers of the trip hop scene.

Somerset

Bath

Sometimes you can't move in Bath for writhing groups of visiting Italian students and American tourists pounding the pavements, clocking Georgian Bath like it's some kind of Anglo Disney. It's unlikely any of them will visit the large Snow Hill council estate, off the London Road, where one half of the pop duo Tears for Fears grew up.

Curt Smith met Roland Orzabal as a young teenager in Bath, when he lived on Snow Hill, and he later made it the subject of a song, imaginatively called *Snow Hill*. The band and their record company were surprised when their breakthrough third single, *Mad World*, was a hit in 1982. Orzabal wrote it when he lived above a pizza restaurant, overlooking the bustle of Bath city centre. "Not that Bath is very mad," he said in *The Hurting* album liner notes. "I should have called it Bourgeois World."

Muse travelled to the 19th-century St Mary the Virgin church in Bathwick for their 2001 *Origin of Symmetry* album. Matt Bellamy recorded the organ parts on the final track, *Megalomania*, using the church's pipe organ, before the album was mixed at Sawmills Studio (see page 204). The album was a well-received experimental departure from the alternative rock sound of their first album, *Showbiz*.

On the banks of the River Avon lies the city's Riverside Studios, an old coach house two miles east of the city in the village of Batheaston. Artists like Robert Plant, Jeff Beck, Goldfrapp, Siouxsie Sioux, Babyshambles and Basement Jaxx have all recorded here.

Solsbury Hill, just north of Bath, a flat-topped mound between Batheaston and the village of St Catherine, was celebrated in Peter Gabriel's 1977 debut solo single. The stirring views of Bath from the top, or the exertion of getting there, may just make your heart go "boom, boom, boom" (as in the song). But at just 190 m you don't have to be Sir Ranulph Fiennes to climb it. The heartbeats more likely refer to Gabriel's exhilaration at leaving Genesis, as the song is a metaphor for his break from the band. After being "in a rut" Gabriel resolves to "show another me" and walk "right out of the machinery," while the eagle in the first verse mirrors his new sense of freedom. The song's familiar acoustic guitar riff is joined by more and more instruments in each verse, not unlike *Tubular Bells*.

Van Morrison sings lovingly about the county in *Somerset*, a track on 2003's *What's Wrong With This Picture*, released on the fabled jazz label Blue Note. He is accompanied on the song by legendary trad jazz clarinet player, Somerset-born Acker Bilk (Acker being West Country slang for mate):

> 'And we walked, walked all along the sand/
> And it felt, felt like a wonderland.'

Van the Man used an old record shop on the bright side of Walcot Street for the cover of his 2002 album, *Down The Road*. The window of the former Nashers Music Store at number 72 was filled with record sleeves by blues, rock and jazz artists who had influenced the young Morrison. (Sadly, Bath's emporium of second-hand vinyl has since closed.)

Belfast-born Morrison moved to Bath in the mid-1980s and purchased Wool Hall Studios in Beckington, a small village 10 miles southeast of Bath, in 1994. It made sense, as Morrison was one of its best clients, recording five albums there. The historic building was originally converted into a recording studio in the early 1980s, by locals Tears For Fears for their own use. The Bath duo recorded 1985's *Songs From the Big Chair* here, before the studio became a commercial entity, hosting artist such as Joni Mitchell, The Pretenders, The Stereophonics and Paul Weller.

The Smiths' final album, 1987's *Strangeways, Here We Come*, was recorded here, and Morrissey liked the place so much he returned six months later for his solo debut, *Viva Hate*. Morrissey's typically sardonic title refers to the fraught Smiths recording sessions that occurred at the studios. Today the Wool Hall is private property and no longer a recording studio.

Frome

Frome's 850-capacity Cheese and Grain Hall, an old farm produce warehouse, was converted into a music venue in 1997. It puts on regular gigs year round, featuring the likes of The Stranglers, Robert Plant, Babyshambles and, appropriately, The Animals. A few years ago punters threw bottles at Wirral band The Coral when they started slagging off The Wurzels. Sgt. Pepper's Only Dart Board Band is also based in the town. The Beatles tribute band stood in for the Fabs at the 40th anniversary commemorations of Abbey Road in 2009. Charlie Higson, of the Norwich band The Higsons (and later a TV comedian and novelist), was born here too.

North of Frome, the Tuckers Grave Inn, a real country local on the A366 in Faulkand, near Radstock, was the inspiration for The Stranglers song, *Tuckers Grave*, on their *Norfolk Coast* album. Expect more of a cider and real ale crowd here than Barcardi Breezer yoofs, as some ales are served straight from the barrel.

Taunton

About five miles north of Taunton lies Broomfield, the highest village in the Quantock Hills. This village was home to Joe Strummer and his family, until his sudden death just before Christmas in 2002. He was aged 50 and the victim of an undiagnosed congenital heart defect. Strummer

Above: Van the Man performing live in Hammersmith in 1979. He has been a resident in Bath since the 1980s.
Opposite page: Roland Orzabal and Curt Smith are Bath's Tears for Fears.

(born John Graham Mellor) was famously the leader of 1970s punk band The Clash, who, along with the Sex Pistols, revolutionised British youth culture and music. Their energetic and edgy music lashed out against the stagnation of the musical and political establishment.

In the late 1990s, many years after punk, Strummer returned with his post-Clash band, The Mescaleros. His final regular gig was at Liverpool Academy on 22 November 2002, but his last-ever performance was just two weeks before his death at The Palace, a small venue in Bridgwater near his home. His final album with The Mescaleros, *Streetcore*, was posthumously released in 2003.

glastonbury
Great Mother of all Festivals

WHO would have thought a dairy farm lying between two limestone ridges at the southern tip of the Mendip Hills would become the annual site for Britain's greatest music festival? From an early 1970s hippie convention to the world's largest green field, open-air music and arts event, the Glastonbury Festival of Performing Contemporary Arts is no longer just an annual gathering of crusties and spiritualists. On the weekend closest to the summer solstice in June, most revellers now come for the top bands and the vibe.

The first festival took place in September 1970 on the same site as it does today; Worthy Farm, in Pilton, six miles east of Glastonbury is in the heart of an area famous for its ancient legends and ley lines. It was the day after Jimi Hendrix died in London and 1,500 festival-goers were charged an entry fee of £1 that included a free pint of farm milk. Local Somerset prog rockers Stackridge were the first band to play and Marc Bolan's Tyrannosaurus Rex (later T.Rex) called in to headline on their way to play Butlins in Minehead.

Organiser and local farmer Michael Eavis, even then owner of one of the most famous beards in music, collected the money himself. He had been inspired by seeing hippies and flower power in action at the nearby Bath Festival that June and launched his own version on the family farm three months later. Acts performed on a roofless, makeshift stage tied to an apple tree and hippies wandered naked around the fields.

Nowadays, Glastonbury is a fully-clothed microcosm of society at large, with different camps, tribes and revellers finding a patch that best suits them amongst the crowd. Musos who want to check out new bands head straight for the John Peel Tent, while the Green Fields area, which includes the Healing Field, is evidence that the festival retains some of its laid-back hippy roots. Modern Glastonbury heroes include the likes of David Bowie, the Levellers, PJ Harvey, Pulp, Radiohead and Blur.

When Glastonbury celebrated its 40th anniversary in 2010, the crowds had swelled to nearly 140,000. Tickets that year were sold out in just one hour and 45 minutes. When, in February 2008, it was announced that American hip hop superstar Jay-Z would headline that year's festival, Oasis's Noel Gallagher criticised the organisers for diverting from traditional guitar bands. In a witty riposte Jay-Z opened his set with his rendition of their song, *Wonderwall*. For four decades Glastonbury has survived rain, mud, fires, gatecrashers, disputes with New Age travellers, and charges that the festival has grown too large. But, then again, its critics were saying that back in the early 1970s.

Other Somerset festivals

If you don't fancy Glastonbury, or missed the ticket scrum, here are a few other festival options:

All Tomorrow's Parties
Named after The Velvet Underground song, the annual All Tomorrow's Parties series of music festivals, held each December at Butlins holiday camp, pride themselves on being non-corporate and fan-friendly. Festivals are curated by a band or artist, such as Belle & Sebastian, who choose the line-up of influential acts from every musical genre. The resort also hosts The Bloc Weekend electronic music festival each March.

Sunrise Celebration
Along with a diverse line-up of artists spread over six music stages and room for 6,000 revellers, the accent at the uncommercial Sunrise Celebration is on ethical living, with more than half of the profits going to community causes. It's held at an organic farm in Bruton, southeast of Shepton Mallet, and with water fountains, compost toilets and a renewable energy source, it's little surprise it's been voted the most eco-friendly of all Britain's festivals. It began in 2006 as an alternative to the Glastonbury festival which was cancelled that year and now takes place in late May to avoid a clash with the Great Mother of all festivals.

Tribe Of Doris Intercultural Summer School
This is summer school meets world music festival. What started as a drumming convention with 75 participants in 1991 now attracts more than 1,000 visitors over five days. It takes place near the Wellington Monument on the Somerset-Devon border. Featuring musicians from Africa, South America and Asia, there are over 40 drumming, dance and song workshops a day. All abilities welcome from complete novices to advanced drummers.

A good friend of Strummer's was the noted film and documentary-maker Julien Temple, who also lives in the Quantock Hills. In 2006, Temple made a documentary about Strummer called *The Future Is Unwritten*. He's also made acclaimed films about Madness, Dr Feelgood and a trio of films about the Sex Pistols: *The Great Rock 'n' Roll Swindle*, *The Filth and the Fury* and *There'll Always Be An England*, a film of the band performing at London's Brixton Academy on a reunion tour.

At early Clash gigs Strummer wore a T-shirt supporting Brigade Rosse, the Italian Red Brigades who murdered the former Italian prime minister Aldo Moro. Such provocative acts were a cornerstone of the punk ethos and, as an outspoken freethinker, Strummer was trying to get people to think for themselves. "The spirit of rock 'n' roll helped to stop the Vietnam War," he told *The Times* the year before he died.

"Perhaps it's a bit crazy for me still to feel like that. But I can't help it. Someone's got to keep the faith."

A charitable trust, Strummerville, established soon after his death by his widow Lucinda, helps creative kids from disadvantaged backgrounds put musical projects together, providing funding for rehearsal space and studio time.

Bridgwater

Trouble Over Bridgwater was a 2000 album by Half Man Half Biscuit, a clear quip on the name of Simon and Garfunkel's famous song and album (see Tiverton, page 199). Targets on this album included BBC sports commentator Tony

Gubba (*Gubba Look-a-Likes*), legendary TV presenter Noel Edmonds (*Visitor For Mr Edmonds*), techno heads (*Twenty Four Hour Garage People*) and goths on *With Goth On Our Side*, about a Welsh goth called Dai Young:

'Now this Land Of My Fathers/
It don't suit my needs/
I'd rather be some place/
Like Bradford or Leeds.'

Weston-super-Mare ➤

The sleeve of the 1995 Oasis single, *Roll With It*, was photographed on the beach here with the band sitting in deckchairs watching television sets, with the historic Grand Pier in the background. Not for the first time Oasis were following The Beatles. The Fab Four were famously photographed at the seaside resort in July 1963, fooling around on the beach dressed in Victorian bathing costumes. For six nights The Beatles appeared at the Odeon, the single-screen cinema that stopped showing films to make way for the mop-tops. The Oasis single represented one corner in the so-called Battle of Britpop, in which Oasis and Blur fought it out for top spot in the charts, with Blur's *Country House* emerging victorious. Weston's Grand Pier was destroyed by fire in July 2008 and was still undergoing redevelopment at the time of writing.

The seaside town was lauded in the song *Sunny Weston-Super-Mare* (sic) by Somerset's legendary comic folkies, The Wurzels. The Scrumpy 'n' Western band also recorded such classics as *Rock Around The A38*, about the major road that runs through Somerset connecting Bristol to the West Country, and *Somerset Born And Proud*. Album titles have included *I'll Never Get A Scrumpy Here* and *Never Mind The Bullocks, Ere's The Wurzels*.

In 2007, they re-recorded their 1970s hit, *I Am A Cider Drinker*, with legendary DJ Tony Blackburn in aid of a Bristol-based cancer charity. In the video a jolly Blackburn does a proper job amid clichéed 'Zummerzet' rustic life, featuring hay-filled cowsheds, scrumpy tankards and impossibly buxom milkmaids. Phwoar… Ooh-arr.

When Weston-super-Mare's Winter Gardens on the seafront opened in 1927, its Pavilion Ballroom hosted elegant dances and parties. One look at today's programme of tea

Left: Rick Parfitt and Francis Rossi of Status Quo first met at the Minehead Butlins in 1965.
Opposite page: Joe Strummer, leader of The Clash, lived near Taunton until his untimely and sudden death in 2002 at the age of just 50.

dances and it's hard to believe anything has changed, but much has gone on in the intervening years.

In the 1960s and early 1970s the venue became a revolving door of thriving rock talent. The West Country musical hotspot hosted the likes of David Bowie, T.Rex, a five-piece Pink Floyd – with both Syd Barrett and new guitarist Dave Gilmour – and Deep Purple, with Weston-born homeboy Ritchie Blackmore on lead guitar. Before one gig, King Crimson played a game of football on the beach against their support band. Ziggy Stardust and his Spiders paid a visit, as did The Nice (featuring Keith Emerson), whose 1969 album, *Nice*, has photographs of the band along Weston's seafront on the cover. When Atomic Rooster blew a fuse during a gig, their suitably prog rock response was for drummer Paul Hammond to play on his own until everything was fixed. The last bumper year of appearances came in 1972 before it closed as a venue in 1973.

Minehead ➤

Minehead's Butlins holiday camp was pivotal in the long-standing musical partnership of Francis Rossi and Rick Parfitt of Status Quo. They first became friends when the young pair met at the Minehead Butlins in 1965. Parfitt was a teenage cabaret singer at the holiday camp when he came into contact with Rossi's band The Spectres, also playing Butlins. They got on brilliantly from the start, so well that when Rossi was expelled from his accommodation for sneaking a girl back, Parfitt left his digs in protest. Instead they made a little camp on the beach and slept on deckchairs. Parfitt was later invited to join The Spectres, who would change their name to Status Quo.

Wiltshire

Swindon ⟩

The Wiltshire town's Oasis Leisure Centre, a swimming pool, sports centre and 3,000-capacity concert venue, inspired Britpop giants Oasis to change their name. They were previously called The Rain until singer Liam Gallagher saw the venue's name on a concert poster for The Inspiral Carpets, when brother Noel was a roadie for the band.

The former frontman of The Smiths, Morrissey, collapsed on the Oasis stage in October 2009. Moments after performing his opener, *This Charming Man*, he fell to the ground with breathing difficulties and was dragged offstage by worried roadies. Arriving on stage minutes earlier he had announced: "Good evening… probably."

The venue also welcomes chart-topping acts such as Sugababes, Hard-Fi, Beverley Knight, Pet Shop Boys, Paolo Nutini, McFly and *X-Factor* winner Shayne Ward. Meanwhile, Swindon's annual music festival is called the Swindon Shuffle and it plays across venues like The Beehive and the 12 Bar.

The town lays claim to Justin Hayward of The Moody Blues, actress and singer Billie Piper and Supertramp's Rick Davies. Davies can be seen reading a copy of Swindon's *Evening Advertiser* (now the *Swindon Advertiser*) in an American diner on the sleeve art of their album, *Breakfast in America*. But easily one of the finest bands to come from the Wiltshire town were XTC.

The band's guitarist, singer and chief songwriter, Andy Partridge, has lived in Swindon since he was two years old. He once described the town to *Rolling Stone* magazine as "a little gritty industrial blob in the West Country" and was criticised by his local newspaper. Partridge gave up live performance in 1982 due to stage fright. In 2003 he set up his own label, Ape Records: "Artists get a 50 per cent royalty of any net profit," he told the *Independent*. "I'm proud of not screwing the artist, whereas a lot of record companies are quite the opposite." Like Ray Davies of The Kinks, Partridge has soundtracked the banality of everyday life in suburbs and small towns. He celebrated the ordinariness of towns like Swindon particularly well in his 1980 song, *Respectable Street*:

> 'It's in the order of their hedgerows/
> It's in the way their curtains open and close/
> It's in the look they give you down their nose/
> All part of decency's jigsaw I suppose.'

Chalkhills and Children, the final track on XTC's 1989 album, *Oranges & Lemons*, recounts a balloon ride over the English countryside and mentions the old Roman road of Ermin Street which skirts Swindon en route to Cirencester.

Chippenham ⟩

A car crash on Rowden Hill in April 1960 robbed the world of rock 'n' roll legend Eddie Cochran. During a five-week English tour, the 21-year-old was in a taxi to Heathrow Airport after

with crazed fans chasing the north London quartet out of a gig at the Neeld Hall in Borough Parade. Teenage fans of the band were in such a frenzy that The Kinks legged it for fear of being torn to pieces.

In June 2006, The Verve's former frontman Richard Ashcroft was arrested after an unannounced visit to a Chippenham youth club. He burst into the Bridge YMCA youth club, looking less than focused, and demanded to give a music lesson to the 60-odd teenagers inside. The police were called and the singer was taken into custody for a couple of hours and given an £80 fixed penalty for disorderly behaviour, before being released. Ashcroft said later he wanted to see if the kids in there were being taught music, and, if they weren't, could he help?

Malmesbury

The annual celebration of music and dance, the Womad festival (World of Music Arts and Dance), takes place each year at Charlton Park on the last weekend in July. The family-oriented festival moved to Wiltshire in 2007 after it outgrew its Rivermead site in Reading. Lasting three and a half days, from Thursday evening to Monday morning, the line-up majors on world music performers, but also hosts jazz, blues, rock and hip hop artists with usually a few household names.

Melksham

It's not immediately apparent what Melksham's claim to rock 'n' roll fame is. The newsagent in the town, seven miles south of Chippenham, may sell copies of the *NME* but that hardly counts. Its notoriety goes back several decades when now-disgraced pop star Gary Glitter appeared here. In mid-July 1972, the Assembly Hall (now Melksham Labour Club) was the venue for the first-ever performance of The Gary Glitter Rock 'n' Roll Spectacular, featuring the performer studded with sequins, alongside two sax players and two drummers called Pete. A plaque marking the event was removed in 1999 following Glitter's fall from grace.

a gig at the Bristol Hippodrome, when the car blew a tyre and crashed into a lamppost on the A4. Cochran died later in Bath's St Martin's hospital.

The crash also injured his songwriter fiancée, Sharon Sheeley, and left another rock 'n' roll star, Gene Vincent, injured and scarred for life. Several days before the crash a gypsy in Blackpool had told Cochran that he would never leave England. A memorial stone to Cochran is located near the crash site that claimed his life, and Chippenham still commemorates him with regular Eddie Cochran Weekend festivals.

Dave Dee of the 1960s band Dave Dee, Dozy, Beaky, Mick & Tich was a young police cadet in the Wiltshire Constabulary who was called to the fatal crash scene. He salvaged Cochran's Gretsch guitar and kept it safe, later confessing that he'd given the guitar some good strums before forwarding it to the rock 'n' roll star's mother. Dee was born David Harman in Salisbury in 1941 and was famous for cracking a whip while singing about *The Legend of Xanadu*. He helped establish the Nordoff-Robbins Music Therapy charity in the 1970s. As a record company executive for WEA Records, he secured the deals that brought AC/DC, Boney M and Gary Numan to the label. Dave Dee died from prostate cancer in 2009.

Back in September 1964, Beatlemania was in full swing but Chippenham suffered more from a dose of Kinksmania,

Box is the HQ of rock musician and producer Peter Gabriel. His Real World Studios are housed in a former mill he had converted in 1988 in the quiet rolling hills along Wiltshire's border with Somerset. The following year, the former Genesis star founded his Real World label to record and promote world music artists internationally. The residential recording studios boast some of the most high-tech and state-of-the-art recording equipment in the world. The Stereophonics, Tom Jones, Oasis, Jamie Cullum, Midge Ure, Kylie Minogue and The Beautiful South have all recorded there. Gabriel paid for a public footpath behind the studios to be re-routed after bands in the recording rooms complained about being spied on by groups of fans.

Tragically, in January 2004, James Lawrence, guitarist with the band Hope of the States, hanged himself from a wooden beam in one of the studios.

Marlborough

Radiohead decamped deep into the Wiltshire countryside on the edge of Savernake Forest in October 2006 to record their seventh album, *In Rainbows*. The band temporarily converted Tottenham House, a crumbling old Palladian mansion at Great Bedwyn, seven miles southeast of Marlborough, into a recording studio. *In Rainbows* was released the following year as a digital download that buyers could order for whatever price they liked.

No more albums will be recorded at the Grade I-listed country house that was commandeered by the American Armed Forces during World War II. The country mansion will become The Savernake Club, a posh hotel and golf club opening in 2015, with close to 300 bedrooms and suites.

Avebury

A visit to Avebury stone circles inspired Julian Cope to write a book about Britain's megalithic heritage. Published in 1998, *The Modern Antiquarian: A Pre-Millennial Odyssey Through Megalithic Britain* is a guide to stone circles, megalithic monuments, barrows and hill forts. The Arch-Drude now lives near Avebury with his wife and wonderfully named daughters, Albany and Avalon. The first part of the medley *Paranormal In The West Country*, on 1994's *Autogeddon*, was recorded in the main neolithic necropolis, of the West Kennet Long Barrow. Before he became one of rock's leading Odinists, Cope formed The Teardrop Explodes in 1978, before going on to record prized acid-pop albums, *World Shut Your Mouth* and *Fried*.

Right: Julian Cope, former frontman of The Teardrop Explodes and Arch-Drude who lives near Avebury stone circle.

Salisbury

The five-day Larmer Tree Festival is held each July at a Victorian estate in the lush Larmer Tree Gardens, Tollard Royal, near Salisbury. The child-friendly annual event features an eclectic line-up: blues, world jazz, roots and reggae. In addition, there are creative workshops and street theatre troupes. The festival's 4,000 capacity translates as a shorter wait for the loos. In fact, previous accolades include Best Toilets and Best Family Festival awards. Another festival, The End of the Road Festival, takes place at the same venue each September. Its major selling point is that bands play longer sets than usual.

The Beatles' second movie, *Help!*, was filmed in exotic locations like Austrian ski slopes and sun-drenched Bahaman beaches and… on Salisbury Plain. In May 1965, The Beatles based themselves in Amesbury's Antrobus Arms Hotel during three days of shooting here. Filming took place at Knighton Down near the Larkhill army base, where The Beatles perform *I Need You* and *The Night Before*, protected by a circle of Chieftain tanks and with Stonehenge visible in the background. Their journey from their hotel to film location attracted huge crowds of teenagers, bringing the streets of Amesbury to a standstill.

Another Chieftain tank appears on the sleeve of *Salisbury*, a 1971 album by hard rockers Uriah Heep.

Tidworth

Situated at the eastern edge of Salisbury Plain, Tidworth is the home-town of the former Household Cavalry officer Captain James Hillier Blount, aka singer James Blunt. In his early twenties, Blunt saw active service in Kosovo as part of NATO's peacekeeping force and also guarded the Queen Mother's coffin. But after six years of British Army service, he left in 2002 to focus on his love of music; he had learnt the violin, piano and guitar in his youth and had been writing songs since his mid teens.

His debut album, *Back to Bedlam*, originally dipped in and out of the Top 100 albums chart until the release of single, *You're Beautiful*. The song became a phenomenal hit in 2005, reaching the number one spot in more than 10 countries.

Even though he changed his surname from Blount to Blunt to sound edgier and more proletarian, many found his well-spoken voice, Harrow public-school education and officer background too posh. Posh or not, he is the most successful British singer-songwriter in the US since Elton John, and *Back to Bedlam* was the biggest selling UK album of the whole of the noughties.

Ashcombe House, in Berwick St John, near Salisbury, was queen of pop Madonna's pad for seven years between 2001 and 2008. A year after moving into the Georgian country estate, Madge and film director husband Guy Ritchie erected 12-foot-high security gates, without obtaining the necessary Listed Building Consent, though they were eventually awarded retrospective permission. In 2004 Madonna got shirty with the great unwashed who crossed her land. Large parts of the estate had been classed as "open downland", to which anyone has access under Right to Roam legislation. The celebrity couple claimed the land was not open, but agricultural, and that ramblers, sightseers and paparazzi could not get within 100 yards of their home. An inquiry ruled ramblers could only access half their land – not getting close to see the mansion. In August 2005, Her Madgesty fell from her horse in the estate grounds, breaking her collar bone and cracking three ribs. The £9 million Ashcombe House went to Ritchie as part of the couple's divorce settlement in 2008.

Stonehenge

Stonehenge is one of the most instantly recognisable monuments in the whole of England, yet the origins and purpose of the giant stone circle remain mysterious. Its mythology influenced Marc Bolan and T.Rex songs, *Dragon's Ear* and *The Children of Rarn*. The ancient site hosted concerts, starting with the summer solstice Stonehenge Free Festival that began in 1972 and lasted for 12 years. And who can forget Stonehenge's inclusion in the classic spoof rockumentary, *This Is Spinal Tap*? When the fictional rockers perform their song, *Stonehenge*, on their comeback tour a misunderstanding about measurements results in a tiny replica of Stonehenge appearing onstage. While Spinal Tap's miniature version was nearly trampled on by the dwarves hired to dance around it, Black Sabbath faced the opposite problem. During the 1983 tour, their life-size stage set of Stonehenge proved too big to fit into many venues.

The Four Seasons (alternate take): SUMMER

A Sky of Honey, Kate Bush
The second half of Kate Bush's 2005 double album, *Aerial*, is a 42-minute meditative suite. It's Bush at her free-spirited, experimental best and as ever, the album is a total rejection of any prevailing pop trends. Sunrise, sunsets, the recurring sounds of birdsong and nature, the rain, the stars, the beach, the ocean, a moonlight swim… the delights of summer are all here (even Rolf Harris pops up as a street painter at work in changeable light). Sumptuous string arrangements and piano chords summon up a beautiful summer soundscape that begins, on *Prelude*, with birdsong and the voice of Bush's young son:

> 'Mummy… Daddy/
> The day is full of birds/
> Sounds like they're saying words.'

Club Tropicana, Wham!
Wham!'s 1983 hit was so evocative of hedonistic summer package holidays that its inclusion here is mandatory. With the sound of cicadas and the mention of soft white sand, blue lagoons and panama hats, it is clearly set abroad, though.

Southern Freeez, Freeez
An unforgettable slice of classic British jazz-funk from 1981 that summons up those long summer nights when you don't have a care in the world. Health and safety alert: trying to master the song's cracking bass breaks on your air bass without supervision may result in a hernia.

The First Picture of You, The Lotus Eaters
"Seeing the flowers scream their joy." Few hits capture the endless possibility of long, warm summer nights as well as this one-hit wonder from Liverpool's The Lotus Eaters. An evocative ode to summer's dreamy exuberance.

Wild Wood, Paul Weller
Weller's peaceful acoustics on the title track of his second solo album, borrowed from children's classic *The Wind in the Willows*, provide a perfect accompaniment to a hot summer's afternoon in the English countryside, but with the sound of the traffic never far away.

Hear also:
The Rain Song and *Down By The Seaside* by Led Zeppelin; *Sun Hits The Sky* by Supergrass; *Cruel Summer* by Bananarama; *In the Summertime* by Mungo Jerry; *Long Hot Summer* by The Style Council; *Staying out for the Summer* by Dodgy; *Lazy Sunday* by Small Faces; *Hot In The City* by Billy Idol; *Pain Killer* by Turin Brakes; *Flowers In The Rain* by The Move; *Sunny Afternoon* by The Kinks; *Diamond Day* by Vashti Bunyan; *The Lazy Sunbathers* by Morrissey; *Little Bird* by Goldfrapp; *Mr Blue Sky* by the Electric Light Orchestra and *Summer's Cauldron* by XTC (or anything else on their *Skylarking* album).

Westbury ⟩

You don't need to be brothers in a Mancunian Britpop band to loathe each other. In June 1985, the long-standing spat between Hawkwind founder members Nik Turner and Dave Brock was still much in evidence. At a free festival at Westbury's White Horse, an artwork of a horse carved into chalk, the twice-sacked Turner jumped on stage uninvited while his old band were playing. He told the crowd that he and Brock had buried the hatchet. A few seconds later Turner heard Brock say behind him: "In your f***ing head you c***!"

In 2007 Brit Award-nominated five-piece The Feeling recorded their second album, *Join With Us*, at Bradley House, in Maiden Bradley, near Warminster. The Tudor country house is normally used as a wedding venue (and provided a notable contrast to the production of their 2006 debut album, *Twelve Stops And Home*, which was largely made in a shed belonging to the parents of the band's brothers Ciaran and Kevin Jeremiah). The band slept in beds that had previously belonged to King Henry VIII and claimed they saw a ghost.

Above: Hawkwind – as famous for their well documented spats as for their music.
Left: The 2005 Summer Solstice at Stonehenge.

Gloucestershire

Cheltenham ⟫

Brian Jones, founder of The Rolling Stones, is buried in Cheltenham's Priory Road Cemetery, a (rolling) stone's throw from his parents' home, across from the Parish Church on Hatherley Road. At Cheltenham Grammar School for Boys (now Pate's Grammar School), he excelled in academic subjects and sports, even though he suffered from asthma. Ironically, one of these sports was swimming; he drowned in the swimming pool of his home in July 1969 (see page 77).

Born in Cheltenham in 1942 as Lewis Brian Hopkin Jones, the middle class son of an aeronautical engineer, it was Jones who put an ad in *Jazz News* looking for musicians for an R&B group that became The Rolling Stones in 1962. By 1969 his appetite for drink and drugs left him often incapable of playing in the studio, let alone of embarking on an imminent US tour.

In 2004, Cheltenham Borough Council decided the proposed Brian Jones Close, a road named after the dead Stone, and part of a new housing development, should be renamed in honour of Gloucestershire writer and naturalist John Moore instead. Builders Bryant Homes told the council open-minded buyers didn't want to live on a road named after a drug user. The chairman of the Brian Jones Fan Club said Stones fans everywhere were disappointed, but the regret was only short-lived. The following year Cheltenham commemorated its famous rock star son with a statue in the town's Beechwood Shopping Centre. Proud fan club members unveiled a green and gold bronze bust entitled Golden Boy, created by local sculptor Maurice Juggins.

The origins of post-punk warlords Killing Joke were in west London but the band's frontman Jaz Coleman, son of a high-caste Brahmin Indian mother and English father, hails from Cheltenham. Their provocative single sleeves featured the likes of Fred Astaire tap-dancing over a trench full of First World War bodies and the Pope given a Nazi salute by German troops and blessing them in response.

Killing Joke's gloomy world view appealed to goths, but their music straddled many genres, inspiring future generations of bands. After Killing Joke, multi-instrumentalist Coleman became a classical composer and focused on his multi-cultural approach to music, including Maori folk songs and Arabic music. He co-wrote an album of Middle Eastern instrumental music and released three albums of symphonic rock music.

Cheltenham racecourse is not exclusively the domain of National Hunt horse racing and the Cheltenham Festival each March. In early June there's plenty more jumping (but no fences), when the racecourse swaps lean equine racing machines and the not-so-elegant and usually inebriated Irish and English punters for several thousand music fans at its annual Wychwood Festival. Launched in 2005, this smallish, family-friendly festival (there's a nappy service and a new toddler area) veers towards indie, roots and world music. In addition to music, there are also workshops: previous years have included comedy, yoga and African drumming classes. And, if the music won't change your life, perhaps a life-coaching workshop might.

Upcote Farm in Withington, southeast of Cheltenham, is the venue

Left: The funeral of The Rolling Stones guitarist Brian Jones at St Mary's Parish Church, Cheltenham in 1969.
Opposite page: Post-punk outfit Killing Joke.

for the 2000 Trees Festival each July. Starting in 2007, this sponsorship-free and non-branded festival was born out of disappointment with the undiluted profit motive of larger, mainstream festivals. Its name comes from the number of tickets on sale and the organisers' promise to plant a tree for every reveller who attends. The line-up offers an eclectic mix, from rock, metal and indie to folk and pop. In keeping with its strong environmental ethos, the main stage is The Treehouse and there are DJ lounges called The Greenhouse and Leaf Lounge. A Big Green Shuttle Bus transports festival-goers from Cheltenham Spa train station to the festival site and two campsites mean there is also plenty of grass for revellers to enjoy.

Aust

The abandoned Vauxhall Cavalier car belonging to troubled Manic Street Preachers guitarist Richey Edwards was found near the Severn View service station in February 1995, leading to speculation of his suicide. Afterwards there were reported 'sightings' of Edwards every few months: in the Canary Islands, Goa and even Newport public library just a few miles from his hometown in Gwent. His disappearance followed a long period of depression during which he cut '4REAL' into his arm (see Norwich, page 121). He was officially pronounced dead in November 2008.

Stow-on-the-Wold

Quarwood, the Victorian Gothic mansion that stands atop the highest hill on the edge of the Cotswolds market town of Stow-on-the-Wold, was the home of one of Britain's greatest rock 'n' rollers, John Entwistle of The Who. Quarwood appears in The Who biopic, *The Kids Are Alright*, and was home to the legendary bass player for 27 years, until his very rock 'n' roll death in Las Vegas on the eve on a 2002 US tour: a cocaine-induced heart attack after a night with a stripper at the Hard Rock Hotel and Casino. His 42-acre estate contrasted greatly with Stow's genteel atmosphere, its antique emporiums and teashops. Stone pillars adorned by lion plinths guarded the entrance to the long gravel driveway. Inside, a suit of armour stood guard at the foot of the stairway and, for baronial effect, Entwistle had the walls painted to look like stone. Aside from bedrooms and guest rooms, the 55-room mansion housed his collection of pinball machines, while other rooms accommodated his huge collection of guitars and basses, and his train set. Another room was dedicated to stuffed fish suspended from the ceiling: sharks, barracuda,

swordfish and marlin he had caught in Mexico and Florida. Despite having no driving licence, Entwistle owned some luxury cars, including a Cadillac Eldorado and a Rolls Royce Silver Shadow customised to take his dogs. He installed two recording studios and recorded two of his solo albums in the larger one on the ground floor. He would surprise visitors with two human skeletons called Mr and Mrs Bones; alarmed guests would find the fleshless figures grinning at them from cupboards and beds.

Entwistle was an influential and accomplished musician who played the bass almost as a lead instrument. He was The Who's anchor – while the rest of the band romped around the stage, he stood firm – hence his nickname of The Ox. Entwistle's funeral was held at St Edward's Church in Stow-on-the Wold in July 2002.

Gloucester

Gethsemane, Again, a song on Al Stewart's 1970 album, *Zero She Flies*, was the singer-songwriter's no-holds-barred response to a visit he made to Gloucester Cathedral.

Stewart was appalled by the merchandise for sale and the blatant commercialisation of the church and saw it as the second betrayal of Jesus:

> 'And the outstretching hands of the swains of the Lord/
> Sold the communing commuters the word/
> With LPs of Mary and photos of God/
> In the hall.'

A thriving local live venue is Gloucester Guildhall in Eastgate Street, in the heart of the city. Both big-name bands early in their career and established acts warming-up for bigger venues seem to play here, all in an intimate setting in front of a couple of hundred people.

Gloucester-based train company Cotswold Rail has a habit of turning music lovers into trainspotters. Three of its fleet of railway locomotives are named after famous musicians and radio DJs. The company, which hires out its stock to railway companies, including Virgin Trains, has named three of its Class 47 locomotives after Joe Strummer, John Peel and Captain Sensible.

Newent

Northwest of Gloucester, the small market town of Newent was the birthplace and home of pioneering record producer and songwriter Joe Meek. His best-known creation was the hit record *Telstar* by The Tornados; incidentally, the favourite record of former prime minister, Margaret Thatcher. During his career Meek invented many recording techniques; *I Hear a New World*, a concept album he made for shops to test new stereo equipment, was admired for its groundbreaking use of electronic sounds. Not bad for someone widely known to be tone deaf. Meek suffered from chronic depression and his problems worsened as his career failed. In 1967, a paranoid Meek, convinced someone was trying to harm him, shot his landlady before turning the gun on himself at his home/studio (see North London). He was buried in Newent Cemetery.

Clearwell

Clearwell Castle, near Coleford in the Forest of Dean, is an 18th-century mock Gothic castle with terraced gardens and a gateway formed by two tall towers. It is now a posh hotel that hosts wedding receptions, but standard wedding fare like Robbie Williams' *Angels* was not always the only music to be heard here. The castle was made of harder stuff as a favourite rehearsal and recording studio for many top 1970s heavy rock bands. It attracted the likes of Led Zeppelin, Black Sabbath, Deep Purple and Bad Company. In 1973, Deep Purple created part of their album, *Burn*, here, and the same year Black Sabbath rented the castle and wrote their *Sabbath Bloody Sabbath* album here, some of it in the castle's dungeon.

Cinderford

Another popular wedding song comes care of the best band ever to come out of the Gloucestershire town of Cinderford, dance-rockers EMF. Their catchy dance hit, *Unbelievable*, conquered the British charts in 1990 and the US charts the following year. They formed and were based in the Forest of Dean town. The band's name was an acronym of Epsom Mad Funkers, although many fans, especially devotees of the Madchester music scene, thought it stood for Ecstasy Motherf***ers. Their record label, Parlophone, however, insisted it stood for Every Mother's Favourites. The band's 1991 debut album sold two million copies but courted controversy and its release was delayed when John Lennon's widow Yoko Ono objected to the sampled voice of his killer Mark Chapman on the track, *Lies*. The album's name, *Schubert Dip*, was inspired by the main songwriter Ian Dench's view that if he were ever short of a chord sequence, he'd borrow one from the Austrian composer.

Right: Cinderford's EMF.
Opposite page: John Entwistle of The Who at home.

Dorset

Swanage

Many southwest seaside towns pride themselves on offering visitors a wide range of active pursuits to burn off the ice creams; 1980's band Big Country embarked on some of them around Swanage and the Purbecks in their video for *In a Big Country*. The four-piece were from Fife in Scotland but in their 1983 promo they tore around green fields on all-terrain trikes before putting on wet suits on Swanage Pier and heading out into Swanage Bay on a motorboat. The band were also seen at Corfe Castle station on the restored six-mile heritage Swanage Railway before some of the tracks were re-laid. The video has an incomprehensible narrative but plenty of product placement of the band's logo throughout.

Lulworth

Aptly, the natural limestone arch Durdle Door, near Lulworth, on the spectacular Dorset coastline known as the Jurassic Coast, resembles a prehistoric monster quenching its thirst in the sea. Some more dinosaurs, rock legends Pink Floyd, were photographed at Durdle Door for the lyric book artwork of *The Division Bell* album. The arch also appears on the cover of Ocean Colour Scene's 2003 album, *North Atlantic Drift*.

Several pop videos have been filmed at Durdle Door and around. Roland Orzabal and Curt Smith of Tears For Fears explore the area in the first half of their video for 1984's *Shout*, while the coastline features prominently in Cliff Richard's 1990 Christmas number one, *Saviour's Day*. The video's finale, in which the evergreen Richard is joined by locals for some elevated seasonal swaying, has eerie echoes of the build-up to the climax of the classic British horror flick, *The Wicker Man*.

Durdle Door and the coast also appear briefly at the start and end of Billy Ocean's 1985 single, *Loverboy*. Punk band Tenpole Tudor travelled to nearby Lulworth Cove to film the promo for their 1981 single, *Throwing My Baby Out With the Bath Water*, which reached a whopping number 49 in the charts.

The grounds of Lulworth Castle, nearby, are the location for the annual Camp Bestival, a three-day family-friendly music festival in July, which exports the ethos of Isle of Wight's Bestival to the mainland. This, too, is organised BBC Radio 1 DJ Rob Da Bank. As the festival name implies, the emphasis is on camping, with sleeping options as diverse as the festival line-up: luxury tepees and yurts, camper vans, or even a solar-powered pod-pads with fitted carpets.

Bournemouth

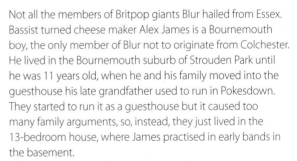

Not all the members of Britpop giants Blur hailed from Essex. Bassist turned cheese maker Alex James is a Bournemouth boy, the only member of Blur not to originate from Colchester. He lived in the Bournemouth suburb of Strouden Park until he was 11 years old, when he and his family moved into the guesthouse his late grandfather used to run in Pokesdown. They started to run it as a guesthouse but it caused too many family arguments, so, instead, they just lived in the 13-bedroom house, where James practised in early bands in the basement.

He once bunked off school for a week to sit on Bournemouth beach, looking out to sea and strumming his guitar. At other times, James joined his sixth form Bournemouth School mates and skipped lessons at the top-floor café at Dingles department store in Old Christchurch Road. There they would smoke filterless cigarettes and pose with their Jean-Paul Sartre and Albert Camus books, eyeing up the local girls. He bought his first bass guitar at Southbourne

Exchange & Mart, in Christchurch Road. James originally wanted to buy some keyboards but they were too expensive.

Blur's Britpop rivals Oasis travelled south to the Victorian seaside town for the cover sleeve of their 1998 number one single, *All Around the World*. The band were photographed on Bournemouth beach, with the name of the song written in the sand.

Between Bournemouth and Christchurch lies Hengistbury Head, a nature reserve full of herons, skylarks and a lily pond that attracts a magnificent array of beautiful dragonflies. Perfect images for an album cover you might think. US rockers Phish completely ignored this beauty spot and headed straight for the beach below for the striking cover of their 1997 live album, *Slip Stitch and Pass*. Designed by graphic artist, Storm Thorgerson, best known for his Pink Floyd covers, the mammoth-sized ball of purple wool featured on the sleeve was actually heavy rope.

Bridport

Dorset diva Polly Jean Harvey (PJ Harvey) was born in Bridport in 1969 to a stonemason father and sculptress mother; in the early 1990s she moved to London to study sculpture herself at Central St Martins. She was raised on a sheep farm in Corscombe, near the Somerset border, where her music-loving parents introduced her to American blues legends and Bob Dylan, Jimi Hendrix and Captain Beefheart, sometimes waking the young Polly and her brother with loud music at 3am. (Her songs are published by Hot Head Music, named after a Beefheart track.) She saw Dylan and The Rolling Stones in concert before she was 10 years old. The songs on her Mercury Prize-winning 2000 album, *Stories From the City, Stories From the Sea*, were written in Dorset and New York and pay tribute to her Dorset roots. The beautiful title track of her 2007 album of ethereal piano ballads, *White Chalk*, evokes the Dorset coastline and chalk hills.

Wimborne

The legendary guitarist and producer Robert Fripp hails from the Dorset town of Wimborne, or Wimborne Minster to give it its full name. In addition to being the only constant in the ever-changing line-up that was King Crimson, he's collaborated with Brian Eno, Andy Summers, David Sylvian, and his wife, singer and actress Toyah Willcox. They married in 1986 in nearby Poole. When, in 2003, she was voted out of TV series *I'm a Celebrity, Get Me Out of Here!*, Fripp was there to meet her: "…and here's your husband, Robert," presenters Ant and Dec told Toyah and viewers, making no mention of who he was. Maybe they were too young to know.

The market town also claims Scottish-born singer-songwriter, Al Stewart, who grew up here having moved south with his mother, and, in complete contrast, the heavy metal/doom metal band Electric Wizard.

Just like sub-editors at the *Sun* newspaper, it seems music festival promoters can't resist a good pun. North of Wimborne, the annual rural Endorse-It-In-Dorset music festival takes place at Oakley Park, near the village of Sixpenny Handley in the heart of Dorset's historic and picturesque Cranborne Chase. The line-up includes an eclectic mix of ska, dub and punk bands on two tented stages, and there's also an open-air stage for music and comedy and a chill-out area, ideal for tired parents given the run-around by their darlings.

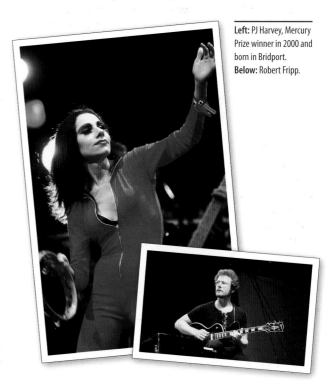

Left: PJ Harvey, Mercury Prize winner in 2000 and born in Bridport. **Below:** Robert Fripp.

Devon

Exeter ▶

For a city of its size, Exeter punches above its musical weight. Its brightest musical luminary is Coldplay lead singer Chris Martin, who comes from the village of Whitstone to the city's west. Until recently, his father ran a caravan sales place just outside Exeter at Sandygate roundabout, while Martin's grandfather was both Sheriff and Mayor of Exeter. Portishead singer Beth Gibbons was also born and raised here, moving to Bristol to pursue a singing career aged 22. Former University of Exeter students include the first *Pop Idol* winner Will Young and Radiohead's Thom Yorke, who between studies was a DJ at the Lemon Grove, better known as the Lemmy. The Cavern Club, in Queen Street, is a popular indie live venue, where Muse played some early gigs. The live music club The Hub, in Mary Arches Street, is now Mama Stone's, run by soul singer Joss Stone's mother, Wendy Joseph and her husband.

Bideford ▶

Devon's contribution to punk was The Adverts, regulars at the legendary London punk club, The Roxy. They were formed in Bideford in 1976 by the Devon art school duo of singer and guitarist TV Smith and his bass-playing girlfriend, Gaye Advert. As punks they committed the cardinal sin of working alongside the old guard, producer Tom Newman, who had worked with progressive rock acts, and in punk eyes the biggest yawn-fest of all, *Tubular Bells*. For their second album, The Adverts recorded at Richard Branson's Manor Studios in Oxfordshire, where *Tubular Bells* was made.

Right: Jimmy Cauty of KLF.
Opposite page: Joss Stone performing live at Glastonbury festival in 2004.

Saunton Sands ▶

One of Devon's greatest beaches is a three-mile curl of flat sand enclosed by a huge expanse of sand dunes. Pink Floyd made great use of the expanse of sand for the cover of their 1987 album, *A Momentary Lapse of Reason*. Floyd enlisted their old sleeve designer Storm Thorgerson, who arranged for 800 beds to be sent from London to Devon. They were lined up along the beach to make the striking cover. The beach also proved a draw for Robbie Williams who shot the black and white video for his most popular song, *Angels*, here.

Totnes ▶

In recent years Totnes has become a magnet for healers, herbalists and New Age types, a phenomenon that's not gone unnoticed by Birkenhead's finest, Half Man Half Biscuit. The ancient market town was honoured in the song, *Totnes Bickering Fair*, on the band's 2008 album, *CSI:Ambleside*. It's typically humorous fare that includes the memorable final lyric: "Not long now before lollipop men are called Darren." The song also includes the line: "I want a sun tan, not Vashti Bunyan," a reference to the cult English folk legend. Totnes was the birthplace of Rockman Rock (aka Jimmy Cauty), one half of The KLF (aka The Justified Ancients of Mu Mu).

Ottery St Mary

Brighton-based folk-punk band The Levellers enjoyed Glastonbury so much they started their own festival. They created Beautiful Days in 2003 because they wanted an old-fashioned festival rich in community spirit and without corporate sponsorship. With a capacity of 10,000, Beautiful Days is a former winner of the Best Grassroots Festival and showcases folk, roots and punk. Recent line-ups have included The Stranglers, Echo & the Bunnymen, Steeleye Span, The Pogues and Hawkwind. And, every year without fail, some band called The Levellers also turns up, and not just to sample the homemade Beautiful Daze beer. The action takes place near Ottery St Mary, just off the A30 between Exeter and Honiton, at Escot Park, on land designed by Capability Brown.

Clovelly

In the last two weeks of 1970, Deep Purple, featuring the band's classic MKII line-up of Ian Gillan, Ritchie Blackmore, Ian Paice, Roger Glover and Jon Lord, retreated to north Devon to an old farmhouse miles from anywhere. The rented farmhouse was The Hermitage on Welcombe Manor, located about six miles from Clovelly. It was here, between drinking sessions and séances, and with their wives, girlfriends and roadies in tow, that they began recording sessions for their album, *Fireball*. It was the second of a trio of albums recorded between late 1969 and 1971 that secured their reputation and defined hard rock for several generations.

Tiverton

For years, Bickleigh, near Tiverton, was subject of a Devonian legend to rival the Hairy Hands of Dartmoor. It was claimed that the village's medieval bridge over the fast-flowing River Exe inspired Paul Simon to write *Bridge Over Troubled Water*. As inspiring as the ancient grey stone bridge is, and as much as local tourism chiefs probably want it to be true, it was a long-running urban myth created by music journalist Pete Frame. The man behind the *Rock Family Trees* books, later developed into a TV series narrated by John Peel, has admitted it was a deliberate mistake to catch out plagiarists, or "ensnare pirates" as he put it. Paul Simon's singing partner Art Garfunkel has stated that Simon took the song title from a gospel phrase in a Baptist church hymn. What is beyond doubt is that Paul Simon and Garfunkel did visit the Tiverton area in the 1960s.

Ashill

West Country soul diva Joss Stone hails from the tiny village of Ashill, east of Tiverton, on the northern edge of the Blackdown Hills. Born Joscelyn Stoker in Dover, Stone lived in the Kent port town until she was eight, when her parents moved to Ashill in rural Devon seeking a better quality of life. Her parents' home was alive with the sound of music: a mix of Anita Baker, Whitney Houston, The Clash and The Jam. She went to Uffculme Comprehensive School five miles away, where she made her first public performance, singing Jackie Wilson's *Reet Petite* at a 1950s-themed variety show in the school hall. When she burst onto the music scene as a young teenager in the early noughties, Stone was enthusiastically touted as the new Aretha Franklin and the best white female soul singer to emerge from Britain since Dusty Springfield more than 40 years ago. When she first appeared on MTV in the US, geographically confused yanks described her as "the 16-year-old girl from the little English town of Devon."

The three members of Muse met as teenagers when they were students at Teignmouth Community College. Guitarist and singer Matt Bellamy, drummer Dom Howard and bassist Chris Wolstenholme were all originally members of different bands, before Muse formed in 1994. Wolstenholme was in a covers band but was kicked out for liking Status Quo. All of the trio were born elsewhere in England but grew up in Teignmouth after their families moved to Devon. Matt Bellamy's father, George, was the guitarist in the 1960s band The Tornados who had a huge international hit with *Telstar*, the first US number one by a UK group.

Muse prepared for their 2004 *Absolution* tour with practice sessions at Coombeshead College in nearby Newton Abbott, where Matt Bellamy attended sixth form. By now recognised as global rock gods, in September 2009, the Teignmouth trio returned to their Devon home-town to kick off their world tour. They played two open-air concerts at The Den seafront park, a decade after the release of their debut album. It was the biggest thing to happen to the seaside town since 1943, when the American Navy practised manoeuvres for the D-Day Landings here.

"The only time the town came to life was during the summer when [Teignmouth] turned into a vacation spot," frontman Bellamy told the *Guardian*, talking about growing up there. "When the summer ended they left and took all the life with them. My friends were either getting into drugs or music, but I gravitated towards the latter and learned how to play. That became my escape. All we used to do was hang around, smoke and listen to music. There wasn't anything else to do."

Bellamy now divides his time between a house in Devon and a villa by Lake Como in Italy, where the 19th-century composer Vincenzo Bellini lived.

Dartmoor ➤

Folk who couldn't bear progressive rockers Yes had wanted to throw tomatoes at the band for years and, in the late

Seth Lakeman's Dartmoor

DARTMOOR-based folk singer and fiddler Seth Lakeman writes stirring songs about local legends and folklore. While they have traditional arrangements and influences, there's a bite that gives them a modern feel. Lakeman himself describes his pounding rhythms and songs as "handmade music with an edge." He is a contemporary folk singer-songwriter with a pop heart. "There is obviously a stereotype against English folk music that stops it entering pop world but I do think that seems to be changing," he told your author.

To Lakeman, Devon is a wonderful place to create songs. "The people and places have had a very important impact on me and my music. I've been inspired by the space, the beautiful and varied countryside." He was born, and still lives in, Yelverton and comes from strong folk music stock; he first picked up the fiddle because his mother played. "I was inspired to become a musician because I was always surrounded by it and loved playing music and communicating with other performers."

Lakeman's breakthrough record, 2004's Mercury Prize-nominated *Kitty Jay* was recorded in his brother's kitchen in Horrabridge for just £300. "We had to pause the recording at night whenever the local farmer was working next door!" Lakeman recalls. The songs on the album capture the spirit and wilderness of the moor and were inspired by local stories and the legends of Dartmoor. "A very dramatic and sometimes mysterious landscape surrounds us here on the moor," says Lakeman.

The *Kitty Jay* sleeve sees Lakeman pictured in tiny Wistman's Wood on Dartmoor, one of the last ancient sessile oak forests left in England. Here the oaks grow between large moss-covered boulders and moorland granite, with ferns growing from the branches.

His 2006 album, *Freedom Fields*, drew again on West Country legends, telling of stricken ships and lovers lost in civil war. *Lady Of The Sea* was about the area's naval traditions. The album and title track explore the factions created by the English Civil War and take their name from the site of a massive battle in the middle of Plymouth in December 1643, which changed the course of English history, when the Roundhead Garrison of Plymouth made their final rally, routing the King's army of Cavaliers. "I've written a number of songs inspired by this battle," says Lakeman. "*1643*, on *Freedom Fields*, is the best representation of this."

Lakeman named the album after Plymouth's Freedom Fields Hospital, where he was born. The former workhouse turned city hospital was torn down in 1998 and the site redeveloped as affordable housing. *Freedom Fields* also contains the song, *Childe the Hunter*, about the legend of a wealthy Saxon lord who became separated from his hunting party and stranded on Dartmoor by a violent storm. He was forced to take desperate measures to avoid dying from exposure. "I have written a lot of songs inspired by the moors but my favourite is probably *Childe the Hunter*. A very evocative tale."

And it doesn't seem as though Lakeman will run out of local folklore to write about anytime soon. "I tend to research further a field these days too, but I'm sure there's enough material on Dartmoor to write about forever!" In fact, when we spoke, he had just written a song about Bowerman's Nose, a stack of heavily weathered granite on Dartmoor, near Hound Tor, reputed to be the inspiration for Sir Arthur Conan Doyle's *The Hound of the Baskervilles*.

1970s they got their chance, at least visually. Gone were the fantastical landscape sleeves designed by graphic artist Roger Dean, instead the band chose the aptly named Yes Tor, near Sourton Cross, on a picturesque corner of Dartmoor to appear on the cover of their 1978 album, *Tormato*. The inner sleeve shows the band pictured in front of Dartmoor's second highest point, 619 m above sea level. The album was originally due to be called just Yes Tor but another Devonian legend has it that keyboard wizard Rick Wakeman wasn't fond of the cover photos so he threw a tomato at them. The title and its cover were duly changed.

Yes Tor lies on a British Army firing range and subsequently is out-of-bounds when live firing is taking place. Unless you want to end up resembling the album sleeve yourself, check the nearby firing notice for the all clear.

Whiddon Down on the edge of Dartmoor is the venue for the annual Chagstock Festival that started in 2003 as a private party and made its public debut in 2007. The site's three 10-acre fields, with panoramic views of the Dartmoor National Park, have capacity for 3,000 revellers with no plans to grow any bigger. Chagstock has a chilled-out atmosphere with an eclectic music line-up and plenty of children's activities to occupy the little ones when worse-for-wear Daddy starts to rant.

Opposite page: Muse playing The Pyramid Stage at Glastonbury Festival, 2010.

Cornwall

Truro ⟩

In late June 1970, Truro's City Hall claimed itself a little bit of rock history, when future rock royalty Queen made their world debut here, albeit also under a different name. The venue billed them as Smile, their previous moniker. Their first-ever gig came about after drummer Roger Taylor promised his mother the band would play a charity event she had organised in aid of the Red Cross.

Taylor's musical career started in Truro after his family moved to the Cornish town from their native Norfolk. He was enrolled as a junior at the local Bosvigo School and then Truro School, the local public school, after winning a scholarship. Taylor learnt the ukulele and formed a skiffle group called the Bubbling Over Boys. Then, five years before Queen's first gig, a young Taylor appeared at the same venue keeping beat for local band Johnny Quale and The Reactions. In March 1965, the band entered the annual teen contest, the Rock and Rhythm Championship of Cornwall. Some 800 teenagers crammed into Truro City Hall that night, paying the sixpence entrance fee.

Redruth ⟩

Another legendary English rock drummer, the towering colossus that is six-foot-six-inch Mick Fleetwood, hails from Cornwall. Fleetwood was born in Redruth in 1947 to the son of an RAF officer, which led to a nomadic childhood as his family were posted abroad to countries like Norway and Egypt. He was discovered by keyboard player Peter Bardens, who invited him into his band The Cheynes. This led to work in John Mayall's Bluesbreakers and, finally, he teamed up with guitarist Peter Green and bassist John McVie in Fleetwood Mac.

In 1970, Fleetwood married and, rather dizzyingly, later divorced, remarried and divorced again, Jenny Boyd, sister of model Pattie Boyd, who was wife of George Harrison and, famously, the object of Eric Clapton's affections.

His late sister was the actress Susan Fleetwood who starred alongside Spandau Ballet's Kemp brothers in *The Krays*, as their aunt.

North of Redruth, Porthtowan Beach was the location for the cover image of 1993's *Surfing on Sine Waves* by Polygon Window, an alias of maverick ambient and electronic dance music guru, Richard James, aka Aphex Twin. Born in 1971, James grew up in the village of Lanner, near Redruth, and paid homage to his Cornish roots on the 2001 US re-release of *Surfing on Sine Waves*. The track *Redruth School* was named after his secondary school and *Portreath Harbour* is in honour of the nearby fishing port. "I'm just some irritating, lying, ginger kid from Cornwall who should have been locked up in some youth detention centre," he told the *Guardian* in 2001. "I just managed to escape and blag it into music."

He started in music early, building his own synthesisers in his bedroom aged 14 and writing his own computer programmes. He has worked with avant-garde composer Philip Glass and has been cited as a major influence on Radiohead. His recordings are also regularly used in films and TV adverts. Aphex Twin is known for his memorable music videos, notably 1997's brilliantly scary *Come to Daddy*, described as *The Exorcist* of pop videos, in which hordes of grinning replica Aphex Twins frighten passers-by, including a frail old lady. This was followed by 1998's infamous *Windowlicker*, a 10-minute hip hop send-up. The uncut version of the video uses the f-word 44 times in just under four minutes.

Opposite page: The giant Mick Fleetwood live in concert behind the drums in 1970.

Solomon Browne, a song on folk singer and fiddler Seth Lakeman's 2008 album, *Poor Man's Heaven*, tells the story of the 1981 Penlee lifeboat disaster, when eight volunteer lifeboatmen from the Cornish village of Mousehole, near Penzance, died. The week before Christmas, lifeboat *Solomon Browne* went to the aid of the stricken shallow-hulled coaster *Union Star* in stormy waters and hurricane winds. Two boats were lost in heavy seas, resulting in 16 dead, eight from each vessel. As a young boy Lakeman knew some of the bereaved: "I grew up with one of the boys who lost his dad in the disaster. They lived next door."

Porthcurno Beach is one of the best beaches in Cornwall and can be found on the Penwith Peninsula, near Land's End. The beach was the inspiration for Richard Hawley's sumptuous song, *The Ocean*, on his 2005 album, *Coles Corner*.

Billed as Cornwall's theatre under the stars, the open-air Minack Theatre, set on the cliff side at Porthcurno, predominantly stages plays, but also concerts. "I always love playing the Minack Theatre," says Seth Lakeman. "It's a stunning location." While Porthcurno simply means Port Cornwall, Minack derives from the Cornish for 'rocky place' (not to be confused with rock 'n' roll place).

Lizard Point ⟩

Using a mix of synthesiser noises and recorded nature and animal sounds, *Lizard Point*, the opening track on Brian Eno's 1982 ambient *On Land* album is an evocation of a specific place: the tip of Cornwall's Lizard Peninsula, mainland Britain's southernmost point.

Liskeard ⟩

Many Echo & The Bunnymen fans consider the band's 1983 album, *Ocean Rain*, to be their finest. The cover sleeve was shot in man-made caves hewn by local slate miners. They're called the Carnglaze Slate Caverns and can be found near the village of St Neot, just northwest of Liskeard. The cavern in which the band are seen in a rowing boat is the lowest of the three caverns, with a clear-watered subterranean lake that lies 60 m below the ground. The lake's blue-green hue is thanks to the presence of minerals in the rock. The upper cavern was used during the Second World War as a Royal Navy rum store. Nowadays the caves are sometimes used as a concert venue and auditorium, with seating for 400 people.

The cover image continued the theme of elements explored in the band's sleeve artwork. While *Ocean Rain* clearly represented water, previous covers depicted earth (*Crocodiles*), air (*Heaven Up Here*) and ice (*Porcupine*). Somehow they never got around to portraying fire. Upon its release, head Bunny Ian McCulloch modestly described *Ocean Rain* as "the greatest album ever made".

The Hurlers, the opening track on Seth Lakeman's *Poor Man's Heaven* is named after Cornwall's answer to Stonehenge, the ancient stone circles near the village of Minions on Bodmin Moor, north of Liskeard. As legend has it, some locals preferred to play hurling here rather than attend church and so were turned to stone, leaving them to play hurling forever on the moor. Another legend says if you correctly count the number of the Hurlers, misfortune will befall you. For his *Poor Man's Heaven* sleeve, Lakeman was pictured northwest of Bodmin Moor on the dramatic and windswept Atlantic coastline near Tintagel.

Fowey ⟩

At times the small port village of Fowey (pronounced 'foy') on the Cornish Riviera can seem like Hampstead-on-Sea. An influx of well-heeled visitors and new residents have pushed up house prices, forcing out locals. Bands are known to visit the village when staying a couple of miles north at Sawmills Studios, located in a converted 17th-century water mill, near the village of Golant. One of the UK's first residential recording studios, its picturesque location on the banks of the River Fowey means it's only accessible by boat or by the Lostwithiel and Fowey Railway. Many albums have been recorded at Sawmills since it was started in 1974 by record producer, Tony Cox, including Oasis's debut album *Definitely Maybe*, as well as *I Should Coco* and *In It For the Money* by Supergrass and The Verve's *A Storm in Heaven*. The studios have also hosted Wet Wet Wet, Catatonia, Ocean Colour Scene, The Stone Roses, Razorlight and Robert Plant. Muse started their career at Sawmills, recording parts of their first two albums, *Showbiz* and *Origin of Symmetry* here. New Model Army once said they didn't want to record albums anywhere else.

St Ives ⟩

St Ives, the former pilchard fishing port turned artists' colony, proved to be an important transitional place for one musician at least. The Cornish seaside town was a turning point in the career of singer-songwriter Donovan. High on bohemian thought, Buddhism and beatnik ideals, he answered the troubadour's call of the open road in the early 1960s, hitchhiking from his Hertfordshire home down to Cornwall. Donovan lived the wandering minstrel life and ended up in St Ives, where he lived and slept on the beach. It was here he started to write many of his songs and find his voice. Donovan was joined by a group of other folk musicians, like Ralph McTell and John Renbourn, who also spent their summers here in the early '60s.

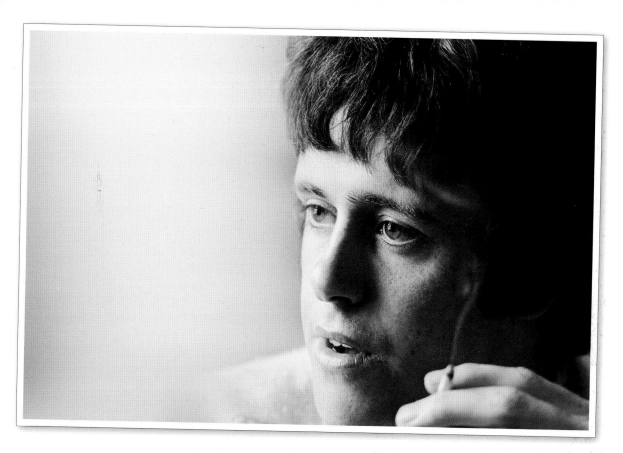

St Austell

A couple of miles from St Austell, the now-famous biomes of the Eden Project form a backdrop for the Eden Sessions, a season of one-day summer gigs at the tourist attraction each July. Kicking off in 2002, the annual Sessions have attracted line-ups of top names, including Paul Weller, Muse, Editors, The Verve, Moby, PJ Harvey and Amy Winehouse. Oasis had to cancel their performance in the summer of 2008, after Noel Gallagher cracked three ribs when a crazed fan knocked him over at a Toronto gig. Gallagher promptly hired British boxer Ricky Hatton as his bodyguard for future gigs. The Eden Project also took part in the Live 8 series of concerts in the summer of 2005, hosting the Africa Calling event.

Above: Bohemian troubadour Donovan settled in St Ives after making his way there from his Hertfordshire home in the 1960s.

Newquay

Starting back in 1987 with a group of Volkswagen campervan owners driving to the Cornwall seaside, the annual Run to the Sun festival has morphed into one of Europe's largest VW, custom car and dance festivals. Three days of live music and some of the biggest DJs in the world come here every May. True to its *Wacky Races* origins, the festival still kicks off with VW campervans and Beetles assembling at Heston motorway services on the M4 and picking up vehicles en route to Cornwall's surf and party central, Newquay. In previous years, the convoy of vehicles has grown to several miles long.

Newquay also hosts the annual Relentless Boardmasters each August, a five-day music festival, in a picturesque cliff setting, overlooking nearby Watergate Bay. The festival is run alongside the Rip Curl Boardmasters surfing championships.

The Midlands

Birmingham
West Midlands
Warwickshire
Worcestershire
Hereford &
** Shropshire**

Staffordshire
Derbyshire
Nottinghamshire
Lincolnshire
Leicestershire
Rutland
Northamptonshire

Birmingham

To some, the least palatable sound emanating from Birmingham is the accent. Sniffy types like nothing more than poking fun at a dialect that's probably the most ridiculed in England. And it's not beyond mockery by its own either; Black Country comedian Frank Skinner once described the Brum burr as not so much an accent as a speech impediment. (For readers unfamiliar with it, just envisage a normal-looking Ozzy Osbourne, without the crazed rabbit-caught-in-the-headlights demeanour.)

Everyone knows Birmingham through its near-art installation-like Gravelly Hill Interchange, better known as Spaghetti Junction. Birmingham was the cradle of the Industrial Revolution and has been a centre of manufacturing and engineering ever since its own Matthew Boulton joined forces with Scottish engineer James Watt to create steam engines to power the nation's factories. But the city's image as a grim, industrial landscape is outmoded.

Not so well known is the fact the UK's second city has more miles of canals than Venice and more parks than any other European city. Free-thinking, diversity and individuality have long flourished here, from 18th century clergyman Joseph Priestley, who is often credited with inventing oxygen, to heavy metal gods Judas Priest, who were hell-bent on bursting eardrums – just one of the city's many contributions to rock and pop music. Birmingham was once known as the UK's Motor City; although it didn't produce a soul factory to rival Detroit's Motown its contribution to popular music has been significant.

As well as being described as the birthplace of heavy metal music (see Heavy Metal box on page 214) and Birmingham provided fertile ground during the 1960s beat boom, serving up The Moody Blues, The Spencer Davis Group, The Fortunes and The Move. Never mind bitching about the Brum accent, it's the other sounds of England's second city that concern us here.

Birmingham supergroup The Move formed in 1965 at one of Brum's most famous venues, the Cedar Club on Constitution Hill. The band was formed from the cream of Birmingham's finest beat groups: Roy Wood, later of ELO and Wizzard, lead guitarist in Mike Sheridan and The Nightriders; guitarist Trevor Burton, from Danny King and the Mayfair Set; and bassist and singer Chris 'Ace' Kefford, from Carl Wayne and the Vikings. Before long the trio invited singer Carl Wayne and drummer Bev Bevan to join them. Jeff Lynne later joined the band in 1970, until they disbanded two years later and he, Wood and Bevan morphed into the Electric Light Orchestra (see below).

Cedar Club owner Eddie Fewtrell's next venture was the former factory, Barbarella's, in Cumberland Street, off Broad Street, which hosted many top acts, straddling eclectic musical genres; it was a vintage soul club and a major punk venue. It closed in the autumn of 1979, after skinhead violence at a Sham 69 gig. Barbarella's was bulldozed in 1981 to build a car park for the city's International Convention Centre. To paraphrase Joni Mitchell's *Big Yellow Taxi*, Birmingham city council paved a punk paradise and put up a parking lot.

Below: The Electric Light Orchestra in 1970.
Opposite page: Duran Duran.

Musically, Birmingham has always been a hotbed of hairy heroes: Robert Plant, Roy Wood, Slade, Black Sabbath and Judas Priest (see page 214 for more on the last two), but one of the hairiest were the Electric Light Orchestra. At their most hirsute, the band were the UK's answer to Hanna-Barbera's 1970s cartoon characters, the Hair Bear Bunch. Their violin-laden pop operas, classic rock suites and catchy pop songs were imbued with a clear love of early rock 'n' roll. ELO were formed in 1971 by Jeff Lynne and Roy Wood, after The Move disbanded, and were widely rounded on by music critics for being a watered-down version of The Beatles. (The *NME* loathed them so much they refused to review their albums.) They were the band that rock aficionados probably listened to when their friends and colleagues weren't about. Some musos must have bought their music, since, despite their lack of critical acclaim, they became one of the UK's biggest-selling bands.

Originally a British Invasion R&B-based band, The Moody Blues embraced 1960s pop and rock, psychedelia and early prog rock. They became The Moody Blues by way of the Birmingham brewery, M&B (Mitchells and Butlers), who owned most of the big dance venues. Hoping for some funding from the brewery, and to get on their circuit, the band named themselves The MB 5 after the brewery. When sponsorship didn't happen, they came up with The Moody Blues: Moody after the Duke Ellington composition, *Mood Indigo*, a favourite of the band's co-founder Mike Pinder; and Blues because they had been a backing band for visiting blues stars like Memphis Slim and Sonny Boy Williamson. The band appeared as The Moody Blues for the first time at the Erdington's Carlton Ballroom in early May 1964.

Duran Duran were created in Spring 1978 by keyboardist Nick Rhodes and bassist John Taylor in Birmingham, taking their name from the Milo O'Shea character Dr Durand-Durand in the 1968 sci-fi film, *Barbarella*. They came up with the band's name over a couple of drinks in the Hole in the Wall pub (now Saramoons), in Dale End. Rhodes and his childhood friend Taylor lived near each other and had similar tastes in music. Both had been in punk bands but were propelled to form Duran Duran by a combined love of punk, glam-rock and electronica. Looking for a gig, they targeted the Rum Runner club, in Broad Street, in Birmingham city centre, which had a growing reputation for dance music.

First opened in 1964, the Rum Runner had recently relaunched itself, after owners – brothers Paul and Michael Berrow – had visited New York's famous Studio 54 club. They introduced moving lights, palm trees, a big pink neon flash and clown pastels on the wall. Duran Duran got much more than just a gig. The Berrow brothers liked what they saw so much that they offered a rehearsal room and a place to play gigs – and also offered to manage the band. Duran Duran became the club's resident band and even helped run the place. While the rest of the band polished mirrors, collected glasses and helped out in the kitchen, the 18-year-old Rhodes got the best gig as a DJ every Tuesday night, spinning tunes by the Human League, Tubeway Army and David Bowie.

While the band wrote and rehearsed songs for their first album in their room at the Rum Runner, Dexys Midnight Runners, The Beat and UB40 were in a rehearsal room next door, taking advantage of the club's offer of free space for Birmingham bands. The video for The Beat's *Mirror In The Bathroom* was filmed at the Rum Runner, making use of the club's mirrorflex decor.

The classic Duran Duran line up was completed when Andy Taylor moved down to Birmingham from Newcastle. Rhodes and Taylor found drama student Simon Le Bon through the club. Before they achieved world domination, an early Duran Duran song, *Late Bar* (B-side of debut single *Planet Earth*, which mentions the words 'New Romantic') was based on the Rum Runner. The club was levelled in 1987 to make way for the Hyatt Hotel.

Left: UB40, among Digbeth's finest exports.

urban music and arts festival which takes place at the Custard Factory, Gibb Street: old factory warehouses and art galleries that used to belong to the Bird's instant custard company.

Good venues include The Rainbow, a Victorian pub on the corner of Adderley Street and High Street; the Wagon and Horses in Adderley Street, which hosts a mixed musical bag of live acts, including punk, reggae, jungle and ska; and the traditional Irish boozer, The Spotted Dog, where Warwick Street meets the High Street, featuring anything from punk to Irish folk.

For UB40 fans The Eagle & Tun, in Banbury Street, was their answer to Abbey Road. The pub's interior featured on the cover of *Best of UB40 Volume One*, and took a starring role in the black-and-white video for their 1983 chart-topping cover of Neil Diamond's *Red Red Wine*. Closed at the time of writing, The Eagle & Tun is just over the road from the site of UB40's recording studios, DEP International (also known as Abattoir Studios), set up after the release of their 1980 debut album, *Signing Off*, so the band could control their output and release music by other artists. The studios, on the corner of Fazeley Street and Andover Street, were bulldozed in 2008.

Digbeth ⟩

Southern snobs who scoff that the UK's second city is a cultural vacuum have clearly never set foot inside the vibrant heart of Digbeth. Musically, it certainly seems to have its finger on the cultural pulse. Digbeth was a major player in the UK's folk scene in the 1960s, and a leading light was Ian Campbell, father of UB40's Ali and Robin Campbell. A decade on and Digbeth Civic Hall rocked to the raucous sounds of The Damned, The Ruts and Killing Joke, before embracing the rave and drum and bass scenes. Digbeth is a cultural hybrid of creative spaces, live music and festivals.

One weekend each November, Digbeth becomes Gigbeth, a diverse music festival of free concerts, showcasing Birmingham's music profile. Launched in 2006, Gigbeth features acts from a myriad of genres: indie, pop, classical, jazz, bhangra, reggae, gospel, hip hop, folk and blues, with bands playing gigs at venues across the Digbeth district. The three-day Supersonic Festival is an annual

Balsall Heath ⟩

UB40 themselves hail from the inner city area of Balsall Heath, where Ali Campbell and his brother Robin were born and grew up. Founding members Campbell, Earl Falconer and Jimmy Brown all met at Moseley School of Art in February 1979 (where ELO's Roy Wood and Jeff Lynne had also attended years earlier). United by their love of reggae, they hung around Balsall Heath together and, with their dole money, the yet-to-be popular UK reggae band set their sights on musical fame. They hired a room at the Cannon Hill arts centre in which to practise and hone their sound.

here comes the son
...and daughter

Jason Bonham

Oliver Wakeman

Zak Starkey

Jason Bonham, son of the late Bonzo, is a heavy rock drummer in his own right and has successfully followed in his father's drumsticks, playing at Led Zeppelin's 2007 reunion gig at London's O2 Arena (see page 50). He first took the drummer's chair aged four, and appears alongside his dad in *The Song Remains The Same*.

Keyboard wizard Rick Wakeman's sons have followed their father behind the keyboards. **Adam Wakeman** has played with Black Sabbath and Ozzy Osbourne's band, while his older brother **Oliver Wakeman** replaced his dad in Yes. In 2009, he toured and recorded with another of his father's old bands, The Strawbs, before returning to Yes.

The daughter of British rock 'n' roll godfather Joe Brown is singer-songwriter **Sam Brown**. A solo artist, she is also a hugely successful backing singer, recording and performing with the likes of the Small Faces (aged just 12), Pink Floyd and David Gilmour, Nick Cave and Dave Rotheray of The Beautiful South.

Zak Starkey taught himself how to drum after only one lesson from his famous father, The Beatles' Ringo Starr. He has worked with Johnny Marr, The Icicle Works and The Lightning Seeds and, most famously, Oasis and The Who.

The Sex Pistols drummer Paul Cook's daughter **Hollie Cook** has continued the skin-beating family tradition and drums with The Slits.

As a boy, **Baxter Dury** appeared alongside his late father Ian Dury on the cover of 1977's *New Boots And Panties!!*, outside a long-gone shop in London's Vauxhall Bridge Road. Now an indie musician, he released his debut album, *Len Parrot's Memorial Lift*, in 2002.

Other musical progenies include: John Lennon's sons Julian and Sean Lennon; Pete Townshend's daughter Emma Townshend; Judie Tzuke's daughter Bailey Tzuke; folk icons Richard and Linda Thompson's son Teddy Thompson.

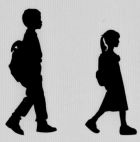

Ocean Colour Scene formed in 1989 after seeing a gig by The Stone Roses at Digbeth's Irish Centre Birmingham. Inspired by the sounds coming from John Squire's guitar, the Moseley indie band gigged around the local pub scene and the following year were signed by local label, Phffft Records. Their second album, 1996's *Moseley Shoals* – and their Moseley Shoals Studio where it was recorded – is named in honour of the Alabama soul factory, Muscle Shoals, and the south Birmingham suburb where three of the band were born (see also Leamington Spa on page 224). Inspired by Moseley, *The Riverboat Song*, the first single from the album, provided the theme tune to the popular 1990s Channel 4 show, *TFI Friday*, hosted by Chris Evans. Though Britpop contemporaries Oasis and Blur eclipsed them, as far as the Scene's fervent following was concerned, the Brum boys outshone them both.

Moseley is the birthplace of Duran Duran's Nick Rhodes, as well as Fyfe Dangerfield, founding frontman of indie rockers Guillemots. His solo version of Billy Joel's *She's Always a Woman* featured in the popular TV ad for department store John Lewis. From the age of eight, Dangerfield grew up in the Worcestershire town of Bromsgrove, southwest of Birmingham.

UB40's first gig was at the Hare and Hounds pub in leafy Kings Heath's High Street in February 1979. Toyah Willcox – actress, singer and wife of Robert Fripp – was born and brought up in Kings Heath. She trained at the Old Rep Drama School and her first performance of note was in Derek Jarman's 1977 punk film, *Jubilee*, the same year as she assembled her own band.

Handsworth

The members of Steel Pulse grew up together, forming their roots reggae band in 1975 at Handsworth Wood Boys School, which most of the band attended. As 16-year-olds some of them sung in the school choir, before playing gigs in 1975 and 1976 at the Rialto in Handsworth's Soho Road. Birmingham's West Indian community increased in size in the 1970s, contributing to the popularity of reggae. Steel Pulse started out mostly doing covers of Bob Marley songs, but developed into one of the most successful UK reggae acts. They were associated with the punk scene and supported the Rock Against Racism movement, touring with a number of punk acts. At other times they were sometimes refused gigs because of their militant Rastafarianism. Their groundbreaking 1978 debut, *Handsworth Revolution*, not only name-checked their origins but was soon hailed as a classic of British reggae. The album's political debut single, *Ku Klux Klan*, saw the band speak out against the potential visit of the Klan's Grand Wizard to Britain in the wake of the rise of the right-wing National Front.

In the early 1990s, Handsworth also produced reggae DJ Apache Indian, pioneer of bhangra and ragga fusions.

Aston

Although music scholars will argue that the birthplace of heavy metal was The Kinks' north London living room on the day they created *You Really Got Me*, Aston is its spiritual home. Ozzy Osbourne was born and grew up in working-class Aston (see page 214), as were all the original members of Black Sabbath.

Birmingham's most notorious son was born at 14 Lodge Road in 1948 and worked a series of unsavoury jobs, including in a local slaughterhouse, killing cows by firing a spike into their brains with a pressurised bolt gun (see box on page 101), and even spent six weeks in nearby Winson Green prison. But when Ozzy heard The Beatles he knew music would be his future. In 1968, he advertised himself as a wannabe singer, Ozzy Zig. The rest of Sabbath, already in a band, visited him at home and were alarmed at his short hair.

You can raise a glass in honour of Ozzy and the rest of Black Sabbath at The Bartons Arms, in the High Street, which was saved from dereliction in 2002. This Grade II-listed building was Ozzy's drinking den in the early days of Sabbath. Ozzy was not the only singer to imbibe in this Victorian boozer with its grand staircase and palatial archways. The Italian tenor Enrico Caruso was a regular here when appearing at the Aston Hippodrome, as were Charlie Chaplin, and Laurel and Hardy. Ozzy Osbourne was inducted into Birmingham's Walk of Fame in July 2007.

With such a soulful voice, many people couldn't believe future singing legend Steve Winwood was actually a white kid from Birmingham. Winwood was a teenager when he first caught the world's attention as the singer in The Spencer Davis Group, which had the hits *Gimme Some Lovin'* and *I'm a Man* and also featured his bass-playing brother Muff. Traffic were formed in April 1967 when drummer Jim Capaldi and songwriter, guitarist and sitar player Dave Mason made the trek to the Midlands to see Winwood play at The Elbow Room club in Aston High Street. The line-up was completed with another West Midlands musician, the late saxophone and flute player, Chris Wood. From the blues and R&B-influenced grooves of The Spencer Davis Group, Winwood was soon part of Traffic's collective spirit and had the financial backing of Island Records. Using their melting pot of influences, Traffic created a sound that blended R&B and soul with folk and psychedelic-tinged pop.

Top right: Steve Winwood surprised many with his incredible voice.
Bottom right: Reggae legends Steel Pulse.
Opposite page: Fyfe Dangerfield, perfoming at the Moseley Folk Festival.

SATAN'S COME AROUND THE BEND:
BLACK SABBATH AND JUDAS PRIEST

THE origins of heavy metal lie in the early 1960s British blues explosion, the distorted guitar sound of The Kinks classic, *You Really Got Me*, and the heavier power chords of The Who's Pete Townshend. Black Sabbath just cranked it up to 11.

The band didn't come from hell – "the only black magic we ever got into was a box of chocolates," said frontman Ozzy Osbourne – they came from Aston. But they are now largely credited with inventing a whole genre of music. Sabbath were four working-class lads (or "four dickheads from Aston," as Ozzy once described them), who saw heavy rock as an alternative to a life spent working in factories. Left-handed guitarist Tony Iommi even worked in heavy metal – as a metal sheet worker. A factory accident that cut off the tips of two fingers could have ended his musical career, but undeterred he carried on, making plastic thimble-like tips.

Strictly speaking, Sabbath didn't so much invent heavy metal as redefine it; they were heavier than anything that had come before. They started as a struggling blues band called first Polka Tulk, then Earth, on the dark, depressing streets of Aston in the late 1960s. Looking for a singer, guitarist Tony Iommi, bassist Terry 'Geezer' Butler and drummer Bill Ward found skinhead Ozzy, an old school adversary of Iommi's. Renamed Black Sabbath in 1969 by Butler, after a Boris Karloff horror movie, they recorded their 1970 eponymous album in 12 hours en route to a gig in Germany (see page 166 for the sleeve location).

Clocking in at just 30 minutes long, the album introduced Iommi's groaning, leaden guitar riffs and Ozzy's vocals. Their evil, doom-laden sound flew in the face of the prevailing flower power hippy ethos of the late '60s from the opener in which church bells toll amid the sound of driving rain and a clap of thunder, followed by a huge moaning power chord… Black Sabbath set out their stall from the start. *Paranoid*, released just seven months later, set the blueprint for heavy metal for generations to come, and the title track became the band's first hit single. In the mid-'70s Sabbath handed the baton over to another west Midlands metal band who grew up within earshot of foundries pounding away.

Judas Priest, from West Bromwich, also saw heavy metal as their passport out of the factories. They took the genre away from its blues roots into a faster, riff-laden form of metal, with a dual guitar sound, double-kick drumming and, in Rob Halford, a lead singer with a four octave vocal range.

They were the precursors of speed metal and influenced the likes of Van Halen, Metallica and Slipknot. Halford's father had been a Walsall metalworker and guitarist, Glenn Tipton, an apprentice at British Steel. Named after a Bob Dylan song, *The Ballad of Frankie Lee and Judas Priest*, they were once voted by MTV viewers as heavy metal's second most important band (behind Black Sabbath).

Heavy metal was never cool or fashionable and didn't receive airplay on mainstream radio. When its critics weren't ignoring it, or covering their ears, they ridiculed it and, without any sense of irony, called it the devil's music. But metal fans didn't care; those that didn't get it could go to hell. They grew their hair even longer, sewed more band patches on their denim jackets and banged their heads to the music within an inch of their lives.

Opposite page: Heavy metal legends and pioneers Judas Priest (top) and Black Sabbath.
Right: New wave heavy rockers Diamond Head.

JUDAS Priest are also credited as pioneers of the music genre known as the New Wave of British Heavy Metal, which went under the catchy acronym NWOBHM (pronounced Neh-Wobham like Cobham), which swept the land in the early 1980s. Inspired by punk's do-it-yourself ethos, many bands welded the 1970s heavy rock of Deep Purple and Led Zeppelin with the energy and attitude of punk.

NWOBHM's originators were the Cardiff rockers Budgie, but the movement soon became a nationwide English phenomenon: Motörhead from London; the demonic Venom from Newcastle; the exotically named Tygers of Pan Tang from Whitley Bay; Barnsley five-piece Saxon (originally called Son Of A Bitch, they changed their name to try and sell records in the US); and glam rock-inspired Def Leppard from Yorkshire. Diamond Head, from Stourbridge in the Midlands, were hyped by *Sounds* as "the new Led Zeppelin," and were a huge influence on future US metal gods Metallica and Megadeth. They could be loud in the south too: Girl, Angel Witch, Samson, the all-female Girlschool and the undisputed kings of British heavy metal, Iron Maiden, all came from London.

Samson's frontman Bruce Dickinson would later replace Paul Di'Anno in Maiden – many of the bands were good friends. Legendary venues included Bridge House in Canning Town, east London, The Ruskin Arms in East Ham, London, Porterhouse in Retford (between Nottingham and Sheffield) and Spread Eagle in Birmingham. You could locate the venues just by the smell: a curious mix of patchouli oil, spilt lager and body odour.

Championed by weekly music newspaper, *Sounds*, the nerve centre of the NWOBHM scene was a back room in a now-demolished mock-Tudor Prince of Wales pub in Kingsbury, northwest London. The Soundhouse and its pioneering resident DJ Neal Kay had hosted a heavy rock disco here since 1975. Fans turned up with hardboard fake guitars, and the squeak of their leather jackets was only drowned out by the deafening music. NWOBHM gigs were so loud it felt like a million hairdryers were turned in your direction, and a good night usually meant fans went home drenched with sweat and other fluids. And, you couldn't hear anything for days afterwards.

THE RIFF VALLEY:
THE NEW WAVE OF BRITISH HEAVY METAL

West Midlands

Wolverhampton

The culture of reinvention in rock and pop music is nothing new. Black Country boys Slade went from struggling late-1960s skinheads to chart-topping glam rockers. Slade were formed in Wolverhampton in 1966 as The 'N Betweens. Bassist Jim Lea, who had auditioned to join the band earlier that year, was born in the city (in the long-gone Melbourne Arms pub) and Devon-born guitarist Dave Hill grew up here from an early age. Drummer Don Powell was born and raised in Bilston; the town's Trumpet pub in the High Street was a regular watering hole for the band in their early days. (Slade conventions have been held here in the past, though the venue now focuses on jazz gigs.)

Lead singer Noddy Holder hailed from nearby Walsall, where, as Ambrose Slade, the band were pictured on the sleeve of debut album, 1969's *Beginnings*. The band were captured in the snow at Pouk Hill, which overlooks the Beechdale housing estate where Holder grew up. The hill would provide inspiration for a song of the same name, and, as The 'N Betweens, the band held their first rehearsal together, in the spring of 1966, in the estate's Three Men In A Boat pub.

To capitalise on the 1969 boot-boys fashion trend, their manager Chas Chandler got the band to shave their heads and wear Ben Sherman shirts and Dr Martens boots. For their later glam rock image, they shortened their name and adapted their skinhead image to become more showbiz and pantomime-like. They replaced jeans with tartan trousers, bovver boots with platform boots and grew their hair but kept true to their skinhead origins with braces and hairstyles favoured by skinhead girls: cropped tops and long sides. Dave Hill's more individual dazzling and glittery look came later.

The band then embarked on their trademark misspelt glam rock anthems, which made them the bane of English teachers everywhere: *Coz I Luv You*, *Skweeze Me Pleeze Me*, *Cum On Feel The Noise*, *Gudbuy T' Jane*, *Take Me Bak 'Ome* and *Mama Weer All Crazee Now*. These song titles were almost text-speak decades before SMS messaging was invented. Their almost perfectly spelt 1973 Christmas number one, *Merry Xmas Everybody*, was recorded at New York's Record Plant studio in the summer of 1973, as John Lennon worked on *Mind Games* next door.

Soul diva Beverley Knight was born and raised in Wolverhampton by Jamaican parents. She found her voice early on in gospel music and began singing in the Pentecostal church her family attended every Sunday. She became a singer-songwriter as early as 13 and was performing in local clubs three years later. She also learnt to sing by memorising the harmony parts to Michael Jackson's *Off the Wall* and *Thriller*. But at 19 she turned down a recording contract to take a theology degree in Cheltenham in order "not to end up an R&B chicklet," Knight told the *Daily Telegraph*. "I knew that people would automatically see me differently with a degree than if I had come out of school at 16 and gone straight into the industry."

At the age of 21, after Cheltenham, she concentrated on a career in the music industry. She landed a record deal with Dome Records in 1995 and released her debut album, *The B-Funk*. Apart from chart success, she has since won three Mobo Awards, sung *Happy Birthday* to Muhammad Ali and started her own record label, *Hurricane Records*.

Dudley

Success does allow for certain indulgences. The world's biggest rock band, Led Zeppelin were able to release their fourth album in 1971 without their name on the cover. It became commonly known as 'Led Zeppelin IV' and its gatefold sleeve featured a painting of an old man (see Reading, page 150) attached to the wall of a derelict house in Butterfield Court, a high-rise tower block off Salop Street in Dudley's Eve Hill area.

JB's club on Castle Hill, near Dudley Zoo and Castle, claims to be the longest-running live music venue in the country, hosting every genre of music. So many bands have passed through JB's before they hit the big time, including Dire Straits, Judas Priest and U2. No one had heard of Bono and his mates when they were booked; regulars were told they were an Irish blues band. Since opening in 1969, the club – named after the initials of local DJ John Bryant – has had three different homes, first at Dudley Town Football Club, then in King Street in the early 1970s, before a later incarnation opened in nearby Walsall but closed in the early 1990s. The Castle Hill club has been in operation since 1994 but is threatened with closure at the time of writing.

Below: Slade performing on *Top of the Pops*.

While Led Zeppelin guitarists Jimmy Page and John Paul Jones were seasoned London session musicians, it took the recruitment of a younger drummer and singer from the Midlands to complete their rock powerhouse. John Bonham hailed from Redditch, (see page 226) and singer Robert Plant was born in West Bromwich.

With words that pay homage to forests, trees, snow and ice, Plant's Zeppelin lyrics were strangely prescient, a long time before saving the planet became fashionable. Years before he gave us every inch of his love and eco-friendly verse, Plant fell in love with the blues; he was first exposed to the music via package tours that appeared at the Wolverhampton Gaumont. In 1963, he saw a concert there that included Little Richard, Bo Diddley, The Everly Brothers and The Rolling Stones. Plant left school aged 15 to pursue a career in music and his fondness for the blues supplied him

with first band names: The Black Snake Moan (after a Blind Lemon Jefferson song) and The Crawling King Snakes (after a John Lee Hooker track). Plant used to stock up on blues records at The Diskery in Bromsgrove Street, Digbeth – still selling second-hand and rare vinyl today.

A later group was called Band of Joy, formed with John Bonham after they'd met at the Old Hill Plaza (see Halesowen, below). The band's roadie was Slade's Noddy Holder, and the band used to travel to gigs in his father's window-cleaning van, complete with buckets crashing and sloshing around. Band of Joy were successful locally but failed to secure a record deal and broke up in spring 1968. (In 2010 Plant revived the name of this band for an album and tour as Robert Plant and the Band of Joy.)

In search of a new singer for The Yardbirds, Jimmy Page and Peter Grant travelled to the West Midlands in August 1968 to see Plant sing with the curiously-named Hobbstweedle at Walsall's West Midlands College of Higher Education. Their first choice singer, Terry Reid (see Huntingdon, page 116) declined and recommended Plant instead. They liked what they saw and the rest is a whole lotta history.

Thin Lizzy's late frontman Phil Lynott was brought up in Dublin by his grandmother, but was born here in 1949. He emerged into the world at West Bromwich's Sandwell General Hospital (then Hallam Hospital) and was christened at St Edwards Church in Selly Park. His mother was Irish and his father came from Guyana.

Anorak fact alert: West Bromwich has supplied *Top of the Pops* with two of its theme tunes. Even though Led Zeppelin never appeared on the show, an instrumental version of the band's *Whole Lotta Love*, played by the *Top of the Pops* orchestra, provided its theme music for many years. Then later, for much of the 1980s, it was Phil Lynott's electro-rock track *Yellow Pearl*, from his 1980 album *Solo in Soho*.

Halesowen

One of the West Midlands' legendary music venues was the Old Hill Plaza Ballroom in Halesowen Road, two miles north of Halesowen. Adored by a generation of rockers and soul fans, as its famous revolving stage hosted famous bands such as Bill Haley and the Comets, The Rolling Stones, The Beatles, Jimmy Ruffin and The Drifters, The Moody Blues,

The Spencer Davis Group and The Kinks. And, when Black American soul and Tamla Motown was all the rage, the Plaza Ballroom attracted acts like Ben E King, Geno Washington, Edwin Starr and Jimmy James and the Vagabonds. The Midlands half of Led Zeppelin – John Bonham and Robert Plant – first met at the venue. The Ballroom was the brainchild of the enterprising Joe and Ma Reagan, who owned other venues like the Handsworth Plaza and the Birmingham Cavern, which became known as 'the Ma Reagan Circuit'. In 1972 it was turned into a bingo hall and, at the turn of the 1990s, a fire destroyed the revolving stage. In 2008 the doors were shut on the bingo hall after Ma Reagan's death, but the former ballroom re-opened in 2010, after a major redevelopment by a new entrepreneur owner, and the revamped venue promises to combine live acts with wedding receptions.

Smethwick

One way of giving yourself an edge and getting noticed in the music industry (see page 287 for more) is to bestow yourself with just one name: Madonna; Prince; Donovan; or even just Lawrence, frontman of Birmingham's 1980s indie darlings, Felt.

Another one-name wonder is R&B and soul popstress Jamelia, who was born Jamelia Davis in Smethwick in 1981 and raised in the Winson Green area by her Jamaican mother and Zimbabwean father. Aged just 15 she signed to Capitol Records (but soon shifted to Parlophone) when label executives were impressed with her self-penned a capella songs. She released her first album, *Drama*, in 2000 at the age of 18 and went on to win four MOBO Awards.

Walsall

Likewise, if you were born Clifford Joseph Price you can always rename yourself Goldie. Multifaceted Goldie was raised in Walsall children's homes and with abusive foster parents, from the age of three. His mother was an alcoholic Scottish pub singer, who put Goldie into care while keeping his younger brother, Melvin. His possible salvation was the Wolverhampton skating rink, Whispering Wheels, where he

Above: Robert Plant, frontman of rock 'n' roll legends Led Zeppelin, is from West Bromwich.
Right: Another frontman, this time of Thin Lizzy, also came from West Bromwich.

played roller hockey for the England B team and learned to breakdance. He also took up graffiti, and his artwork around Birmingham and Wolverhampton was featured in *Bombin'*, a 1988 documentary film about hip hop and the graffiti scene. He then painted murals for television adverts and designed artwork for Soul II Soul before he became the diamond-encrusted gold-toothed face of drum and bass/jungle, the British-born genre that mixed bass-heavy reggae sound systems with early 1990s rave music and breakbeats.

The jungle innovator has never been content to be pigeonholed with just drum and bass. He was runner-up in the 2008 BBC TV series, *Maestro*, in which celebrities learned to conduct a concert orchestra. But he was composing lengthy orchestral pieces as early as his second album: the hour-long track *Mother* on 1998's *Saturnz Return*. He is friends with Prince Harry, has dated Björk and Naomi Campbell, and tried his luck at acting, playing a Bond villain

in 1999's *The World Is Not Enough*, and in Guy Ritchie's 2000 film, *Snatch*, as well as a gangster in the long-running soap, *EastEnders*. Always up for a challenge, Goldie has also appeared in *Celebrity Big Brother* and, more recently, *Strictly Come Dancing*, not long after his son, Jamie Price, was jailed for life in September 2010 for stabbing to death a rival gang member in Wolverhampton.

Walsall Town Hall was the venue for the first and last gigs by Black Country rockers Slade. Their first-ever show, as The 'N Betweens, took place in 1966, featuring their original line-up of singer Johnny Howells, Noddy Holder on rhythm guitar and vocals, backed by the familiar line-up of Dave Hill, Jim Lea and Don Powell. Slade's last live performance was in exactly the same place 25 years later when, in April 1991, they played only one song, *Johnny B Goode*, to adoring fans at a Slade 25th Anniversary Convention.

Left: From drum and bass wildman to classical composer: there's much more to Goldie than his golden teeth.
Below: Ned's Atomic Dustbin were made up of former students at Halesowen College.
Opposite page: Rick Astley with his producers, Matt Aitken and Pete Waterman in 1988.

Stourbridge

Stourbridge was where Led Zeppelin's Robert Plant went to school. In his early teens he was an excited youngster who went to see Gene Vincent play at Stourbridge Town Hall. The Midlands glass-blowing town was also home to Diamond Head who changed the course of heavy metal (see New Wave of British Heavy Metal, page 214).

Stourbridge was briefly in the limelight as the birthplace of the Black Country grebo scene in the late 1980s and early 1990s. For a brief period of time, before the arrival of grunge and Britpop, Stourbridge briefly became the focal point for the music business and the nation's youth. The epicentre of the scene was Stourbridge's town centre pub, The Mitre Inn in Lower High Street. With a thriving student clientele, it hosted early performances by grebo bands Pop Will Eat Itself, Ned's Atomic Dustbin, and The Wonder Stuff.

The latter were local boys who enjoyed chart success in 1991 with *The Size of A Cow* and even a number one, *Dizzy*, accompanied by comedian Vic Reeves. The band and their fans were regulars in The Mitre and played gigs in the upstairs room.

Named after a classic *Goon Show* script, which singer Jonn Penney had had read to him as a child, Ned's Atomic Dustbin were leading lights of the Stourbridge-based grebo scene. Formed as students at Halesowen College, the band had two bass players in their line-up. They had a hit album and several hit singles before they split in 1995.

Grebo's other major players were Pop Will Eat Itself (or The Poppies), featuring frontman Clint Mansell. They had songs called *Oh Grebo I Think I Love You* and *Grebo Guru*. In true indie music style, in 1986, they produced an EP themselves – *Poppies Say Grrr!* – releasing it in a rubber-stamped paper bag for just £1. They soon bid freewill to their indie status by singing to a major label, RCA Records. Their name came from an article in *NME* written by David Quantick.

Coventry ❯

The Specials' Jerry Dammers met his band's future bassist Horace Panter, aka Sir Horace Gentleman, as an art student at Coventry's Lanchester Polytechnic (now Coventry University) in 1973. Back then, Dammers was a mod with sideburns who wore tartan trousers and whistled skinhead reggae songs. (For more on The Specials and 2-Tone see The Dawning of a New Era, pxx). Pauline Black also studied biochemistry at Lanchester Poly before she became lead singer of The Specials' 2-Tone label-mates, The Selecter.

Coventry's biggest band since The Specials are The Enemy, a three-piece from Holbrooks who formed in 2006. The title track of their 2007 debut album, *We'll Live and Die in These Towns*, is seen as the band's answer to The Specials' *Ghost Town* and paints a bleak a picture of life in noughties Britain, while offering a positive message about being proud of your origins. The song's video is a definite nod towards *Ghost Town*, albeit with the band appearing in a more fancy vehicle. Bassist Andy Hopkins drives the less cramped Jaguar (a Coventry icon, of course), drummer Liam Watts is in the front passenger seat, while frontman Tom Clarke sings from the back seat. The band didn't stray as far as the actual *Ghost Town* video (shot in East London) – Coventry is prominent on the road signs.

Major league record producer Pete Waterman has been a leading light of Coventry music. As a third of the 1980s songwriting pop powerhouse, Stock Aitken Waterman, he is best known for a roll-out of hits by the likes of Kylie Minogue, Rick Astley and Mel & Kim. But long before he created his PWE

(Pete Waterman Entertainment) empire, Coventry-born Waterman was an early champion of The Specials. He was briefly their manager in 1979 and helped them set up the 2-Tone label. After hearing the band rehearse at Holyhead Youth Centre, Waterman offered them recording time at Soho's Berwick Street Studios. Even with only a few songs, Waterman knew they stood out at this early stage. The connection first came about when Specials singer and dancer Neville Staple met Waterman, who was resident DJ at the Locarno ballroom (Coventry's answer to northern soul venue The Wigan Casino). The Locarno is now the site of Coventry's central library but was immortalised in The Specials lyrics, in *Ghost Town*: "All the clubs have been closed down," and in *Friday Night, Saturday Morning*, which even namechecks the Locarno: "I'm going watch my money go / At the Locarno, no".

> 'Bouncers bouncing through the night/
> Trying to stop or start a fight/
> I sit and watch the flashing lights/
> Moving legs in footless tights'.

Waterman penned the foreword to Staple's 2009 autobiography, *Original Rude Boy*.

The record producer was also mad keen on Tamla Motown and heavily involved in the 1970s British reggae scene. In 2010, he wrote and produced *That Sounds Good To Me*, the UK's entry for the 2010 Eurovision Song Contest in Oslo, sung by Josh Dubovie. The judges didn't share the sentiments of the song's title however and placed it last.

Coventry's contribution to the punk revolution was a band called Squad, formed at the end of 1977. The band's original lead vocalist was Terry Hall, later of The Specials, who was replaced by the late frontman Gus Chambers. The band had a compilation aptly named *Sent From Coventry*. After punk, Chambers recorded on Neville Staples' Shack Records label with the band 21 Guns.

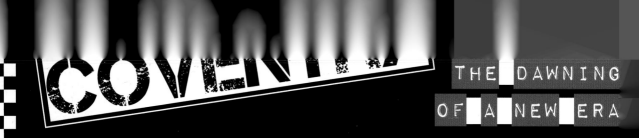

COVENTRY

Coventry was bombed beyond recognition by the German Luftwaffe in World War II, yet, in the late 1970s and early '80s, the city became an unlikely nucleus of British pop music. The city helped rejuvenate a grim post-punk landscape and took centre stage in a pop and cultural revolution. For a brief period, it even eclipsed the more established musical hubs of London, Liverpool and Manchester.

In the late 1970s Coventry was indeed a ghost town: a depressing, forgotten-about place, nose-diving into recession. People queued for the dole, rather than gigs and the bleak inner city was a wasteland of boarded-up shops and litter-strewn streets. The local motor industry was on its knees, hit hard by cheap overseas competition and, as a consequence, Coventry had one of the highest unemployment rates in the country. The despair of jobless parents filtered through to their children, and increasing unemployment halved the chances of school leavers gaining a job. These were prime breeding conditions for extreme right-wing politics; social decay threatened to complete what Nazi bombers had started in 1940. The response to the gloom came in the form of the 2-Tone record label – and pop culture movement.

The movement's home was the West Midlands and it was led by seven-strong band, The Specials: two black and five white Coventry youths led by a gap-toothed, militant socialist, the son of a clergyman and an English teacher, Jerry Dammers.

Two years before Dammers founded 2-Tone Records, the keyboardist formed The Hybrids (with guitarist Lynval Golding and bassist Horace Panter, aka Sir Horace Gentleman), which became the Automatics,

then the Coventry Automatics, then The Specials. The band featured black and white musicians performing together, and their exuberant live performances combined original songs with material by artists like Prince Buster, The Maytals and The Skatalites. Blending politically aware lyrics – usually about society collapsing around them – with foot-stomping tunes, The Specials created a welcome rarity in pop: energetic music, with something to say, that you could dance to.

Using Berry Gordy's Tamla Motown record label as a blueprint, The Specials set up 2-Tone Records in 1979. The label helped boost a radical, multi-racial movement offering fresh hope at a time when punk had failed to deliver and mainstream politics gave little optimism. 2-Tone was exciting pop music with a social agenda which perfectly captured the frustration of the late '70s. Bands fused punk's passion and politics with the pounding rhythms and brass instrumentals of old Jamaican ska music of the 1950s and '60s.

The fashion of this ska revival was three-button tonic suits, pork-pie hats, braces and Harrington jackets and loafers or Dr Martens – and to top it all, a tidy suedehead.

Dammers saw 2-Tone as a revolutionary instrument for social change and racial harmony (the two 'tones' being black and white). The logo was a black and white

chessboard pattern, while inspiration for the man who adorned all the label's releases was based on a suited young Peter Tosh as he appeared on the *Wailing Wailers* album sleeve. Dammers' master plan was to overthrow the establishment while making great music and having fun along the way.

Playing music that combined black and white influences, 2-Tone's anti-racist stance was a direct response to prominent right-wing skinhead gangs in and around Coventry in the late '70s, and to the rise of the National Front nationwide. Some second-generation Asian and black kids, and like-minded whites, weren't prepared to put up with what their immigrant parents had suffered. With their Jamaican musical influences and multi-racial line-up, 2-Tone acts sought racial unity – to unite black and white through music – and rescue skinhead reggae back from the far right.

Early demonstrations of Dammers' revolutionary zeal saw him try to hacksaw through his art school railings, declaring that art was for all, and being banned from student union gigs for opening the fire doors during performances, to demonstrate that music wasn't just for students.

Soon The Specials were supporting The Clash on their 1978 On Parole tour which ended with four nights at Camden's Music Machine. The band's two front men were a priceless Jekyll and Hyde combination of Jamaican-born toaster Neville Staple, a former roadie for the band, and singer Terry Hall, who grew up listening to his skinhead sister's Motown and ska records. While Hall stood motionless, staring sullenly at the audience from behind a mike, manic extrovert Neville Staple charged around the stage shouting like town centre nutcase. (Staple later had two knee operations as a result of his stage antics, which included jumping off speakers.)

The Specials delivered the skank and groove of reggae with the velocity of punk it wasn't long before packed venues became a sea of sweaty, like-minded youngsters, their hair matted with perspiration. Stage invasions by their rude boy fans became an integral part of gigs, and followers who travelled the length of the country to see them often slept on the band's hotel room floors.

An exciting mix of punk and ska, their first single, *Gangsters*, was recorded at Coventry's Horizon Studios. The song featured screeching car tyres from Prince Buster's *Al Capone*, and Dammers ranting at the music industry. Neville Staple's opening toast: "Bernie Rhodes knows! Don't argue!" namechecks The Clash's manager, their own boss for a brief while. *Gangsters* reached number six in the singles chart.

Produced by Elvis Costello, The Specials' debut album capitalised upon the sound of their first singles. The songs combined pithy social comment and politics with catchy dance rhythms. *Nite Klub* and *Too Much Too Young* were brooding depictions of inner-city life, laced with a reggae bass sound, while *Doesn't Make It Alright* drew directly upon the racial violence experienced by the band's guitarist, Lynval Golding.

The album's opener, *A Message to You, Rudy*, was a version of Dandy Livingstone's *Rudy, A Message to You*, and it included Jamaican trombonist Rico Rodriguez, a member of legendary ska band The Skatalites. He'd performed on the Livingstone original, as well as many '50s and '60s Jamaican recordings.

The Specials opened the doors for other 2-Tone bands who played a mixture of punk, ska and reggae. The Selecter, also from Coventry, were fronted by musician Neol Davies and singer Pauline Black. They took their name from the title of their debut single; an instrumental tune that Specials drummer

John "Brad" Bradbury had recorded with Davies. Dammers asked Davies to add a ska rhythm to it, and the result became the B-side of the first 2-Tone single, *Gangsters vs. The Selecter*, in July 1979. They recorded several later singles, including *On My Radio* and *Three Minute Hero*, and their debut album, *Too Much Pressure*, was written as Davies worked at Lucas Aerospace in Coventry.

The 2-Tone label operated with autonomy as an independent entity within Chrysalis Records. Later acts signed to 2-Tone included the indie-funk sound of The Higsons, The Apollinaires, The Friday Club and The Bodysnatchers, a seven-piece all-female band from London. Most of the latter band would merge into The Belle Stars and sign to Stiff Records in 1981. Both Birmingham's The Beat and Madness from London's Camden Town recorded one single on the 2-Tone label before signing elsewhere. But Madness soon ditched the ska-influenced scene in favour of a more commercial pop sound. It proved hugely successful, netting them over a dozen top 10 hits in the 1980s.

The Specials' *Ghost Town* (see The Margaret Thatcher Songbook, page 242) captured a dark moment in post-war British history. The song went to number one in 1981, just as inner-city riots engulfed the UK. The B-side, *Why?*, written by Lynval Golding, was a call for racial harmony.

By the time of The Specials second album, *More Specials*, the band were yielding to in-fighting. The original line-up split in 1981. Singers Terry Hall and Neville Staple and guitarist Lynval Golding departed to become Fun Boy Three. The Specials guitarist Horace Panter left to join The Beat's Dave

Wakeling and Ranking Roger in General Public, while Dammers continued, reverting to The Special AKA.

He revised the band line-up, recruiting singer Stan Campbell, and Rhoda Dakar from The Bodysnatchers. He turned his attention to injustices further afield and wrote 1984's *Free Nelson Mandela*, which raised consciousness about apartheid in South Africa and the then jailed African National Congress leader. Produced by Elvis Costello, it was another upbeat protest song you could dance to.

On the 30th anniversary of 2-Tone in 2009, The Specials embarked on a nationwide reunion tour – albeit without Jerry Dammers in the line-up. Commemorative plaques were also unveiled at key locations associated with the label in Coventry: the Holyhead Youth Club building (now Artspace, in Lower Holyhead Road), where early jam-sessions took place, and the Mr George nightclub (now T J Hughes), where The Specials (then The Automatics) started their rise to fame with a residency.

The 2-Tone sound may have only been a short-lived pop phenomenon but its output still sounds remarkably fresh today – and it got British youngsters dancing again. Its inspirational fusion of ska rhythms and street observations remain an influence on some of today's artists, in particular Lily Allen and Amy Winehouse.

Above and opposite page: The Specials.
Below: The Selecter.

Warwickshire

Tanworth-in-Arden

Cult singer-songwriter Nick Drake died in 1974 at the age of just 26, having released only three albums. Many artists have achieved posthumous fame but Drake's renaissance has been extraordinary; ignored in his lifetime, he is now widely adored, even canonised in some quarters.

He grew up, and spent the last depressed months of his life, in the quiet leafy Warwickshire village of Tanworth-in-Arden, surrounded by an almost picture-book bucolic English landscape of rolling hills, hedgerows, endless meadows and serene country churchyards.

Drake was discovered in Cambridge by legendary producer Joe Boyd, who signed and managed Drake and produced his first two albums for Island Records. His albums were commercial flops and ignored by critics, not helped by Drake's loathing of touring and doing interviews. After his second album, 1970's *Bryter Layter*, was a commercial failure, Drake descended into clinical depression.

He died in his sleep from a fatal overdose of the prescription anti-depressant Tryptizol, which may have been accidental or deliberate. The coroner ruled his death as suicide but Drake's family and friends dispute this. He was cremated at Solihull Crematorium, and his ashes were buried beneath an oak tree in the cemetery of the church of St Mary Magdalene in Tanworth. Inside the church there is a small brass plaque in honour of Drake attached to a pipe organ, ensuring the village's most famous son is remembered every time the church choir performs hymns. The words, "Now we rise and we are everywhere," that appear on the back of his gravestone are a line taken from *From The Morning*, the last song on his final album, *Pink Moon*, released in 1972, featuring only Drake and his finger-picked guitar.

Drake's death went virtually unnoticed, yet his trio of albums are now universally celebrated and have been a huge influence on many songwriters and musicians. The Dream Academy's 1985 hit, *Life in a Northern Town*, was written as a tribute to Drake, even if Warwickshire is in the Midlands rather than the North. Since 2003, The Annual Nick Drake Gathering has happened each summer in Tanworth-in-Arden, celebrating the singer-songwriter's life and music. Nick Drake's estate is run by his sister, the actress Gabrielle Drake.

Leamington Spa

Ocean Colour Scene's 1996 album, *Moseley Shoals*, was a pun on the famous Alabama soul recording studios, Muscle Shoals, where Bob Dylan, Aretha Franklin, The Rolling Stones and many others recorded classic songs until it closed in January 2005. The album sleeve was not shot in the Birmingham suburb of Moseley, birthplace of some of the band, but in the Warwickshire town of Leamington Spa, famous for its gardens and parks. The four-piece are pictured in the Jephson Gardens, in front of the memorial to Victorian physician Dr Henry Jephson, a leading light in the Regency town's early 19th-century development as a health spa.

Stratford-upon-Avon

The late wannabe MP and 1960s musician Screaming Lord Sutch first stood for election at the 1963 Stratford-upon-Avon by-election sparked by the resignation of John Profumo (see Taplow, page 151). His party, the National Teenage Party, polled just over 200 votes. Two decades later he formed the Official Monster Raving Loony Party to fight the 1983 Bermondsey by-election in south London, and was

a welcome oddball amongst the stuffed shirts at subsequent by-elections and general election nights until his suicide in 1999. Sutch was immortalised in the lyric, "All dressed up just like a Union Jack," in The Rolling Stones song, *Get Off Of My Cloud*, a UK chart-topper for three weeks in 1965.

Rugby

The Warwickshire market town that helped introduce rugger buggers, scrums and fly-halves to the world has also scored a few musical drop-kicks. The origins of the band Spiritualized date back to 1982, when two art school friends (born on the same day in 1965), Jason Pierce and Pete Kember, formed Spacemen 3 in their hometown of Rugby. When disagreements and breakdown followed, Pierce defected with other members of the band to form Spiritualized in 1990 (though Pearce is now the only original member), while Kember formed Spectrum. Spiritualized's third album, 1997's *Ladies and Gentlemen We Are Floating in*

Above left: Jason Pierce performing live with Spiritualized.
Above right: Nick Drake on his now legendary Five Leaves Left album cover.

Space, was a spacey, critically acclaimed – NME's 1997 Album of the Year– contemporary slice of psychedelia. And the numerous mind-altering references start as early on as the sleeve, designed to look like a pharmaceutical prescription.

Singer-songwriter James Morrison was born on a run-down drug- and crime-ridden council estate in Rugby, in 1984. Growing up, he didn't enjoy much stability, moving house frequently. When his alcoholic father left home, the family was made homeless and moved to Northampton, where he was brought up by his mother, Suzy, who wrote songs and poems and was in a band. Morrison believes it's from her that he gets his creativity: "She was a hippy and believed in doing what was in your heart," he told *The Times* in 2009. "She didn't worry about money, parents' evenings and cooking, but she was always supportive." It was when the family moved to a house in the Cornwall village of Porth, near Newquay, that Morrison started singing, and people took note. He began busking and playing gigs on the beach.

Worcestershire

Stourport

Not quite rock 'n' roll but Worcestershire's most famous musical son is still Sir Edward Elgar, to many the owner of the best moustache in English recorded music. The celebrated composer is not the only one to have drawn inspiration from the Worcestershire countryside.

Stourport-born Clifford T Ward may be unfamiliar to some, but the 1970s singer-songwriter enjoyed a cult following, and his songs have been recorded by Art Garfunkel and Ringo Starr. He found his singing voice as a choirboy at Stourport Secondary Modern School, and later fronted local band Cliff Ward and the Cruisers in the mid-1960s. He trained to be a teacher and, while teaching English (to Sting's future wife Trudie Styler amongst others) at North Bromsgrove High School, he started his solo recording career on the late DJ John Peel's Dandelion label before it went bust. Indeed, the children's voices heard on Ward's early songs belong to young students at North Bromsgrove High School. Ward failed to capitalise on his early success by his refusal to perform live and fans consider his second album, 1973's *Home Thoughts*, to be his finest hour. It featured the singles, *Gaye*, which sold over a million copies worldwide and reached number eight in the charts, and *Home Thoughts From Abroad*, a homesick ode to his beloved Worcestershire:

> 'How is Worcestershire?/
> Is it still the same between us?/
> Do you still use television to send you fast asleep?'

He also waxed lyrical about Birmingham (see page 209). Ward was constructing a home-based recording studio in 1984 when he was diagnosed with multiple sclerosis and confined to a wheelchair. He continued to work however, completing his final album in 1994. But in November 2001, he was taken ill with pneumonia and died a few weeks later.

Led Zeppelin's fabled drummer John Bonham, born in 1948, was a builder's son from Redditch, the Worcestershire new town once famous for needle-making. Bonham – affectionately known as 'Bonzo' – became a multi-millionaire after the successes of *Led Zeppelin III* and 'IV', allowing him to buy a 100-acre ranch-style farm, The Old Hyde, Cutnall Green, near Stourport. There he bred prize-winning Hereford cattle and pursued his passion for cars. Part of Bonham's fantasy sequence in the Led Zeppelin movie, *The Song Remains The Same*, was shot at his white-fenced Worcestershire estate. Zeppelin broke up a few months

Above: Clifford T Ward of Stourport.
Opposite page: Jim Capaldi. He formed Traffic with Steve Winwood in 1967.

after Bonham's drink-related death in September 1980 (see page 152). His last resting place is just north of his farm, in St Michael's Church, in the village of Rushock, between Kidderminster and Bromsgrove. Bonham's legacy as one of rock's greatest-ever drummers remains firmly intact.

Evesham

Another famous Worcestershire drummer was Evesham's Jim Capaldi, who formed Traffic with Steve Winwood in 1967. They wrote many of Traffic's best-known songs together (for more on Traffic, see Birmingham, page 213; and Oxfordshire, page 171). Born Nicola James Capaldi to a musical Italian immigrant family who settled in Worcestershire, Capaldi was set to drum in the rock supergroup Blind Faith with Eric Clapton but lost out to Clapton's Cream colleague, Ginger Baker. After Traffic reformed – and then disbanded again – he struck out alone with a string of solo albums and collaborations, including Bob Marley and Carlos Santana. His soulful voice could be heard on his cover of the Everly Brothers' *Love Hurts*, a number four in 1975, and he worked with Brazilian composers when he lived in Bahia at the end of the 1970s. Capaldi succumbed to stomach cancer in January 2005; two years later the famous Roundhouse venue in London's Camden hosted a musical celebration in his honour called Dear Mr Fantasy (named after the Traffic album). Many musician friends turned up to celebrate his life, including Pete Townshend, Gary Moore, Paul Weller and, of course, Steve Winwood. All proceeds from the event went to a charity, supported by his Brazilian wife Aninha, which helps street children in her native country.

Malvern

Nestling under the Malvern Hills, the Malvern Winter Gardens was an important venue from the 1960s through to the 1980s, hosting many gigs, from prog rock to punk. The venue, which includes a garden and bandstand, ensured there was at least one regional place where Worcestershire's rock fans could see top bands. Dozens of big-name acts played this small town, from Black Sabbath and Hawkwind to Joy Division and The Jam. Electric Light Orchestra played its first sell-out concert here. The theatre complex now mostly hosts plays, opera and pantomime, quite a contrast from a Hawkwind gig.

Great Witley

For such a mammoth hit as Procol Harum's 1967 *A Whiter Shade of Pale* (six weeks at number one during 1967's Summer of Love), perhaps it's only right there should be three different versions of the video to accompany the song. Arguably the most memorable one, which was banned from *Top of the Pops*, intersperses footage of them performing and newsreel footage of the Vietnam War with scenes of the band walking amongst the spectacular and ghostly ruins of the stately home Witley Court, northwest of Worcester.

Another version shows black-and-white performance footage of the band, while a third features no live action and is more of a snapshot of late 1960s fashion, with scenes of the musicians amid everyday life in central London, including Trafalgar Square and Piccadilly Circus. It also shows the band, including singer and founder Gary Fisher dressed in a monk's cloak, gallivanting across fields. All very 1960s. Three videos and over four decades on from its release, the song retains an air of myster, and most listeners still don't have a clue what the lyrics are about.

A wing of the Grade I listed Witley Court was gutted by fire in 1937 and is today administered by English Heritage. The ruins attracted other musicians: Bob Dylan went ghost-hunting here in the 1960s, and members of Traffic hung out together here and went on road trips around Worcestershire, soaking up the atmosphere of its natural and ancient places.

Hereford & Shropshire

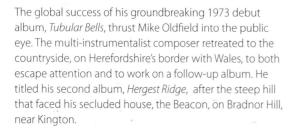

Ledbury

As locations for annual music festivals go, The Big Chill in early August takes some beating. Surrounded by the beautiful Malvern Hills, four lakes and thick woods and with the large 19th-century Eastnor Castle as a backdrop, it can be hard to remember it's a music festival. The 5,000-acre estate near Ledbury hosts top artists, dance events, films, cabaret and comedy acts across several outdoor stages in the castle's Deer Park. The laid-back, family-friendly festival has space enough for 30,000 revellers and its diverse music line-up ranges from rock legends to up-and-coming bands, top headliners to obscure indie bands. There's also folk, world music, jazz and DJs spinning chilled-out beats in honour of The Big Chill's ambient and dance roots. Most revellers camp and those with stacks of cash can book into their own yurts (which some genius has dubbed a Yurtel, geddit?), with individual toilets.

Just as the mock Gothic castle is something relatively new trying to be old, the reverse scenario was the case when Slade shot their video for *Run Runaway* at Eastnor in 1984. The band have a fun time even if, at times, they resemble town centre nutters on the loose.

Kington

The global success of his groundbreaking 1973 debut album, *Tubular Bells*, thrust Mike Oldfield into the public eye. The multi-instrumentalist composer retreated to the countryside, on Herefordshire's border with Wales, to both escape attention and to work on a follow-up album. He titled his second album, *Hergest Ridge*, after the steep hill that faced his secluded house, the Beacon, on Bradnor Hill, near Kington.

Below: Mike Oldfield retreated to the countryside to make *Tubular Bells*.

Like *Tubular Bells*, 1974's *Hergest Ridge* was another long suite in two parts and a glorification of the countryside. Once again, Oldfield played many instruments himself (including a nutcracker) but this time he employed the services of other musicians. The new album met with a critical mauling, not entirely unconnected with the fact that Oldfield refused to talk to the music press or promote it. This led to him being dubbed: the 'Rock and Roll Hermit Millionaire'.

Oldfield turned parts of the Beacon into a recording studio and recorded his next album, 1975's *Ommadawn*, there. The sleeve features a Christ-like image of Oldfield taken by David Bailey. Both albums were reissued in June 2010, although *Hergest Ridge* has a new cover. Oldfield was never fully happy with the original sleeve, which is a fish-eyed lens photograph of his glider and dog atop Hergest Ridge. The new artwork still features a glider and the ridge, but Google Earth's view of it.

They helped pave the way for punk and were the only band for whom Queen were ever a support act. From The Clash, The Smiths, Oasis, Blur and Primal Scream to Kiss and REM, numerous bands cite them as influential. Mott The Hoople's significance to modern rock music is incalculable.

The 1970s rockers garnered a huge cult fan base because their gigs felt like a genuinely communal thing. The band broke down the barriers between performers and crowd and made the audience feel part of the action.

Their roots lie in two early 1960s pub bands who learned the ropes in and around Herefordshire: Ross-on-Wye's The Soulents, with drummer Dale 'Buffin' Griffin and his bassist school friend Pete Overend Watts, and Hereford-born guitarist Mick Ralphs' band The Buddies. Meanwhile, frontman Ian Hunter, born in Oswestry, was following his own musical path.

As his father was a member of the British Military Intelligence agency MI5, the family moved around regularly, finally settling in Shrewsbury. Before he was a junior reporter on the *Wellington Journal*, Hunter went to Shrewsbury's Priory Grammar School and, later, left home when his delinquency forced him out. He recalled this time on two much later songs: *23A, Swan Hill* (from 1996 solo album *The Artful Dodger*), his address in Shrewsbury town centre, and *The Loner* (from 1989's *YUI Orta*), one of his collaborations with Mick Ronson.

Mott The Hoople finally came together in London in 1969, when Hunter joined the band, initially called Silence and under the clutches of svengali-like rock impresario Guy Stevens. He promptly renamed them after a 1966 American novel.

On stage, Mott's glammed-up bassist Overend Watts wore eight-inch, white, thigh-length platform boots, while Hunter's ever-present Aviator shades became his rock star trademark and images of him without sunglasses are rarities. Hunter has since said the shades were not for affect or to look cool: "I have weak eyes, studio lights are bright."

Hunter's acclaimed 1974 autobiography, *Diary Of A Rock 'n' Roll Star*, penned during the band's 1972 US tour, has been lauded by *Q* magazine as "the greatest music book ever written." An exhausted Hunter quit to pursue a solo career in 1974, a year after guitarist Mick Ralphs had left to form Bad Company.

Some 35 years later the original Hereford line-up (plus Hunter) played a string of 40th anniversary reunion shows at London's Hammersmith Apollo. Due to demand the original three shows in October 2009 were extended to five nights.

The 1980s popsters T'Pau were a Shropshire band named after a *Star Trek* character. Singer Carol Decker was born in Liverpool but grew up and went to school in Wellington from an early age, while guitarist Ronnie Rogers came from Shrewsbury and other members from Telford. While studying art at Shrewsbury's Wakeman College, Decker was in a ska band, then gigged around the area with her then partner Rogers, performing Brotherhood Of Man covers, before writing their own material.

They formed T'Pau in 1986 and were rewarded with a huge hit the following year with *China In Your Hand*, a UK number one for five weeks. The song title was inspired by a fragile china tea set given to them by Rogers' mother. Jazzman David Sanborn was originally earmarked to do the song's sax solo but plans fell through. At times the song's accompanying video resembles a dentistry training video, as the camera nearly enters Decker's mouth.

Below: Mott the Hoople live.

Staffordshire

Stoke-on-Trent ⟩

Before he adopted his trademark top hat, big hair and shades, former Guns N' Roses guitarist Slash was raised as Saul Hudson in Stoke-on-Trent. Born in Hampstead, London, in 1965, to a white English father and African-American mother, the guitar hero lived in Stoke until he was six years old and the family moved to Los Angeles. He hasn't been back to Stoke since. "When I have some time I will pop over there," Slash told *Q* magazine. "I'm interested to see what it's like. I loved it when I was little but I guess I had nothing else to compare it to." One of his sons is called London.

An early band of Slash's was called Road Crew, after the Motörhead song, *(We Are) The Road Crew*. Motörhead's singer and bassist Lemmy is another rock 'n' roll icon from the city. Born in Burslem as Ian Kilmister, the son of a Protestant vicar, Lemmy was a former roadie for Jimi Hendrix who formed Motörhead in 1975, after his sudden ejection from Hawkwind.

His band were originally called Bastard, until he decided on the name for a speed freak. Motörhead were the heavy metal band that even the punks liked; their punk cred was aided by their debut album being released on the Chiswick label, alongside label-mates The Damned. Chiswick Records boss Ted Carroll signed Lemmy and his band after seeing them at London's Marquee Club.

Another hardcore Stoke outfit were punk four-piece Discharge, formed in the city in 1977 and still going today. But Stoke's most famous musical son is Robbie Williams. Growing up, he lived in Burslem's Red Lion pub in Moorland Road, which his parents ran, very close to his beloved Port Vale Football Club. On open mike nights he sang with his father, comedian Pete Conway. When his parents split up

Right: A crazed-looking Lemmy. Enough said.

Williams moved to a Victorian terrace in Greenbank Road in nearby Tunstall, with his mother and older sister.

Stoke doesn't just celebrate its sporting heroes like footballer Sir Stanley Matthews. In Hose Street, Tunstall, there's a commemorative plaque in honour of The Golden Torch, a long demolished but still fondly remembered Northern Soul club, which hosted The Drifters, Edwin Starr, Junior Walker and The Stylistics. At its height, some 1,300 northern soul fans attended an all-nighter at The Torch.

Stafford ⟫

When the Wigan Casino closed, in 1981 many said northern soul had had its day. It was not to be. Like a moveable feast, northern soul simply found a new home in Stafford, and the Midlands town continued where the Wigan Casino left off with its now legendary Top of the World ballroom.

The members of indie band Editors are dubbed a Birmingham-based band but their origins lie in Stafford. The four-piece met as music technology students in the early noughties at the Beaconside campus of Staffordshire University. The entire band relocated to Birmingham when they graduated.

Fran Healy of Travis (named after the main character in the film, *Paris*, *Texas*, rather than *Taxi Driver*) was born in Stafford in 1973, but grew up in Glasgow.

Weston ⟫

A natural limestone cavern in the Peak District took a starring role on the sleeve of The Verve's first album, *A Storm In Heaven*, released in 1993. The cover was shot at Thor's Cave in the Manifold Valley, inside a rock that rears up out of the hillside. The cave's entrance is 10 metres high by seven-and-a-half metres wide – so big enough to accommodate Bono's head if U2 ever fancy shooting a cover here – and as it's located some 80 metres up the rock, there are excellent views of the valley. Excavations found remains of extinct animals and stone tools, meaning it was inhabited in the Stone Age.

Weston-under-Lizard ⟫

The grounds of Weston Park country house in Staffordshire are the venue for the Midlands sector of the annual V Festival each August (also see Chelmsford, page 140). This is one of the UK top summer festivals, and continues to attract big name acts as headliners.

Tamworth ⟫

It's possible some home-grown musicians thrive because of the English penchant for the ever-so-slightly mad. This country's pop culture would be so much poorer without maverick eccentrics and outsiders like ex-The Teadrop Explodes frontman Julian Cope. Born in Wales, before he fled to Liverpool as a student, Cope grew up in Tamworth, and the area has been a source for lyrics and album sleeves.

The memorable cover for 1984's *Fried* album shows the singer with a toy truck, crouching naked underneath a giant turtle shell bought from a Cambridge antique shop. For the shoot Cope and photographer Donato Cinicolo travelled to the Alvecote mound, a slag heap near Tamworth that overlooks the M42. "It was f***ing freezing and I was naked for most of the day," Cope commented later.

He chose different attire during most of the recording of the album, preferring to wear a Royal Mail postal sack. The album's opener, *Reynard the Fox*, conjures up childhood memories of the countryside near Tamworth – and ritual sacrifice; a reference to the night at the Hammersmith Palais in March 1984, when Cope stabbed himself in the stomach with a broken microphone stand, while quoting Kenneth Williams as Julius Caesar: "Infamy, infamy, they've all got it in for me." The sleeve for 1987's *Saint Julian* was shot in a Tamworth scrapyard.

Derbyshire

Swarkestone

Just outside the village of Swarkestone, south of Derby, is the twin-turreted Swarkestone Hall Pavilion, location of the 1968 Rolling Stones photoshoot for the *Beggars Banquet* album. Images of the band playing cricket in and around the Pavilion, taken by the South African photographer Michael Joseph, are considered among the most iconic of the band.

Swarkestone was as far south as Bonnie Prince Charlie's army reached during the 1745 Jacobite Revolution. It was here they realised his attempt on the English throne was futile and turned back towards Scotland, only to meet defeat at Culloden. Swarkestone Hall itself had been demolished by 1750 but the Pavilion survived, and it's been renovated by current owners The Landmark Trust. It now has a roof and can be rented by tourists and Stones fans alike (bring your own cricket whites for Stones re-enactments).

Beggars Banquet was the first album produced by Jimmy Miller and the last to feature Brian Jones. Featuring *Sympathy for the Devil* and *Street Fighting Man*, it was a commercial triumph and a return to blues after their experimental psychedelic sound on the previous album, *Their Satanic Majesties Request*. Despite all the prancing around in cricket gear, the album was finally released with sleeve artwork from inside a house in Hampstead.

Billy J Kramer and the Dakotas – and was approached by Elvis Presley, but the Dakotas' managers didn't forward the message. In later years, Green worked alongside Bryan Ferry, Paul McCartney, The Animals and Van Morrison. Although never a famous name, Green was hugely influential; fellow guitarists admired his distinctive staccato style and ability to play lead and rhythm guitar at the same time. He inspired guitarists like George Harrison and Pete Townshend and also the likes of Wilko Johnson of Dr Feelgood, who based his style on Green. In fact, the R&B band got their name from a Pirates cover of the song, *Dr Feelgood*. And, Uriah Heep's guitarist Mick Box cites Green as the reason he picked up the instrument. Green's funeral in early 2010 ended with the words: "Heaven's just got a little bit louder."

Matlock

One of rock's original guitar heroes hailed from this Derbyshire town, situated beside the Derwent Gorge. Matlock was the birthplace of the late rock guitarist Mick Green, member of the 1960s rock 'n' roll group Johnny Kidd and the Pirates. When that band faded, he played with

Staveley

Derbyshire claims another renowned guitarist: session guitarist, solo artist and producer Chris Spedding. His only solo hit was 1975's *Motor Bikin'*, which saw him perform on TV dressed in classic rock 'n' roll garb: greased hair and full biker gear. For a performance on TV show, Supersonic, he was backed by punk band The Vibrators, with whom he had released an early single, called *Pogo Dancing*. His association with punk did not end there; he produced the Sex Pistols' first demo sessions in May 1976. Versatility was clearly Spedding's trademark; just before his involvement with punk he was Wellington, one of The Wombles. He toured with the all-singing furry pioneering environmental activists in the 1970s in full costume, complete with his Gibson Flying V guitar.

Cromford ⟩

The village of Cromford was originally built to house the workers of Richard Arkwright's first water-powered cotton mills. Its claim to a place in rock folklore is a little more recent and lies in the shape of Cromford railway station. Part of the branch line between Derby and Matlock, the station looks virtually the same today as when it took a starring role on the cover of the Oasis single, *Some Might Say*. The Gallagher brothers appear on the sleeve: Liam on the railway bridge,

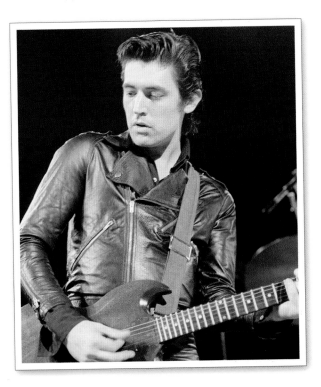

while Noel empties a watering can. In 1995 the song was the band's first UK number one single, taken from their *(What's the Story) Morning Glory?* album (for that cover, see Central London, page XXX). The station, constructed by the Midland Railway in 1860 in a French style, was once part of the main line to Buxton and Manchester.

Buxton ⟩

The Peak District spa town of Buxton is the birthplace of former BBC Radio 1 DJ Dave Lee Travis (nicknamed the Hairy Cornflake because he had a beard and did the breakfast show) and singer-songwriter Lloyd Cole, now solo but formerly frontman of 1980s darlings, Lloyd Cole and the Commotions.

An incident near Buxton in the late 1950s inspired a classic folk song. Stockport train driver John Axon was posthumously awarded the George Cross for bravery, after he attempted to save others in a rail crash in 1957. He died trying to stop a runaway freight train after a brake failure. His heroic death became the inspiration for a famous radio ballad, *The Ballad of John Axon*, one of a series created by folk legends Ewan MacColl and his wife Peggy Seeger and radio producer Charles Parker.

The Echo & The Bunnymen concert held at Buxton's Pavilion Gardens in St Johns Road in January 1981 ended up as their *Shine So Hard* EP. The gig was kept secret, with fans driven to the venue by coach or given maps, and was later made into a video.

Swanwick ⟩

One of England's most inventive music festivals must surely be the annual Indietracks, the successful and yet improbable coupling of indie music with England's railway heritage. Each summer since 2007 the Midland Railway Centre in the village of Swanwick hosts indie bands on several stages: a converted engine shed, a railway platform and a church. For festival-goers there's a free ride on a 1950s steam train through the Derbyshire countryside included in the ticket price. Money raised goes towards the Midland Railway Trust.

Left: The renowned guitarist from Staveley, Chris Spedding.
Opposite page: Mick Green of Johnny Kidd and the Pirates.

Nottinghamshire

Nottingham

An unlikely anti-war song came courtesy of Nottingham's most successful band, the 1970s three-hit-wonders, Paper Lace. Formed in 1969, they were regulars on the small venue circuit and the resident band at Tiffany's club in Rochdale before they struck gold, winning 1974's *Opportunity Knocks* TV talent contest, *The X-Factor* of its day. The band spent three weeks at number one that year, with a tear-jerking song about the American Civil War, *Billy Don't Be a Hero*, with the band appearing on *Top of the Pops* dressed in the dark blue uniforms of the Union army.

Deep Purple's drummer Ian Paice hails from Nottingham. Born in the city in 1948, his first musical instrument of choice was the violin before switching to percussion aged 15. Before turning to the eardrum-pounding, heavy stuff, he kept the beat in waltzes and quicksteps in his pianist-playing father's dance band.

Born four years earlier, guitarist and singer Alvin Lee of Ten Years After started playing guitar at 13, inspired by rock 'n' roll guitarists Scotty Moore and Chuck Berry. A worldwide audience saw his performance at the 1969 Woodstock Festival on the following year's documentary film, propelling his band to global stardom.

Also from the city was the late Elton Dean, Soft Machine's jazz fusion saxophonist, who supplied Elton John with his first name when they played together in Long John Baldry's band, Bluesology.

Nearby, Editors lead guitarist Chris Urbanowicz hails from Aslockton, east of the city, while Rob Birch and Nick Hallam of the Stereo MCs come from Ruddington, south of Nottingham. Stereo MCs are best known for their 1992 song, *Connected*, used in Vodafone TV commercials in the late noughties.

It is not all hard rock in the Midlands. In the past three decades Nottingham has metamorphosed from a live music backwater into one of the country's best cities for live venues. The 400-capacity Bodega (formerly The Bodega Social and still called 'the Social' by many) in Pelham Street is Nottinghamshire's number one magnet for indie hipsters wearing skinny jeans and Converse trainers. Its name means winery in Spanish and derives from the venue's origins as a warehouse owned by the Bodega Wine Company, and later the Bodega pub. It majors on showcasing British indie bands on the rise and critically acclaimed foreign acts on their first UK tours. Amongst many others, The Libertines, The Kooks,

Above: Ian Paice, drummer of Deep Purple, hails from Nottingham.
Opposite page: Nottingham's Rock City has been hosting gigs since the 1980s.

Hard-Fi, Mumford & Sons and Coldplay have all graced the stage here in recent years. The venue is run by DHP, the Midlands club operator, who also has Nottingham's Rock City and the Rescue Rooms in their live venue portfolio.

Since 1980, the 1,900-capacity Rock City venue in Talbot Street has been the proud, throbbing heart of rock and pop in the Midlands. When it opened, the world's top rock and pop acts no longer had an excuse to bypass Nottingham.

Its name is a bit of misnomer as its booking policy takes in so many more genres and styles than just rock: The Specials, White Lies, Gary Numan and Slayer, at just a random glance. Rock City hosts chart acts, indie bands, synth-pop duos, punk and ska legends. In fact, a snapshot of its diversity came as early as its first salvo of artists in December 1980. Because its opening was delayed a few weeks, gigs by emerging giants of their genres, Iron Maiden and The Human League, were cancelled but punk legends The Undertones were the first to perform, followed by rock

'n' roller Shakin' Stevens, a huge star at the time. Both Nirvana and Pearl Jam stopped off at Rock City on their first UK tours in the early 1990s. Not bad for an old bakery, and, later, a cabaret venue called The Heart of the Midlands, which put on variety shows starring the likes of Marti Caine.

The Nottingham Boat Club is such an unassuming a venue, it looks more like it should be hosting school discos than rowing crews or rock gigs. Located on the bank of the River Trent, in the shadow of Nottingham Forest's City Ground, its wooden boards have been trodden by rock behemoths such as Elton John, Rod Stewart, the Sex Pistols, Led Zeppelin and Black Sabbath since the late 1960s. As the venue doesn't have links with any promoters, there's no list of forthcoming gigs but it's always available for hire, so you never know.

Named after Echo and the Bunnymen's second single, The Rescue Rooms in Goldsmith Street opened in 2003 and is Nottingham's top venue after the legendary Rock City. The .

480-capacity venue puts on an eclectic array of bands, some of whom, like Bloc Party and Razorlight, used the venue to try out their new albums. If the sold-out gigs feel a little too intimate and the elbows of too many students have bruised your ribs, there's indeed rescue in the form of a balcony where older folk can stretch, re-shape their cadres and wipe the beer off their slippers.

Nottingham's big boy is the multi-purpose Nottingham Arena, which stages conferences, indoor sports events and gigs. Its 10,000 capacity ensures it nets the big cats, acts like Bob Dylan, Oasis and Rod Stewart.

Below: Soul legend Edwin Starr died in Beeston in April 2003.
Bottom: Mansfield's very own Alvin Stardust.
Opposite page: Bruce Dickinson and Iron Maiden.

Beeston >>

Rock royalty Led Zeppelin drew upon a huge range of influences: the blues of Howlin' Wolf and Muddy Waters, the rock 'n' roll of Little Richard and the folk of Bert Jansch and influential singer Anne Briggs, born in 1944 in the Nottinghamshire town of Beeston, three miles southwest of Nottingham.

The soul legend Edwin Starr (born Charles Edwin Hatcher, in Nashville) lived for many years in the UK, breathing his last at his home in Beeston, in early April 2003. Only a few weeks earlier, as a multinational force, including soldiers from Starr's homeland and adopted homeland, invaded Iraq, anti-war protesters around the country were singing his biggest hit, *War*.

Originally written by Motown songwriters Norman Whitfield and Barrett Strong as an anti-Vietnam War protest, the song famously asked, "What is it good for?" and answered, "Absolutely nothing! / Say it again!" It was a US number one in 1970 and number three in the UK, before being covered by Frankie Goes to Hollywood and Bruce Springsteen. More hits followed for Starr in the late 1970s, with the Top 10 disco hits, *Contact*, and *H.A.P.P.Y Radio*. The US-born star started making records in the 1950s and was one of the first artists to be signed to the Motown record label. His grave is located in the Southern Cemetery and Crematorium, Wilford Hill in West Bridgford, Nottingham.

Mansfield >>

David Bowie and Madonna didn't pioneer the culture of pop reinvention, it was originally done with stardust. Alvin Stardust was plain north London-born Bernard Jewry when he moved to Mansfield at the age of two with his family. He was destined for the stage from an early age, as his mother ran a boarding house, and many of the guests were musicians and actors appearing at the Mansfield Theatre. Consequently, the young Bernard showed an interest in music and acting, making his stage debut at the age of four in a pantomime. When he was older, he changed his name to Shane Fenton and had some hits in the 1960s with his band The Fentones. But when they broke up, he disappeared until the early 1970s, reappearing with dyed

blond hair, kitted out in black leathers and with a new mean and moody image borrowed from Gene Vincent, Dave Berry and Lee Marvin. Reborn as Alvin Stardust, his new chart career took off with his debut single, 1973's *My Coo-Ca-Choo*.

Clipstone

As the sun slowly disappears behind the trees in this woodland beauty spot in the heart of Robin Hood country, you may spot bemused local fauna, like deer and squirrels, maybe even a lost American tourist searching for a Lincoln green-clad outlaw. But in recent years you also might have seen Paul Weller, Simply Red, Keane, Pulp and Status Quo. Since 2001, Sherwood Pines Forest Park, close to Clipstone, near Mansfield, has hosted a series of open-air summer gigs usually in June and July. The forest park venue, owned by the Forestry Commission, is the largest woodland open to the public in the east Midlands.

Live in Sherwood Forest '75 by space-rockers Gong was recorded in November 1975, not in Sherwood Forest but at Nottingham University. Originally broadcast as a live radio broadcast, it was issued as an album release until 2005. It's an important gig for Gong fans, as the set features guitarist Steve Hillage on his farewell tour before he embarked on his solo career.

Worksop

This Nottinghamshire town on the River Ryton can claim rock's premier multi-faceted polymath as its own: fencer, broadcaster, writer and airline pilot Captain Dickinson, better known as Iron Maiden singer Bruce Dickinson. When he's not thrilling fans with the band's take on Samuel Taylor Coleridge's *Rime of the Ancient Mariner*, Maiden's frontman regularly flies jets for the UK charter airline Astraeus. Dickinson flew his band mates and crew in a specially painted Boeing 757-200 for Iron Maiden's 2008 Somewhere Back in Time world tour, which started in Mumbai. (Rock bands are no strangers to being flown around in their own huge passenger jets; Deep Purple, Led Zeppelin and The Rolling Stones did it in the 1970s, but no one in any of those bands actually flew the plane). Dickinson also presented 6 Music's *Friday Rock Show*, until it was axed in May 2010.

Lincolnshire

Scunthorpe

Scunthorpe's musical sons include Howard Devoto, frontman of both the Bolton punk band Buzzcocks, and later of Magazine. A key mobiliser in the Manchester punk scene, Devoto was inspired to form Buzzcocks with Pete Shelley after seeing a Sex Pistols gig.

Guitar virtuoso and celebrated folk singer-songwriter Martin Simpson was born in Scunthorpe in 1953; his blend of folk and country blues has spanned four decades.

Also from the town: singer-songwriter Stephen Fretwell whose song, *Run*, provided the theme tune to the BBC sitcom, *Gavin & Stacey* (and once described by *Q* magazine as "Scunthorpe's finest export… ever") and Iain Matthews, the former leadsinger of Fairport Convention. He left the folk-rockers in 1969 to form Matthew's Southern Comfort; his country-rock, steel-guitar-laden cover of Joni Mitchell's *Woodstock* spent three weeks at number one in the UK in 1970.

Cleethorpes

The musical genius who gave the world *Thriller* hails from the seaside town of Cleethorpes. No, not the late Michael Jackson, but Grammy-winning songwriter, producer and musician, Rod Temperton. He wrote some of Jackson's most famous songs, including *Off the Wall*, *Rock With You* and the title track of *Thriller*, the biggest-selling album of all time. Temperton played keyboards in 1970s disco outfit Heatwave, with free-spirited flyaway lapels, and had hits like *Boogie Nights* and *Always and Forever* until he was recruited by Quincy Jones as a songwriter for Jackson.

Growing up, Temperton studied at De Aston comprehensive in Market Rasen and his first job was in a Grimsby fish factory. Originally a drummer, he switched to keyboards and joined Heatwave via the time-honoured route of answering an ad in *Melody Maker*. Temperton also penned hits for the likes of Donna Summer, Anita Baker, Herbie Hancock, Quincy Jones, The Brothers Johnson and George Benson. He came up with *Thriller* in a taxi en route to the studio.

Cleethorpes' 16-car Big Wheel on the beach and Corporation Bridge, a lifting bridge in the town's former fish docks, were featured in Erasure's video for *The Circus*, the synth-pop duo's 1987 fanfare for the working man shut out of employment by big corporations. Yorkshire crooner Richard Hawley visited Cleethorpes for the cover of his eponymous 2000 debut album. The 'Sheffield Sinatra' is pictured on Cleethorpes' North Promenade.

The Wigan Casino, the Blackpool Mecca and Stoke's Golden Torch did not hold the monopoly on the 1970s northern soul scene. Another leading northern soul club

Left: Howard Devoto, frontman of the Buzzcocks and product of Scunthorpe.
Opposite page: Cleethorpes pier's legendary 'Talk of the North' all-nighters.

was the 700-capacity ballroom dance floor on Cleethorpes Pier, which housed 'Talk Of The North' all-nighters. Starting in February 1975, these ran every fortnight for just over a year, attracting ecstatic soul fans and spinning dancers. Its success was partly due its eclectic music policy, with as many as 12 DJs a night spinning a diverse mix of unknown rarities, classic soulful stompers and breaking new sounds. Several live acts also appeared including The

Trammps and Viola Wills. Soul boys and girls danced all night to everything from traditional 1960s soul to funk, before staggering their way home with arms raised to protect their eyes from the sunrise over the River Humber as huge tankers navigated their way up the estuary. In fact, the all-nighters proved so popular, promoter Mary Chapman had to hire the nearby 500-capacity Winter Gardens on the seafront to accommodate the extra revellers. Talk Of The North managed to celebrate its first birthday before the authorities pulled the plug on the all-nighters, worried the pier might fall into the sea due to all the stomping.

With its domed roof, Cleethorpes Winter Gardens could be seen from many vantage points around the town – and heard if AC/DC were in town – it was also a rock venue,

Left: Bernie Taupin, Elton John's hugely successful writing partner and lyricist.
Below: Dexy's Midnight Runners.

firmly on the live circuit for touring bands. Appearing here were the likes of Queen, The Bay City Rollers, Genesis, Free and Chris 'Motorbikin' Spedding (accompanied by local Grimsby bassist, the late Steve Currie, formerly of T.Rex), as well as punk groups like the Sex Pistols, The Damned and The Stranglers. Wearing their stage-garb of donkey jackets and woolly hats, 1960s soul-inspired Dexys Midnight Runners appeared at The Winter Gardens in 1980, on the same evening that they appeared on *Top of the Pops*, performing their number one hit single, *Geno*, a homage to the 1960s soul singer Geno Washington.

Despite huge local objection, in 2007 Cleethorpes council called time on the venue and it was demolished the following year, finally slamming the door on a treasure trove of musical memories.

Market Rasen ❯

Elton John's writing partner and lyricist Bernie Taupin was born at Flatters Farmhouse between Sleaford and Anwick, near Market Rasen, north of Lincoln. When he was a boy, his family moved to Maltkiln Farm in the village of Owmby-by-Spital, but he attended secondary school in Market Rasen. Later Taupin worked at dead-end jobs until, aged 17, he answered an ad in the *NME* that led to his lifelong collaboration with Elton John.

Lady What's Tomorrow, on Elton John's 1969 debut, *Empty Sky*, was one of the first songs the duo wrote together and it plaintively recalls the rural beauty of Taupin's Lincolnshire childhood. It was a theme the lyricist returned to on the title track of 1973's *Goodbye Yellow Brick Road*, a lament for the Lincolnshire countryside and the culture clash experienced by a country kid heading to the big city. The lyric "back to my plough" is a clear reference to growing up on a farm.

Taupin's lyrics for the classic ode to drinking and fighting – *Saturday Night's Alright For Fighting*, on the same album – were inspired by teenage Saturday evenings spent in Lincolnshire dance halls, like the Boston Gliderdrome and Mecca Ballrooms, and pubs like the Aston Arms pub in Market Rasen (a framed newspaper article on a wall inside commemorates its role in the song). These were all locales where Taupin and friends partook in underage drinking and inevitably ended in England's other national sport, pub fighting.

Tell Me When the Whistle Blows, on 1975's *Captain Fantastic And The Brown Dirt Cowboy*, sees Taupin reflect on the pull of his mother's "apron strings" as he takes a train home to Lincolnshire. The autobiographical concept album is about two struggling young songwriters, Captain Fantastic (Elton John) and The Brown Dirt Cowboy (Bernie Taupin), who take on the Tin Pan Alley music industry ("those old die-hards in Denmark Street"). The original album artwork included photographs of Flatters Farmhouse and the Aston Arms. Other Taupin lyrics featured specific Lincolnshire locales, like *Grimsby* on 1974's *Caribou*, a homage to the nearby seaport.

Along with Bernie Taupin and his mates, the Gliderdrome in Boston, southeast of Market Rasen, drew some of the biggest names in the world of music. Boston's 'Palace of Pop' attracted massive crowds in its 1960s and 1970s heyday, hosting Motown acts as well as soul legend Otis Redding. T.Rex's *Live at the Boston Gliderdrome* was recorded at the venue in 1972 at the height of their fame.

Skegness ❯

One of Lincolnshire's best venues is The Farm at Chapel St Leonards on the Lincolnshire coast, a few miles north of Skegness. Located in its own grounds and surrounded by farmland, countryside and nature reserves, it's a stone's throw from large, sweeping, unspoilt beaches.

A few miles inland, near Alford, the county boasts a cutting-edge residential recording studio in the form of Chapel Studios in the village of South Thoresby in the heart of the Lincolnshire Wolds. The two studios here have hosted some of the UK's top artists, including Kaiser Chiefs, Simple Minds and Paul Weller. The first studio complex is spread across restored village buildings like farm cottages, a Wesleyan Chapel (hence its name), school rooms and a blacksmith's workshop, while the second studio is housed in what used to be the post office and village shop. Some of the albums recorded here have included The Darkness's *Permission To Land*, Editors' *The Back Room* and Arctic Monkey's *Whatever People Say I Am, That's What I'm Not*.

MARGARET THE THATCHER SONGBOOK

SHE was a humble grocer's daughter from the Lincolnshire market town of Grantham, but few political leaders divided opinion like Baroness Thatcher, the prime minister formerly known as Margaret. Some feel Britain's first woman PM was a saviour of the nation who made Britain great again, while others feel the country is still reeling from her influence. By the turn of the 1980s, Thatcherism was having a dramatic effect. There was a crippling miner's strike, inner city riots, three million people out of work for the first time since the 1930s and the country was at war. Naturally, songwriters queued up to have their say:

Ghost Town The Specials (1981)
"Can't go on no more / The people getting angry" – Britain's bleakest ever number one? Few songs capture the grimness of the Thatcher era as well as The Specials' eerie, atmospheric ode to Coventry and anthem for a nation ill at ease with itself. As the single went straight to number one in July 1981, many inner cities around the UK were erupting in social unrest and widespread rioting. Jerry Dammers tapped into this inner city alienation and anger, drawing upon scenes he'd witnessed during a UK tour. These lyrics were made even more haunting by the trombone playing by ska elder statesman and Jamaican trombone legend Rico Rodriguez, an original member of Jamaica's Skatalites. (For more about the *Ghost Town* video, see Southeast London, page 42).

King's Cross Pet Shop Boys (1987)
Neil Tennant uses London's King's Cross station as a metaphor for Thatcher's Britain. It's a song about hopes being dashed, about a place where people look for opportunities that don't happen. King's Cross is the station where Geordies like Neil Tennant would arrive in London when travelling from the northeast. The song proved somewhat prophetic: just a few weeks after it was released on the album, *Actually*, the King's Cross fire occurred, killing 31 people, a disaster many attributed to Tory government cuts.

Little Beast Elbow (2001)
Elbow frontman Guy Garvey has said this song, from *Asleep in the Back*, is about Thatcher's "general sacking" of the north of England. He wanted to look at how the generation before him was badly treated by her government and what it was like growing up in one of the northern towns "she tried to wreck".

One In Ten UB40 (1981)
Although their reggae was deemed too straight-ahead to be aligned with the British ska revival or 2-Tone, UB40 commented on similar social ills and frustrations. *One In Ten* was partly a biting critique of unemployment, but also explored the way official figures were thought to be manipulated. The multi-racial Birmingham band named themselves after a DHSS unemployment benefit document and

their 1980 album, *Signing Off*, even used the old claim form as its cover artwork.

Shipbuilding Robert Wyatt (1983)
The former Soft Machine drummer and singer-songwriter offers a grim yet beautiful take on Elvis Costello's deeply ironic song about Britain's ravaged shipyards suddenly thriving thanks to the 1982 Falklands War. In the song, Wyatt (who lives in the Lincolnshire town of Louth) inhabits the role of a Tyneside dockworker employed to make warships for a conflict at the expense of his own son, who'll be sent to the frontline.

Sowing the Seeds of Love
Tears For Fears (1989)
"Politician granny with your high ideals / Have you no idea how the majority feels?" The Bath duo wrote this as a rallying call to the working class to take a more active role in politics and as a protest against the re-election of Thatcher as prime minister.

Stand Down Margaret The Beat (1980)
"Stand down please / Our lives seem petty in your cold grey hands." A brand of anti-Thatcherism you could dance to, from the Birmingham band (known in the US as The English Beat). This rousing anthem was a political plea for the British prime minister to resign, but also to get off her soap box and stop talking down to people. It would be another decade until the Brum band would get their wish.

Thatcher's Children
Wild Billy Childish And The MBEs (2008)
"Thatcher's Children / Only tied to the purse / It ain't gettin' better / It's just gettin' worse." The Kentish garage rock legend and his band, the Musicians Of The British Empire, paid homage to the generation born under Thatcher. The sleeve was designed by legendary Sex Pistols cover artist Jamie Reid and featured the Iron Lady.

The Fletcher Memorial Home
Pink Floyd (1983)
The theme of much of Pink Floyd's *The Final Cut* album was Roger Waters opposition to the Falklands War and other perceived betrayals by post-World War II leaders.

Fletcher refers to Waters' father, Eric Fletcher Waters, who died at the 1944 Battle of Anzio, south of Rome.

Walls Come Tumbling Down
The Style Council (1984)
Paul Weller was the impassioned angry voice who spoke for a generation opposed to Thatcherism, and many tracks on the 1985 album, *Our Favourite Shop*, could be included here. This single was soul pop with a socialist conviction which starts with the emphatic line: "You don't have to take this crap." The call to arms then takes on government youth training schemes, broken communities and the miners' strike.

Bonus tracks:
Between the Wars Billy Bragg (1985)
This song conveyed the experience of the miners' strike and their year-long battle with the Thatcher government.

Sanctuary Iron Maiden (1980)
Political comment was not beyond heavy metal either. This single sleeve showed the band's mascot Eddie knifing the prime minister.

Tramp The Dirt Down
Elvis Costello (1989)
This song on *Spike* pulled few punches: "When England was the whore of the world / Margaret was her madam. "

Extra bonus tracks:
How Does it Feel?, Crass (1982); *Think For A Minute*, The Housemartins (1986); *Bury Me Deep*, Chumbawamba (2008); *Pills and Soap*, Elvis Costello (1983); *Leper Skin*, Julian Cope (1991); *Margaret On The Guillotine*, Morrissey (1988); *She'll Have to Go* and *Wonderland*, Simply Red (1989, 1991).

Leicestershire

Leicester ⟩

In 2007, a plaque in honour of late ska legend Laurel Aitken was unveiled at his Leicester home. Cuban-born Aitken, who would later be known as the Godfather of Ska, grew up in his father's homeland of Jamaica from the age of 10. There he sang as part of a calypso band that performed for cruise ship passengers arriving on the Caribbean island.

He was one of the earliest artists to release a ska record: his double A-side, *Little Sheila / Boogie in My Bones*, was the first single released on Chris Blackwell's Island label. A massive hit in Jamaica, where it topped the charts for nearly three months, it later became the first Jamaican record ever released in the UK.

Encouraged by the popularity of his records in England, Aitken moved to London in 1960, joining the West Indian community in Brixton. He recorded over 15 singles for Blue Beat, the first British-based record label to cater to the musical tastes of Jamaican immigrants. He moved north and settled in Leicester in 1971.

The 2-Tone ska revival movement of the late '70s (see Coventry, page 222) thrust Aitken in the limelight again. The Beat's song, *Ranking Full Stop*, was a rewrite of Aitken's *Pussy Price (Gone Up)*, while UB40 covered his *Guilty*, which he had released under the pseudonym Tiger, on their album *Labour Of Love*. Aitken recorded sessions with punk band The Ruts (see Hayes, page 103) and went back into the studio in 1981 to record *Rudi Got Married*, his first UK chart single. In 1986, Aitken also appeared alongside David Bowie in *Absolute Beginners*, Julien Temple's musical adaptation of Colin MacInnes's novel about life in late-fifties London. He died in July 2005.

Four-piece Kasabian are the biggest thing to come from Leicester since 1970s chart regulars and teddy boy revivalists, Showaddywaddy (an eight-piece with two drummers, bassists and singers). Kasabian were originally called Saracuse but renamed themselves after a gang member involved in one of the 20th century's most frenzied killings.

Linda Kasabian was the getaway driver of Charles Manson's 'Family' cult, who murdered film director Roman Polanski's heavily pregnant wife Sharon Tate and four others in Los Angeles in August 1969. (To many, the horrific murders pinpointed the moment the Sixties ended.)

The band were formed when singer Tom Meighan met guitarist and vocalist Serge Pizzorno at Countesthorpe Community College in the Leicestershire village of the same name. Their first public performance was at the clubhouse of Vipers Rugby Club on the Blaby bypass, southwest of Leicester.

The city can also lay part claim to Arnold Dorsey (no relation to American jazz band leader Tommy) who changed his name to the multi-syllabled Engelbert Humperdinck, after the 19th-century German composer most famous for his opera, *Hansel Und Gretel*. Humperdinck was born in India into a British army family but later grew up in Leicester. The change of name was the idea of his manager Gordon Mills. Humperdinck went on to sell well over 100 million records worldwide. The late music impresario Mills also name-changed his other charges: Thomas Woodward became Tom Jones and Raymond O'Sullivan was reborn as Gilbert O'Sullivan.

Progressive rockers Family formed in 1966 out of two bands, The Roaring Sixties and The Farinas, with origins in Leicester Art College (now De Montfort University) in the early 1960s.

Cornershop's Tjinder Singh was born in Wolverhampton but moved to Leicester, where his siblings lived, in 1992. He spent his time looking around charity shops, writing his own songs and working as a barman at Leicester's now-defunct live music pub, Magazine, where he developed the promising indie-pop band he'd formed with Ben

Ayres at university in Preston. Joined by his brother Avtar, Cornershop's first gig was at O'Jays at Belgrave Gate. It was their 1997 song, *Brimful of Asha* – a tribute to the Bollywood legend Asha Bhosle – that made their name, reaching number one on the singles chart. Or rather, it was a version of their original song, remixed by Fatboy Slim (aka Norman Cook). Cook had heard Cornershop's slower version on the radio and asked if he could mix it. Cook ordinarily charged lots of money for a remix but did it free of charge.

Leicester also claims two top bass players, John Illsley from Dire Straits and Queen's John Deacon.

Leicester's Granby Halls venue is no more, bulldozed in 2001, but still going strong is the city's famous neo-classical De Montfort Hall, in Granville Road. The venue is named not after a local cheese but a local big cheese: Anglo-French nobleman Simon de Montfort, the 13th-century Earl of

Above: Kasabian.
Right: Laurel Aitken.

Leicester. Beyond its white, Grecian-style colonnaded frontage, this all-purpose venue stages a wide-ranging repertoire of comedy, jazz, ballet, opera and classical concerts, and still plenty of rock and pop gigs to warrant inclusion here. Many top rock acts played here when starting out: The Rolling Stones, The Clash and Joy Division to name just a few. De Montfort Hall's parkland grounds are the setting for the annual Summer Sundae Weekender music festival each August. Starting in 2001 as a one-day festival, the focus is definitely on the music, with over 100 acts appearing across six stages.

Ashby-de-la-Zouch

You'd be nuts to go there? Not necessarily. The nation's snacks and biscuit capital has probably provoked hours of drunken wonderment in pubs up and down the land as punters clock the address of KP Nuts on the back of packets. The town is hardly a hotbed of English rock 'n' roll but has produced the indie rock trio, Young Knives.

Now based in Oxford, the band formed in Ashby-de-la-Zouch in 1998, playing Ned's Atomic Dustbin covers. Their

2006 debut album, *Voices of Animals and Men*, produced by Gang of Four's Andy Gill, was full of English themes and put provincial Britain on the map in tracks such as *Loughborough Suicide*, *Weekends And Bleak Days (Hot Summer)* and *Coastguard*.

The band – drummer Oliver Askew, singer and guitarist Henry Dartnall and his brother Thomas 'House of Lords' Dartnall (so named because he supposedly vetoes the best ideas) – returned to their Leicestershire hometown in May 2008 to play a one-off gig at the Ashby Venture Theatre.

Castle Donington

Welcome to the spiritual home of heavy metal. You could ask for directions to the Download Festival, Europe's foremost heavy rock and metal get-together, but you're better off just following the legions of longhairs in denim and leather and the wafts of petunia oil.

Held in the grounds of the Castle Donington racetrack in Leicestershire, Download started life as the Monsters of Rock Festival in 1980, as a rival to the then heavy rock-dominated Reading Festival. This was at the height of the new wave of British Heavy Metal (or NWOBHM, see page 215), when skin-tight spandex trousers were all the rage. All of the biggest names in heavy rock have performed there, including Iron Maiden, Guns N' Roses, AC/DC, Metallica, Whitesnake and Slayer.

The 1986 festival saw the triumphant return of Sheffield's Def Leppard and their drummer Rick Allen for his first UK show after losing an arm in a road accident. Tragedy struck two years later, when two fans were crushed to death during a Guns N' Roses performance. When the band came off stage they were elated about their show but were instantly numbed when told the news. Guitarist Slash said later that hearing about the deaths just "erased everything". After 1996, there was a break of several year before Monsters of Rock was reborn as the two-day Download in 2003. Nowadays there are over 100 bands on the bill, appearing across four stages.

Castle Donington also hosts the child-friendly Off The Tracks festivals, two separate spring and summer events in May and August or September, at which bands playing any musical form except heavy metal compete with circus workshops, tai chi and meditation. Just a slight contrast from Download, then.

Rutland

If nothing else, England's smallest county has given its name to The Beatles spoof pop band, The Rutles. Created by two former members of the Monty Python team, Eric Idle and Neil Innes (also of The Bonzo Dog Doo-Dah Band), The Prefab Four – Dirk, Nasty, Stig and Barry and their manager, Leggy Mountbatten – were born out of a sketch for the 1975 BBC show, *Rutland Weekend Television*. The Rutles might just have been the best tribute band ever: John Lennon gave them his approval and George Harrison liked them to such an extent he even appeared in The Rutles 1978 movie, *All You Need Is Cash*.

The name of American soul and R&B icon Geno Washington's band, The Ram Jam Band, derives from the Ram Jam Inn, a pub and restaurant on the Great North Road in Stretton near Oakham. In the early 1960s, Washington was stationed in East Anglia with the US Air Force, as well as being a regular performer in and around London.

To provide sanctuary and focus during the recording of Kasabian's 2004 eponymous debut album, the Leicester band lived communally in an isolated farmhouse at Rutland Water. They slept in the same room and saw no one but each other for several weeks.

Below: The Rutles, from er... Rutland.
Opposite page: The Download Festival has been held at Donington Castle since 1980.

Northamptonshire

Oundle

The Northamptonshire market town of Oundle is home to one of the oldest public schools in the country, Oundle School, founded in the 16th century. Old Oundlians include Iron Maiden frontman Bruce Dickinson and Nick Garvey of Ducks Deluxe and later The Motors. But not Billy Bragg, though he did reside in the town in the late 1970s.

His band Riff Raff also lived at the isolated farmhouse Bearshanks Lodge, on the edge of Bearshanks Wood, near Pilton. Surrounded by flat arable fields, this was a country house with a four-track recording studio owned by the late saxophonist and keyboardist Ruan O'Lochlainn and his wife Jackie MacKay. In the mid-1970s, O'Lochlainn played in Ronnie Lane's Slim Chance and pub rockers Bees Make Honey. In 1977, the couple put an advert in the music press for bands to practise and record demos at their farmhouse and a teenage Bragg was the first person to call. Bragg later returned to Barking, but among the songs he wrote during his time in Northamptonshire were *Romford Girls* and *A New England*.

The farmhouse also hosted prog rockers Gong – whose drummer had a penchant for setting up his drum kit in a cornfield – and The Stranglers. The Men in Black resided at Bearshanks in the winter of 1977/78 to write and rehearse songs for their *Black And White* album. Ruan O'Lochlainn took the photograph for the album's monochrome sleeve.

Fotheringhay

In the 16th century, the quiet riverside village of Fotheringhay was a destination of choice for many Scotsmen, who travelled down to Northamptonshire to see if they could rescue their monarch, Mary Queen of Scots, imprisoned locally at Fotheringhay Castle. They failed, and she was tried and executed in 1587. A grassy mound now marks the spot where the castle once stood. The locale inspired singer Sandy Denny's 1969 Fairport Convention song of the same name, albeit spelt *Fotheringay*. When she left Fairport she also named the folk-rock band she formed in 1970 after the place.

Corby

Many centuries later, more Scots made a more permanent passage down south to Northamptonshire, to the town of Corby a few miles west. After a downturn in the Scottish steel industry, a sizeable migrant Scottish workforce of steelworkers crossed the border and settled amongst the Sassenachs in this former steel-making town. The title track of Big Country's 1984 album, *Steeltown*, was a homage to the town and told the story of the Scots who went to work in Corby only to find themselves jobless again when *these* steelworks closed. The nationalised British Steel decided to consolidate steel-making to other areas of the UK and Corby wasn't part of the plan.

Wellingborough

Wellingborough claims the frontmen of two very different but influential bands. Radiohead's Thom Yorke was born in the market town in 1968, before his parents moved to Scotland and finally settled in Oxfordshire when he was 10. Also Peter Murphy, lead singer of goth pioneers Bauhaus, came from Northampton, but grew up in Wellingborough.

The seeds of the band were planted when Peter Murphy struck up a friendship with guitarist Daniel Ash at a Northampton comprehensive school. They formed the band when Ash was going to Nene College and Murphy worked in a printing factory. Emerging out of local groups The Craze and The Submerged Tenth, Bauhaus played their first gig at Wellingborough's Cromwell pub at the end of 1978. Their first single, released the following summer, was the influential 12-inch, *Bela Lugosi's Dead*.

Clocking in at over nine minutes long, it is considered to be the first goth record. Inventive Bauhaus gigs followed: wearing a black-cape, Murphy would sometimes descend from the lighting rig, fastened by his ankles. He dressed up as a vampire or drove across stage in a special hearse, nicknamed the Bauhearse. To many, Bauhaus are seen as the godfathers of goth rock, although the epithet has always sat uncomfortably with the band who reject the label.

Nearby Wollaston's contributions to English culture have been immeasurable: a long-running fashion icon and a fabled venue. Fashion and popular music have always been closely linked but few brands of footwear have signified rebellion as much as Dr Marten boots ('Docs' or 'DMs'), manufactured in Wollaston until 2001, when production was moved to China to cut costs. Since the birth of the company's classic eight-eye 1460 boot in 1960, the boots have graced the feet of rock musicians and fans alike. Wearing a pair of Dr Martens allowed generations of punks, skinheads, mods and, later, grunge fans to send an unfettered V-sign to the authorities. The many English artists who favoured the boots included The Who, The Clash and Madness. Ironically, the Dr Marten boot was never originally designed to be an icon of non-conformity but more a hard-wearing, functional footwear for the likes of police officers and postmen.

The Nags Head (now The Wollaston Inn) looked like a typical village boozer from the outside but for several years harboured one of England's top venues. Many bands started their careers by performing at The Nags Head in the late 1960s and 1970s, including Free. Guided by the landlord 'Big' Bob Knight, this local village pub hosted now-legendary bands and artists like Led Zeppelin, Rod Stewart & The Faces, Yes, U2, Killing Joke, Mott The Hoople and Status Quo. In the early 1970s, the late BBC Radio 1 legend John Peel hosted a regular Friday night DJ spot here, and even sometimes stamped the hands of punters as they entered the venue.

Above left: Sandy Denny's post-Fairport Convention band were called Fotheringay.
Above right: Bauhaus frontman, Peter Murphy, grew up in Wellingborough.

The Northwest

Manchester
Salford
Greater Manchester
Lancashire
Liverpool
Cheshire
Cumbria

Manchester

For more than three decades, Manchester's music scene has been at the forefront of British pop culture. Like Liverpool and London, the city is steeped in musical heritage with defining bands like Joy Division, The Smiths, The Stone Roses, Happy Mondays and Oasis all emerging from the city. Before punk, Manchester was known for the Bee Gees – a group of brothers from Chorlton –10cc and, before them, Manchester beat group The Hollies, who were Britain's third most successful Sixties band, after The Beatles and The Rolling Stones.

After a 3,000-lb IRA bomb ripped through Manchester city centre in 1996 (remembered in Take That's 2006 homage to their home town, *Mancunian Way*), the city underwent an urban redevelopment programme on a scale not seen since the 1950s and '60s. Sandwiched between two of England's great landscapes, the Peak District and the Lake District, Manchester looked like a bombsite long before the mid-1990s, and it had nothing to do with terrorism.

The slum clearances of the 1960s created vast areas of decay in the city and, due to the mid-1970s recession, the holes were not filled in. In the 1980s, Conservative governments seemed to share the same relationship with much of northern Britain as Oliver Cromwell had with Ireland. The world's first industrial city, with a rich history of radicalism and a strong trade union heritage, was hit hard with the closure of many factories. Though decay was already evident in the city, the devastation of heavy manufacturing in the 1970s turned Manchester and Salford into post-apocalyptic wastegrounds: abandoned red-brick factories dotted a forgotten industrial landscape. "I don't think I saw a tree until I was nine years old," Joy Division and New Order's Bernard Sumner once said.

Musically, though, there were positives to emerge from the gloom as a generation picked up guitars and translated their disillusionment into song. The bleak post-punk sound of Joy Division seemed to define the spirit of the city (see page 256). And from their ashes rose pioneering dance rockers New Order who would change the future of music as much as the political-tinged pop of The Smiths.

Before that Manchester had embraced punk with open arms. Its main venue was the Electric Circus, a brick cinema in Oldham Road, Collyhurst, opposite a large Mecca ballroom called Rotters. There was often friction outside when it emptied and revellers came face to face with the new spiky-haired subculture. A small basement club on Oxford Road called Rafters also attracted punks.

Manchester's punk scene started when the two founding members of the Buzzcocks, Howard Devoto and Pete Shelley, saw a London gig by the Sex Pistols. Fired up by the band's brash new music and attitude, they enticed the Pistols to Manchester, organising the band's first-ever gig outside the capital.

Central Manchester venue, the Free Trade Hall, in Peter Street (now the Radisson Edwardian Hotel), was originally built to house meetings of the Anti-Corn Law League, but two concerts held there have passed into rock'n'roll folklore. One of these was in early June, 1976, when the Sex Pistols played the upstairs room (the Lesser Free Trade Hall). This gig has now attained mythical status for its pivotal role in the punk and new wave movements. There were just 42 people in the audience (though many who claim to have been there would have been in nappies at the time), including the future members of the Buzzcocks, Peter Hook and Bernard Sumner of Joy Division, The Fall, Morrissey and Mick Hucknall of Simply Red. Perhaps the most influential member of the audience, though, was future Factory Records boss Tony Wilson.

This momentous gig, and the Buzzcocks' debut EP *Spiral Scratch* in 1977, well and truly kick-started the northwest punk scene, inspiring a generation of soon-to-be spiky-haired youths. The four-song EP was recorded in December

THE man who put Manchester on the musical map – and was arguably the most important music business honcho since Brian Epstein – was the son of a tobacconist. Salford-born Anthony Howard Wilson grew up in Marple, near Stockport, and attended De La Salle Grammar School in Weaste, Salford, before studying English at Cambridge University.

His first job was with Granada Television in the 1970s and Wilson fronted the music show *So It Goes*, bringing memorable early performances by The Clash, Siouxsie and the Banshees and the Buzzcocks to the Manchester region viewers. Wilson also gave The Jam, Elvis Costello and the Sex Pistols their TV debuts. "Manchester became the punk city," said Wilson, paraphrasing rock critic Jon Savage. "It took punk to its heart, and the genius of that music and how it moved into Joy Division and The Smiths and everything else was the engine of the glorious example of northern rebuilding that's Manchester today." Most of Manchester's reinvention, as the UK's musical epicentre, can be traced back to Tony Wilson.

The visionary impresario become increasingly active in the city's burgeoning rock scene, helping set up Factory Records in 1978, the label behind Joy Division, New Order and the Happy Mondays. Legend has it that Wilson wrote recording contracts in his own blood, saying the artists owned everything and the label owned nothing. It may be apocryphal, but the principle was a powerful statement of creative freedom – and financial suicide. Wilson once said it "resulted in my entire catalogue being owned by somebody else. I can't regret it, because the idea was not to own the past but to present the future."

In 1982, he established The Haçienda nightclub, which became the heart of the Madchester scene, playing host to bands such as The Smiths, The Stone Roses and other luminaries (even Madonna played her first UK gig here, in 1983.) The club was famous for its dance nights too, particularly house music, where DJs Mike Pickering, Sasha and Dave Haslam regularly played. In 1992, he set up In The City, an influential music forum for finding new talent and discussing the future of the industry.

Dubbed 'Mr Manchester', Wilson loved his city, getting involved in local politics and other cultural events. He was eulogised in the film *24 Hour Party People*, in which he was played by Steve Coogan. Wilson initially disputed aspects of the script but, quoting film director John Ford, said: "If it's a choice between the truth and the legend, print the legend." In the film, Happy Mondays' Shaun Ryder holds the master tapes for the band's new album hostage until Wilson gives him money for his next drug hit.

When Wilson developed renal cancer and couldn't afford the expensive treatment, the Happy Mondays and other local bands chipped in to pay. The day Wilson died, in August 2007, the Union flag on Manchester Town Hall was lowered to half mast as a mark of respect. As with everything else in the Factory empire, Tony Wilson's coffin was given a Factory catalogue number: FAC 501.

"He showed it wasn't poofy to wear nice clothes and use long words," said Coogan. "But above all he was a true civic champion, who found excitement and creativity on his own doorstep. Under his stewardship, Manchester became, and still is, an alternative metropolis. That is his legacy."

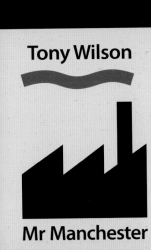

Tony Wilson

Mr Manchester

Above left: The legendary Haçienda exists only in name nowadays.
Above: The Buzzcocks.
Left: The Stone Roses were at the forefront of the Madchester scene.

1976 at Indigo Studios in Gartside Street in just five hours. A month later, the Spiral Scratch EP was released on the band's own New Hormones label. The statue of the founder of Britain's police force, Sir Robert Peel (he of 'bobbies' fame), in Piccadilly Gardens, appears on the cover.

The other legendary Free Trade Hall gig (held in the larger downstairs hall) was a decade earlier, in 1966, when a Bob Dylan show prompted the now famous cry of "Judas!" from a member of the audience during his set. It was an attack on Dylan for 'plugging in', his controversial switch from acoustic folk to electric guitar.

Opposite the Free Trade Hall, the former railway station Manchester Central was converted into the GMEX centre for conventions and concerts and, in 1986, hosted a punk rock festival to celebrate 10 years of the genre, featuring top Factory acts. GMEX has since reverted to its original name.

The former Mecca dance hall, the Ritz, in Whitworth Street West, is Manchester's longest-running club. It's a 1920s traditional ballroom, built with a sprung floor for dancing, with a magnificent mirrored glitter ball suspended above. It was here that The Smiths made their debut, in October 1982. Within a few years Manchester would become Moz-side as Morrissey claimed the city as his own, becoming the musical poet of a generation. Primal Scream, the Happy Mondays and Doves also performed early gigs here. Punk poet John Cooper Clarke's *Salome Maloney* is about the venue and *From The Ritz To The Rubble* by Arctic Monkeys is an ode to its bouncers. As Turner tries to get into the club a bouncer, "wants to give you a duff… secretly they want it all to kick off". Further along Whitworth Street is Manchester's first rock 'n' roll cafe , Cornerhouse. Badly Drawn Boy wrote the soundtrack to *About A Boy*, which starred Hugh Grant, here. On the corner of Whitworth Street West and Albion Street stood the now-defunct Haçienda, the once-legendary nightclub owned by Factory Records. Tony Wilson opened it in 1982 (a few weeks after the Wigan Casino was gutted by fire) to promote the Manchester music scene and America's *Newsweek* magazine would soon call it the most famous club in the world. Defining Mancunian bands such as Joy Division, The Smiths, The Stone Roses and the Happy Mondays all performed here in the Haçienda's early days, and the club would become the epicentre of the 'Madchester' acid house movement (see page 258).

The drug-addled hedonism of the Happy Mondays courted Manchester's blossoming club culture alongside the psychedelic guitar sound of The Stone Roses. "We were supposed to go out and work in factories and we didn't," Stone Roses frontman Ian Brown told *Q* magazine in 2009. "We connected with the people. We elevated ourselves but remained true to ourselves at the same time." When Balearic beats entered the UK from Ibiza in the late 1980s they found a spiritual home in Manchester. The city's rock heritage mixed with the psychedelic sounds from the clubs, and ecstasy diverted youngsters from The Smiths into rave culture.

They ain't heavy, they're the Gallaghers

LOVE 'em or loathe 'em, few could ignore Oasis. For every critic who scoffed at how a band who rhymed supersonic with gin and tonic could become so mega there were legions who adored them. Even to many neutrals, Liam Gallagher had the defining voice of his generation, and those who condemned their music as derivative, couldn't deny its catchiness.

Squabbling siblings are nothing new to the English rock landscape. Most famous are Ray and Dave Davies, but pushing them close in the notoriety stakes are those garrulous Gallagher brothers. Formed in Manchester as The Rain, Oasis played their first live gig at the city's The Boardwalk pub in 1991. Original members Paul 'Bonehead' Arthurs, Paul 'Guigsy' McGuigan and Tony McCarroll soon got rid of vocalist Chris Sutton and replaced him with Liam Gallagher, who immediately suggested they change their name to Oasis (after the Oasis Leisure Centre in Swindon, which he'd spotted on a tour poster for the Inspiral Carpets). Brother Noel was a roadie for the Inspirals and he himself joined soon after, on the condition that he became the band's sole songwriter.

In May 1993, only four days after a gig at King Tut's Wah Wah Hut in Glasgow, in May 1993 – attended by one Alan McGee – Oasis were signed to Creation Records. They released their debut album, *Definitely Maybe*, a year later and never looked back (in anger). Their second album *(What's the Story) Morning Glory?* stayed at number one in the album charts for 10 weeks and would go on to become the third highest selling UK album of all time. Despite their monumental commercial success, releasing irresistible pop songs that rocketed them to fame and fortune, Oasis were constantly dogged by accusations of being little more than a Beatles tribute band. Ironically, they were sued by Neil Innes of the spoof Beatles band, The Rutles, and, for a period in the mid-90s, were never far from the front pages of the tabloids for a series of fraternal spats, drug- and drink-related misdemeanours and high-profile marriages and break-ups. Most infamously, during the so-called 'Battle of Britpop', Noel Gallagher told the *Observer* that he hoped Damon Albarn and Alex James (of Britpop 'rivals' Blur) would "catch AIDS and die". At least he apologised publicly.

Liam Gallagher's malevolent monkey antics would ultimately prove too much for his mastermind older brother and the band finally called it a day in 2009 when Noel quit after yet another backstage bust-up.

•HEART•AND•SOUL•

•JOY•DIVISION•
•AND•NEW•ORDER•

INSTEAD of saying 'f*** off,'" explained the late Manchester music mogul Tony Wilson, "Joy Division said, 'I'm f*cked', and in doing so invented post-punk and regenerated a great art form – rock 'n' roll."

On 20 July, 1976, Bernard Sumner and Peter Hook, mates since the age of 11, attended the legendary second Sex Pistols show at the Manchester Lesser Free Trade Hall (see page 252). The following day Hook borrowed £35 from his mum and bought a bass guitar to form a band with Sumner. The young men had grown up together in Salford, known for its cramped terrace houses and textile factories. They'd been teenage skinheads and mods, hanging out at North Salford Youth Club, listening to rock and soul.

Sumner and Hook placed an advert in Virgin Records for a vocalist and Ian Curtis who worked at Rare Records, still in John Dalton Street today), from Macclesfield, responded. As they'd met at some earlier gigs, Curtis was hired without audition and the rest, as they say, is history. Joy Division's history wasn't a long one, but it couldn't have been more compelling, brilliant or tragic.

Under the name Warsaw, their first public performance was at the Electric Circus (in Collyhurst Street, now demolished) on 29 May, 1977. Drummer Stephen Morris, also from Macclesfield, joined later that year and they signed with Wilson's Factory Records, whose offices were in Palatine Road (their manager Rob Gretton's office was in Whitworth Street).

A crucial stage of development for the band's unusual sound was during 1977 and '78, at TJ Davidson's, a drab, ugly textile warehouse converted to a rehearsal space (now demolished, it was in Little Peter Street, behind Deansgate Station). The video for the band's biggest hit, *Love Will Tear Us Apart*, was also recorded here.

Though lyricist Curtis wasn't one for name-checking city streets and suburbs, Joy Division's sound was uniquely Mancunian. Their post-punk rock was industrial (like the city which spawned it) and machine-like, sparse and gloomy, yet hypnotic, compelling and somehow inescapable. Their unique

bass-lines came from Hook's unconventional playing style. Short for a bass player, he plucked the strings unusually high up saying he couldn't hear himself play otherwise.

Paul Morley, Manchester rock critic, author and early Joy Division evangelist, says their music was borne of "the Manchester damp and the shadows and the omens called into dread being by the hills and moors that lurked at the edge of their vision." Curtis's often-Kafkaesque lyrics were about failure, alienation, disillusionment and desperation. He wasn't making it all up. The young singer was tormented by epilepsy and the prescription drugs he took for it, and torn between his wife and lover. On 18 May, 1980, on the eve of the band's first US tour, after watching *Stroszek*, a film in which the protagonist takes his own life, Curtis did the same.

Buried in Macclesfield Cemetery (87 Prestbury Road) Curtis's memorial stone is inscribed "Love Will Tear Us Apart". It was stolen in July 2008 but has since been replaced. "I'd look at Ian's lyrics and think how clever he was putting himself in the position of someone else," says Morris. "I never believed he was writing about himself. Looking back, how could I have been so bleedin' stupid? Of course he was writing about himself."

Joy Division's influence is unmistakably heard today in bands like U2, The Cure, Editors, Interpol and Bloc Party, plus three Noughties films have added to the cult of the band; *Closer*, *Joy Division* and *24 Hour Party People*.

In the wake of Curtis's death, Sumner, Hook and Morris formed New Order (with Sumner reluctantly assuming singing duties), who would go on to affect British electronic dance music as powerfully as Joy Division had British guitar music. The band's seminal 1983 hit *Blue Monday* saw New Order master anthemic dance hits; synthesizers, drum machines et al. It's the best-selling 12-inch single of all time.

New Order's history is intertwined with legendary club The Haçienda (11-13 Whitworth Street West), for a while the world's most famous nightclub. Opened in 1982, with financial backing from the band and Factory, the club became synonymous with the Madchester scene in the late 1980s and early 1990s. Yet The Haçienda, owned by Factory Records, struggled financially and was supported by New Order's record sales for most of its lifetime. The club spun its last discs in 1997, with, according to Hook, loses of, "£18 million, or something".

MADCHESTER

and the second summer of love

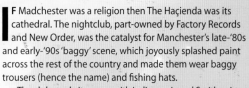

IF Madchester was a religion then The Haçienda was its cathedral. The nightclub, part-owned by Factory Records and New Order, was the catalyst for Manchester's late-'80s and early-'90s 'baggy' scene, which joyously splashed paint across the rest of the country and made them wear baggy trousers (hence the name) and fishing hats.

The club made its name with indie music and Smiths gigs, but as the '80s progressed it featured more disco, hip hop and electro, switching focus from being a live venue to a dance club. In 1986 it was the first UK venue to take house music seriously, with DJs Mike Pickering, Graeme Park and 'Little' Martin Prendergast all spinning discs here. Other clubs like The Boardwalk and Devilles followed suit and clubbers took those influences back to their bedrooms – and their embryonic bands.

In the autumn of '88, The Stone Roses released *Elephant Stone* (produced by New Order's Peter Hook) as a single, the Happy Mondays released their *Bummed* album and the national music press sensed something was up. *NME's* Sean O'Hagan said, "There is a particularly credible music biz rumour-come-theory that certain Northern towns – Manchester being the prime example – have had their water supply treated with small doses of mind-expanding chemicals."

With rave and acid house on the rise, drugs were playing a part in the escalating Madchester scene. "Ecstasy use changed clubs forever," said DJ Dave Haslam. "A night at the Haçienda went from being a great night out, to an intense, life-changing experience." The ecstasy-fuelled partying of 1988 and '89 would become known as the Second Summer(s) of Love.

It was early in 1989, with the release of the Stones Roses, eponymous debut album, that things really took off. Critics loved it, with the *NME* instantly proclaiming the album one of the UK's all-time greats. Soon Inspiral Carpets, 808 State, A Guy Called Gerald, The Mock Turtles and The Charlatans would all be chipping in, along with James, who'd been around for a while without chart success.

The music was different because it crossed genres. Madchester had tunes that both acid-head ravers and indie kids could dance to, together. The dance influence came from '70s funk, disco bass-lines and wah-wah guitar, which melded triumphantly with indie jingle-jangle and that signature Mancunian swagger. As the '80s became the '90s, the sound spread across the country, with bands such as The Farm, Flowered Up, Candy Flip and Blur joining the baggy conga line.

The Inspiral Carpets were key Madchester members. "Without any collaboration," lead singer Clint Boon told the BBC in 2009, "we were all celebrating colour and psychedelia, with paisley patterns and funky shades. It spread across the nation because what we were doing was so attractive. One of the most exciting moments in my life was when I realised I was in the middle of this hurricane of colourful energy."

Salford

Salford has long been a draw for musicians, with many 'Mancunian' acts hailing from the city to Manchester's northwest: from folk singer and playwright Ewan MacColl – born James Miller in 1915 to communist parents – to Bernard Sumner, of Joy Division and New Order, who grew up in Lower Broughton. Morrissey understood the city's rich musical leanings way back in the 1986 when he and The Smiths were pictured outside Salford Lads Club in St Ignatius Walk, Regent Road, on the inside cover of their classic album *The Queen Is Dead*. Since then it's become a major English rock pilgrimage site every bit as important as the Abbey Road zebra crossing in London's St John's Wood. Thousands of visitors and Smiths fans have positioned themselves outside for a photo and they'll be pleased to know the red-brick Edwardian landmark is now a listed building.

Ewan MacColl wrote his paean to Salford, *Dirty Old Town* (covered by The Pogues in 1985) as a scene-switching interlude for his 1949 play, *Landscape With Chimneys*. It soon became a folk favourite and has been covered by everyone from The Dubliners to the Black Rebel Motorcycle Club. His original lyrics: "Smelled the spring in the Salford wind / Dirty old town, dirty old town," were subject to much criticism by Salford council officials and were changed to the "Smelled a spring on the smoky wind".

Once heard, John Cooper Clarke, or the Bard of Salford, is rarely forgotten. His tales of stark reality and caustic social commentary were delivered in his unmistakeable Salford drawl with a witty twist. And his look was distinct too: a beanpole in drainpipe jeans with a mad explosion of hair. His path to the limelight in the mid-1970s took a very different route than today's premium-rate telephone line pop idols. His first gig was at Manchester jazz club the Black Lion, then he got a residence at cabaret club Mr Smith's. He is a performance poet but was labelled a punk-poet because he achieved recognition during the punk movement and read his work as an opening act for bands like the Sex Pistols and the Buzzcocks. Thanks to him, a whole generation of teenagers growing up in the 1970s saw poetry as accessible and no longer the domain of toffs or something forced down their throats at school. One of Cooper Clarke's finest moments is his famously bleak ode to working-class Salford, *Beasley Street*, with its "smell of yesterday's cabbage", and "the ghost of last year's wife". His work was a major influence on Arctic Monkeys songwriter and frontman, Alex Turner, who got hooked on writing lyrics after seeing Cooper Clarke support The Fall when he was 16.

Talking of The Fall, it's hard to envisage this Salford band at the mercy of today's Saturday night TV audience – even though frontman Mark E Smith was once voted 'The Greatest Mancunian' by readers of the *Manchester Evening News*. He has also memorably been described as a visionary gargoyle. Formed in 1976, The Fall have outlasted all the late 1970s punk and post-punk groups and their output has been prolific. The band's line-up has undergone many changes, with cantankerous vocalist Smith the band's only constant. Before The Fall, Smith worked as an import/export clerk on the Manchester Docks (now Salford Quays) and had failed auditions with several local heavy metal bands. Championed by John Peel, Smith's band became indie rock legends and have occupied the rock 'n' roll margins ever since. And with his snarling, cynical scorn as refreshing as ever, he makes for great telly. (An appearance on BBC 2's *Newsnight*, interviewed by Gavin Esler after the death of John Peel, is well worth a peek on YouTube.)

Salford's healthy contribution to rock and pop doesn't end there. It was in Buzzcocks' Howard Devoto's flat in Lower Broughton Road that he and Pete Shelley hatched the plan to bring the Sex Pistols to Manchester. The boy-girl chart-topping duo, The Ting Tings came together in the Salford arts complex, Islington Mill, a former cotton mill in James Street. Paul and Shaun Ryder of the Happy Mondays grew up in Coniston Avenue in Little Hulton, while Buile Hill High School (formerly Salford Grammar) was where Peter Hook and Bernard Sumner first met in the late 1960s. Kingston Close in Higher Broughton was where 10cc's Graham Gouldman grew up and wrote most of his 1960s songs, while Ordsall's James Henry Avenue was the childhood home of Graham Nash of The Hollies and later Crosby Stills Nash & Young. Finally, The Charlatans frontman Tim Burgess lived in Linkfield Drive in Boothstown until he was nine and his family moved to Northwich (see page 279). R&B veteran, Elkie Brooks was born in 1945 as Elaine Bookbinder to Jewish parents in Broughton and raised in Prestwich. She attended North Salford Secondary Modern School.

Above: The Fall's Mark E Smith was voted The Greatest Mancunian by the *Manchester Evening News*.
Opposite page: John Cooper Clarke.

MANCHESTER," sang Morrissey on *Suffer Little Children*, "so much to answer for". To the many fans of The Smiths, it seems the lyrics should have been: Manchester – so much to thank you for.

Some bands sold more records, but few, if any, were as influential, or as passionately adored, as The Smiths. In 2002 *NME* proclaimed the Mancunians to be "the most influential British band of all time". Without The Smiths, said the *Guardian*, celebrating the band's 25th anniversary, "the entire trajectory of recent British rock music as we now know it would not have been traced." Certainly the likes of Radiohead, Blur, Oasis, The Libertines and Arctic Monkeys would sound very different, if indeed they would have existed at all.

In May 1982 a bequiffed, 18-year-old Johnny Maher (who would soon change his surname to Marr, to avoid confusion with Buzzcocks drummer John Maher) turned up unannounced at the door of 384 Kings Road, a terraced house in Stretford. "It was a sunny day, about one o'clock," he remembers. "There was no advance phone call or anything. I just knocked and he opened the door."'He' was Steven Patrick Morrissey, born in May 1959 in Park Hospital (now Trafford General Hospital) in Davyhulme, to Irish Catholic parents; a hospital porter father and a librarian mother.

Morrissey was initially raised in Harper Street, Hulme, around the time of the infamous Moors Murders – Ian Brady and Myra Hindley abducted and killed four local children during 1963 and 1964 and buried their bodies on Saddleworth Moor, near Manchester. It was a frightening time for children – for everyone – in the city and *Suffer Little Children*, about the murders, would be one of the first songs Morrissey and Marr wrote together, and released on their eponymous debut album in 1984.

In 1965 the Morrisseys moved to Queens Square (still Hulme, near Moss Side), then in 1969 when many of the old terraced streets were being demolished, into Kings Road, Stretford. After St Wilfrid's primary school (in St Wilfrid's Street), Morrissey attended St Mary's secondary modern (in Renton and Christie Roads, Stretford), which closed in the '90s. Morrissey would later "curse his school days with a venom unequalled by

any songwriter of his generation", according to Smiths biographer Johnny Rogan. *The Headmaster Ritual*, on 1985's *Meat Is Murder*, is perhaps the most ferocious tirade against his alma mater. It was inspired by St Mary's headteacher Vincent 'Jet' Morgan (and possibly his PE teacher):

> 'Belligerent ghouls/
> Run Manchester schools/
> Spineless bastards all/
> Sir leads the troops/
> Jealous of youth/
> Same old jokes since 1902'

The shy 23-year-old enrolled at Stretford Technical School, before trying to infiltrate Manchester's music scene with a few eccentric appearances as the lead singer of The Nosebleeds (Morrissey also sent unsolicited Coronation Street scripts to Granada Television and ran the New York Dolls' UK fan club). Marr was also the son of Irish immigrants. Born in Ardwick, he attended St Augustine's Grammar School (which merged with other schools to form St John Plessington High School, which has since closed). A sporty Marr had trials with Manchester City. "I was good enough for City," he said, "but they didn't follow up because I was probably the only player out there wearing eyeliner." Marr was in several short-lived bands: one of these, Paris Valentinos, included future Smiths bassist Andy Rourke (who would later be fired by Morrissey via a post-it note on his car windscreen) and Kevin Kennedy (who would go on to play Curly Watts in Coronation Street for 20 years).

Prior to that fateful day in May '82, Morrissey and Marr had met once before, at a Patti Smith concert at Manchester's Apollo Theatre in 1978, where they'd exchanged the briefest of courtesies. After their second meeting, Morrissey made the return journey to Marr's rented room in Bowdon, where they mapped out a song called *The Hand That Rocks The Cradle*. A songwriting partnership that would alter the course of British rock and pop music had begun, but it was an unlikely one. Marr was the streetwise 'Keef' lookalike, who meticulously layered his guitar tracks in the studio, producing a jaunty, swaying, signature sound that still sounds fresh and unique today. Morrissey,

on the other hand, was a wilful social misfit who opened up his diary to the world. He embraced the poetry of Oscar Wilde, feminist literature and asexual celibacy. The singer would soon perform on *Top of the Pops* wearing NHS spectacles and a hearing aid, with a pocketful of gladioli. Few, if any, frontmen have ever seemed so compelling.

To the non-converts, song titles like *Heaven Knows I'm Miserable Now*, *Last Night I Dreamt That Somebody Loved Me* and *Girlfriend In A Coma* sound ostensibly miserable, but listen a little closer and you'll hear some of the wittiest pop lyrics ever. "Spending warm summer days indoors, writing frightening verse to a buck-toothed girl in Luxembourg" is classic Morrissey (from *Ask*).

John Peel was an early Smiths evangelist and they were soon signed to Rough Trade records. Between 1982 and 1987, The Smiths, now joined by fellow Mancunians Rourke and Mike Joyce (drums), released a string of brilliant singles, four studio albums (*The Queen Is Dead* is roundly acknowledged as their greatest moment) and stirred scenes of fan hysteria not seen since the days of glam rock. Perhaps more importantly, the Smiths revitalised the tradition of the guitar-driven rock group, when keyboards and epic fringes were all the go.

The almost otherworldly creative friction between Morrissey and Marr could never last and Marr finally left The Smiths in 1987, citing a request to cover a Cilla Black song as the last straw. Earlier, there had been a messy court case after a fight over royalties, which Morrissey and Marr lost.

Manchester made The Smiths, and they invoked the city time and again – probably more than any other Manchester band – in their songs.

Greater Manchester

Bury

Five-piece Elbow met at Stand College in Bury in 1990 and formed a band called Soft. When they relocated to Manchester they changed their name to Elbow, after a line in Dennis Potter's television drama *The Singing Detective,* in which a nurse character reckons the word for an arm joint is "the most sensuous word in the world". They started out performing at Bury's Derby Hall and spent years on the edge of the mainstream, using Manchester's Night & Day bar as an office. Their fortune changed for good with their fourth album, 2008's *The Seldom Seen Kid*, which scooped the Mercury Prize and two Ivor Novello awards that year. In many ways Elbow are the antithesis of plastic pop stars. They make honest songs with passionate lyrics and something to say; romantic notions linked to the harsh realities of life. One of the band's finest songs, 2005's *Station Approach*, was an ode to returning to Manchester and beautifully sums up the emotions of many Northerners when their train pulls into Piccadilly Station. But its message is universal; despite the multitude of irritations our home cities throw up, we're proud of our roots and glad to be home:

> 'The streets are full of goths and Greeks/
> I haven't seen my mum for weeks/
> But coming home I feel like I/
> Designed these buildings I walk by'

Wigan

Excluding George Formby, The Verve are Wigan's most famous musical export. The band met at Winstanley College on the outskirts of town. After the 18-year-old Richard Ashcroft saw The Stone Roses live in 1989 he was convinced he could follow a path in life other than a nine-to-five office job or factory work. He walked out of his A-level exams stating he was going to be a musician and formed The Verve with schoolmates Peter Salisbury, Simon Jones and Nick McCabe. Originally called just Verve, the band's first gig was at the Honeysuckle Pub at a friend's birthday party. The culmination of their career was in May 1998, at a massive 'homecoming' farewell gig in the grounds of Wigan's stately Haigh Hall in front of 33,000 people. It was be their last time on stage together – for a few years anyway. The band have broken up and reunited more times than Richard Burton and Elizabeth Taylor, although in July 2010 Ashcroft said it was over for good. The Verve's 1997 *Urban Hymns* (see page 98, for cover location) remains one of the landmark British rock albums of the 1990s.

Wigan is also the original home of Starsailor, featuring the impressive voice of James Walsh. Named after a Tim Buckley album, they have toured with The Rolling Stones and worked with a pre-trial Phil Spector. Limahl, from the 1980s pop act, Kajagoogoo, who had hits with *Too Shy and Ooh To Be Ah*, is also a Wigan native.

Bolton

Bolton can claim beardy indie singer-songwriter Badly Drawn Boy – aka Damon Gough – and the golden-tonsilled Queen of prog rock, Renaissance singer Annie Haslam. Bolton's Buzzcocks kick-started the Manchester punk scene with their debut *Spiral Scratch* EP. It was original singer Howard Devoto and Pete McNeish (later Pete Shelley) who organised one of the most important gigs of all time, the Sex Pistols at the Lesser Free Trade Hall (see page 254). Devoto and Shelley formed Buzzcocks after seeing a Sex Pistols gig in London and Devoto, who would later form Magazine, once lived in

Above: The Verve's *Urban Hymns* was one of the hit albums of the 1990s.
Left: Elbow finally found success in 2008 with the Mercury Prize.

Out On The Floor:
WIGAN AND NORTHERN SOUL

I T began when the eagle landed. In the mid-'60s, DJ Roger Eagle started playing Manchester's Twisted Wheel club. It was primarily a mod club, but as he collected imported American soul, jazz and R&B the 'Wheel' soon became the place to come and hear – and dance to – the latest soul. Youngsters from all over the UK were soon flocking to the place they would later nickname 'the chapel of soul'.

Northern soul mainly meant black American soul music with a heavy beat and fast tempo; mid-'60s Motown, though mainstream hits were usually eschewed. In fact the less well know the artist, the more prized the recording, especially limited editions by small US labels such as Okeh, Cameo-Parkway and Roulette.

As the soul music filled the air, northern soul's trademark dancing was first witnessed at the Wheel. The dolled-up (polyester and crimplene trousers was all the go) boys and girls would gather in circles and take it in turns to move into the middle and perform floordrops, wild spins and backflips. The northern soul dance – a precursor to breakdancing – was born.

Like some sort of happy disease, the movement quickly spread further afield. In the Wigan Casino DJ Russ Winstanley was famous for the 'three before eight' – the last three records played before the casino's eight o'clock (in the morning) closing time. The building was destroyed by fire in 1982, but not before it inspired the 1989 dance record *Wigan*, by Baby Ford. Other legendary venues included Stoke's Golden Torch (see page 231), Wolverhampton's Catacombs and the Highland Rooms at Blackpool Mecca.

There were drugs too, of course. A licensing loophole meant the Wigan casino could be hired from 12.30 am till eight am on a Sunday morning. But as no alcohol could be served during those hours an amphetamine scene burgeoned (not exactly a hindrance to those wanting to dance all night).

Why was the scene such a success? In Wigan, at least, there was a clear contrast between the closed down factories and bleak cobbled streets and the frenzied joy of the ballroom. The scene captured that escapist rush of living for the weekend, of unearthing that rare seven-inch and getting one hell of a workout on the dance floor. After all, what else is there to live for when you're young?

an ex-convent in Bolton. The debut album by Manchester acid house pioneers 808 State, 1988's *Newbuild*, was named after a Bolton housing co-operative and would be a major influence on Richard D James, aka Aphex Twin.

Rochdale

In September 2009, two blue plaques were unveiled in Rochdale, in honour of the town's musical heritage and impact on the Manchester music scene. The first was erected on the former site of the Tractor Sound Studios, in Market Street in Heywood. The studios were financed by John Peel in the early 1970s after Rochdale band Tractor sent him a demo tape. Before he became a DJ, Peel worked at the Townhead cotton mill in the centre of Rochdale. Another plaque was unveiled on the former Cargo Studios, which became Peter Hook's Suite 16 Studios, where the likes of Joy Division, The Fall, Gang of Four and most of the Factory Records and Madchester bands recorded in the 1970s and '80s. The building was also used in the film *24 Hour Party People*. Singer Lisa Stansfield was also born in Rochdale.

Didsbury

"Mr Sifter sold me songs when I was just 16": Sifters Records, in Didsbury's Fog Lane, was the record shop immortalised in the 1994 Oasis single *Shakermaker*. Noel and Liam Gallagher used to shop here for records as kids.

Burnage

Burnage was the early home of Oasis's Gallagher brothers. The city suburb also claims The Durutti Column, fronted by Vini Reilly, who were a favourite of Factory Records' supremo, Tony Wilson. The Happy Mondays song *Cowboy Dave* was written in memory of former Durutti guitarist, Dave Rowbotham who was found dead in November 1991, murdered with an axe.

Stockport

Strawberry Recording Studios, in Waterloo Road, looms large in Manchester musical folklore as the state-of-the-art recording facility associated with 10cc, where their famous *I'm Not In Love* was recorded. The Studios were named after the Beatles song and both Joy Division's *Unknown Pleasures* and The Smiths' eponymous debut album were recorded here. Since opening in 1968, the studios have hosted acts as diverse as The Stone Roses and St Winifred's School Choir. They closed in 1993 and a commemorative plaque was unveiled on the front of the building in 2007.

The Mancunian candidates: songs that mention Manchester

Great Expectations, Elbow (2005)
On *Leaders of the Free World*, Guy Garvey sings about the rain and Stockport supporters as he catches the last bus home on the 135 Bury to Manchester bus route.

Manchester, The Beautiful South (2005)
A single from their last album, *Superbi*, perversely celebrates the idea that Manchester isn't everyone's ideal holiday destination. "If rain makes Britain great," sings Paul Heaton, "then Manchester is greater."

Miserable Lie, The Smiths (1984)
"What do we get for our trouble and pain," laments the Pope of Mope, Morrissey, on their eponymous debut, "but a rented room in Whalley Range?"

Whippin' Piccadilly, Gomez (1998)
"Once upon a time, not too long ago, we took a day out in Manchester" starts the song from Mercury Prize-winning album *Bring It On*. It's about going to Manchester to see Beck while the band were still at university.

Hear also:
Rusholme Ruffians, The Smiths (1985); *Driving Away From Home*, It's Immaterial (1986); *M62 Song*, Doves (2003); *Longsight M13*, Ian Brown (2004); *Matchstalk Men and Matchstalk Cats and Dogs*, Brian and Michael (1978).

Lancashire

Blackpool ⟩⟩

Upon completion in 1896, the late-Victorian Empress Ballroom, inside the Winter Gardens, was the largest dance hall in Europe. Polka dance festivals were all the rage as guests danced underneath its famous chandeliers and arched ceiling. A Rolling Stones gig here, in July 1964 was quite a different ball game. It turned nasty when Keith Richards kicked out at a man in the audience who'd spat at him and the incident sparked a full-blown riot, hospitalising 50 people. Most gigs here are more peaceful affairs, with the venue hosting everyone from The Prodigy to The White Stripes. In August 1989, The Stone Roses played a career-changing gig at the Empress Ballroom and some fans still say it was their best. Roadies kicked the doors open, allowing a massive rush of 4,000 people into the Ballroom, some bringing in beach balls to throw around. When fans got overheated the band threw ice pops into the crowd. Frontman Ian Brown said it was after this gig that he knew the band had made it.

Blackpool was built on the promise of unashamed fun, but of course visitors have different notions of what defines fun. To some it's a kiss-me-quick hat and donkey rides, to others a get-sick-quick drink-a-thon and a closing-time fumble. Seven million people visit Blackpool Pleasure Beach and its numerous rides each year. In 1995, one of them was Simply Red's Mick Hucknall who's video for *Fairground* was filmed here. Most of the video takes place on the Pepsi Max Big One roller coaster ride although there is footage of Blackpool's famous Illuminations too. Many English pop stars, musical acts and DJs have switched on the Illuminations that shine for six miles along Blackpool promenade each autumn, including George Formby, the Bee Gees, Tony Blackburn, Shirley Bassey, Steps, Status Quo, Lisa Stansfield and Geri Halliwell.

Blackpool has been immortalised in song. In The Kinks' 1967 *Autumn Almanac* Ray Davies sings: "I go to Blackpool for my holidays", as if it was as glamorous as the Seychelles (although to many Brits in the late 1960s it probably was). Blackpool can claim Steeleye Span singer Maddy Prior, Little Boots – aka Victoria Hesketh – and Chris Lowe, of the Pet Shop Boys, who could see the Pleasure Beach at the end of his road as he grew up.

Blackburn ⟩⟩

Whether the town of Blackburn likes it or not it will be forever remembered in the lyrics of *A Day In The Life* by The Beatles, the closing track on *Sgt Pepper's Lonely Hearts Club Band* and frequently voted one of the Fab's greatest songs. John Lennon was inspired by a story in the *Daily Mail* newspaper about a plan to fill 4,000 potholes in the streets of Blackburn, Lancashire.

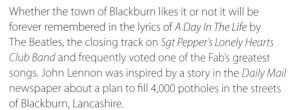

Left: The Empress Ballroom plays host to The Verve in 2007.

Haslingden

The small Lancashire town of Haslingden is mentioned in The Fall's 1980 song *English Scheme*. Commenting on youngsters in the town, and others like it, with little future ahead of them, Mark E Smith urged them to emigrate to Europe:

'They talk of Chile while driving through Haslingdon /
You got 60-hour weeks, and stone toilet back-gardens /
Peter Cook's jokes, bad dope, check shirts, lousy groups /
Point their fingers at America/
Down pokey quaint streets in Cambridge/
Cycles our distant spastic heritage.'

Poulton-le-Fylde

Starting off in the punk scene after seeing a Sex Pistols gig in Manchester, Skrewdriver formed in this Lancashire town in 1976. Led by Ian Stuart, they became one of the first neo-Nazi rock bands and used their music as a way to get their white power message. Fights were common at their shows and their skinhead appearance and reputation for violence got them banned from gigs.

The Police guitarist Andy Summers was born in the town in 1942, in a gypsy caravan on the banks of the River Wyre, before moving to Dorset with his parents.

Burnley

Salford punk-poet John Cooper-Clarke mixed his northernness with punk and frequently came up with dynamite. His ode to Burnley, was called, just *Burnley*:

'I'll tell you now and I'll tell you firmly/
I don't ever want to go to Burnley/
What they do there don't concern me/
I wouldn't even make the journey.'

The Four Seasons (alternate take): SPRING

April, Deep Purple
It can feel like a month goes by listening to Deep Purple's longest studio recording, a largely instrumental 12-minute-plus epic, from their eponymous 1969 album. A long introductory sequence starts with Jon Lord's heavy organ before progressing to strings and woodwind then finally a guitar. This is prog rock with a strong classical bent and at times sounds like a 1960s horror film soundtrack. The spring-tinged lyrics are borrowed heavily from TS Eliot's poem *The Waste Land*, but even they don't kick in until Rod Evans is first heard singing "April is a cruel time" two-thirds in.

April 5th, Talk Talk
Before they retreated to an abandoned Suffolk church to write their fourth album *Spirit of Eden*, Talk Talk had already ditched their synth pop origins. *The Colour of Spring* (1986), the band's best-selling album to date, included this hauntingly beautiful and atmospheric offering:

'Come gentle spring/
Come at winter's end/
Gone is the pallor from a promise that's nature's gift.'

Morning Has Broken, Cat Stevens
The jury was out: blissful harmonies or religious guff redolent of school assemblies? Adapted from a Christian hymn, it appeared on 1972's *Teaser And The Firecat*, an album by Cat Stevens, the artist who's now known as Yusuf Islam. Overtly religious or not, to many it remains a spiritually affirming pop classic.

Hear also:
The First Days of Spring, Noah and the Whale (2009); *Rain*, The Beatles (1966); *Jack-in-the-Green*, Jethro Tull (1977).

Liverpool

Port cities tend to produce three things: a vibrant music scene, rich cultural interchanges and strong women. Some of the world's most exciting ports have strong musical roots; the tango of Buenos Aires, cajun music from New Orleans, Lisbon's fado music, the Greek blues born in the ports of Piraeus and Salonika. Culturally, Liverpool is home to Europe's oldest Chinese and African communities and so much more. (As for port's producing independent women, this stems from the seafaring trade and a self-reliance born from a time when men were absent for long periods and the knowledge that maybe they wouldn't return).

Liverpool is a city that owes its existence and fortunes to the River Mersey and what lies beyond. In the past, all the great liners docked here and most of the trade that came across the Atlantic arrived in Liverpool. Some of this business was human traffic and the city's elegant Georgian-terraced streets were built from the profits of the slave trade. Even Penny Lane itself, made famous by a Liverpool band you may have of, was named after the wealthy slave merchant William Penny (see The Beatles' Liverpool, page 272). The fabled road was also the birthplace of Ian Broudie of The Lightning Seeds.

From legends such as Britain's first great rock 'n' roller, Billy Fury, and four local mop-tops called The Beatles, through to modern-day bands like The Coral, Cast and The Zutons, *The Guinness Book of Hit Singles* calls Liverpool 'The World Capital of Pop' because it's produced more number one singles than any other city in the world.

American blues records found their way into England in the 1950s via Liverpool and caught the attention of young musicians like Keith Richards and John Lennon. Both started their own bands and recorded covers of songs by The Isley Brothers and Muddy Waters. Lennon enthused about the rock 'n' roll records that arrived with returning seamen. At Liverpool docks he once received a copy of *I Put A Spell On You* by Screamin' Jay Hawkins from a 'Cunard Yank' seaman. They were British pop's unsung pioneers who imported American records to a nation still mired in post-war austerity.

Merseyside musicians have always been connected with the water. From Gerry & the Pacemakers' *Ferry Cross The Mersey* (later covered by Liverpool's Frankie Goes to Hollywood), to Echo & the Bunnymen's *Ocean Rain* and The La's' *Liberty Ship* (La's frontman Lee Mavers once called the Mersey 'the Mersey-sippi').

Even the word Scouse derives from the sea. It was an early 19th century term derived from lobscouse, a popular dish amongst visiting sailors made from boiling leftover meat, vegetables and potatoes. For some Scousers Liverpool has always felt apart from the rest of England – some even consider it a Celtic city, a bit of Ireland dumped in the UK.

The city is a proud place that always showcases itself through music, poetry and football. And its rich culture has often been its salvation. An active skiffle scene in Liverpool mixed with imported American rock 'n' roll records created a new sound in the early 1960s: Merseybeat. The Beatles didn't invent Merseybeat – the phrase was coined in 1961

Right: The Beatles.
Above: Gerry & the Pacemakers at the Cavern club, which is still open today (shown opposite).

by a Liverpool fanzine of the same name referring to smart, young, smiling men in suits playing harmony-based guitar pop – but they were certainly part of it. Other Merseybeat bands included The Searchers, Gerry & the Pacemakers, The Swinging Blue Jeans, plus Brian Epstein's stable of acts, including Cilla Black and Billy J Kramer. Together with the Fab Four, Merseybeat made Liverpool a world music city and many early Merseybeat venues, such as the Cavern, the Grapes and the Jacaranda, are still around today.

Ironically, one of London's best-known songs was originally written about Liverpool. The Kinks' *Waterloo Sunset* was first called *Liverpool Sunset* – about the decline of Merseybeat – but Ray Davies relocated the song to the capital after The Beatles released *Penny Lane/Strawberry Fields Forever*. He deemed another tune about Liverpool surplus to requirements.

After The Beatles had inspired millions with their songs, bands inevitably followed in their wake. In the late '70s, when punk swept Britain, Liverpool responded with a new wave style of its own. For a while, in the mid-1980s, Echo & the Bunnymen were arguably the biggest band in Britain (U2 being Irish of course), a fact that belies their inauspicious beginnings. The Bunnymen were formed after Ian McCulloch met Will Sergeant outside the ladies' toilets of legendary Liverpool punk establishment Eric's Club (more anon).

McCulloch was raised in the Norris Green area of the city and the road on which he originally lived, Parthenon Drive, is the title of a song on the 2005 Echo & the Bunnymen album, *Siberia*. Another song, 1980's *Rescue*, is about the house's back wall falling down.

In the mid-'80s Ian Broudie was standing at a bus stop in the rain when Echo & the Bunnymen stopped their van to offer him a lift. In conversation Broudie wound up telling them how they could improve their songs and went on to become their producer (as well as producing albums for The Fall and Icicle Works). Broudie would then go on to lead The Lightning Seeds to considerable chart success, before discovering and developing latter-day Liverpudlian rock bands The Coral and The Zutons.

Before all that though, in the Seventies, a much younger Broudie was a member of punk band Big In Japan (a 'supergroup' that included future members of The KLF, Siouxsie and the Banshees and Frankie Goes To Hollywood). The band played many early gigs, including their last in August 1978, at Eric's Club (in Matthew Street, opposite The Cavern).

Eric's was the epicentre of the Liverpool music scene in the late '70s and early '80s: The Teardrop Explodes, Wah! (Pete Wylie had been in Crucial Three with McCulloch and Julian Cope, who would go on to form The Teardrop Explodes), Echo & the Bunnymen and Orchestral Manoeuvres in the

IN MY TIME
THE BEATLES' LIVERPOOL

The Beatles Shop, 31 Mathew Street
The specialist shop contains the largest range of original 1960s Beatles memorabilia in the world, ranging from T-shirts, maps, posters and postcards through to watches, toys, mugs and jewellery. Since it opened in 1984, fans have browsed through thousands of original items, all to a backdrop of Beatles singles on an original 1959 jukebox.

The Beatles Story, Albert Dock
An award-winning museum called The Beatles Story, located at Liverpool's historic Albert Dock, is another tour bus favourite. You can visit 'Abbey Road', go underwater in a yellow submarine and much more.

The Cavern Club, 10 Mathew Street
First opened as a jazz cellar in 1957, this is probably the most famous club in the world; certainly it was the country's most important venue in the early 1960s. The Beatles made their debut performance in the Cavern in February 1961 and it was the following November that Brian Epstein first heard them play, in the crowded basement. In all, The Beatles played here 292 times. It was sweaty and smelly, and the toilets overflowed. Determined to be a star, one Priscilla Black (Cilla Black) worked as a cloakroom attendant until she was spotted by Beatles manager Epstein. In 1973 the venue stood in the way of a planned ventilation shaft for the new underground rail loop line and the club was shut. But the shaft was never constructed and a new Cavern opened in 1984. It retains the original address of 10 Mathew Street, even though the entrance is 15 yards or so from the old one. The new Cavern was carefully rebuilt using bricks from the first club to recreate the cellar arches. The tiny floodlit stage was repainted just like the original and has been signed by many of the stars who played the venue in the Sixties. The Cavern still hosts upcoming bands: Wirral's The Coral started out here.

The Cavern Pub, 5 Mathew Street
Opened in 1994 opposite the Cavern Club with authentic Beatles instruments on display, there's live music seven nights a week here.

Eleanor Rigby statue, Stanley Street
Dedicated to "all the lonely people", the statue depicting a forlorn Eleanor Rigby sitting on a bench was sculpted in 1982 by fellow 1960s singer, Tommy Steele. It's a tribute to the Liverpudlian pop icons and a thank you to the people of Liverpool for all the happy times Steele spent here.

The Empress pub, 93 High Park Street, Dingle
This pub features on the cover of Ringo Starr's first solo album, *Sentimental Journey*. Ringo was brought up in the area and used to drink in this pub; his mother, Elsie, worked here.

20 Forthlin Road, Allerton
The former home of the McCartney family is now owned by the National Trust. The front

room of this 1950s suburban terraced house is where The Quarrymen rehearsed, and The Beatles wrote many of their earliest songs. In fact more than 100 songs were written here, many of them in the bathroom where the acoustics were better. McCartney lived here until 1964.

Four Lads Who Shook The World, 21 Mathew Street

The Four Lads Who Shook The World statue, on the wall above the Mood Indigo bar, portrays the Fab Four as cherubs made from plastic dolls. Erected in 1974, it was made by local sculptor Arthur Dooley. The figure representing McCartney mysteriously disappeared one day, never to be replaced. A guitar-carrying cherub, surrounded by a halo and the words "Lennon Lives", was erected next to it, following Lennon's murder in 1980.

The Grapes, 25 Mathew Street

A few yards down from the Cavern Club, this became the Fab Four's favourite hang-out after gigs, as the Cavern didn't have a licence to sell alcohol. It was also a safe refuge from teenage fans too young to enter. In August 1962, after being fired by Brian Epstein, Pete Best famously drowned his sorrows here with road manager Neil Aspinall. Their first manager, Allan Williams – known as 'the man who gave the Beatles away' – still drinks here sometimes.

The Hard Days Night Hotel, North John Street

The world's first Beatles-themed hotel opened in 2008 on the corner of Mathew Street and North John Street. The hotel's 110 bedrooms include two suites: The Lennon Suite, painted all white and featuring a white grand piano – a copy of the one from the *Imagine* video – and the McCartney Suite, which has a suit of armour, signifying Sir Paul's status as a knight. Located next to the rebuilt Cavern Club, where The Beatles first rose to fame, one of the hotel's restaurants is called Blakes, after pop artist Sir Peter Blake, who designed the iconic *Sgt Pepper's Lonely Hearts Club Band* album sleeve. There's also a wedding chapel called Two Of Us, named after the track on *Let It Be*, The Beatles' final album.

68 Hope Street

Nowadays it's part of Liverpool John Moores University, but the building was formerly the Liverpool College of Art where John Lennon attended between 1957 and 1960.

John Lennon Airport

New Orleans airport is named after jazz trumpeter Louis Armstrong; Rio de Janeiro's after composer and father of bossa nova, Antonio Carlos Jobim; and in 2002, Liverpool renamed the city's old Speke Airport in memory of Lennon. Yoko Ono attended the official opening by the Queen during her Jubilee celebrations. A seven-foot bronze statue of Lennon now stands overlooking the check-in hall and his lyrics "above us, only sky" from *Imagine* have been painted onto the airport's roof.

Oasis single sleeve, *Don't Go Away*, from the album, *Be Here Now*, features a photograph of the old Speke airport, where thousands of excited fans greeted the Fab Four on their return home from touring in the Sixties. The old terminal building (now a hotel) also appears in the Oasis video for *Supersonic*.

'Mendips', 251 Menlove Avenue, Woolton

This is John Lennon's childhood home, where he lived with his aunt Mimi and uncle George. Now also a National Trust property, which opened to the public in 2003, it's been restored to what it would have looked like when Lennon lived here between the ages of five and 23. Lennon wrote *She Loves You* in the living room here and the house appears on the cover of Oasis single *Live Forever*.

Mount Pleasant, Waterloo

The registry office where John Lennon married Cynthia Powell in August 1962.

Penny Lane, Mossley Hill

Made famous by the song of the same name, Penny Lane is an unremarkable road of red-brick terraces. Situated off Allerton Road, you'll find the bank, fire station and "the shelter in the middle of a roundabout" that provided The Beatles with inspiration. None of the places mentioned in the song exist in the street itself, but they're all nearby. The Penny Lane barbershop at 11 and 11a Smithdown Place – mentioned in the lyrics – where

John, Paul and George had their haircut as kids went under the hammer in 1997. The property is still a barber's shop today, albeit a unisex one. In 2006, an ambitious Liverpool Councillor, keen to erase the darker aspects of Liverpool's history, suggested any city streets named after people linked with slavery should be renamed. This included Penny Lane, named after 18th-century ship owner, James Penny who made a stash out of shipping slaves from Africa to the West Indies. But the suggestion was rejected and Penny Lane kept its moniker, much to the relief of Beatles bus-tour operators.

St Peters Church, Woolton

Paul McCartney and John Lennon first met here when they played at a church fête. On 6 July, 1957, when McCartney was 15, his friend Ivan Vaughan persuaded him to come to the Woolton Parish Church summer fête across town to watch a skiffle band, The Quarrymen, led by a student from Quarry Bank High School. The first thing McCartney did was pick up Lennon's guitar and tune it.

Eleanor Rigby's grave is also located here. McCartney has denied that was the source of the inspiration for the song, though he has agreed the name may have been a subconscious recollection from his youth.

Strawberry Fields, Beaconsfield Road

Located in Liverpool's Victorian suburbs, the now-closed Strawberry Field was a Salvation Army orphanage. John Lennon wrote the song *Strawberry Fields Forever* about playing here as a child. He loved the large Gothic house and the privacy that it offered. It's sadly now demolished.

12 Whitechapel

Now an Ann Summers shop, this is the site of the former office of Brian Epstein and NEMS (North End Music Stores), a musical instrument shop. McCartney's father's piano was bought from Brian Epstein's father – Harry Epstein – when none of the McCartneys had ever heard of the Epstein family.

Dark (OMD) all have strong connections to the club and its scene. Eric's staged music rarely heard in other city centre venues; from jazz, reggae and folk to performance art, poetry and punk. Recognisable regulars included Jayne Casey (with a lampshade hat on her shaved head), Holly Johnson and actress Margi Clarke, and on busy nights people would queue along the length of Mathew Street. It was Liverpool's Haçienda – the place to be.

Today, the Liverpool music scene is as vibrant as ever, with bands like Ladytron, Sugababes and The Zutons once again giving the city a fair shout as the UK's Capital of Pop.

Super-club Cream is another Liverpool legend. Set up in 1992, it's now a dance brand that has crossed continents. Liverpool still has a healthy live scene, with venues such as Korova, Barfly and Magnet acting as launch pads for the best new locals bands.

Above: Echo & the Bunnymen.
Below: The multi-talented Ian Broudie.

Stories from the city, stories from the sea: songs that mention Liverpool

Ferry Cross The Mersey, **Gerry & the Pacemakers (1964)**
Gerry Marsden's song was a hit on both sides of the Atlantic, reaching number six in the US and number eight here. The song also features in the film of the same name.

Liverpool Girl, **Ian McNabb (2004)**
"She's a Liverpool girl," sings Liverpudlian McNabb on his album *Mersey Boys and Liverpool Girls*. And continues with:

> 'She likes her crisps, she likes a drink/
> She likes to think she's/
> Headed somewhere better then the place she is.'

Heart As Big As Liverpool, **Pete Wylie (1998)**
Perenial favourite of Liverpool FC and a fitting tribute to the city by one of its best-loved sons.

Kardomah Cafe, **Cherry Boys (1983)**
Liverpool's own Cherry Boys were largely ignored in the UK but this haunting melody remains a classic tale of their home city.

Hear also:
Liverpool Tide, PJ Harvey (2008); *In Liverpool*, Suzanne Vega (1992); *Going Down To Liverpool*, The Bangles (1984); *Liverpool Lullaby (Oh You Are A Mucky Bird)*, Cilla Black (1969); *Stanhope Street*, Real Thing (1977); *Long Haired Lover From Liverpool*, Little Jimmy Osmond (1972); *Mersey Paradise*, The Stone Roses (1989).

The Wirral

Birkenhead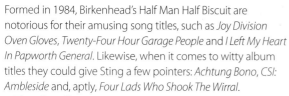

Formed in 1984, Birkenhead's Half Man Half Biscuit are notorious for their amusing song titles, such as *Joy Division Oven Gloves*, *Twenty-Four Hour Garage People* and *I Left My Heart In Papworth General*. Likewise, when it comes to witty album titles they could give Sting a few pointers: *Achtung Bono*, *CSI: Ambleside* and, aptly, *Four Lads Who Shook The Wirral*.

Their first album, 1985's *Back in the D.H.S.S*, became a firm favourite of DJ John Peel and the best-selling indie record of 1986. Half Man Half Biscuit eschew the limelight; they play live but have shunned several offers to perform on TV, including one from the now-defunct music show *The Tube* (see page 277).

They're led by singer/guitarist Nigel Blackwell who frequently talks over beats like he's making up lyrics on the hoof. For nearly three decades their observations about the foibles of English society have struck a chord with fans. Furthermore, they've spoofed, punned and satirised their way into the hearts of a cult following with numerous mentions of TV personalities and modern English folk heroes in their lyrics.

Perhaps most memorable of all was the glorification of comedy actor and Benny Hill straight man, Bob Todd, in *99% Of Gargoyles Look Like Bob Todd*. In the world of sports they targeted England cricket legend Fred Titmus in *F***in' 'Ell It's Fred Titmus* and former sports presenter Dickie Davies, in *Dickie Davies Eyes*. The closing track on *CSI: Ambleside* is *National Shite Day*, a mini-masterpiece of Wirral wit:

> 'I try to put everything into perspective/
> Set it against the scale of human suffering/
> And I thought of the Mugabe government/
> And the children of the Calcutta railways/
> This works for a while/
> But then I encounter Primark FM'

Hoylake

With the Wirral Peninsula jutting into the Irish Sea between Liverpool and Wales, inevitably Hoylake's origins are nautical with many local family histories anchored in sea-fishing or lifeboats. Wirral five-piece, The Coral, formed at Hilbre High School in West Kirby in 1996 and evoked the peninsula's strong association with the sea on two songs on their 2002 self-titled first album; *Spanish Main* and *Skeleton Key*.

Heswall

Two lads that shook the Wirral were synth-pop duo OMD (Orchestral Manoeuvres in the Dark), namely singer/bassist Andy McCluskey and keyboardist Paul Humphreys. McCluskey went on to form Atomic Kitten in 1997. He co-wrote *Whole Again* and managed/produced them until the all-girl group, that included Kerry Katona, showed him the cat-flap and he was sacked.

Above: Half Man Half Biscuit playing live in 2004.

SING WHEN YOU'RE WINNING: FOOTBALL & POP MUSIC

IN a secular society like England, football teams can attract near-religious followings and many pop and rock stars are regular worshippers. Here's a selection of English clubs and their rock music links:

Arsenal Gooners include Finsbury Park's finest, John Lydon, Dido, Dave and Ray Davies of The Kinks and Spandau Ballet.

Aston Villa Amy Winehouse, Ozzy Osbourne and Geezer Butler from Black Sabbath are fans. Duran Duran played a charity concert at Villa Park in 1983.

Birmingham City The Electric Light Orchestra's *Mr Blue Sky* is played before each Blues home game. Jeff Lynne is a life-long supporter and friends with club hero, Trevor Francis.

Brentford Fan of Celtic, Scotland and tall blondes, Rod Stewart, was once an apprentice at Brentford.

Charlton Athletic Squeeze co-songwriter Glenn Tilbrook supports The Addicks and in 1998 the band released *Down in the Valley* in honour of his boyhood team.

Chelsea The Blues and their fans get a mention in the Fall's *Theme From Sparta FC*: "English Chelsea fan this is your last game (Hey!) / We're not Galatasaray we're Sparta FC (Hey!)." The song is the theme music to BBC 1's *Final Score* programme on Saturday afternoons. Chelsea fans include Led Zeppelin's Jimmy Page, while Canadian singer-songwriter Bryan Adams dedicated the song *We're Gonna Win*, from his 1996 album *18 Til I Die*, to the club.

Leicester City Die-hard City fan Kasabian's Serge Pizzorno once had a trial for Nottingham Forest, although he wore Leicester socks under his kit.

Liverpool Anfield's Kop is in good voice on the song *Fearless* on Pink Floyd's album *Meddle*. Floyd attended a match and were impressed with the famous stand's vocal output. Fans can be heard singing *You'll Never Walk Alone*, although this is not exclusive to football. At their Knebworth concert in 1979, crowds serenaded Led Zeppelin with the same song after the encores. Liverpool fans also appear on the sleeve of Ace's *Five-A-Side* album, featuring their transatlantic hit *How Long*. Liverpool

fans include Peter Gabriel, Elvis Costello and US gangster rapper Dr Dre. He discovered the team on a tour with NWA in 1988. (At least that's one American welcome at the club.)

Luton Town Thin Lizzy's *The Boys Are Back in Town* is played as the teams run out at the start of games at Kenilworth Road.

Manchester United Status Quo hit the charts again in 1994 with their song backing United: *Come on You Reds*. United's mixed bag of fans includes Simply Red's Mick Hucknall, Queen's Brian May, ex-Stone Roses frontman Ian Brown and rapper Tinchy Stryder.

Manchester City Oasis are the club's most famous fans and Noel Gallagher bought turnstiles and turf from Man City's old Maine Road stadium to install in his Buckinghamshire estate. The cover of *Definitely Maybe* features a picture of City hero Rodney Marsh (and United legend George Best). Factory Records man, Mike Pickering – who M People were named after – is also a City fan, as were Joy Division's late manager and frontman, Rob Gretton and Ian Curtis.

Nottingham Forest In early 1978, local pop heroes Paper Lace remerged from the wilderness to record a version of *He's Got the Whole World in His Hands*, with the team, changing the first word to 'We've'. It was a top 10 smash in Holland.

Port Vale A life-long supporter, Robbie Williams bought £240,000 worth of shares in the club in 2006, making him the majority shareholder. A performance by Motörhead at Vale Park in 1981, headed by local boy Lemmy, was so loud it could be heard 12 miles away. The gig landed the band in the *Guinness Book Of Records* as the world's loudest band (though they've since been topped by AC/DC). The band produced 135,000 watts of power, causing a local sub station to blow up.

Queens Park Rangers When he's not in prison or court Pete Doherty supports west London team QPR. As a teenager Doherty produced a Rangers fanzine called *All Quiet on the Western Avenue*.

Sheffield Wednesday Wednesday musos include singers Paul Carrack and Joe Elliott of Def Leppard, and two Arctic Monkeys; Alex Turner and Jamie Cook.

Tottenham Hotspur Spurs fans Chas and Dave recorded three FA Cup final songs with the team, including *Glory Glory Tottenham Hotspur/Ossie's Dream* (1981) and *Tottenham Tottenham* (1982). Dave Clark grew up in London N15 and is also a big Tottenham fan. His band The Dave Clark Five were at the vanguard of the early Sixties beat sound, and the north Londoner was marketed in the US as "the Mersey sound with the Liverpool beat".

Tranmere Rovers Birkenhead's Half Man Half Biscuit may have had a song called *All I Want For Christmas Is A Dukla Prague Away Kit* but they are Tranmere fans. They once turned down an appearance on *The Tube* because it clashed with a fixture.

Watford Sir Elton John is life-long Watford fan and has been involved with Watford since the 1970s. The former chairman is currently the club's life president.

West Bromwich Albion Baggies fans include two guitar supremos. Eric Clapton draped a Baggies scarf across his guitar on the back sleeve of his album *Backless* and played a concert for former captain John Wile's testimonial year in 1982. Rolling Stone Ronnie Wood also has a soft spot for the team after his brother supported WBA when he was a child.

West Ham United Two Hammers fans, 1970s heartthrob David Essex and Iron Maiden bassist and founder Steve Harris, both also played for West Ham juniors. At gigs Leytonstone lad Harris has proudly displayed a West Ham sticker on his bass and worn their kit. The Bard of Barking, Billy Bragg, is also a fan.

Wolverhampton Wanderers Life-long Wolves fans include Led Zeppelin frontman Robert Plant who became the club's third vice president in 2009. He officially received the honour at Molineux before the 2009/10 season's opening fixture. He's said Wolves nearly ruined his marriage.

Cheshire

Wilmslow ➤

The indie rock trio Doves hail from this comfortable Cheshire dormitory town best known for its resident footballers, 15 miles south of Manchester. The band's 2005 single *Black and White Town* was about their native Wilmslow, but its sentiments – feeling suffocated by your surroundings and wanting to break out of a small-town England – could apply to any number of places:

> 'In satellite towns/
> There's no colour and no sound/
> I've been 10 feet underground/
> I gotta get out of this satellite town.'

Doves frontman Jimi Goodwin grew up in Handforth and met twin brothers, Andy and Jez Williams at Wilmslow High School in the 1980s after three schools merged. They enjoyed humble beginnings, playing at Wilmslow Leisure Centre, The Assembly Rooms in Alderley Edge and a youth club in Handforth, where they stored their gear and practiced for 25 pence a day. All the trio were in bands from an early age; Goodwin debuting at Wilmslow Leisure Centre in a band called The Risk when he was 14. The Wilmslow boys later formed a group when Goodwin bumped into his childhood friends at the legendary Haçienda nightclub in Manchester in 1989.

They enjoyed chart success in 1993 as the dance act Sub Sub, reaching number three with the catchy dance number *Ain't No Love (Ain't No Use)*, featuring singer Melanie Williams. But on the Williams twins' birthday, in February 1996, the band's Ancoats studio burned down. They made a radical shift in sound in 1998 and were reborn as guitar trio Doves.

Northenden, a track on their compilation *Lost Sides*, was named after the Manchester district and its "kids who love guns and kidnap" (the song also name-checks Levenshulme, Stockport and Hulme) while *The Greatest Denier* and *Kingdom of Rust*, from 2009's album of the same name, sees the group look at Manchester's regeneration. *Kingdom of Rust* paints a picture of a road trip to Preston, complete with cooling towers. "There's an aspect of searching for something, going to a place that you've lost, or a person perhaps," Goodwin has said.

Left: From early 1990s dance act to guitar trio, Doves.
Opposite page: The Charlatans.

Northwich

Although honorary Mancunians because of their association with the 1990s Manchester music scene, The Charlatans formed in Northwich where lead singer Tim Burgess grew up. The cover of their 1998 compilation album *Melting Pot* is a photograph of The Weaverdale café in Witton Street, Northwich, where the band convened after signing to the Beggars Banquet label in 1990. The greatest hits album includes psychedelic, live favourite *Sproston Green*, a song named in honour of the village near Holmes Chapel, southeast of Northwich, near their Big Mushroom studios in Middlewich. Nearby Budworth Mere, a popular angler's lake near Northwich, graced the cover of the band's 2004 album *Up At The Lake*.

Macclesfield

None of Joy Division came from Manchester proper. Peter Hook and Bernard Sumner hailed from twin-city Salford, while Stephen Morris and Ian Curtis came from the Cheshire market town of Macclesfield, which used to produce finished silk for some of the world's finest wardrobes. So much for rock stars burning out in a haze of amphetamine and adrenalin; in May 1980, the day before they were due to embark on a crucial US tour, 23-year-old Curtis hanged himself at his Macclesfield home, at 77 Barton Street, where he wrote many of his songs. His wife Deborah had spent the night at her parents' house after a row, but returned the following morning to find her husband's lifeless body in their kitchen, hanging from their floor-to-ceiling clothes rack. He had been listening to Iggy Pop's *The Idiot* when he committed suicide – the record was still spinning on the turntable.

A memorial stone laid at Macclesfield Cemetery and Crematorium bearing words from the song *Love Will Tear Us Apart*, commemorates the life of the Joy Division frontman and has become a pilgrimage site for fans around the world. His gravestone was stolen in 2008 but has since been replaced.

Curtis was brought up in Hurdsfield, on the outskirts of Macclesfield, and as a teenager lived at 11 Park View, a grey block of council flats behind the railway station. They were demolished in 2003. Prior to success with the band, Curtis worked at a Macclesfield job centre in Armitt Street, helping disabled jobseekers claim benefits.

The small Cheshire town in the foothills of The Pennines once provoked the wrath of The Fall's frontman Mark E Smith. When he tried to stub out a cigarette in the face of *Loaded* writer John Perry, Smith cried: "From Macclesfield, are you? Think you're f***in' hard, do yer?"

Widnes

This Cheshire industrial town isn't just famous for its rugby league team. A small plaque at Widnes railway station commemorates the fact that US singer-songwriter Paul Simon wrote his song *Homeward Bound* in 1965. A homesick Paul Simon (whose "love lies waiting" was Kathy Chitty in Essex) was stranded overnight on the platform of Ditton Junction railway station after following another time-honoured English tradition of misunderstanding a British

Rail timetable. The plaque was erected at Widnes station because the actual Witton station was closed by Railtrack in 1994, after the privatisation of British Rail. Explaining the song some years later, Simon said: "If you know Widnes, then you'll understand how I was desperately trying to get back to London as quickly as possible."

Widnes was also the location for the legendary outdoor concert by The Stone Roses in 1990, which rocketed them to stardom. In 1990, 27,000 fans converged on a Widnes field opposite a cement factory at Spike Island, a kind of Woodstock for the baggies. The Oldham rock band Puressence met on the way to the gig and featured Spike Island on the sleeve of their self-titled first album. The gig also inspired Pulp song *Sorted for E's & Wizz*. A girl Jarvis Cocker met in Sheffield had attended the gig, but all she remembered was scallys walking around asking: 'Is

Above: Paul Simon.

everybody sorted for E's and wizz?' When the single was released in 1995 the sleeve notes demonstrated how to conceal amphetamines in a makeshift wrap and tabloid newspapers called for the single to be banned. The furore helped the song get to number two in the UK charts.

Music festivals have always been as much about self-expression as about chilling-out in a field with friends and listening to some great sounds. Southeast of Widnes, the village of Daresbury in Halton hosts the annual Creamfields dance festival each August Bank Holiday weekend. The two-day festival is the UK's biggest dance and electronic event and attracts some of the world's best DJs plus major live acts. The festival moved to the Daresbury estate in 2006 after revellers had attended the Liverpool airfield for the previous six years.

Altrincham

The pioneering inventor of skiffle, Glasgow-born Lonnie Donegan, who kick-started the British folk revival, was evacuated to Altrincham to escape bombing during World War II. He attended St Ambrose College in the town, when it was located in Dunham Road.

Stone Roses masterminds, Ian Brown and John Squire, both went to Altrincham Grammar School for Boys, although frontman Brown left, aged 16, with only two O-levels. He later claimed punk rock was his education. "I couldn't get into revision. Those summer nights were too tempting, plus we had bands like The Clash. I went to see them the night before geography and maths O-level. Amazing!"

Before moving to Wales, Sale-born singer-songwriter David Gray grew up in Altrincham.

Cumbria

over the band's guitar sound. The critics seem to like them; the band's second album, 2009's *Two Dancers*, was widely praised and nominated for the 2010 Mercury Prize.

Ambleside

Wordsworth was wrong. Clouds don't wander lonely in this part of the world; they gang up and soak you at every opportunity. This Lake District town is hardly the rock 'n' roll centre of the universe but Ambleside's Priest Hole restaurant, set in the restored 16th century Kelsick Old Hall in Church Street, appears on the cover of Half Man Half Biscuit's 2008 album *CSI: Ambleside*.

Kendal

Home of mint cake, British Sea Power and indie band Wild Beasts, until they moved to Leeds. The four-piece grew up here, on the edge of the Lake District, and have known each other since Queen Katherine secondary school. Frontman Hayden Thorpe has a distinctive falsetto voice which towers

Carlisle

The Crown and Mitre Hotel's contribution to rock 'n' roll trivia is a night in early 1963 when The Beatles were thrown out for not being properly attired. At a sponsored dance by the Carlisle Golf Club held at the English Street hotel, their crime was to wear leather jackets in the ballroom. The Fabs were supporting Helen Shapiro on tour and had played the town's ABC Cinema earlier in the evening.

Bouth

Rock stars and visitors can wear what they like in the small village of Bouth, just south of the Grizedale Forest Park. It harbours no rock 'n' roll secrets just a musical claim to fame as the birthplace of Fleetwood Mac's Christine McVie (née Perfect) in 1943.

Yorkshire & the Northeast

Durham
Northumberland
Newcastle
Tyne & Wear
North Yorkshire
East Yorkshire
West Yorkshire
South Yorkshire

Durham

Easington

Regularly voted one of the greatest-ever album covers, the soiled monolith on the front sleeve of The Who's 1971 *Who's Next* was located near the old mining town of Easington. The band were returning from a gig in Sunderland, in May 1971 when they noticed a large concrete block in a nearby slag heap. A film canister full of rainwater did the honours when band members couldn't urinate. The photograph on the back cover was taken a few days earlier, backstage at the De Montfort Hall in Leicester. An alternative cover featured drummer Keith Moon wearing a wig and black lingerie.

Langley Park

From Moon the Loon to Paddy McAloon: the much-loved 1980s/1990s pop band Prefab Sprout put the village of Langley Park, near Durham, on the music map with their 1988 album *From Langley Park to Memphis*, which included Pete Townshend and Stevie Wonder. Frontman singer-songwriter McAloon and his bass-playing younger brother, Martin, were born and grew up in former mining village of Witton Gilbert, a few miles northwest of Durham. Guitarist and backing singer Wendy Smith came from Middlesbrough. Formed in Newcastle in 1977, it's thought the band's name was McAloon's homage to the fatuous band names of his youth, in the late '60s and early '70s. The cover of the Prefabs' previous album, 1985's *Steve McQueen*, was shot a couple of miles west of Langley Park and Witton Gilbert in Lanchester. The motorbike was a clear reference to the chase scene in the classic McQueen film *The Great Escape*. Now partially blind and sporting one of the great beards in rock, McAloon has been likened to Elvis Costello and Paul McCartney and

even dubbed 'the Geordie Brian Wilson'. McAloon wrote songs for his friend and fellow Geordie Jimmy Nail, for his TV show and spin-off album, *Crocodile Shoes*.

Durham

Durham itself claims troubadour Martin Stephenson, who started out in music at the age of 15, busking in Newcastle. The band he set up in the early 1980s, Martin Stephenson and The Daintees, spanned folk, rockabilly, punk and pop. Stephenson moved to Scottish Highlands when they split up in 1992. Some of his songs were far from the usual love song fodder, instead they dealt with issues such as having a gay sister (*Coleen*) and a miscarriage (*Caroline*).

Stockton-on-Tees

Singer-songwriter Claire Hamill learned to play the guitar and write songs in her early teens. She hails from the small village of Port Clarence on the north bank of the River Tees. Island Records boss Chris Blackwell signed her to his label, and in 1971, aged just 17, she released her debut album, *One House Left Standing*. She appears on the cover sleeve with her hometown Port Clarence and the Tees Transporter Bridge in the background. The bleak Middlesbrough landscape of the cover is reflected in the album itself with many of the songs based on her experiences of growing up in the northeast. Before long she was touring North America with Jethro Tull and Procol Harum and she later recorded with Wishbone Ash. In the early '80s she formed her own band, named Transporter after the famous bridge.

The Durham port of Hartlepool is the birthplace of two useful guitarists: one who was lost to the Lord, and another whose band were named after a torture device for those who insulted Him. First, Jeremy Spencer, slide guitarist in the original Fleetwood Mac line-up in the late 1960s. During a US tour in 1971, Spencer left the band's hotel to go shopping, never to return. After several days' search, involving the FBI, Interpol and psychics, a spaced-out Spencer was located in a warehouse occupied by religious sect, The Children of God (now known as The Family International, or TFI). He told his bandmates he had no intention of rejoining the tour, or the band and he remains a member of TFI.

Hartlepool's other famous axeman is Janick Gers, currently one of three guitarists in Britain's premier heavy metal band, Iron Maiden. He joined the rockers in 1990 in time for the band's seven-month No Prayer On The Road world tour.

In March and April 1965, many Motown greats toured the UK for the first time, extending their Stateside success to Blighty. The three-week Tamla Motown Revue saw 20-odd performers and musicians – including Martha and the Vandellas, The Supremes, Smokey Robinson and Stevie Wonder – travelling up and down the country on a coach tour of ABC, Odeon and Gaumont theatres. They experienced the culture clash of inclement weather, dubious English cuisine and the good old class system.

Before heading to working class Liverpool, performers were invited to dinner at the stately home of Wynyard Park, west of Hartlepool, as the guests of Lord and Lady Londonderry. At the country house they got a chance to see how the other half lived and were introduced to the delights of sherry and English tea. Even though the Motown stars sung and played their hearts out, the tour was a failure, with disappointing ticket sales and the Revue sometimes performing to less than half-full auditoriums. Motown performers nicknamed it the 'Ghost Tour'. Ostensibly a flop, it still broke Motown music in the UK.

Above right: The cover shot of *The Who's Next* album was taken in Easington.
Below right: Jeremy Spencer (right) performing with Fleetwood Mac. He left the group in 1971 in favour of life with the religious sect, The Children of God.

Northumberland

Corbridge ❯

One of the surprise nominations on the 2008 Mercury Prize shortlist was *The Bairns*, by Northumberland-based folk group Rachel Unthank and the Winterset (now called The Unthanks). The album included traditional melodies and versions of songs by Robert Wyatt and Bonnie 'Prince' Billy. Their 2005 debut album *Cruel Sister* was followed by a show-stealing performance at the Cambridge Folk Festival. The Unthanks' manager Adrian McNally told the BBC that in the last decade the public and media have become more receptive to folk music. "I think what people are searching for essentially from folk music is some sense of authenticity."

Holy Isle ❯

Formerly known by the name Lindisfarne, this North Sea island is where Christianity is believed to have started in England, in the 7th century. In 635AD, St Aidan travelled from the Scottish island of Iona and founded his monastery here. A little like news of the 2007 Led Zeppelin gig at London's O2, the Christian message flourished and word was spread further around the world. Many centuries later, in 1970, a group of Newcastle musicians were inspired by the holy island, calling their folk-rock band Lindisfarne.

Hexham ❯

Although now a fully-fledged Londoner, tabloid fodder and bad boy of English rock, Pete Doherty, frontman of The Libertines and Babyshambles, was born in the market town of Hexham in 1979. The son of a British army officer, he spent much of his childhood moving between military bases in the UK and Germany. The first sign of his lyrical prowess was at the age of 16 when he won a poetry competition.

Wark ❯

Northumbrian pipes and fiddle player, Kathryn Tickell comes from the small village of Wark in the North Tyne Valley. Inspired by her father, who was deeply involved in the local music scene, she took up the traditional Northumbrian small pipes at the age of nine. Tickell was also influenced by the older generation of folk musicians, including Will Atkinson and Billy Pigg (the Northumbrian piper who inspired folk-rockers Fairport Convention to integrate more traditional music into their repertoire). Through her work she's helped take away traditional folk music from its stuffy and old-fashioned image.

Since Tickell's first album in 1984 – when she was just 16 – she has toured extensively and collaborated with jazz, folk and rock musicians. She has played on four Sting albums, with The Chieftains, and a 2001 piece Tickell wrote with jazz saxophonist Andy Sheppard was premiered at the opening of Gateshead's Millennium Bridge. Her pipes have been seen on *Later With Jools Holland* and *Last Night of the Proms*. She was awarded 2005 Musician of the Year at BBC Radio 2's Folk Awards and in 2009 she received the Queen's Medal for Music.

Folk has always been strong element in the northeast, maybe due to the fact the region has a musical instrument all of its own – those Northumbrian small pipes. Northumbrian music is a mix of indigenous English folk and traditional Irish music, that draws upon the sea, the countryside and the mines, amongst other things, for material.

TOP TIPS FOR ASPIRING BANDS

An irreverent guide to making it

Think ahead Give an early song a title that will also make a suitable name of a live album or DVD later on in your career. For example, The Rolling Stones and *Let's Spend the Night Together*.

Art for art's sake Nurture an interest in art, or at least pretend to. It'll make you look more intelligent than you really are. If you become mega-rich, then it'll also give you something to spend your money on, other than coke.

Grow a beard This is obligatory if you want to be taken seriously as an artist. Not only will a bit of fluff make you look deep and distinguished, it will also keep your face warm in winter when your gas is cut off. Applies to male acts only.

Make a sex video The more controversial, the better. Nudity and sex have been done, so try some other taboos. Maybe involving animals.

Create a scene Find some similar local bands, or get some untalented friends to form one. Then contact a friendly journalist to write about 'The Loughborough Sound' or 'The Billericay Beat,' but ensure the other bands are useless. One band apart from your own will probably be enough.

Design a unique costume If you're unsure about your music, make a bizarre costume out of angular bits of cardboard and tinfoil and wear a small birdcage on your head. During live performances this will distract attention from the fact you're a bit crap.

Check out early Achieve a degree of rock 'n' roll immortality by expiring early. It will make you instantly more interesting. If possible, leave some indecipherable, self-indulgent scribbles on napkins or loo paper. Your premature departure may assure a measure of longevity – and hopefully increased sales. Legions of new fans may suddenly find you fascinating.

Better look down Try to look broody and as miserable as possible, especially if you sense a paparazzi lens trained upon you, and definitely

during any authorised photography sessions. You'll give the impression there's more going on up top than there is. Image is an all-important element in pop, as important as the music itself, especially if you're not that good.

Enigma variations Create yourself as an enigma. Give wrong or conflicting information to music journalists. Contradict yourself frequently.

A hidden track Include one on your first album. Maybe make it so hidden it doesn't even exist. Either that or include a *Blazing Saddles*-style flatulence session by the band after several minutes of humming.

Children of the revolution Name your children after classic pop icons: Joni, Strummer, Elton, Dylan, Chesney. Or maybe even try two names: Louie Louie, Rebel Rebel…

Mind your space Hire someone to run your personal MySpace page and a graphic designer to fabricate some unprofessional-looking personal snaps to put on it to show that you're a real person trying to keep in touch with your fans.

I want to hold your hand Be evasive about your love life in interviews. This is a nifty old trick that dates back to The Beatles. Pretend you don't have anyone to go home to so fans can fantasise they're in with a chance.

Write a blog / twitter regularly But watch what you say after nine pints. Good example: "OMG we're on *Later With Jools Holland* tomorrow night! V. nervous but v. excited!" Bad example: "Got off my tits on free champagne at a party for some record company twats. Kicked a fan in the balls LOL!" Buy a computer plug-in that will introduce the right degree of spelling mistakes to make you seem approachable and human – and so busy. Again, probably best to hire a professional to do this.

Be a location scout Keep your eyes peeled for striking locations for your album artwork, so, if nothing else, you can appear in books like this.

Why not be photographed underneath The Angel of the North, or even better, on top of it. Just be clear what statement you are making. If there isn't one, just make one up. If you can't find anywhere inspiring, just put a scooter on your first sleeve.

And if those don't work…

- Do that difficult second album first.
- Start wearing a braided military jacket.
- Make it clear early on that you are not puppets of your record company.
- If you want to get it together in the country with bandmates, do it while you still like them.
- Get a supermodel girlfriend or famous partner so you can be seen in the newspapers. Break up. Get back together. Break up again.
- Have an easily imitated image: flowers in your trousers, war paint, a funny hat, etc.
- As tempting as it might be, at gigs don't alienate the audience with comments like "put down those f***ing phones and just watch the gig!"
- Leave any Nazi insignia well alone.
- Keep your band to a trio or quartet. Too many members make it harder to become a millionaire.
- Have unshakeable self-belief. (You can develop charisma later.)
- If you feel like murdering your drummer, ask him or her to leave the band, then on your band website say they left due to "artistic and creative differences."
- Walk out of radio interviews.
- It's hard to be a true original, so try to find a musical direction of your own. If not, just copy the bands you like.
- Finally, if it all goes wrong, or you are ever in doubt, blame the record company.

Newcastle

His trademark Fender Stratocaster made him almost as instantly recognisable as his black, horn-rimmed glasses. Hank Marvin, Newcastle-born guitarist of The Shadows, inspired a whole generation of guitarists, including Ritchie Blackmore and Jeff Beck. Marvin and fellow Geordie guitarist, Bruce Welch met at Rutherford Grammar School in Newcastle and played in the same skiffle group. Marvin taught himself guitar, boogie-woogie piano and banjo (bought from a Rutherford schoolmaster) at school before his father gave him a guitar for his 16th birthday. When his Crescent City skiffle group won a South Shields Jazz Club talent contest he received an invite to join Bruce Welch's own skiffle band, The Railroaders, which he'd formed aged just 14. When the duo moved to London they started hanging around skiffle central: Soho's 2i's Coffee Bar, the in-place that spawned the likes of Tommy Steele and Wee Willie Harris. They briefly performed as the Geordie Boys before joining an act called The Drifters, which, for legal reasons, evolved into The Shadows (see Ruislip, page 109). They became famous as Cliff Richard's backing band even though the four-piece recorded independently and became Britain's top instrumental act. In the early 1970s Marvin and Welch were joined by an Aussie songwriter, John Farrar, and went under the name of Marvin, Welch & Farrar. They recorded two albums, including 1971's *Second Opinion*, the cover of which sees the trio stood on the dried mud of the Tees estuary.

The Shadows reformed once again in 2004 for a farewell tour that ended in September at Wembley with the Stratpack concert that celebrated the 50th Anniversary of the Fender Stratocaster. Marvin appeared alongside fellow English guitar greats – Brian May, David Gilmour, Ronnie Wood and Phil Manzanera.

Marvin also influenced Dire Straits frontman Mark Knopfler, not least in his choice of guitar. As a young teenager young Knopfler wanted an expensive Fender Stratocaster like Marvin's trademark Fiesta Red. Born in Glasgow, Knopfler's family moved to Newcastle when he was young and grew up there. He and his younger brother David formed Dire Straits in 1977 and went on to sell over 120 million albums. They began playing in London pubs, and sometimes asked landlords to turn down their amps so drinkers could chat more easily. Their first, and breakthrough, single, *Sultans of Swing* was the story of a jazz band that played small clubs and didn't give two hoots how unpopular they were (and inspired the name of the Irish punk band The Sultans of Ping FC). Knopfler's evocative *5.15am*, the opening track his 2004 solo album, *Shangri-La*, is a real slice of Tyne Delta blues, the story of a beleaguered Tyneside mining community and one-armed bandit gangland murder, which inspired the original *Get Carter* film.

> "5.15 A.M. snow laying all around/
> A collier cycles home from his night shift underground/
> Past the silent pub, primary school, working mens club/
> On the road from the pithead/
> The churchyard packed with mining dead"

In November 1970, Geordie miner's son, ex-ceramics teacher and aspiring rock musician, Bryan Ferry wanted to form a band based round himself and bassist Graham Simpson, who he'd performed with in Newcastle R&B act The Gas Board. Andy Mackay replied to Ferry's ad for a keyboard player, even though he was a saxophonist and oboist, and once he'd persuaded a friend, Brian Eno, to join as synth operator and technical wizard, the seeds of pioneering avant-garde glam-rockers Roxy Music were planted. Their first single, 1972's *Virginia Plain* was genuinely different and introduced the world to their unique mix of art rock and electronics. Starting with the sound of a motorbike revving up (recorded outside Command Studios in London's Piccadilly) and a sudden ending to outfox the DJs, it was inspired by a brand of cigarettes featured in an old painting by former art student Ferry and namechecks Warhol superstar, Baby Jane Holzer. In the mid-1960s, Ferry had studied at Newcastle College of Art under pop artist Richard Hamilton, whose influence on Roxy Music would echo that of The Velvet Underground and Andy Warhol.

Newcastle five-piece Maxïmo Park burst onto the music scene with their 2005 debut album *A Certain Trigger*. Led by singer Paul Smith and his distinctive bowler hat, their song *Another World (You'd Have Found Yourself By Now)* on 2009's *Quicken the Heart*, references The Tuxedo Princess, Newcastle's infamous floating nightclub, a former car ferry berthed on the Tyne until the summer of 2008.

Formed in Newcastle in 1962, The Animals, fronted by Tyneside bluesman Eric Burdon, cut their teeth at city venues like the Club A-Go-Go on Percy Street. When producer Mickie Most spotted them playing there in 1963 he offered to pay the band royalties if they allowed him to produce their records. Most was able to strike a deal with record label, Columbia Records. Their breakthrough was a 1964 recording of *House of the Rising Sun*, which had long been part of the band's live set. The single clocked in at over four minutes, breaking all the industry rules about singles being three minutes long, but Most persuaded the label to go ahead and release the single, which topped the charts on both sides of the Atlantic.

In the following year, 1965, Most brought a touch of New York back to Newcastle when he secured recording rights to *We Gotta Get Out of This Place*, written by the Brill Building songwriting duo Barry Mann and Cynthia Weil, and originally earmarked for The Righteous Brothers. Back on Tyneside, Burdon and band revamped the song as a rebellious rallying

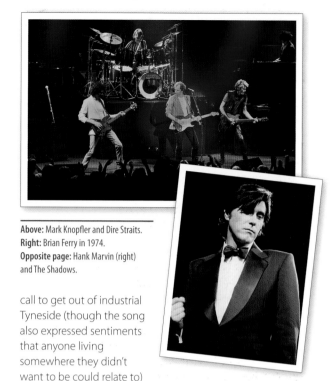

Above: Mark Knopfler and Dire Straits.
Right: Brian Ferry in 1974.
Opposite page: Hank Marvin (right) and The Shadows.

call to get out of industrial Tyneside (though the song also expressed sentiments that anyone living somewhere they didn't want to be could relate to) and became a firm favourite among American GI's in Vietnam. Shortly after, in 1969, The Animals split and Eric Burdon teamed up with Californian funk band War to create one of the first multi-racial groups, mixing Burdon's blues spirit with War's funky Latin rhythms. Jimi Hendrix appeared on stage with them just two days before his death. The Seattle guitarist had been discovered and managed by ex-Animals bassist Chas Chandler, who brought him over to the UK. Hendrix spent time in Newcastle in the 1960s, and busked in the Heaton area of the city.

Okay, so it's not quite the mighty Mississippi, but the River Tyne has also inspired a handful of songs, including two by local lads, Dire Straits: *Southbound Again* and *Down to the Waterline* (which mentions Newcastle landmarks Dogleap Stairway and the Quayside) as well as Jimmy Nail's *Big River*. Most famously perhaps the river was immortalised in Lindisfarne's 1971 *Fog on the Tyne*. The sleeve of the band's album of the same name shows a Victorian depiction of a spectacularly unfoggy Newcastle quayside and the River Tyne, decades before the Tyne Bridge was built. A reworked version of *Fog on the Tyne* became an unlikely hit years later in 1990 for local-born footballer Gazza, the footballer formerly known as Paul Gascoigne. The famous arch of Tyne Bridge graced the cover of *Five Bridges*, a 1969 suite about Newcastle, recorded live by Keith Emerson's progressive rockers The Nice and released in 1970.

The 1968 song *Rene* by the Small Faces immortalises Tyneside docks and some of its characters. It is one of the band's best music hall numbers, with lead singer Steve Marriott at his jauntiest:

'Love is like an 'ole in the wall/
A line-up in the warehouse no trouble at all/
If you can spare the money, you'll have a ball/
She'll have your oars out!'

Other Newcastle musical luminaries include actor-cum-singer Jimmy Nail and Cheryl Cole (née Tweedy) from Girls Aloud who was born and brought up in the rundown neighbourhood of Walker. There's also folkie singer-songwriter Beth Jeans Houghton and dance-pop trio Dubstar, featuring singer Sarah Blackwood, who formed in Newcastle in 1992, as well as early punk quartet Penetration, formed in 1976 and who were all from Ferryhill, a small pit village near Newcastle.

Neil Tennant of the Pet Shop Boys was born in North Shields and attended Newcastle's St Cuthbert's Grammar School, which inspired his lyrics to *It's A Sin*. A whole decade before he ended up as assistant editor of *Smash Hits* magazine in London, Tennant was in the audience when Led Zeppelin played Newcastle City Hall in 1971. Soul duo The Lighthouse Family – singer Tunde Baiyewu and keyboardist Paul Tucker – formed in 1993 after meeting at Newcastle University. Their 1995 album *Ocean Drive* sold 1.6 million

copies in the UK, and provided the background music for many a dinner party in the late 1990s. They split up in 2003.

Up until 1987, Channel 4 broadcast the weekly live rock music programme *The Tube*, produced at Tyne Tees TV studios in Newcastle's City Road. The main hosts were Jools Holland and the late Paula Yates. The first edition of the show in 1982 featured the last ever TV appearance by The Jam before Paul Weller broke up the band at the end of the year. When, in January 1987, Jools Holland let slip the words "ungroovy f***ers" it caused a national outrage and hastened the programme's demise. It was axed later the same year. Tyne Tees' City Road studios went the same way 22 years later, and were demolished in 2009.

Newcastle has no shortage of live venues. The Carling Academy opened in October 2005 with a sell-out live performance by local band The Futureheads, providing the region with a much-needed mid-size venue. Once the legendary Majestic Ballroom, famous for a Beatles concert in 1963 when they wrote *She Loves You* after the show, the venue has been restored to its former art deco glory, with original ceiling features, stairways, stage and balcony. There's also a 'Carling Academy 2', an upstairs venue designed to break new local bands.

Newcastle's Metro Radio Arena is the northeast's largest concert venue, with an 11,000 capacity, and the brainchild of former Animals bassist, the late Chas Chandler. It opened in November 1995, albeit with the not-very-rock 'n' roll Premier League Basketball, but soon established itself as a concert venue when its first gig a few weeks later was David Bowie. Newcastle City Hall on Northumberland Road is a legendary 2,000-seater concert venue, one of the oldest in the region. It's where the Animals broke up and Emerson Lake and Palmer recorded their *Pictures at an Exhibition* album in 1971. Nowadays the venue straddles classical music and pop and rock acts.

Both the city's universities – Newcastle University in Kensington Terrace and Northumbria University in Ellison Place – have large performance venues, each with capacity for around 2,000 people and host a variety of bands from the indie scene. Other popular music venues in the city include The Head of Steam, The Cluny in Lime Street, which hosts up-and-coming bands, and Trillians Rock Bar at Princess Square, a pub venue with live gigs at least three nights a week.

Far left: The Animals.
Left: Paula Yates and Jools Holland were the presenters of Channel 4's The Tube.

THOSE ROXY COVER GIRLS

Rather than opt for a dull photo of band members dressed in jeans, Roxy Music added a touch of glamour to their 1970s album artwork…

Roxy Music (1972)
Kari-Ann Muller was first in the long line of models to grace a Roxy sleeve. Their eponymous debut album saw a 1950s-style high-fashion shot of Muller draped across the gatefold sleeve, with a gold disc tucked behind her evening stole. Muller was the first of several cover stars to date Bryan Ferry and later became Mick Jagger's sister-in-law when she married his brother, Chris.

For Your Pleasure (1973)
French model and singer Amanda Lear poses with a black panther on this cover, while Ferry appears on the back sleeve as a chauffeur. Lear and Ferry were dating at the time of the shoot, before she caught the eye of David Bowie. To create some hype about her they invented a story that Lear was a transsexual.

Stranded (1973)
The woman in the red dress stranded in the jungle, nestled amongst tropical foliage, was Marilyn Cole, a former *Playboy* magazine Playmate of the Year. At the cover shoot, in a small studio off London's Edgware Road, the band's fashion guru, Antony Price, cut slashes in her red dress and sprayed her with gold paint. And yes, Cole and Ferry dated. She later married the former Playboy executive Victor Lownes (see Aldbury, page 158).

Country Life (1974)
More foliage on the sleeve of Roxy's fourth album, this time with two scantily-clad German girls Ferry met on holiday in the Algarve – Constanze Karoli and Eveline Grunwald – standing in a forest. They were both Roxy fans and were more than happy when Ferry asked if they would pose for the sleeve. They even translated the lyrics to the track *Bitter-Sweet* into German for him. Karoli's brother is the late Michael Karoli, a founding member of krautrockers Can. Some shops in the US refused to display the album because of the raunchy cover.

Siren (1975)
Jerry Hall was a 19-year-old embarking on her modelling career when she posed on the rocks in front of Ellins Tower. The area is a Royal Society for the Protection of Birds reserve on the cliff tops at South Stack in Anglesey, just over the border from England in a little place called Wales. Roxy's fashion guru Price painted Hall blue and gave her winged feet for the photoshoot. Hall and Ferry dated and the model later famously married Mick Jagger.

Tyne & Wear

Gateshead

Proud Geordie Brian Johnson has led a more successful career as a heavy rock frontman than when he used to make bogus tax discs from Newcastle Brown Ale labels. When AC/DC's Aussie singer Bon Scott was found dead after an all-night drinking session in early 1980 (see page 49) the spotlight fell on Johnson, singer with glam rockers Geordie, as replacement. He first honed his voice in a church choir growing up in the Tyneside industrial town of Dunston, Gateshead. His family lived near the ship breakers yard where wooden staithes loaded coal from the North Durham coalfield onto ships. He seems to have spent a lot of the 1960s courting in Tynemouth. "The car park at Tynemouth was legend," Johnson recalled to music journalist James McNair in 2009. "Sometimes you'd look out and the sea would be perfectly calm, but all the parked cars would be bobbing up and down. The windows would steam up and the coppers would come by and bang on the window." Another rock writer, Sylvie Simmons, once memorably described Johnson as "Andy Capp after a *Cosmo* makeover and sounds like he gargles drain-cleaner." During a short break from AC/DC in 2001, Johnson rejoined his old band Geordie on a short reunion tour of the UK; one of the venues they played was the Newcastle Opera House in Westgate Road.

Since 2005, Newcastle and Gateshead have hosted Evolution, the northeast's biggest annual music festival. Spread over 10 days there are loads of live gigs in indoor and outdoor venues ending with a huge free concert on the May Bank Holiday alongside the River Tyne. Gateshead's Quayside development is a good example of how public art and innovative architecture can regenerate an area after industrial decline. Opening in 2004, the £70 million Lord Norman Foster-designed Sage Concert Hall is a conference and music development centre but is primarily a live music venue containing two concert halls and a rehearsal space. It is home to the Northern Sinfonia chamber orchestra but hosts a diverse concert programme, from Morrissey, Elbow and Van Morrison to the late James Brown, jazz legend Herbie Hancock and the Brazillian singer-songwriter who became the country's culture minister, Gilberto Gil. The futuristic-looking building also houses Folkworks, a programme of classes designed to develop interest and participation in folk and traditional music through classes and performances. The Northumbrian piper Kathryn Tickell is the programme's artistic director (see page 286).

Wallsend

Singer/songwriter, activist and actor Sting was born Gordon Sumner in 1951 in a terraced house beside the Swan Hunter shipyard on the banks of the Tyne in Wallsend (named after its location at the eastern end of Hadrian's Wall). Growing up, the young Sting often rose in the early cold to help his milkman father Ernie (the fastest milkman in the northeast?)

The Police were formed in London in 1977, with the former drummer of prog rockers Curved Air, Copeland, keen to make inroads into the London punk scene. While early releases veered towards punk, their first album *Outlandos D'Amour*, in 1978, featured enough catchy pop songs to suggest they wouldn't remain in the genre for long. In many ways they were the antithesis of punk; while most bands could barely play their instruments, The Police were seasoned musicians, allowing them the freedom to dabble with other genres, most notably reggae. Their unique brand of white pop-reggae became their trademark and they were soon one of the biggest bands in the world.

Whitley Bay

Mark Knopfler often referred to northeast landmarks in his autobiographical lyrics. The Spanish city mentioned in the Dire Straits epic song *Tunnel Of Love* is not Madrid, Seville or Barcelona; nowhere even in Spain, in fact. It was the former Spanish City fairground in the seaside resort of Whitley Bay, near Newcastle, an important location for thousands of children who grew up in the northeast during the heyday of the British seaside holiday. One of those children was Dire Straits frontman, Knopfler, whose song summons up nostalgic visions of waltzers, ghost trains and, of course, a tunnel of love ride (there's probably a metaphor in there somewhere too). The Spanish City later fell on hard times – partly because Geordies started going to real Spanish cities for their holidays – and was later demolished in the 1990s. The song was written by Knopfler, except for a sample of Rodgers and Hammerstein's *Carousel Waltz* at the start. Whitley Bay is also the hometown of the new wave heavy metal band Tygers of Pan Tang (see page 215), who took their name from one of novelist sci-fi writer Michael Moorcock's novels. Another guitarist who could never be considered heavy metal, Duran Duran's Andy Taylor, is also from here.

on his round. "I remember the soft snowfall of so many dark winter mornings as we drove silently through the empty streets," Sting wrote in the sleeve notes to his 2009 album *If On A Winter's Night*. In March 1967, the 15-year-old Sting sneaked in to see a Jimi Hendrix gig at Newcastle's Club A Go Go. It was the first time he'd ever seen a black person in the flesh and it would change his life. The Police drummer Stewart Copeland and guitarist Andy Summers had similar life-changing experiences at a Hendrix gig at the London club Blaises the previous year. Sting worked as a primary school teacher, a football coach and ditch digger before he gave it all up for music. He played jazz bass with a Newcastle jazz act Last Exit and was rechristened Sting by fellow musicians because he wore a yellow and black hooped sweater that made him resemble a bee.

South Shields

One of the UK's most politically charged bands hailed from the once iconic shipbuilding town of South Shields.

Top: Sting and the Police.
Above: The Angelic Upstarts looking a little less than angelic live on stage.
Opposite page: Brian Johnson (left) on stage with AC/DC.

The Four Seasons (alternate take):
WINTER

I Believe in Father Christmas, Greg Lake
A crimbo song had to be here, so, with Christmas bells, a backing choir and sumptuous acoustic guitar, they don't come more atmospheric than this Christmas 1975 number two, which was kept off the top spot by Queen's *Bohemian Rhapsody*. Written by Greg Lake and Pete Sinfield, his lyricist in prog rockers King Crimson (who went on to write hits for Bucks Fizz), the Christmas-sounding instrumental in-between verses was borrowed from the *Troika* section of Russian composer Sergei Prokofiev's *Lieutenant Kijé* suite. The song has been accused of atheism but Sinfield has claimed his lyrics are about the loss of innocence.

Snowbound, Genesis
From 1978's *And Then There Were Three*, named after the band were reduced to a trio thanks to the departure of guitarist Steve Hackett, the album marked the start of the band's transition from progressive rock to pop. While the album contained the singles *Follow You Follow Me* and *Many Too Many*, this evocative wintry number sees them clinging onto prog:

'Here in a world of your own/
In a casing that's grown/
To a children's delight/
That arrived overnight'

Under Ice, Kate Bush
This chilling, in both senses of the word, song is from 1985's *Hounds of Love*, her most successful album and widely seen as a classic. It's about a woman skating on ice who realises she's actually trapped underneath it in a dreamlike state:

'It's wonderful/
Everywhere, so white/
The river has frozen over/
Not a soul on the ice'

Winter, The Rolling Stones
This bluesy number from their lesser-known follow-up to *Exile On Main Street*, 1973's *Goat's Head Soup*, sees Sir Mick clearly wishing he was in much warmer climes. Although recorded in Kingston, Jamaica, Jagger does a thoroughly convincing job of someone in the cold pining for sunshine. The jangly piano that plays throughout was the late Nicky Hopkins, one of rock's most in-demand session pianists in the late-1960s and 1970s.

Hear also:
Immigrant Song, Led Zeppelin (1970); *The Last Of The Melting Snow*, The Leisure Society (2008); *Winter*, The Cure (2004); *Cold Wind*, Galliano (1994); Christmas Time (Don't Let the Bells End), The Darkness (2003); *Last Christmas*, Wham! (1984); *Always Winter But Never Christmas*, XTC (1992); *Victorian Ice*, British Sea Power (2005); *The Chill Air*, Brian Eno and Harold Budd (1980); but not *Snowblind* by Black Sabbath (1972), that one's about a different type of white powder.

Formed in 1977, The Angelic Upstarts had to sail upon waves of right-wing extremism. Made up of former miner frontman Mensi (Thomas Mensforth), shipyard electrician-turned guitarist Mond (Ray Cowie), bassist Ronnie Wooden and a drummer called Sticks, The Angelic Upstarts set out their stall early on: their 1979 debut single *The Murder of Liddle Towers* was an indignant attack on police brutality after the death in police custody of an amateur boxer. When the band's popularity increased, so did the violence at their gigs, which attracted support from fascist National Front supporters who misconstrued their socialist songs as a defence of their cause. In fact, though technically a skinhead band, their songs attacked the racism that ran through the skinhead community. Chart bands such as Sham 69, The Specials and Madness also had concerts disrupted by far-right *seig-heiling* skinheads.

Along with The Cockney Rejects, the Upstarts were leading lights of the Oi! movement, coined by Sounds writer Garry Bushell after the Rejects song *Oi! Oi! Oi!*. While the rest of the music press more or less ignored these bands Bushell championed Oi! as a sub-genre of punk played by working-class bands and the true sound of Britain's streets in the late 1970s. In addition to the Upstarts and the Rejects Oi! bands included Peter and the Test Tube Babies and Red Alert.

The legendary Johnny Cash did his famous Folsom and San Quentin prison concerts; bluesman Taj Mahal entertained death row inmates at Wilmington State Penintentary… and, in April 1979, the Angelic Upstarts did their own prison gig at Acklington Prison in Northumberland. When the band hoodwinked a prison chaplain into letting them play, some 150 inmates turned up and listened to Upstarts anthems like *Police Oppression* and *Borstal Breakout* (specially refashioned for the occasion as *Acklington Breakout*). The band's stage set included a Union Jack scrawled with the words 'Upstarts Army', the motto 'Smash Law And Order' and a pig in a helmet entitled 'PC F*** Pig'. Naturally, the powers-that-be weren't overly impressed, with both the prison governor and local Conservative MP for Tynemouth, Neville Trotter, condemning the gig.

Sunderland

The cream of Wearside's indie scene are two interlinked bands that record in the same studio; Field Music and The Futureheads, the northeast's most successful musical export of recent years. Sunderland three-piece Field Music formed in 2004, emerging from the same northeast scene that spawned Maxïmo Park and The Futureheads. At the band's core are songwriting brothers, Peter and David Brewis, who are long-time friends with Wearside four-piece The Futureheads, formed in 2000 and part of a so-called angular movement that included Bloc Party and Franz Ferdinand. While Peter Brewis was the original drummer with The Futureheads, the latter's frontman/guitarist Barry Hyde was in an early line-up of Field Music. Both Brewis and Hyde taught at the lottery-funded Sunderland City Detached Youth Project which was designed to get kids off the street through music. The other Futureheads band members were also part of this project.

Eurythmics musician and record producer Dave Stewart hails from Sunderland and he's quite distinctive from the other musicians called Dave Stewart as he's the only one who didn't play in a progressive rock band. Other musicians of the same name have played guitar, drums and keyboards in Egg, Hatfield and the North, Camel and with Gong guitarist Steve Hillage. Baz Warne, replacement singer and guitarist with The Stranglers, was born in Sunderland and previously fronted local punk band Toy Dolls, as was heavy rock keyboardist Don Airey who has played with Deep Purple, Whitesnake, Black Sabbath and Rainbow amongst others.

Sunderland's leading music venue is the 450-capacity Independent club in Holmeside which took over the 'Bar 36' venue in 2006. The venue's impressive roll call includes Maxïmo Park, Snow Patrol, Kaiser Chiefs, Kasabian, Jamie T and Bloc Party. There's another smaller venue upstairs at the Independent club called The Little Room.

Above: The Futureheads live.

North Yorkshire

Middlesbrough

Several of Middlesbrough-born singer and guitarist Chris Rea's songs have been inspired by his hometown, including *Stainsby Girls*, on 1985's *Shamrock Diaries*, about the secondary modern high school in Acklam where his wife Joan was a pupil. The album's opener *Steel River* sees a plaintive Rea return to Middlesbrough after a few years absence. He likens the re-development of the town centre to that of a recent war.

> 'Ten thousand bombers hit the steel river/
> And many died to keep her running free/
> And she survived but now she's gone forever/
> Her burning heart is just a memory'

Paul Rodgers, the gravel-voiced frontman of 1970s hard rock acts Free and Bad Company, is also from Middlesbrough. In recent years he's recorded and toured with Queen alongside original members Brian May and Roger Taylor.

Since 2000, Middlesbrough Music Live, a free festival held in the town centre in the first week of June has showcased up-and-coming bands.

Saltburn-by-the-Sea

Like a musical dating agency, numerous band members have found each other through the pages of *Melody Maker*, the weekly music newspaper that closed in 2000 just short of its 75th birthday when it merged with its IPC Media rival, *NME*. Erasure found each other; guitarist Steve Hackett's ad was picked up by Genesis frontman Peter Gabriel; and Deep Purple found a new singer in David Coverdale.

The Saltburn-born and -bred singer had been singing locally for several years, fronting local rock acts like Denver Mule, The Government and The Fabulosa Brothers. In 1973, he was working as a salesman in a Redcar boutique called Gentry, and looking for a gig. When he opened the pages of *Melody Maker* he read that Deep Purple were looking for a replacement for Ian Gillan and auditioning unknown singers. He remained in the band until they imploded in 1976. In the late 1980s he married his girlfriend, Tawny Kitaen, the American actress who appeared in several Whitesnake music videos, most notably 1982's *Here I Go Again* in which she cavorts over the bonnet of his Jaguar in a white negligee. They divorced in 1991. He currently lives in Nevada, a long way from his seaside resort hometown east of Middlesbrough.

Scarborough

Scarborough Fair was made famous as a hit song by Simon & Garfunkel, based on an ancient English folk ballad dating back many centuries to when the Fair was an important trading event – an ancient Expo even. Paul Simon learnt the tune from English folk singer Martin Carthy in 1965 but failed to acknowledge it as 'traditional' and copyrighted it, receiving full royalties. "Martin Carthy had a beautiful arrangement of it," Paul

Simon once commented. "And my arrangement was like my memory of his arrangement." The song had revelled in obscurity until Carthy revived it in the early 1960s and taught it to Bob Dylan, borrowed parts of the melody from Carthy's arrangement and turned it into *Girl From The North Country* on 1963's *The Freewheelin' Bob Dylan*, and later as a 1969 duet with Johnny Cash on *Nashville Skyline*. *Elizabeth My Dear*, a short 1989 song by The Stone Roses, also shares the same melody.

York ❯

York's fortified walls couldn't contain the shaven-headed local four-piece The Redskins, who evolved from the York punk band, No Swastikas. They burst out of the ancient city with an explosive mix of Socialist Workers Party politics and a soulful horn section. They were proud, left-wing skins, keen to show not all skinheads had right-wing tendencies.

In 1984, when they performed on Channel 4's Newcastle-produced music show *The Tube*, they brought an out-of-work Durham miner on stage with them, introducing the appropriately named Norman Strike: "on tambourine, additional percussion and on strike for 35 weeks, a Durham miner". When he started to make a speech about the strike he couldn't be heard, as the microphone was dead. Viewers jammed the Channel 4 switchboard with complaints, screaming conspiracy. In all likelihood it was a publicity coup for The Redskins and the miners as they got more coverage out of the confusion than they might have otherwise.

Fibbers, in The Stonebow, in the heart of York city centre, is a cafe/bar during the day and a music venue at night. Located in the basement of one of York's tallest buildings, Stonebow House, its music varies from acoustic folk and death metal to the inevitable guitar-based indie bands.

After leaving The Stone Roses, songwriter/guitarist John

Squire formed The Seahorses in 1996, recruiting bass player Stuart Fletcher after he saw him here in York covers band, The Blueflies. Nirvana, Oasis, Stereophonics and Coldplay have all played here – the latter two as support acts.

Britpop contenders Shed Seven are also from York, though success never smiled on them the way it did on Britpop contemporaries Blur and Oasis. They played a 20th anniversary gig at the refurbished Fibber in September 2010.

Ripon ❯

The 1982 pop video for *Maid of Orleans (The Waltz Joan of Arc)* by Merseyside synth-poppers Orchestral Manoeuvres in the Dark was shot outside Fountains Abbey, a ruined monastery near Ripon. Directed by Steve Barron, the snow was real and the song sounds like it's itching to launch into the theme tune to Channel 4 soap *Brookside*. It was written by OMD frontman Andy McCluskey on 30 May, 1981, the 550th anniversary of Joan of Arc's death.

Fountains Abbey is the largest and best-preserved monastery in Yorkshire. It was founded in 1132 by 13 Cistercian monks, who'd fled an abbey in York, after a riot, in search of a stricter spiritual code of isolation, poverty and… no underwear. As their superior, St Benedict, hadn't mentioned if wearing undergarments was allowed all the monks simply went commando. From austere early intentions, the monks became medieval moguls who got rich by fleecing visiting merchants with supplies of local high quality wool. Within half a century Fountains Abbey was one of the richest monasteries in England.

Skipton ❯

Another 12th century ruin in the Yorkshire Dales appears on the front sleeve of The Cure's 1981 album *Faith*. The Augustinian Bolton Priory appears cloaked in a thich fog.

Much easier on the eye is the stunning countryside around Heslaker Farm, near Skipton, site of the 3,000-capacity annual Moor Music Festival each August. Three music stages offer everything from rock to reggae via rave, as well as a drumming workshop and a cycle-powered disco, in which revellers have to pedal if they want to party.

Above: Fountains Abbey near Ripon.
Opposite page: Many of Chris Rea's hits are inspired by his hometown, Middlesborough.

East Yorkshire

Hull ⟩

A city without a cathedral that was built up around its seafaring industry, Hull, or Kingston-upon-Hull for folk with time on their hands, can be fiercely proud of its pop and rock offspring.

West of the city, The Grafton Hotel pub, in Grafton Street off Newland Avenue, is the birthplace of The Housemartins and The Beautiful South. *Old Red Eyes Is Back*, a song on 1992's *0898 Beautiful South* was inspired by a Grafton regular affectionately known as Swiller.

Paul Heaton, the frontman and songwriter for both groups, lived in a flat at 70 Grafton Street and was a regular at the pub. His mid-1980s four-piece The Housemartins enjoyed chart success with soulful pop mixed with radical socialism. The title of their 1986 debut album, *London 0 Hull 4* was a dig at the capital, but the band were soon targeted by the tabloid press for other matters; their objection to the Conservative government and the royal family.

After The Housemartins split bassist Norman Cook junked pop in favour of dance music and recast himself as Fatboy Slim with global success (and married TV entertainer Johnny Ball's daughter, Zoë). Meanwhile Heaton and drummer Dave Hemingway formed the six-piece cooperative The Beautiful South. Guitarist Stan Cullimore became a children's author and previous drummer Hugh Whitaker was detained at Her Majesty's Pleasure (see next page).

In the spring of 2010, Heaton returned to his east Yorkshire roots for an intimate gig in Hutton Cranswick, near Driffield. More than 200 fans packed into The White

Horse Inn, in the Main Street. The gig was part of Heaton's nationwide Pedals And Beer Pumps Tour, which saw him cycle hundreds of miles across England to promote cycling, a new solo album and the importance of the traditional British pub.

One of Hull's most-loved musical sons is late guitarist Mick Ronson. With his trademark Gibson Les Paul guitar, he was the first point of reference for generations of glam rock guitarists and David Bowie's faithful lieutenant. The Spiders From Mars were actually from Hull. Before connecting with Ziggy's orbit the three down-to-earth east Yorkshiremen –

Right: From Hull to Mars with David Bowie: Mick Ronson.
Left: Paul Heaton (third from left) and the Housemartins.

Ronson, bassist Trevor Bolder and drummer Mick 'Woody' Woodmansey – played together in the late 1960s Hull band The Rats. After a disastrous French tour a disgruntled Ronson returned to Hull to work for the Hull City Council parks department. He was a gardener until one day in 1970 he took a call from Bowie and was asked to join the Spiders.

As a guitarist, songwriter and producer Ronson recorded with Ian Hunter from Mott The Hoople and Bob Dylan; he also produced Morrissey's *Your Arsenal* (1992) and co-produced Lou Reed's *Transformer* album (1972), with Bowie in London's Trident Studios. Reed praised Ronson's work on the album, in particular the fading out of vocals to highlight the strings, even though he sometimes struggled to understand Ronson's Hull accent.

In the early 1990s Ronson was working on a solo album called *Heaven and Hull* when he was diagnosed with liver cancer. He passed away in 1993 and is buried at Hull's Eastern Cemetery, in Preston Road, alongside his father George. Gone but far from forgotten: in his honour there is a Mick Ronson Memorial Stage in Hull's Queens Gardens and a street named after him on Bilton Grange Estate, not far from where Ronson lived.

Throbbing Gristle's Christine Newby – better known as Cosey Fanni Tutti – hails from Hull. Her pioneering industrial group were formed in the city in the late 1970s when she met Genesis P-Orridge (Neil Megson) at Hull University.

Plait-haired American-born singer Lene Lovich, who had a hit in 1979 with *Lucky Number* on Stiff Records, was born Lili-Marlene Premilovich in Detroit to a Yugoslav father and English mother. Her family moved to Hull when she was 13 years old and enrolled at Greatfield High School. In 1968, six years later, she travelled south to attend art college in London where she also started busking.

Born in Birmingham, actor and singer Roland Gift grew up in Hull and was singing in a local ska revival band when he was invited to join Fine Young Cannibals by two former members of the Brummie ska group The Beat.

In the early 1980s the UK charts were regularly invaded by Sade and Everything But The Girl, who both fused pop with smooth jazz. Three musicians in Sade's band – saxophonist Stewart Matthewman, bassist Paul Denman and drummer Paul Cooke – were all originally from Hull. Cooke was 'let go' from the band just before the release of one of the biggest selling albums of the 1980s, *Diamond Life*. Duo Everything But the Girl formed while Ben Watt and Tracey Thorn were studying at the University of Hull. They named

Above: Roland Gift.
Right: Ben Watt and Tracey Thorn formed Everything But the Girl after meeting at Hull University in the 1980s.

themselves after the well-known slogan of Turners furniture shop in Beverley Road: 'for your bedroom needs, we sell everything but the girl.'

Hull's legendary live venue is The Adelphi, in De Grey Street, an old Victorian house and one of the last remaining underground live music venues in the country. A small venue with a tiny stage, it has achieved recognition outside Hull for hosting everyone from The Stone Roses to Oasis, Green Day to Radiohead (who once supported the Hull band Kingmaker). The Adelphi was the first venue Pulp played outside their native Sheffield and in October 2009 Jarvis Cocker returned to perform a largely acoustic, secret gig here in honour of its 25th birthday, scrawling some lyrics on a poppadom packet so as not to forget them. Cocker first visited the Adelphi in 1985 and played there with Pulp seven times.

Freedom, Hull's annual free live music, arts and dance festival, features live performances from a wide range of acts. No gigs by Pink Floyd, but set the controls for chart-toppers, plastic pop stars and Mercury Prize nominates, who share the bill with avant-garde arts companies and colourful dance displays. The action happens at Humber Quays and Queens Gardens, which are renamed Freedom Gardens for the weekend festival each September.

JAIL GUITAR DOORS

FOR some performers a court appearance followed by prison is just another venue and part of the rock 'n' roll tour. Here's a selection of jailhouse rockers.

Dan Treacy

Founder and frontman of new wave band Television Personalities was incarcerated on the Dorset prison ship HMP Weare for six years in 1998 on drug-related offences. The UK's last floating jail was berthed at the disused Royal Navy dockyard at Portland Harbour to ease prison overcrowding, but was sold off in 2006.

George Michael

The singer was sentenced to eight weeks in Pentonville Prison in 2010 after crashing his Range Rover into the Hampstead branch of Snappy Snaps while stoned. Afterwards some local wag daubed 'WHAM!' on the shop's wall, while Snappy Snaps said they were happy to welcome the singer back to its Hampstead store – but preferably during opening hours.

Guy Stevens

Producer extraordinaire and impresario, and once dubbed England's Phil Spector, Guy Stevens was a record producer with Island Records in the 1960s. He gave the bands Mott The Hoople and Procol Harum their names and produced punk's last great record, The Clash's *London Calling*. When his protégés Procol Harum had a number one in 1967 with *A Whiter Shade Of Pale* he wasn't around to join the celebrations. He was spending eight months in Wormwood Scrubs for drug possession.

Hugh Cornwell

The former singer of The Stranglers has been imprisoned twice – in the same year. In 1980 he spent two months in Pentonville for drug possession, an experience he recounts in his book *Inside Information*. Later that year Cornwell and bandmates, JJ Burnell and Jet Black, were banged up after French police arrested them on an incitement to riot charge after the audience rioted at a show in Nice.

Hugh Whitaker

The Housemartins drummer took the notion of sharp business practice a little too literally in 1993 when he attacked a former business partner with an axe – and firebombed his house. The drummer was convicted of assault and banged up for five years.

Ian Brown

The former Stone Roses frontman was sentenced to four months in Strangeways in 1998 for air rage, after threatening a stewardess. Still, he emerged intact and with a lifetime of tales, including one of dead pigeons stuffed with marijuana 'flying' over the prison walls into the gym yard.

Lew Lewis

In 1987, the harmonica virtuoso and former member of Eddie and the Hot Rods robbed a post office of £5,000 with an imitation pistol, on a shopping bike, in a disguise. The post office was in West Road, Westcliff-on-Sea, the same road he lived on. He got seven years (see page 138) and would later be diagnosed with mental health problems.

Pete Doherty

The Libertines and Babyshambles frontman was sentenced to six months in 2003 for burgling his Libertines bandmate Carl Barât. Doherty's time in Pentonville wasn't entirely fruitless as he wrote the song *Pentonville*, which moaned about a "lumpy mattress". Doherty also spent time inside in 2008 for breaching the terms of his probation.

West Yorkshire

Leeds ➤

Synth-pop duo Soft Cell were formed when Marc Almond and Dave Ball met at Leeds Polytechnic in October 1978. Ball was a northern soul fan who also liked Kraftwerk and his mix of electronic music and catchy hooks would prove irresistible to many. The odd couple's first show was at Leeds Art College, in February 1979, when Almond asked Ball to provide some musical accompaniment to his 'Industrial Cabaret' performance. Their big break came when Some Bizzare Records boss Stevo Pearce spotted them later that year at Futurama, an annual music festival held at the Queens Hall in Leeds. Futurama in September 1979 is now

the stuff of legend, with a stellar line-up that included Joy Division at their peak, Public Image Ltd, The Fall, The Teardrop Explodes and Throbbing Gristle.

Leeds-born singer-songwriter, Corinne Bailey Rae met her jazz saxophonist husband, Jason Rae in 1998 at the city's Underground jazz club, where Bailey worked in the cloakroom while studying English literature at the University of Leeds. Before her self-titled 2006 debut album went straight to number one, winning two Grammys, she fronted a grunge band called Helen. In March 2008, she was confronted with the sudden death of her husband from an accidental methadone and alcohol overdose. Jason Rae's eight-piece band, The Haggis Horns, had been enjoying their own success and backed Amy Winehouse and Mark Ronson at the previous month's Brit Awards. Bailey Rae made an emotional comeback in November 2009 with a gig at The Wardrobe, a Leeds jazz and soul club, where she previewed tracks from her second album, *The Sea*, released in 2010. It was a poignant choice of venue: it had hosted her 2001 wedding reception and Jason Rae's 2008 wake.

Having struggled for several years as a band called Runston Parva – a deliberate misspelling of east Yorkshire hamlet Ruston Parva – the Leeds five-piece changed their name and burst onto the music scene in 2005 as Kaiser Chiefs. The band's best-known song, *I Predict A Riot*, is a paean to English town centres everywhere but in particular a tribute to Leeds nightlife. The lyrics deal with urban aggro, including police and locals fighting each other, and another time-honoured English ritual, the cab queue altercation.

The Who's *Live at Leeds* has long been regarded as one of the greatest live albums (for other contenders see next page). The landmark records, which captured the raw energy of The Who's live show, was recorded on Valentine's Day 1970 in The Refectory of the University of Leeds. The venue was packed with 2,000 students, plus around another thousand fans on the roof. Opening in 1955, The Refectory is a student cafeteria by day but come sunset it morphs into one of Leeds's largest live venues. The Who returned in June 2006 to recreate the original show. Billed as Live at Leeds 2, devoted Who fans queued overnight for tickets, which sold out within half an hour. During the gig Roger Daltrey swirled his microphone around and played catch with it while Pete Townshend leapt around the stage indulging in his trademark windmilling in-between mighty power chords, before the performance ended with *Won't Get Fooled Again*. Before the show The Who unveiled a Civic Trust blue plaque in honour of the venue and the band's momentous performance there back in 1970.

University campuses were the bedrock of the live rock scene in the 1960s and '70s. After The Who's gig everyone wanted to play Leeds Uni: Led Zeppelin, Pink Floyd, The Rolling Stones, Elton John, Fleetwood Mac, Bob Marley and The Clash to name a few. More recently The Refectory has hosted the likes of Muse, Radiohead, Keane and Arctic Monkeys.

Three members of post-punk band Gang of Four – singer Jon King, guitarist Andy Gill and drummer Hugo Burnham – formed at the University of Leeds in 1977. Before they took their 2005 reunion tour worldwide they returned to their alma mater as part of a UK tour, introduced by former fellow student, broadcaster and world music guru, Andy Kershaw (also the ex Leeds student union entertainments secretary). And they went back to their former campus again in the summer of 2009 to take part in a seminar on new wave and post-punk. While they continue to record as Gang of Four, Gill is also a prolific producer and Burnham lectures on the music industry at a college in Boston, Massachusetts.

Other acts emerging from Leeds have included indie bands The Wedding Present and The Pigeon Detectives, punk survivors The Mekons, The March Violets, The Mission and The Sisters of Mercy (see page 306). There was also post punk band Delta 5, important vanguards of the Rock Against Racism movement, Melanie Brown of the Spice Girls and two singer-songwriters: folkie Michael Chapman and Jake Thackray. The latter was born in Leeds but told many people he was from rustic Swaledale in the Yorkshire Dales, where he set many of his songs.

Wakefield ➤

Twins Gary and Ryan Jarman and younger brother and drummer Ross played music together as children and released their first single as indie rock band The Cribs, in 2003. Originally a three-piece, the band from Wakefield became a quartet when ex-Smiths guitarist Johnny Marr joined them on stage at the 2008 Reading Festival. He's now a full time member. Songs on their 2009 album, *Ignore The Ignorant*, addressed everything from lad mag culture to the British National Party's success at the European parliamentary elections in their home county of Yorkshire.

Be Bop Deluxe were formed in Wakefield in 1972 by the band's lead singer and guitarist and local boy Bill Nelson.

Top: Post-punk outfit Gang of Four.
Above: Be Bop Deluxe.
Opposite page far left: Soft Cell.
Opposite page left: Leeds' very own Corrine Bailey Rae.

Growing up, he would make cardboard replicas of Duane Eddy's Gretsch guitar and mime along to records in front of a mirror. Nelsonica, an annual Bill Nelson fan convention, takes place each November at York's Park Inn hotel.

Wakefield also claims composer Noel Gay who wrote the show *Me And My Girl*, which includes the song *The Lambeth Walk*, and *Loose Women* host and singer Jane McDonald.

Wakefield was economically devastated when the mines closed in the 1980s, something not lost on Chumbawamba. Inspired by the music of The Fall, the Leeds anarcho-rock band were never tongue-tied on political issues. The group's 1987 album *Never Mind the Ballots…* featured songs critical of all UK political parties and was released prior to the general election. During the 1984-85 British miners' strike they picketed on the frontline and released a three-track cassette dedicated to the miners to raise money for their hardship fund. One of the songs, *Fitzwilliam*, honoured the village of the same name, southeast of Wakefield, and the economic decline it faced after the strike. The village was originally built to house colliery workers at the local Fitzwilliam Main mine.

> 'Twelve months of bribery, 12 months of lies/
> Cops in the village to truncheon your bride/
> Scabs down the back roads to break up the strike/
> Come out of your houses there's a war on outside'

The sleeve of The Smiths'1988 single *Barbarism Begins at Home* placed 1960s Football Pools winner cum *Spend Spend Spend* singer Viv Nicholson at the pithead of Castleford's Wheldale Colliery. The last of the town's mines to close, in 1987, it was nicknamed the 'the sunshine pit' because if the sun shone miners had a 'sunshine break' and went home. Today, the site retains the pit wheel as a feature and there is a memorial to mineworkers killed in World War II. Smiths frontman Morrissey had quite a thing for Nicholson. A wild-looking photo of her sporting a troll-like hairdo was used as the sleeve of 1984 single *Heaven Knows I'm Miserable Now* and later another image of her appeared on 1988 single *The Headmaster Ritual*.

Batley ❯

Like many places in west Yorkshire Batley, was known as a woollen mill town, but for several years it also became known as 'Las Vegas of the north', thanks to the biggest variety club in Europe. Anyone who was anybody in the

rock and pop world played The Frontier Club, in Bradford Road, when it was known as the Batley Variety Club. Batley might have been the back of beyond, but it attracted some of the biggest names in showbiz: Tom Jones, The Everly Brothers, Dusty Springfield and Cliff Richard were all there in the late 1960s and early '70s. Roy Orbison even released a 1969 album called *Live from Batley Variety Club,* and Shirley Bassey performed regular three-week residencies. The man behind the club was entertainment entrepreneur James Corrigan, who hailed from a Yorkshire fairground family. In the early '70s ambitious Corrigan attempted to attract Elvis Presley, who had never appeared in England, to perform in the Yorkshire mill town. He offered Elvis's manager Colonel Tom Parker in the realm of £100,000, a huge amount of dosh in those days. "Well, that will do for the manager," said Parker, "now what about my boy?" Similarly, invites to Frank Sinatra and Dean Martin also failed to materialise. However, opening in 1967, one of the club's early coups was Louis Armstrong. In his wonderful book, *Bringing It All Back Home*, west Yorkshire-born writer Ian Clayton tells a story of when the jazz trumpeter was chauffeur-driven from the airport

Above: Anarcho-rockers, Chumbawamba.

BEST LIVE ALBUMS

LADIES AND GENTLEMAN — WOULD YOU PLEASE WELCOME...

The Who's Live At Leeds is touted as the greatest live album ever, but which other albums by English acts capture the passion and energy of a live performance?

Get Yer Ya-Ya's Out!, The Rolling Stones (1970)
Honky Tonk Women also appears on what the influential American rock critic Lester Bangs called the greatest live album. It was recorded in November 1969 over two nights at New York's Madison Square Garden when Ike and Tina Turner and BB King opened for the Stones. With their new, ex-John Mayall's Bluesbreakers guitarist Mick Taylor on board after the death of Brian Jones, the band thrilled fans with covers of Chuck Berry's *Carol* and *Little Queenie* and a nine-minute-plus rendition of their own *Midnight Rambler*. The live album was released in the middle of the Stones' most fruitful period – some would say the greatest series of albums in rock history: *Beggars Banquet* (1968), *Let It Bleed* (1969), *Sticky Fingers* (1971), and *Exile on Main St* (1972).

Less than two weeks after these New York concerts the Stones would be party to an event that hastened the end of the Sixties' love and peace ethos. The final date of their 1969 American tour was due to be a free concert in San Francisco's Golden Gate Park but the city council pulled out at the last minute and the venue was changed to Altamont in northern California. In a disastrous move, the Stones elected to use Hell's Angels as de facto security staff. Amid rising tensions a festival-goer was stabbed to death in an altercation with the Angels. Farewell to the Sixties.

Mad Dogs & Englishmen, Joe Cocker (1970)
Sheffield singer Joe Cocker introduced lots of white teenagers to the music of Otis Redding, Ray Charles and Solomon Burke. His deep and soulful voice is much in evidence on this recording at New York's Fillmore East in March 1970, part of the Mad Dogs and Englishmen tour, in which Cocker played over 60 gigs in two months. A 34-strong backing band, led by singer-songwriter and pianist Leon Russell featured multiple drummers and guitarists and a huge choir. Songs included covers of The Rolling Stones's *Honky Tonk Women* and Bob Dylan's *Girl From the North Country*. The tour almost wiped Cocker out mentally and physically.

Strangers in the Night, UFO (1979)
Named after the famous 1960s underground London club (see Central London, page 13), English hard rockers UFO influenced loads of bands, including Sheffield stadium rockers Def Leppard and Californian heavy metal giants Metallica and Megadeth. Ex-Guns N' Roses guitarist Slash also cites this as one of his favourite albums. Recorded at the band's peak, during a 1978 US tour when the band opened for Blue Oyster Cult, the critically-acclaimed album was also a commercial success, reaching seventh spot in the UK album charts. There's an amusing moment halfway through when singer Phil Mogg forgets where he's from. He starts to introduce fan favourite, *Love To Love* in a laid-back American accent but suddenly remembers he's English and corrects himself.

Hear also:
Live and Dangerous, Thin Lizzy (1978); *Live Killers*, Queen (1979); *Rockin' the Fillmore*, Humble Pie (1971); *I Might Be Wrong: Live Recordings*, Radiohead (2001); *How the West Was Won*, Led Zeppelin (2003); *Alive!*, Slade (1972); *Les Bains Douches 18 December 1979*, Joy Division (2001); *Space Ritual*, Hawkwind (1973); *Made In Japan*, Deep Purple (1972); *Dig The New Breed*, The Jam (1982); *Frampton Comes Alive!*, Peter Frampton (1976); *No Sleep 'Til Hammersmith*, Motörhead (1981).

Bring out your undead

T'S ironic that a musical genre with such a strong affiliation with death refuses to die itself. From its origins in glam rock, punk and the New Romantic movement, goth rock has been around since 1979 when Bauhaus (pictured) unleashed the bats from the bell tower with their debut single *Bela Lugosi's Dead* and launched a whole new genre.

The elder statesmen of goth were Manchester post-punk band Joy Division who blazed the trail for goth with their bleak, existential songs, followed by The Cure, Killing Joke and Siouxsie and the Banshees. Many fans were disaffected and alienated youngsters who enjoyed being outsiders and were attracted by the gloomy music with dark lyrics.

Goth central was the Batcave club in London's Soho, where self-expression through dressing up was as important and exciting as the doom-laden music.

Androgynous, black-clad, pasty-faced followers wore crucifixes, painted their nails black and bought Boots out of eyeliner and blood-red lipstick. The original goth heroes opened the door for a second wave of bands in the early 1980s and goth thrived away from the capital in places like Northampton, Bradford and Leeds, where The Sisters of Mercy, Fields of the Nephilim and The Mission would take over from the goth godfathers. The genre lives on with the popularity of its sound and iconography inspiring a new generation of moody, eyeliner-wearing youths.

to Batley in a Rolls-Royce. Accompanied by club manager Alan Clegg, the Roller stopped outside an abandoned wool mill in the middle of Batley where children were running around, chucking bricks at windows and trying to hit a rat with a stick. "This is the club, Mr Armstrong," the New Orleans legend was told. There was an elongated pause, until Clegg added: "only kidding." The Batley Variety Club finally closed its doors in 1978 as a result of competition, changing tastes and appearance fees required to attract the stars. It reopened as The Frontier Club in 1981 and became a nightclub, hosting comedy acts, tribute bands – and darts tournaments.

The town's most famous musical son is the late singer-songwriter Robert Palmer. Born in Batley in 1949, he died suddenly of a heart attack in Paris in September 2003, aged 54.

Huddersfield

The day the Sex Pistols came to Huddersfield is now the stuff of rock 'n' roll folklore. After swearing live on TV, dissing the Royal Family, and being demonised by the establishment and the popular press, the Pistols had been banned from gigs just about everywhere, except one place: Ivanhoe's club in Huddersfield. On Christmas Day, 1977, the band turned up for an afternoon benefit gig for Huddersfield's striking firefighters and their children. The gig got off to a shaky start when the Sex Pistols took to the stage with *Holidays In The Sun* and bassist Sid Vicious promptly started gobbling on the children. John Lydon had to remind him the audience were just kids. The Pistols also paid for a Christmas party for the children and even acted as Santas, handing out skateboards and a bicycle as Christmas presents to kids who probably wouldn't get many presents that year. The venue was awash with cake, sweets and copies of the band's album. Many young children walked around the venue wearing T-shirts emblazoned with the *Never Mind the Bollocks* logo. Along with pieces of cake, Lydon also gave one lucky fireman's daughter a gold disc of their last record. 'Johnny Not So Rotten After All' said local newspaper *The Huddersfield Examiner*. The Christmas Day gig would prove to be their last gig in Britain (until they re-formed in 1996).

Holmfirth

Best known as the setting of the BBC's long-running comedy, *Last of the Summer Wine* (until it was axed in 2010), the town's cinema, the Holmfirth Picturedrome, is an excellent small venue that hosts regular gigs by acts as varied as Richard Hawley and Saxon.

Bradford

Bradford's melting pot of musical talent includes beneficiaries of two 2002 ITV talent shows; Girls Aloud's Kimberley Walsh, from *Popstars: The Rivals*, and *Pop Idol* runner-up Gareth Gates. The city also claims some acts who weren't voted for by Saturday night TV viewers on premium rate telephone lines: singer Tasmin Archer, post-punk act New Model Army, who named themselves after Oliver Cromwell's anti-royalist military force, and Terrorvision, formed in 1987 in Keighley, before moving to Bradford.

Menston

Kasabian's 2009 album, *West Riding Pauper Lunatic Asylum*, was inspired by the name of an old Victorian mental hospital south of the village of Menston, north of Bradford. Founded in 1888, it was the country's first mental institution for the poor (previously it was mainly rich people who got treatment). Kasabian songwriter Serge Pizzorno first heard about the place in a TV documentary and says its name reminded him of a 1960s concept album "where each song was a member of this madhouse". In 1963, its name was changed to High Royds Psychiatric Hospital and the institution closed in 2003. Is the place being renovated into a concert venue for upcoming bands? No chance. The site will be converted into a new housing development, called High Royds Village. The Kaiser Chiefs penned a song about the same place; their 2007 track *Highroyds*. Three members of the band – Nick Hodgson, Simon Rix and Nick Baines – once attended St Mary's Catholic Comprehensive opposite.

Halifax

The New Orleans-born blues singer and boogie boogie pianist, Champion Jack Dupree, who influenced Fats Domino and many early British blues stars like Chris Barber, John Mayall and Eric Clapton, settled in west Yorkshire. In the 1970s and '80s Dupree lived in the village of Ovenden, near Halifax, after marrying a Yorkshire woman. He died in 1992. An upright piano used by Dupree was later found by pianist Matthew Bourne, in the drama department at Halifax's Calderdale College.

West of Halifax, the market town of Hebden Bridge receives a shout in the 2008 Half Man Half Biscuit song, *Lord Hereford's Knob*:

> 'Ever since the chattering classes invaded Hebden Bridge/
> And priced the likes of me and mine/
> To the pots of the Pennine Ridge/
> To South East Wales I was forced to flee/
> And now I have no job/
> That's why tonight I'm sitting on top of
> Lord Hereford's Knob.'

Much loved by ramblers and giggly teenage schoolboys, Lord Hereford's Knob is a mountain in the Welsh Black Mountains.

And finally, east of Halifax, who can forget the nearby Pennine villages of Brighouse and Rastrick, whose Brass Band was formed in 1881 and nearly a century later had a number two hit with *The Floral Dance*. The 1977 song was only kept off the top spot by *Mull of Kintyre* by Wings. Another version of *The Floral Dance*, featuring broadcaster Sir Terry Wogan, also charted.

Below left: Born in Batley, Robert Palmer.
Below right: Hebden Bridge, Halifax.

South Yorkshire

Sheffield ⟫

For years the most regular beat to emerge from Sheffield was the crunching sound of the drop hammers of the city's steel forges. But as one of the UK's musical nerve centres it has long had a more melodic touch, producing esteemed acts from The Human League and Arctic Monkeys to the 'Sinatra of the North', Richard Hawley via stadium rockers Def Leppard and the unrelated Cockers, Joe and Jarvis. Despite its 1980s synth-pop explosion and raw young Noughties guitar bands with witty lyrics, the Steel City continues to live in the musical shadow of Manchester, Liverpool and London.

Ironically, in spite of Sheffield's love affair with the synthesiser in the 1980s (see page 312) with bands like the Human League, ABC and Heaven 17, the city's most successful musical export that decade were heavy rockers Def Leppard.

They formed at the height of punk, with their first rehearsal happening in 1977 in an old spoon factory in Sheffield's Bramall Lane. It should have been all over for the band on New Year's Eve 1984 when Leppard's 21-year-old drummer,

Rick Allen, crashed his new Corvette Stingray in a country lane just off the A57 road near Sheffield. He lost his left arm in the near-fatal smash and was taken to Sheffield's Royal Hallamshire Hospital. After recuperation Allen learned to play on a specially adapted electronic drum kit. Released in 1987, their next album *Hysteria* became hard rock's answer to Michael Jackson's *Thriller* and their Americanised sound made Leppard one of the world's biggest rock bands. Their original guitarist Steve Clark wasn't so fortunate. He was on a six-month leave of absence from the band when he was found dead in his Chelsea flat from a mix of drugs and alcohol in January 1991. His grave is in Loxley's Wisewood Cemetery, west of the city.

Def Leppard have been inducted into the Sheffield 'Hall of Fame', on the pavement outside the Town Hall, alongside fellow Steeltown hero, Joe Cocker, Sheffield's former gas fitter and plumber turned soul man.

Four-piece Little Man Tate honoured a beloved Sheffield musical landmark on the sleeve of their debut album. The independent record shop pictured on 2007's *About What You Know* is Record Collector, in Fulwood Road in the city's Broomhill student quarter. The shop is still around, unlike the band (named after a 1991 Jodie Foster film) who split up in 2009.

Sixties rock 'n' roller Dave Berry first took to the stage as an entertainer in the late 1950s when pop singers were a novelty. He is still performing today and at the time of writing was touring the UK on a 63-date Solid Silver 60s show. The former Sheffield welder's biggest hit was 1964's haunting *The Crying Game*.

Now defunct dance-pop duo Moloko – Róisín Murphy and Mark Brydon – formed

Far left: Sheffield's Def Leppard.
Left: Dave Berry, the former Sheffield welder.

PULP & JARVIS COCKER

LIKE many acts, Jarvis Cocker, the lanky pop-nerd hero adored by pretty much everyone, except the Michael Jackson faithful, was influenced by punk's ethos of inclusion and accessibility. He realised he wouldn't need to be a virtuoso to play; just a few chords would do.

Aged 15, Cocker formed Pulp (originally Arabacus Pulp) in 1978 at Sheffield's City School, in Stradbroke Road, where his fellow high school friends paid to see them during their lunch hour. The band's name was shortened to Pulp by the time Cocker handed over a demo tape to BBC Radio 1 at a John Peel Roadshow at Sheffield Polytechnic (now Sheffield Hallam University). This led to a Peel Session in 1981 but the band struggled to make any headway in the '80s.

Cocker moved to the capital and enrolled at "Saint Martins College" (now called Central Saint Martins, a constituent college of University of London Arts) on a film studies course. He emerged with a BA and inspiration for the 1995 Pulp song *Common People* (see Central London, page 11), covered brilliantly nearly a decade later in a duet by singer-songwriter Joe Jackson and *Star Trek*'s Captain Kirk, actor William Shatner.

Pulp's breakthrough came when they signed to Island Records, releasing the album *His 'n' Hers* in 1994. But they became Britpop legends with their 1996 Mercury Prize-winning *Different Class* album, in which Cocker's dry Sheffield humour was unleashed on a diverse range of subjects including drug use, class and sex. The band parted company with Island after 2001's *We Love Life* and Pulp disbanded. The former Pulp frontman with the droll Sheffield accent has since recorded two solo albums, *Jarvis* and *Further Complications*.

Before Pulp hit the big time and Cocker became a geeky icon he worked at a wet-fish stall in Castle Market, Sheffield's largest indoor market (see box on previous page). The unlikely pop idol has written several songs about Sheffield, including *Babies* and *Joyriders* on *His 'n' Hers*, and pre-Britpop songs such as 1992's *Sheffield: Sex City* (which namechecks numerous suburbs) and *My Legendary Girlfriend*, first released in 1991:

> 'So I woke her/
> And we went walking/
> Through the sleeping town/
> Down deserted streets/
> Frozen gardens grey in the moonlight/
> Fences, down to the canal/
> Creeping slowly past the cooling towers/
> Deserted factories/
> Looking for an adventure'

Richard Hawley's Sheffield

HIS father was a Sheffield steelworker, his uncle Frank was in Sheffield rockers, Dave Berry and The Cruisers and he was in numerous local bands: Treebound Story, the Longpigs and Pulp. He even played guitar on the All Saints' cover of Red Hot Chili Peppers song *Under the Bridge*. Sheffield singer-songwriter Richard Hawley has been dubbed 'Sinatra of the North' and 'the Steel City Bard'. Whatever you want to call him, his albums enshrine his native Sheffield:

Late Night Final (2001)
Inspired by the call of vendors selling Sheffield's Star newspaper, the sleeve shows a pre-smoking-ban Hawley, head down in a newspaper at Sharon's Snack Bar in Sheffield's Castle Market. When a young Jarvis Cocker worked on the wet-fish stall, Hawley and his friends would amble past and shout: "Have you got any crabs on yer cock?"

Lowedges (2003)
Named after one of the oldest districts in Sheffield, now a southern suburb of the city. Hawley has been curious about the name ever since he saw it on the destination board of a bus.

Coles Corner (2005)
Inspired by a popular meeting point for generations of friends and lovers, young and old – including Hawley's parents and grandparents – on the corner of Fargate and Church Street. Coles used to be a big Sheffield department store and although it was demolished in 1963 the junction is still known as Coles Corner. With the original setting no longer available the sleeve showed an anticipatory, flowers-laden Hawley outside Scarborough's Stephen Joseph Theatre.

Lady's Bridge (2007)
Named after another central Sheffield landmark, the oldest bridge in the city, which arches over the River Don, traditionally the transition point from the poor area of the city to the rich bit.

Truelove's Gutter (2009)
Inspired by another hidden gem of the Sheffield cityscape and named after an ancient Sheffield street name (now Castle Street). An 18th-century local innkeeper called Thomas Truelove once owned a gutter where Sheffield folk could dump their rubbish in the River Don.

after they met at a party in Sheffield in 1994. Irish singer Murphy introduced herself to mixer/producer Brydon with the chat-up line, "Do you like my tight sweater? See how it fits my body." The band's debut album *Do You Like My Tight Sweater?* was released the following year.

In addition, Sheffield can claim the five-piece indie rockers The Long Blondes, as well as Reverend and the Makers. Chris McClure, the brother of the latter band's outspoken frontman Jon 'Reverend' McClure, is the slightly worse-for-wear figure on the sleeve of Arctic Monkey's debut album *Whatever People Say I Am, That's What I'm Not*. There's also singer-songwriter Paul Carrack who was in Ace, Roxy Music, Squeeze and Mike & the Mechanics. *Waiting for a Miracle*, the1980 debut album by post-punk four-piece The Comsat Angels, features a night-time photograph of the Sheffield Parkway dual carriageway on its sleeve.

Of course, to produce a supply of local bands it helps if you have a vibrant live scene and the steel city certainly has this. There's live music every night of the week at The Boardwalk, in Snig Hill, in the heart of Sheffield city centre. In many ways it is Sheffield's answer to the Cavern; a small, intimate venue that's big on history. At its previous incarnation as the Black Swan, The Clash played their first live gig here in July 1976, supporting the Sex Pistols. It has hosted early shows by local growler Joe Cocker and the near-local west-Yorkshireman Robert Palmer. Unsigned talent share the listings with larger, more established acts. Many movers of Sheffield's recent resurgent music scene worked here: Arctic Monkeys frontman Alex Turner and Jon 'Reverend' McClure were barmen, while Little Man Tate lead singer Jon Windle checked tickets at the door.

Another leading light in the Sheffield music scene is The Leadmill club, or the 'Leady', in Leadmill Road. Since opening in autumn 1980, countless bands have cut their teeth here with early gigs including Pulp, Cabaret Voltaire, Killing Joke, The Fall and The Human League. The venue also hosted early gigs by four of the UK's biggest bands of recent years: Muse, Coldplay, Oasis and Arctic Monkeys. The new Steel Stage hosts smaller acts on the rise; The Maccabees and Kate Nash have played here. Now three decades old, the Leady is one of the UK's most enduring venues and after three decades it's older than many of the clientele it attracts.

The Grapes pub, in Trippett Lane, featured the world debut of local heroes, Arctic Monkeys, in June 2003, when they played mostly cover versions, rather than urban tales. They received just £27 from ticket sales. Gigs

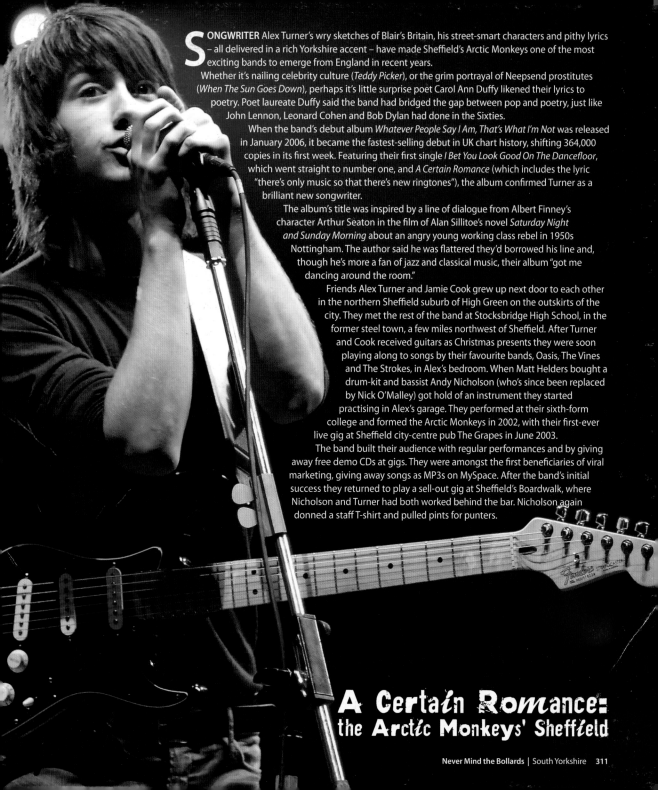

SONGWRITER Alex Turner's wry sketches of Blair's Britain, his street-smart characters and pithy lyrics – all delivered in a rich Yorkshire accent – have made Sheffield's Arctic Monkeys one of the most exciting bands to emerge from England in recent years.

Whether it's nailing celebrity culture (*Teddy Picker*), or the grim portrayal of Neepsend prostitutes (*When The Sun Goes Down*), perhaps it's little surprise poet Carol Ann Duffy likened their lyrics to poetry. Poet laureate Duffy said the band had bridged the gap between pop and poetry, just like John Lennon, Leonard Cohen and Bob Dylan had done in the Sixties.

When the band's debut album *Whatever People Say I Am, That's What I'm Not* was released in January 2006, it became the fastest-selling debut in UK chart history, shifting 364,000 copies in its first week. Featuring their first single *I Bet You Look Good On The Dancefloor*, which went straight to number one, and *A Certain Romance* (which includes the lyric "there's only music so that there's new ringtones"), the album confirmed Turner as a brilliant new songwriter.

The album's title was inspired by a line of dialogue from Albert Finney's character Arthur Seaton in the film of Alan Sillitoe's novel *Saturday Night and Sunday Morning* about an angry young working class rebel in 1950s Nottingham. The author said he was flattered they'd borrowed his line and, though he's more a fan of jazz and classical music, their album "got me dancing around the room."

Friends Alex Turner and Jamie Cook grew up next door to each other in the northern Sheffield suburb of High Green on the outskirts of the city. They met the rest of the band at Stocksbridge High School, in the former steel town, a few miles northwest of Sheffield. After Turner and Cook received guitars as Christmas presents they were soon playing along to songs by their favourite bands, Oasis, The Vines and The Strokes, in Alex's bedroom. When Matt Helders bought a drum-kit and bassist Andy Nicholson (who's since been replaced by Nick O'Malley) got hold of an instrument they started practising in Alex's garage. They performed at their sixth-form college and formed the Arctic Monkeys in 2002, with their first-ever live gig at Sheffield city-centre pub The Grapes in June 2003.

The band built their audience with regular performances and by giving away free demo CDs at gigs. They were amongst the first beneficiaries of viral marketing, giving away songs as MP3s on MySpace. After the band's initial success they returned to play a sell-out gig at Sheffield's Boardwalk, where Nicholson and Turner had both worked behind the bar. Nicholson again donned a staff T-shirt and pulled pints for punters.

A Certain Romance:
the Arctic Monkeys' Sheffield

While my guitar gently sleeps

UNTIL The Human League's 1981 album *Dare*, synthesisers were experimental instruments usually operated by boffins and lab technicians. They were hidden away at the back of the stage like an embarrassing uncle.

The Human League's mission not-so-impossible – which they decided to accept – was to banish guitars from pop music, replacing them with tape machines and synthesizers. In the late 1970s it was the turn of Sheffield's young bands to take punk's do-it-yourself ethos and apply it to the synth-based music they liked the most. They wanted to create a new music as cutting-edge as that of the punk bands they had deposed. The Steel City's synth revolution was started by the original Human League, and Cabaret Voltaire, who

turned the city into a hotbed of electronic musical experimentation. And it really took off in 1980 when the arty, experimental first incarnation of the League split up. Synth boffins Martyn Ware and Ian Craig Marsh recruited their singer friend, Glenn Gregory and formed Heaven 17, while singer Phil Oakey and his lop-sided haircut revamped The Human League as pop chart contenders, inviting two teenage schoolgirls – Joanne Catherall and Susan Ann Sulley – he'd spotted dancing at the Crazy Daisy nightclub on the High Street (now a branch of the Bradford & Bingley Building Society). While Heaven 17 racked up a great success with *Penthouse and Pavement*, the reinvented feminised version of the League went global with *Dare*. In response to this Sheffield synth success, a concerned Musician's Union launched a

campaign called Keep Music Live in the belief that electronic music would make many of its members redundant. *Dare* went on to sell five million copies. Sheffield suddenly found itself in the musical limelight with The Human League, Heaven 17 – and ABC – all enjoying mainstream chart success. They were joined by Merseysiders Orchestral Manoeuvres in the Dark and Essex's Depeche Mode.

take place in a tiny low-ceilinged room upstairs with a stage barely bigger than an A4 piece of paper.

Increasing in capacity, Sheffield City Hall, at Barker's Pool, bills itself as Yorkshire's premier music venue hosting larger mainstream acts, as does the Hallam FM Arena in Broughton Lane. The Octagon at Sheffield University, in Glossop Road, hosts large bands who've outgrown the Leadmill.

Below left: Joe Cocker growling away.
Below right: The crooner from Conisbrough, Tony Christie.

Conisbrough ❯

Made in Sheffield, a 2008 album by south Yorkshire's easy listening crooner Tony Christie, honoured the musical talent of the steel city. The sleeve shows Christie perched on the stage of Conisbrough Castle Working Mens Club, the venue where he performed his first show in his late teens. Christie was born in Conisbrough and grew up in the Sheffield area. The album features Christie's covers of songs by some of Sheffield's most lauded artists including *The Only Ones Who Know* by the Arctic Monkeys, *Louise* by The Human League, *Born To Cry* by Pulp and *Coles Corner* by the album's co-producer, Richard Hawley. A whole new generation discovered Christie's voice in 2005 when comedian Peter Kay lip-synched along to Christie's 1971 hit *Is This the Way to Amarillo?* to raise money for Comic Relief.

Rotherham ❯

Apart from being the home town of Muse bass player Chris Wolstenholme and chart-topping cartoon rabbit, Jive

Bunny and the Mastermixers (whose first three singles went to number one in 1989), Rotherham's only real claim to rock 'n' roll fame is hosting the first gig by Pulp. In July 1980, Jarvis Cocker led his Britpop band on stage for the first time at Rotherham Arts Centre in Walker Place.

Barnsley

Folk singers Kate Rusby and Kathryn Roberts are both Barnsley born and bred. Rusby attended Barnsley College in the early 1990s, a bit before two Arctic Monkeys – frontman Alex Turner and drummer Matt Helders – both studied music at the Honeywell Centre campus. As did the Jarman twins – frontman Ryan and bassist Gary – from The Cribs. New Wave of British Heavy Metal band Saxon (see box) are also from Barnsley. Each summer since 2004 Barnsley has hosted BOM Fest – or Barnsley Original Music Festival – which caters for unsigned local and national artists. The Arches, in Pitt Street on the edge of the town centre, is Barnsley's best live venue.

Grimethorpe

For softy southerners who have never set foot further north than Milton Keynes, there can be few more northern-sounding places than Grimethorpe, east of Barnsley. The South Yorkshire mining village takes a proud place here thanks to its Grimethorpe Colliery Band, one of several traditional northern brass bands formed at social clubs for mining communities. Grimethorpe's band found international fame with the film *Brassed Off* and have recorded on some of The Beautiful South's hits. They were also the 'backing band' on Roy Harper's much-loved, quintessentially English, 1975 song, *When An Old Cricketer Leaves The Crease*. The song captures the atmosphere of English village cricket match while lamenting a nostalgic age; never before has cricket been such a metaphor for life. Both John Peel and his long-running producer John Walters wished the song to be played at their funerals.

> 'The hallowed strip in the haze/
> The fabled men, and the moonday sun/
> Are much more than just yarns of their days.'

This is Barnsley Tap

FORMED in 1976, Barnsley heavy metal band Saxon were at the forefront of the New Wave of British Heavy Metal and are still rocking today, albeit with vastly different line-up. Whilst other bands of that era have been forgotten, Saxon have achieved a level of immortality. The reason is they are largely credited to be the inspiration behind Rob Reiner's 1984 spoof rockumentary *This Is Spinal Tap*. While other metal bands were also parodied in the film, the Barnsley band were the main source of inspiration. And one member of Saxon in particular has been elevated to British heavy metal legend, if not nation hero status; former bassist, Steve 'Dobby' Dawson. He was a key inspiration for Spinal Tap's moustachioed bassist Derek Smalls. Shortly before Spinal Tap shooting began, American actor Harry Shearer shadowed Saxon during a UK tour and found Dawson to be the ideal role model. The bassist wore tight striped trousers, sported a handlebar moustache and would pluck the bass with his right hand whilst raising his left fist in the air. As for the scene where the band get lost backstage, that wasn't made up either. That happened to Saxon's lead guitarist Graham Oliver at London's Hammersmith Odeon in 1979. Since 1995, both guitarist Oliver and bassist Dawson have performed together as the metal band Oliver/Dawson Saxon.

Below: Saxon (top) and Spinal Tap (below).

Index

Footprint credits

Project Editor: Alan Murphy
Design and production: Angus Dawson
Cover design: Pepi Bluck
Picture Editors: Angus Dawson,
Alan Murphy
Editor: Damian Hall
Proofreader: Sophie Jones

Managing Director: Andy Riddle
Commercial Director: Patrick Dawson
Publisher: Alan Murphy
Publishing Managers: Felicity Laughton,
Nicola Gibbs
Digital Editors: Jo Williams,
Jen Haddington
Marketing: Liz Harper
Sales Manager: Diane McEntee
Advertising: Renu Sibal
Finance & administration: Elizabeth Taylor

Print

Manufactured in Italy by Printer Trento
Pulp from sustainable forests

The views expressed in this book are the views of the contributors and do not necessarily reflect the views of the author or the publisher. While every effort has been made to ensure that the facts in this book are accurate, the author and publisher cannot accept responsibility for any loss, injury or inconvenience however caused.

Publishing information

Never Mind the Bollards
1st edition
© Footprint Handbooks Ltd
October 2010

ISBN 978-1-907263-14-9
CIP DATA: A catalogue record for this book is available from the British Library

® Footprint Handbooks and the Footprint mark are a registered trademark of Footprint Handbooks Ltd

Published by Footprint

6 Riverside Court
Lower Bristol Road
Bath BA2 3DZ, UK
T +44 (0)1225 469141
F +44 (0)1225 469461
footprinttravelguides.com

Distributed in North America by
Globe Pequot Press

All images courtesy of Getty Images except:
pages: 6, 7, 8, 9, 10, 11, 14, 29, 83 (all courtesy of Max Wooldridge).
page 177 (courtesy of Kevin Russell).

Front cover images: Getty Images, Alamy, Max Wooldridge, Alan Murphy, Carol Browne, Oliver Ledbury, Michael Smith, Diane Livesey, Ian Dockry, Jeff Keen and Kevin Russell.

Front cover flap image: Tony Day

Back cover image: Robert Roberts

Author acknowledgements

Many thanks to: Seth Lakeman, Emily Enright, David Courtney, Keith Altham, Sue Garvock, Oliver Bennett, Steve Daley, Jamie Fox, Robbie Vincent, Rick Kenny, Stephen Cviic, Stephen Bagness, Ian Belcher, Frank Barrett, Wendy Driver, Courtney Pine, Martin Dimery, Chris Haslam, Gerry Dawson, Hunter Davies, David Smyth, Nick Roberts, Clayton Hartley of The Furbelows, Malcolm McLaren (RIP), Keith Morris (RIP) and Binary Man Mike: have you forgiven me yet for spreading butter on your Crass records?

Additional thanks are due to friends, contacts and fellow music anoraks who took the time to suggest nuggets of trivia, places where album covers were shot and locales that have inspired lyrics. At Team Bollards I would particularly like to thank Alan 'McGee' Murphy, Damian 'Mozza' Hall and Angus 'Thumbs' Dawson who helped steer me back onto the slopes whenever I went off-piste. Any mistakes are my own unless they are glaringly obvious then they are the fault of my two-strong editorial team who should have picked it up. Thank you to one friend for pointing out to me that Chichester is actually in Sussex and not Hampshire.

This book is dedicated to my parents: my late father, Ian, who died in 2007, an inspiring man and brilliant writer who unwittingly got me hooked on rock and pop music when he banned anything but Beethoven from the family home, and my mother Veronica who since childhood has been a tower of support and from an early age was "a vision of love in Marigold gloves".

And with much love to Tina. You have the worst taste in music.